The Maroons of Prospect Bluff

and Their Quest for Freedom

in the Atlantic World

CONTESTED BOUNDARIES

UNIVERSITY PRESS OF FLORIDA

Florida A&M University, Tallahassee
Florida Atlantic University, Boca Raton
Florida Gulf Coast University, Ft. Myers
Florida International University, Miami
Florida State University, Tallahassee
New College of Florida, Sarasota
University of Central Florida, Orlando
University of Florida, Gainesville
University of North Florida, Jacksonville
University of South Florida, Tampa
University of West Florida, Pensacola

University Press of Florida

Gainesville/Tallahassee/Tampa/Boca Raton/Pensacola/Orlando/Miami/Jacksonville/Ft. Myers/Sarasota

The Maroons of Prospect Bluff

and Their Quest for Freedom

in the Atlantic World

Nathaniel Millett

A Florida Quincentennial Book

First cloth printing, 2013
First paperback printing, 2015

Library of Congress Cataloging-in-Publication Data
Millett, Nathaniel.
The Maroons of Prospect Bluff and their quest for freedom in the Atlantic World /
Nathaniel Millett.
p. cm.
Includes bibliographical references and index.
ISBN 978-0-8130-4454-5 (cloth: alk. paper)
ISBN 978-0-8130-6086-6 (pbk.)
1. Maroons—Florida—Franklin County—History. 2. Black Seminoles—Florida—Franklin
County—History. 3. Seminole Indians—Florida—Franklin County—African influences.
4. Slavery—Florida—Franklin County—History. 5. African Americans—Florida—
Franklin County—Relations with Indians. 6. Nicolls, Edward. I. Title.
E450.M64 2013
975.9'91—dc23
2013007077

The University Press of Florida is the scholarly publishing agency for the State University
System of Florida, comprising Florida A&M University, Florida Atlantic University, Florida
Gulf Coast University, Florida International University, Florida State University, New
College of Florida, University of Central Florida, University of Florida, University of North
Florida, University of South Florida, and University of West Florida.

University Press of Florida
15 Northwest 15th Street
Gainesville, FL 32611-2079
http://www.upf.com

Dedicated to Frederick Byrne Millett, 1943–1990

Contents

Figures

Acknowledgments

There are many friends, family members, and colleagues who deserve thanks for their role in this project. During its early research stages I spent a year in Gainesville working at the truly extraordinary P. K. Yonge Library of Florida History. Fitz Brundage, chair of the University of Florida's history department at the time, was very welcoming, as were David Geggus and Jon Sensbach. I would like to thank all the archivists at the P. K. Yonge Library while extending a special thanks to Jim Cusick for sharing his masterful knowledge of the library's Florida history materials. Over the years Jim has taken time from his own excellent research to read and comment on my work.

I would like to thank the staff at Britain's Cambridge University Library, National Maritime Museum, Royal Marine Museum, and the National Archives of Great Britain and the U.S. archivists at the Georgia Department of Archives and History, the Historic Georgia Collection, the Library of Congress, the National Archives and Records Administration, Princeton University Library, the South Carolina Department of Archives and History, the Southern History Collection at the University of North Carolina, and Special Collections at Duke University. Cambridge University, Saint Louis University, Harvard University, and the University of Florida have all provided financial assistance for this project. I would like to thank the Royal Marine Museum for help with illustrations.

Many colleagues have helped to shape this book. At Fresno State, Dan Cady and Eileen Walsh read or discussed my work. At Saint Louis University, Silvana Siddali, Lorri Glover, Flannery Burke, and Charles Parker have closely read and commented on various chapters while Damian Smith has read the entire manuscript on a number of occasions. Richard Price and Canter Brown shared their immense expertise on the topic, much to the book's benefit. Gene Smith has been exceptionally supportive of this project for a long time. Simon Hall, David Milne, Andrew Preston, Dominic Sandbrook, and Jenn Palmer are all good friends and great historians who have shaped my work. Tony Badger has been supportive of it for many years.

Over the years I have presented parts of this project at a number of conferences, including the Omohundro Institute of Early American History's annual conference in 2001, the Southern Historical Association's annual meeting in 2001, Race and Place 2005, the 2005 conference of the Society for Historians of the Early American Republic, the 2006 Allen Morris Conference, the American Society for Ethnohistory Conference in 2009, Early American Borderlands in 2010, and Warring for America in 2011. I would like to thank the audiences at each of these meetings as well as Linda Salvucci, Claudio Saunt, Jane Landers, Celia Naylor, and Kathleen Duvall for their helpful comments.

During the summer of 2011 I was truly privileged to take part in the NEH Summer Seminar titled "The Ethnohistory of the American South" at UNC Chapel Hill. Led by Theda Perdue and Malinda Maynor Lowery, with frequent cameos from Mike Green, the seminar offered me the once-in-a-lifetime opportunity to immerse myself in the Indian history of the South under the tutelage of a masterful pair of teachers and scholars. I would particularly like to thank John Paul Nuno and Laurel Clark Shire, two seminar participants who shared my interest in Florida history.

At the University Press of Florida, Sian Hunter has been a fantastic editor. Immediately responding to my array of questions and concerns, Sian has skillfully guided the manuscript toward publication. I would also like to thank Robert Paquette for his incredibly detailed and constructive pair of reports that shaped the project much for the better; thanks go as well to an anonymous reviewer from UPF.

So many friends and family have made this journey worth taking and, indeed, possible. My mother and sister, Liza and Amy, have always been supportive of my career. Seal Grandma was a tremendous supporter of my academic career. Uncle Elliot and Aunt Jill never failed to make me feel welcome when I was in London. My friends from New Jersey and New York have certainly provided me with a lot of laughs, as have my friends from Scotland, England, and across Europe. In many ways Jonathan Greenburg and Chris Schorr made this entire project possible. While working on this book, I was lucky enough to meet my future wife. Remarkably, Lina's father and brother are both historians and her paternal great uncle was the most famous historian in her native Lithuania. Perhaps Lina was destined to marry a historian, but I was nothing other than lucky to marry her. Most remarkable of all, our daughter Simone was born just days before the manuscript was due to be sent for copyediting. I love both of my girls very much and hope that this book makes them proud.

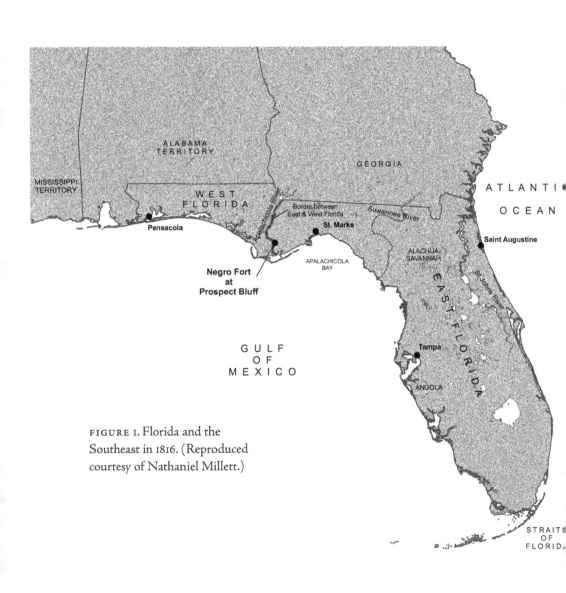

FIGURE 1. Florida and the Southeast in 1816. (Reproduced courtesy of Nathaniel Millett.)

➤ Introduction

THE APALACHICOLA RIVER twists and turns lazily through the Florida Panhandle as it makes its way toward the Gulf of Mexico. Along its banks in present day Franklin County lies Prospect Bluff, situated fifteen miles from the Gulf and forty miles south of Tallahassee in a remote area densely covered in sandy flatwoods, with stands of sixty-foot-high longleaf pines, black gum, pop ash, red maple, myrtle-leaved holly, and various cypresses.[1] It was to this corner of the continent that Thomas Wentworth Higginson, the radical anti-slavery proponent and leader of the First South Carolina Volunteers, the first federally authorized black military unit during the Civil War, turned his gaze and wrote: "I used seriously to ponder, during the darker periods of the war, whether I might not end my days as an outlaw,—a leader of Maroons."[2]

Higginson was forced to make this association, because in the second decade of the nineteenth century a large and well-organized maroon community (an independent settlement of escaped slaves and/or their descendants) emerged at Prospect Bluff. The inhabitants of the "Negro Fort," as it came to be known in popular parlance, were able to define a cutting edge version of freedom that fought to reject fully their prior enslavement because of the intersection of a triad of forces: exceptional geopolitics, tradition, and exposure to an unusual set of ideas about radical anti-slavery and the nature of the British Empire.[3] These forces, when combined with the former slaves' own worldview and desire for freedom, would have remarkable results. How these former slaves constructed their freedom, I argue, sheds much light on slave consciousness and the extent to which slaves would and could fight physically and intellectually to claim their freedom.

In 1972 Prospect Bluff became a National Historic Landmark. In spite of the federal government's recognition of the historic importance of the maroon community, the settlement of former slaves has been marginalized in and has largely receded from both the scholarly and popular imagination for much of the last century. There was a time, however, when Prospect Bluff was central to the master narrative of American history. Based on intense media attention, the publication of primary sources, and individual and collective memory, the maroons at Prospect Bluff became an important component of nearly every national history of the United States as well as works that focused on the history of Florida, the South, or more specialized subjects, regardless of the author's origins, sympathies, or agenda.[4]

Examples abound of the scholarly and popular attention paid to the maroon community in the nineteenth and early twentieth century. To realize the community's historical importance to past generations, one need only look at a handful of published examples. *Historical Sketches of the United States, from the Peace of 1815 to 1830* by Samuel Perkins (1830) contains a long and detailed chapter that begins with a section titled "Negro fort on the Apalachicola destroyed," which the author ties to the origins of the First Seminole War, before concluding with the American annexation of Florida.[5] As the Civil War began, volume 2 of John Warner Barber's *Our Whole Country, or, The Past and Present of the United States, Historical and Descriptive* (1861) contained an extended account of the origins of "a colony of negro slaves about twenty five miles up the Apalachichola" and the role that the maroons played along with the British in the outbreak of the First Seminole War and annexation of Florida.[6] In the midst of the Gilded Age, Richard Hildreth noted in volume 6 of his *History of the United States of America* (1880) that "loud complaints had been made by the Georgians of the asylum to runaway slaves afforded by the Floridian fort on the Apalachicola." Hildreth then quickly passed over the community's destruction, before concluding that "such was the prelude to the first Seminole war."[7]

The dawn of the twentieth century saw no decline in interest about the maroon community nor in the estimation of its historical importance. For example, Edwin Emerson's exhaustive history of both the United States and the western world during the nineteenth century addressed "Fort Negro" and its connection to American expansion.[8] Perhaps nothing better illustrates the popular regard for the importance of the community during these years than the fact that it featured prominently in works aimed at younger audiences. For example, *The Student's American History* informed its young readers about the "runaway slaves from Georgia uniting with bands of Seminoles [that] seized an empty stronghold which Edward Nicholls . . . [had built, from which] . . . the occupants made raids across the border and plundered the Georgia settlers . . . enticing slaves to join them" at Prospect Bluff.[9] Edward Nicolls (who spelled his surname without an *h*) was a British Royal Marine and radical anti-slavery advocate who was integral in the formation of the maroon community.

In a history of Florida written shortly after the community's 1816 destruction, James Grant Forbes described "three hundred of those misled creatures" who were blown up at Prospect Bluff after having been recruited by the "notorious Colonels Woodbine and Nicolls."[10] (George Woodbine was a Jamaican merchant who assisted Nicolls during his mission to Florida). John Monette's epic *History of the Discovery and Settlement of the Valley of the Mississippi* devoted a great deal of remarkably sophisticated and well-researched attention to the maroon community, the circumstances that led to its creation, and its significance in the coming of the First Seminole War and annexation of Florida. Monette observed that on the eve of the War of 1812, Florida had become a major threat to the United States because the boundary "separate[ed] two races so radically different . . . it was certain the frontier people could never harmonize" if the United States did not acquire the territory. He argued that the "colony of negro slaves," Nicolls's actions with the blacks and Indians (followed by more British intrigues after his departure), and the First Seminole War made matters infinitely worse for residents of the South, who were able to rest easily only after American annexation of Florida.[11]

The maroon community featured prominently in major topical histories. In *Indian Battles, Captivities, and Adventures* (1858) John Frost discussed "a fort, which had been erected by savages on the Appalachicola River . . . [which was occupied] . . . by four hundred savages and negroes."[12] In "Indian Policy Affected by Slavery-Exiles of Florida," chapter 10 of his *History of the Rise and Fall of the Slave Power* (1878), Henry Wilson devotes a tremendous amount of space to criticizing the federal government's role in the destruction of the maroon community and the ensuing First Seminole War, which he regarded as little more than a slave-raiding mission to acquire Florida.[13] Charles Coe's romantic Progressive Era history of the Seminoles, *Red Patriots: The Story of the Seminoles* (1898), contains a detailed account of the community that is, interestingly and correctly, placed in the context of centuries of slave flight and "maroon" activity in Florida.[14] Virtually every book written about Andrew Jackson placed a tremendous amount of importance on the maroon community, its destruction, the First Seminole War, and the annexation of Florida.[15]

During the Civil War era the historical significance and meaning of the maroon community was deeply contested. Most conspicuously, anti-slavery advocates began to reconceptualize the meaning of the community, which in turn reminded a new generation of its importance. For example, William

Jay's sweeping *A View of the Action of the Federal Government on Behalf of Slavery* contained a section titled "The Invasion of Florida, and Destruction of Fugitive Slaves by the Forces of the Federal Government" that stingingly criticized the legality of the community's destruction and the competence of the military officials in charge of it.[16] In 1858 the *Christian Examiner* lamented that "'Uncle Tom's Cabin' is not a more pathetic tale" than the story of the American destruction of the maroon community and that its memory had been distorted "because the aggressors have been telling the story to suit themselves."[17]

No anti-slavery proponent used the community more frequently or more famously than did Joshua Giddings in a series of highly influential anti-slavery publications. Giddings was one of the most important anti-slavery advocates in Antebellum America and was famous for his fiery speeches and writings advocating violence as an acceptable means for blacks and whites to combat slavery. Serving as a congressman from Ohio between 1838 and 1859, Giddings was a leader among the anti-slavery members of the House of Representatives. Together with his colleagues, Giddings relentlessly challenged the expansion of slavery. In the 1850s the congressman was a founding member of the Republican Party and became a national celebrity for the outspokenness of his views. Giddings's most famous book was *The Exiles of Florida* (1858), in which he somewhat naively and idealistically portrayed blacks living in Florida, including those at Prospect Bluff, as simple woodland farmers who inhabited a semi-tropical Garden of Eden for generations.[18] Most of the book is devoted to describing the former slaves' heroic efforts to protect their freedom against the aggressive forces of American slavery, the military, and the federal government. *The Exiles of Florida* was one of the most famous and influential anti-slavery works of this era and brought the memory of the maroon community to the center of the national debate over slavery on the eve of the Civil War. The book was quoted, referenced, reviewed, and plagiarized for years to come.

Given the exalted recognition that the maroon community enjoyed for over a century, it is not entirely clear why the memory of the settlement and the collective estimation of its importance began to recede into relative obscurity around the era of the First World War.[19] Fortunately, scholars have begun to examine the community once again. Even with this turn, however, there was no systematic or exhaustive study, nor do existing studies use the example of the maroon community to understand North American slavery more broadly or to place North American history in a comparative framework within the Atlantic world or African diaspora. Instead, when the settlement has been referenced in modern studies of the Southeast, the community is generally portrayed as of secondary importance to the broader drama of the black and Indian history of the region; as a sideshow to the history of the War of 1812 in the Deep South that was somehow tied to American expansion; or it is overshadowed by the story of Fort Mose.[20]

I find this an unsatisfactory state of affairs for two main reasons. First, and simply, I argue that the story of the maroon community is an essential component in a full and balanced understanding of the black, white, and Indian history of the Southeast, the War of 1812, the First Seminole War, the American annexation of Florida, and the expansion of the plantation complex. Thus the maroon community deserves a more prominent place within the broader narrative of North American history that would have been recognized by Americans in the century after its destruction.

Second, and more important, I propose that a close examination of the maroon community can shed much light on the subject of slavery and the lives of slaves both within a North American framework and from a comparative Atlantic or African diaspora perspective. This study reveals the settlement of escaped slaves as a clear, yet exceptional, example of a maroon community by carefully analyzing the inhabitants' demographics, backgrounds, culture, economy, military structure, political system, and, more broadly, their society. In other words, life at Prospect Bluff is here re-created in the fullest possible detail allowed by the extant primary sources. Historians of slavery have long argued that when viewed against instances of maroon settlement and rebellion in slave societies across the Western Hemisphere, North American slaves faced too many obstacles to form large and functional maroon communities.[21] This perception has endured in part because of the difficulty in finding good cases of successful or viable maroon communities (organized settlements with hundreds of members who created a functional society) in the southern British colonies, Spanish Floridas, Mississippi Valley, or, later, the southern United States. I argue that Fort Mose, which was a settlement of former American slaves located on the outskirts of St. Augustine during the middle of the eighteenth century, did not qualify fully as a maroon community. Fort Mose never achieved the status of a fully independent community, because it always came under the jurisdiction of the Spanish, nor did the residents of Fort Mose ever achieve full political or legal equality with their Spanish neighbors, who regarded the former slaves as second-class subjects and racial inferiors. As important as Fort Mose was in the history of the Southeast and in the African diaspora, it was a fundamentally different phenomenon than Prospect Bluff. Accordingly, the two communities are intentionally not compared in this book.

As historians have correctly argued, North American slaves indeed faced immense obstacles in establishing and sustaining themselves in functional maroon communities. Most North American "maroons," even those in the Great Dismal Swamp, were not much more than desperate bands of runaways who struggled on a daily basis to survive. Octave Johnson's experience in the bayous of Louisiana during the Civil War was typical of would-be North American maroons. For a year and a half Johnson and thirty others struggled to survive only four miles from the plantation from which they had fled, stealing livestock and trading meat for corn bread from field slaves who might easily "betray those in the swamp, for fear of being implicated in their escape." The maroons "slept on logs and burned cypress leaves to make smoke and keep away mosquitos." For months the "master of hounds" hunted the fugitives until one day twenty bloodhounds trapped them, leading to a terrifying and bloody encounter in which the escaped slaves killed eight of the dogs before jumping into "Bayou Fanfron; the dogs followed us and the alligators caught six of them . . . [because they] . . . preferred dog's flesh to personal flesh."[22]

Eventually Johnson escaped to the Union Army, but most American maroons were not so lucky. Even maroon communities that appeared to be more stable, such as one located along the Savannah River in South Carolina during the 1760s—described as a "Town . . . [with] . . . a Square Consisting of four Houses seventeen feet long and fourteen wide. . . . [that was supplied with]. . . . about fifteen Bushels of rough Rice Blankets Potts Pales Shoes Axes and many other Tools all of which together with the Town they set fire too"—could sustain only small numbers, had to be located in deeply inhospitable terrain, and lived a precarious and fleeting existence.[23]

This was not the case at Prospect Bluff. At its peak the community's population numbered hundreds of men, women, and children whose origins lay in numerous societies from across the African diaspora and Africa itself. They lived in and around a formidable British-built fort in well-constructed houses, cultivated their fields, participated in an exchange economy, enjoyed flourishing cultural lives, served in an organized militia, and constructed a political system. Ultimately the inhabitants of the maroon community came to regard themselves as constituting a complete polity with limitless horizons.

When comparing the maroon community with well-documented and well-studied examples of *grand marronage* from across the Western Hemisphere, the settlement at Prospect Bluff clearly emerges as part of the same phenomenon, albeit with a number of important differences that I analyze closely. Two of the most notable differences between the Prospect Bluff community and the most successful maroon settlements elsewhere were its relationship with the British (Edward Nicolls in particular) and its relatively brief duration of fifteen months as a fully independent community once the British departed Prospect Bluff in May 1815. I maintain that neither of these points makes the Prospect Bluff settlement less of an example of marronage, and nor do they undermine the usefulness of the community as a tool for studying slavery and black life during this era.

In July 1816 hundreds of American and Creek soldiers destroyed the fort at Prospect Bluff. However, the vast majority of the maroons successfully fled the assault. Accordingly, an analysis of the thought and actions of hundreds of refugees from Prospect Bluff over the course of the next fifty years provides further insights into exactly what had been achieved at Prospect Bluff, and the extent to which the settlement was a distinct variation of marronage, as well as revealing much about slavery and the lives of slaves.

The settlement at Prospect Bluff also reveals much about slave resistance during the Age of Revolution—a time of rapid and profound intellectual, social, and political change across the Western Hemisphere and Europe.[24] At the heart of this change was a sustained challenge to the old and hierarchical order over topics such as political inclusion, personal freedom, republicanism, rights, sovereignty, and liberty. While these ideas were deeply contested, far from uniformly understood, and not meant to apply equally to various races and classes or both sexes during this period, they nonetheless led to a series of revolutions and reform movements that forever altered imperial maps and fortunes, led to the rise of independent nation-states, and irrevocably altered the intellectual and political landscape of the Western Hemisphere and Europe.

Slaves and free people of color played a vital role in this period of revolution and reform. They shared in the collective wave of fear and hope at the realization that they were living in the midst of a time of profound change, and they also rose in an unprecedented series of rebellions that rocked virtually every corner of the Western Hemisphere during this era.[25] In attempting to understand these revolts, scholars have paid particular attention to analyzing their causes and trying to ascertain the aims of slave rebels.[26]

When examining causes and aims of slave resistance during this era, many historians have attributed a pivotal, yet contested, place to the influence of the Haitian Revolution in providing a watershed example for the potential of slave rebellions that fundamentally changed their frequency and character. Consequently historians have analyzed how slave rebels understood the ideas of the Age of Revolution (rights, liberty, sovereignty, republicanism, freedom, and citizenship, for example) and to what extent they were attempting to claim any of these ideas for themselves. Historians have also leveled a series of questions, such as whether rebels were aiming for the complete destruction of the system of slavery. Were they merely taking advantage of a period of intense and sustained international warfare to lash out violently at an oppressive institution? Did they seek to form maroon communities or to force concessions out of their masters? Were the growing abolitionist and anti-slavery movements a factor? What role was played by Protestant missionaries and the spread of Christianity? How much of a factor was rumor? What type of slave might lead or participate in a rebellion? Did demographic shifts (ratios of Africans to creoles, males to females, and the percentages of different ethnicities) or material, economic, and geographic shifts within slave societies create conditions that led to uprisings, and did these factors shape rebels' aims?

The case of the maroon community at Prospect Bluff, I propose, adds important new dimensions to these discussions as well as to the understanding of the institution of slavery more generally. The diverse collection of rebels at Prospect Bluff, whose actions cannot be explained by age, origin, gender, ethnicity, or former occupation, had one clear and overarching goal: freedom. They did not seek freedom by attempting to destroy the institution of slavery in a violent frontal assault, nor did they attempt to accomplish this by fleeing to the wilderness to carve out a desperate survivalist existence. Rather, the maroons at Prospect Bluff sought to achieve freedom by rejecting their prior condition of enslavement and embracing a belief that they had been granted the rights and liberties of full British subjects.

I also show how the maroons' claim to British status was sponsored by Edward Nicolls, who instructed and radicalized the former slaves. During the War of 1812 Nicolls was ordered to raise an army of slaves and Indians in the Southeast as part of the larger British plan to capture New Orleans. However, because of Nicolls's anti-slavery beliefs, which were fully developed by that time, he quickly came to view his mission in the Southeast as an opportunity to execute an anti-slavery plan. Nicolls explained his original anti-slavery ideology to the former slaves, emphasizing their humanity, Christian virtue, and unlimited potential for racial and political equality and acknowledging the acceptability of violence in combating slavery. At the same time Nicolls explained to the former slaves his understanding of the British Empire as a universal empire of liberalism. When this was done, Nicolls granted the former slaves full political and legal equality within the British Empire. Because of their knowledge of Nicolls's anti-slavery ideology and his understanding of the British Empire, the former slaves never doubted that they were capable of enjoying all the "rights" and "liberties" of "true British subjects," totally equal to those of white Britons. Finally, Nicolls left hundreds of radicalized former slaves who were convinced that they were full British subjects in charge of a British-built fort at Prospect Bluff and its immense store of supplies and military hardware.

Because of the tremendous importance of Nicolls's actions, he factors prominently throughout this book. I emphasize his role as a reflection of the reality of events as they unfolded in the Southeast. Without Nicolls's actions and ideas, I argue, the maroon community at Prospect Bluff would never have existed, nor would the inhabitants have been steeped in radical anti-slavery thought, nor would they have been in a position to believe that they had achieved the status of full subjects of the British Empire. Emphasizing Nicolls's role does not undermine the former slaves' agency—or that of the Red Sticks and Seminoles for that matter. This was because Prospect Bluff was inhabited by a community of former slaves—deep in the heart of Spanish Florida—who had shrewdly realized that Nicolls's ideas, promises, and material support offered the surest route to the fullest version of freedom. This realization and commitment to Nicolls's ideas, which guided the maroon community, continued for decades after the destruction of the physical settlement at Prospect Bluff. Such behavior demonstrates people's conscious and willful embrace of Nicolls's anti-slavery plan.

All totaled, the inhabitants of the maroon community built a version of freedom in spatial, material, economic, cultural, gendered, political, and intellectual terms that was driven by their knowledge of Nicolls's anti-slavery rhetoric, the belief that they were British subjects, and their collective experiences and observations. These actions speak directly to how the former slaves understood freedom and the broader world in which they lived as well as to their desire and ability to achieve the fullest version of freedom that was available to them. Such behavior would have made the maroons the envy of most people of color in the revolutionary Atlantic world; it also demonstrates that the former slaves were resisting slavery as a social institution and deserve to be placed at the fore of contemporary liberationist movements because of their pursuit of such full political, legal, and racial equality.

At face value, the comparative analysis of the Prospect Bluff community adds new and valuable dimensions in the understanding of the Atlantic world, slavery, and the African diaspora. Such an approach emphasizes the extent to which the enslaved both would and could pursue their freedom, as well as the steps taken in this pursuit, when people were presented with any given set of conditions and variables (such as physical environment, available resources, demographics, prior experiences and abilities, the nature of enemies, culture, knowledge of ideas about topics such as politics and anti-slavery thought, broader geopolitics, and timing). Maroons from across the hemisphere sought to navigate these circumstances, but the results varied widely, from bands of desperate survivalists to large and long-lived communities that enjoyed a good standard of living, strong governments, and vibrant cultural lives. As the comparative material demonstrates, the former slaves at Prospect Bluff were able to cultivate an unusually, if not uniquely, full version of freedom mainly because of the remarkable opportunities with which the Prospect Bluff maroons were presented. Finally, the observation that the Prospect Bluff maroons were able to cultivate an unusually full version of freedom, when added to the comparative material, leads to perhaps the most important revelation offered by the Prospect Bluff example: there is no reason to believe that nearly any other North American slave would not have behaved in a manner similar to the Prospect Bluff maroons if provided with similar conditions.

The maroon community at Prospect Bluff stands as a useful tool to understand the broad institution of slavery as well as slave resistance and slave consciousness because it was the rarest of North American phenomena: an example of successful communal slave resistance. The inhabitants of the maroon community had done something of which other slave rebels—including most maroons—could only dream: removed themselves from the broader slave society and established a thriving and prosperous all-black polity. From a hemispheric perspective the community was equally unusual: a radicalized maroon community of people who rooted their freedom in distinctly modern and Atlantic concepts. In this particular case scholars are not left to speculate about what might have happened had a large number of North American slaves successfully thrown off their shackles and formed an autonomous community. Nor are we left to guess about slaves' knowledge of ideas about anti-slavery thought, political inclusion, racial equality, and how this knowledge might have shaped their behavior. Rather, through the careful examination of archival materials found in Europe, across the United States, and in the Caribbean, a clear picture emerges of what slave rebels and the enslaved desired. How the residents of the maroon community found themselves in such a position and how they subsequently behaved both serve to shed valuable light on determining not only the aims of rebel slaves but, more broadly and more important, how slaves understood the contours of freedom and the wider world in which they lived. Put another way, a close examination of the maroon community at Prospect Bluff allows us to see how former slaves wanted to exist when free to live according to their own devices. Thus in many ways the total independence of the Prospect Bluff community allows for more telling insights into the minds of the enslaved than do free black communities such as Fort Mose or those in northern cities or towns. At Prospect Bluff the maroons achieved self-determination, which simply did not happen in formal free black communities. As the evidence from Prospect Bluff demonstrates and the comparative data emphasize, slaves deeply desired the most complete version of freedom possible, and they were shrewd and intelligent realists who fully understood the world in which they lived.

1 ⟹ Edward Nicolls and the Problem of War and Slavery in the Age of Revolution

On June 1, 1812, President James Madison called on Congress to declare war.[1] His message recounted a decade of alleged American grievances suffered at the hands of Great Britain, including impressment, blockades, the Orders-in-Council, and the renewal of Indian warfare on the western frontier. The House of Representatives passed the bill within three days. The Senate narrowly fell in line on June 17, and the next day Madison signed the declaration. Situated squarely within the Age of Revolution, the War of 1812 began at a critical juncture for slavery in North America and the broader Atlantic world. Consequently racial politics shaped the course of "Mr. Madison's War." This was most acute in the Southeast, where the radical anti-slavery thoughts and actions of Colonel Edward Nicolls of the Royal Marines added an extra dynamic to the war.

The Challenge to American Slavery

White Americans emerged from the American Revolution deeply proud of their relatively egalitarian political culture.[2] The young nation was awash with rhetoric and imagery that celebrated republican ideals, though in reality only white male property owners enjoyed full citizenship. Initially the revolutionary era appeared to offer hope for American slaves. The slave community had felt their strength during the conflict, particularly through the service of black soldiers, slave flight, and the promise that "all men are created equal." The spread of Afro-Christianity further strengthened African American communities and the universality of their struggle.[3] Likewise, northern states commenced policies of gradual emancipation, and it appeared that the institution of slavery was on borrowed time in the South. Thus many slaves thought they too would soon enjoy the universal benefits of the Age of Revolution that were sweeping the western world.

However, the intersection of a number of developments conspired against the slaves and dramatically altered the history of North America. At the turn of the nineteenth century, slavery was given a new lease on life with the emergence of cotton as a profitable staple crop, mostly grown in the vast expanses of the Louisiana Purchase.[4] White southerners and their slaves rapidly moved into the interior of South Carolina and Georgia, Alabama, Mississippi, and Louisiana and transformed the area into a vibrant and profitable slave society. In the new century slavery was as central to the southern economy as ever.[5] This was due to the profitability of cotton combined with the growth of the lucrative internal slave trade, the emergence of a sugar industry along the Gulf Coast, and the persistence of plantation slavery in the Chesapeake and Lowcountry. However, American slavery was expanding into direct contact with the Spanish Floridas and into a region where the environment and strong Indian tribes meant that the institution frequently operated on unstable ground.

The 1791 Haitian Revolution, which from the point of view of white southerners was a horrifically violent racial nightmare, provided a vivid example of what could happen when slaves and people of color claimed the inheritance of the Age of Revolution as their very own.[6] The example of Haiti, knowledge of which spread like wildfire fire throughout slave communities across the Western Hemisphere, led to a major upsurge in resistance that lasted well into the nineteenth century.[7] What emboldened slaves terrified white slaveholders, who became even more suspicious of the behavior of their slaves. White anxiety and black hope were further heightened in 1800 by Gabriel's rebellion and in 1811 by the German Coast uprising, both of which were viewed through the lens of the Haitian Revolution.[8]

These domestic political and economic changes, combined with international events, most prominently the Haitian Revolution, redefined American slavery. The institution became more southern, more polarizing, and more rigidly policed.[9] While the American abolitionist movement—centered in the North—was only in its early stages and was dwarfed by its British counterpart, the emergence of an internal and white dissenting voice was nonetheless important. Prior to this period, with few exceptions, white Americans universally accepted slavery. Now a largely southern institution confronted both growing white disapproval and the specter of increasingly rebellious slaves just as white and black settlement was expanding into an unstable frontier region. The result of the internal and external challenges to slavery was a hard-line defense of the institution that rested on race, religion, and economics.[10]

Slavery and the War of 1812

Set against such a tense and turbulent backdrop, slaves and slavery factored prominently in the coming of the War of 1812. In 1811 John Randolph of Virginia took the floor of Congress and famously thundered, "God forbid, sir, that the Southern States should ever see an enemy on their shores, with these infernal principles of French fraternity in the van!"[11] John Calhoun quickly attempted to rebut Randolph's warning that the forces of the Age of Revolution might trigger a major slave rebellion, assuring an audience that "the precise time of the greatest safety is during a war in which we have no fear of invasion—then the country is most on its guard. . . . Even in our Revolution no attempts were made by that portion of our population . . . [to rebel]." Calhoun further stated that regarding "the disorganizing effects of the French principles, I cannot think our ignorant blacks have felt much of their . . . influence. I dare say more than one half of them never heard of the French Revolution."[12] As the words of Randolph and Calhoun demonstrate, many white Americans harbored a fundamental anxiety over slave resistance as the War of 1812 began. This fear derived in part from a powerful realization that "in a state of actual warfare . . . dread and alarm peculiar . . . [to] . . . the Southern states are known to exist . . . [from] . . . a wanton and relentless Enemy, or from an insurrection or internal commotion."[13] When this reckoning was combined with growing insecurities over sectional tensions centered on slavery, the expansion of the institution into new territory, and the past twenty-five years of slave resistance and ideological foment across the Western Hemisphere, many white Americans found Randolph's dire warning more compelling than Calhoun's efforts to ease their anxieties.[14]

White Americans were rightly concerned, because when the War of 1812 spread into the South thousands of slaves fled to the British, who quickly utilized the refugees as guides, laborers, or spies before organizing formal black military units. This was a sensible decision: American slaves proved to be a significant boost to British manpower and highly useful as soldiers.[15] But perception overwhelmed reality: in the southern imagination, arming and recruiting of slaves was tantamount to fomenting a rebellion.

Prior to the War of 1812 North America's most extensive experience with the arming of slaves came during the American Revolution, when both sides utilized slaves.[16] But slaves and slave soldiers played fundamentally different roles in the War of 1812 than they did in the American Revolution. Profound changes had swept the globe during the Age of Revolution, and further shifts had occurred within American slavery and society; taken together, the changes made the arming of slaves a vastly different undertaking in 1813 than it had been in 1776. The very nature of the American Revolution and the War of 1812 fundamentally differed. During the American Revolution the British Army tried to quell a rebellion of fellow members of the British Empire. However, the War of 1812 pitted two sovereign nations against each other. It was certainly the case that both nations shared a number of cultural and historical bonds that might have served to lessen enmity. But other matters eroded this common ground: Britain's resentment that the United States declared war in the midst of the Napoleonic Wars; American humiliation at their recent treatment by the British; and the increasingly testy international rivalry over which nation most fully represented the true spirit of human progress during the Age of Revolution.[17]

Central to these differences was the fact that trained and armed black regiments participated in virtually every conflict across the Western Hemisphere during the Age of Revolution. Whether fighting alongside imperial armies or as slave rebels, black soldiers had become one of the most conspicuous symbols of the changing fortunes of their race during this era. Black soldiers served as clear examples of the complex interplay of race, military service, rights, and freedom.[18] When wars began, whites had to take into account the potential destructiveness of the slave population while grudgingly accepting that slave or free blacks soldiers were a military necessity. Slaves, for their part, clearly understood their role in the balance of power, their desire for freedom, and the various avenues through which freedom could be achieved. As a result, a new type of war emerged in the Caribbean and Latin America during the Age of Revolution.[19] There was a traditional component pitting the armies of European empires against each other in struggles that were anything but new over wealth, power, and influence. Yet these wars were larger and more ideologically infused than ever before, while the role of slaves and slavery greatly influenced the nature of these conflicts in both physical and intellectual terms.

No nation understood the intricacies of this process better than Great Britain. The British military contended with suppressing a number of armed rebellions within its Caribbean possessions during the Age of Revolution, while simultaneously fighting horribly bloody battles against the French across the globe. Most notably, the British military attempted to occupy Saint Domingue between 1793 and 1798 but suffered catastrophic losses and spent much of 1795 and 1796 fighting slave rebels and maroons in Jamaica, Grenada, and St. Vincent.[20] The year 1795 was when the West India Regiments were founded in the British Caribbean, which further illustrates the complex interplay among war, race, freedom, rights, and military service that confronted the British during this period.[21]

The British carried all this dearly bought military experience to the War of 1812. Many of the most important British officers and a large number of the men under their command were veterans of the conflicts in the Caribbean. They entered the war in North America with a deep knowledge of the military usefulness of slaves as well as an understanding of the horrors of slave resistance and the complicated dynamics of this new mode of warfare. This human connection to the revolutionary Caribbean was further enhanced in the Deep South through black and white Haitian refugees.[22]

Because of all of these factors, when it came to the role of people of color, the War of 1812 had more direct continuities with the prior thirty years of international warfare and slave resistance than it did with the American Revolution. This was true in terms of aims, implications, ideas, tactics, and dangers. Speaking with hindsight, Frederic Robinson accurately captured the mood when he told the House of Commons that the opening of the southern theater of the War of 1812 "was one of the most eventful periods of that impolitical war." In Robinson's opinion this was because the "slave population of Virginia amounted to about three millions five hundred thousand of whom a seventh part, at least, might be supposed capable of bearing arms: and as many of them . . . [were] . . . ready to rise against their masters, they were an open enemy in the heart of the country."[23]

Alexander Cochrane and Increased Efforts to Arm American Slaves

No individual had greater personal responsibility for the decision to recruit and arm American slaves than did Alexander Cochrane, who was appointed the commander-in-chief of the British Navy in the newly created American Station in April 1814. Cochrane was no stranger to slaveholding in the Age of Revolution. In 1808 he had raised a corps of black colonial marines in Guadeloupe. As the governor of the Leeward Islands until 1814 he owned a large plantation and many slaves in Trinidad. Cochrane brought to his command of the Royal Navy in North America an intimate knowledge of the precarious balance of power and delicately constructed social fabric that defined slave societies. Because of these experiences, Cochrane felt he could successfully pursue two goals with American slaves. First, by exacerbating the tensions between slaves and whites to some point short of fomenting a large-scale slave rebellion, Cochrane hoped to destabilize southern society and distract slaveholders from supporting the American war effort. Second, he tried to create an organized black fighting force that would complement regular units on the battlefield. Thus Cochrane knew exactly what he was doing in early 1815 when he included blacks in a raid on the Chesapeake in order to "cause alarm among the White population for the insurrection of the slaves and the Revolutionizing of that State."[24] As such he brought one of the living embodiments of the revolutionary Caribbean to the North American mainland.

Cochrane's actions reflected general British policy toward American slaves. British policy focused on the large-scale recruitment and organization of fugitives into formal military units—a policy strongly endorsed by British officers. A number of factors explain the willingness of officers to embrace so radical a stance. Weather was taking a toll on their white troops, especially in the Deep South.[25] The British military believed that black and Indian soldiers were naturally better suited to North America's climate. Vindictiveness played a role as well. Many Britons complained that America had stabbed their country in the back by declaring war while Britain was defending the world from Napoleon.[26] Many Britons further believed that America was waging a dishonorable war. Attacking civilians in Canada, encouraging British soldiers and sailors to desert, ignoring flags of truce, using torpedoes, and poisoning wine were all alleged examples of America's dishonorable tactics.[27] At the same time many Britons, including many soldiers and politicians, regarded Americans as inferior. For example, Rear Admiral Edward Codrington derided Americans as a "detestable race of people" and called the detachment that captured Pensacola "a collection [of] inferior animals."[28] All these factors led Britons to lobby for waging a destructive and punitive war against the Americans. Codrington hoped the Americans would "be chastized even until they excite my pity, by which time they will be sufficiently humbled," while Cochrane wanted "to give them a complete drubbing before Peace is made."[29]

Prior to early 1814 there had been no single galvanizing event equivalent to Lord Dunmore's 1775 proclamation to the slaves of Virginia during the American Revolution.[30] This changed when, only days after his appointment, Cochrane issued a proclamation from Bermuda that read:

A PROCLAMATION
Whereas it has been represented to me, that many Persons now resident in the United States, have expressed a desire to withdraw therefrom, with a view of entering into His Majesty's Service, or of being received as Free Settlers into some of His Majesty's Colonies.
This is therefore to Give Notice,

That all those who may be disposed to emigrate from the United States will, with their Families, be received on board of His majesty's Ships or Vessels of War, or at the Military Posts that may be established, upon or near the Coast of the United States when they will have their choice of either entering into His Majesty's Sea or Land Forces, or of being sent as FREE Settlers to the British Possessions in North America or the West Indies, where they will meet with all due encouragement.

Given under my Hand at Bermuda, the 2nd day of April, 1814.

ALEXANDER COCHRANE [31]

Cochrane's proclamation emphasized military service, family, property, and ultimately freedom in the British Empire. Using such violently contested concepts of the Age of Revolution was bold and provocative to both blacks and whites. Consequently Cochrane's proclamation both challenged American slavery and added a major new dynamic to the war. Specifically, the proclamation forced both black and white southerners to reflect on the uncomfortable ironies inherent in a society in which one part of the population was free while another part was enslaved. Unlike Dunmore's proclamation, which was limited to Virginia, Cochrane's proclamation was circulated across the South for the remainder of the war.

Nobody on either side ever doubted the purpose of the proclamation. In London, John Quincy Adams cornered Henry Goulburn in a tense confrontation as to its real meaning. Adams recorded Goulburn insisting that "the proclamation of Admiral Cochrane referred to gave no such encouragement, there was not a word about negroes in it. It merely offered employment or a settlement in the British colonies to such persons as might be disposed to leave the United States." However, Adams pressed Goulburn on "the import of the term *free* used in the proclamation in connection with the offer of settlements?" According to Adams, Goulburn "answered the question with some hesitation but admitted that it might be understood as having reference to slaves." Adams then "admitted on my part that the word 'negroes' was not in the proclamation, but remarked that he must be as sensible as I was that it could have reference only to them. That certainly no person in America could mistake its meaning. It was unquestionably intended for the negroes."[32] President Madison received word of the proclamation in the middle of May and immediately saw it as "the worst, the Enemy may be able to effect against us"; he complained that it reflected "the most inveterate spirit against the Southern States."[33] The Spanish in Florida were equally nervous about its implications and saw in the proclamation an out-and-out call for American slaves to revolt.[34] Even Britain's *Morning Chronicle* referred to it as "an invitation of the blacks to desert their masters."[35]

In the months after Cochrane issued his proclamation, thousands of slaves joined the British from across the Chesapeake and Lowcountry. Hundreds of these slaves formed military units that fought alongside British soldiers and deeply impressed their white British officers with their ability and bravery. In the end, British aims to utilize American slaves in the upper South and Lowcountry fell short of the military's goals for two reasons. First, both these regions were stable slave societies in which white southerners had become highly effective at policing the slave population and discouraging flight and resistance. Second and more important, British intrigues with the slave population in the upper South and Lowcountry did not begin until the latter stages of the War of 1812. However, across the upper South and Lowcountry, American slaves had aided the British war effort as soldiers, laborers, spies, and guides, while even obedient slaves required extra vigilance from their masters. In the process American slaves vividly illustrated their desire for freedom and their understanding that the conflict with Great Britain presented numerous formal and informal avenues to achieve freedom. The same efforts to recruit slaves and Indians had very different results when the British arrived in the Southeast, making Georgia governor Peter Early correct when he nervously noted that "a storm is gathering in that quarter."[36]

The Radical Anti-Slavery Thought of Edward Nicolls

British efforts to recruit slave and Indian soldiers in the Southeast had different results because of the region's history, population, economy, geopolitics, and physical landscape. The single most important reason for the different recruitment results was the presence of Edward Nicolls and George Woodbine (whose background is discussed in chapter 2), the two men in charge of the British expedition to raise a black and Indian army in the Southeast. Of great importance in shaping events in the Southeast was the fact that Edward Nicolls was a radical anti-slavery advocate who devoted most of his life to fighting slavery through a unique combination of activism and firsthand action. Nicolls's anti-slavery beliefs, which he had developed long before arriving in North America during the War of 1812, deserve to be considered at length, for these ideas shaped the very nature of the maroon community at Prospect Bluff more than did any other single factor.

Nicolls was the eldest of six sons, the rest of whom died serving in the British military. He was born in Coleraine in the north of Ireland in 1779. In the late eighteenth century Ireland was marked by deeply rooted sectarian tensions as well as concerns that arose from frequently oppressive British rule.[37] Giving testimony to Parliament in 1830, Nicolls sadly noted that the Sierra Leonians "had a kind of patriarchal government, and I am sorry to say they are like the people in my own country, all fighting in clans."[38] During this time even successful Ulster Protestants, who enjoyed the benefits of Great Britain's immense international success, realized that they were peripheral figures in an empire that was fundamentally English at its core. Nicolls's ethnic identity shaped his understanding of the British Empire as well as his anti-slavery thought.

Nicolls's family was of the middling rank (his father was the surveyor of excise in Coleraine) with extensive ties to the British military. In a world where religious practices carried tremendous weight, young Edward received an intense religious upbringing. His mother, whose father was the rector of Coleraine, surrounded herself with "abhorrent" "pet preachers," who "consider[ed] innocent or indifferent acts [to be] *sins*"; she converted from Presbyterianism to Methodism prior to his birth.[39] After leaving home Nicolls converted from Methodism to Presbyterianism.[40] Regardless of these shifts, Nicolls spent his life as an intensely devout Ulster Protestant, which deeply informed an unbending morality that he brought to every facet of his life. The same mindset played into his leadership of the Hibernian Temperance Society.[41] This personal morality was framed in absolute terms and caused Nicolls to attach himself to extreme causes with intense activity, violence, and devotion.

Nicolls's scanty formal education consisted of two years of schooling in Greenwich. At the age of eleven he enlisted in the Royal Navy, and in 1795, at the age of sixteen, he was commissioned as a second lieutenant in the Royal Marines.[42] The age of Nicolls's enlistment was unremarkable, but it is important to consider the brutality of the world he entered as a mere boy. Corporal punishment, self-sacrifice, and rigid discipline under extreme conditions defined his military life. Furthermore the 1790s were a profoundly turbulent time for a young man from the north of Ireland to begin his long military career. The Age of Revolution was entering its most intense stage, with Britain and France locked in an international war on which the survival of both nations appeared to rest, and the Haitian Revolution was sending shock waves across the globe. More pointedly, in 1795 as young Nicolls began his career the British Caribbean was burning in a series of maroon wars and slave rebellions, while thousands of British soldiers were bogged down in the horrors of the Haitian Revolution.

This era of extreme intellectual, political, and social change forced many people to reconsider ideas about political and legal inclusion, rights, race, the

FIGURE 2. Perhaps the only surviving portrait of Edward Nicolls. Photo by Martin Edwards.

state, economics, and social justice. Out of this climate emerged a series of organized movements to abolish the slave trade and, in some cases, slavery itself. Nicolls, with his intense morality and sense of being an ethnic outsider within the British Empire, was quickly drawn to the radical idea of racial egalitarianism and the belief that slavery was an evil institution to be destroyed by any means.[43] Equally important in understanding Nicolls's anti-slavery thought was the fact that the British Empire was rapidly and self-consciously altering many of its ideological foundations as it was forced to reconfigure itself after American Independence and in relation to the threat of the French Revolution.[44] Britons were coming to see themselves as inhabiting an empire of liberty and liberalism that defended the rights of people across the world against French aggression. Ultimately Nicolls embraced extreme, yet intertwined, versions of both empire and anti-slavery that diverged from more mainstream tendencies by combining activism and firsthand violent action, most notably during the War of 1812 and then while serving as governor of Fernando Po between 1829 and 1834. His stance derived from his origins, personality, religious beliefs, and conception as an Ulsterman of his place within the British Empire.

Nicolls quickly earned the life-long nickname "Fighting Nicolls." He gained much of his earliest combat experience in the revolutionary Caribbean, where the seeds of his anti-slavery beliefs began to blossom. In 1803 he distinguished himself at Santo Domingo and in 1804 he led a successful siege of Curaçao.[45] Thus Nicolls first directly encountered Africans and slavery in the midst of one of the most dramatic epochs in western history. He intimately witnessed the collapse of slavery in Hispaniola and the subsequent reverberations across the region that were marked by chaos, black armies, and the general sense of fundamental order having broken down under immense racial and imperial pressures. For a deeply moralistic twenty-four-year-old imperial outsider from Coleraine, this was an extraordinary firsthand introduction to slavery and to anti-slavery in the form of violent black liberation in pursuit of the most radical ideas about racial and political equality that were in circulation during the Age of Revolution.

His own background, when combined with such experiences and the broader intellectual and political climate of the day, had led Nicolls to reflect on questions of race, rights, military service, religion, and empire. The fact that he was exposed directly to slaves and black soldiers at precisely the time when he was going through this intellectual, moral, political, and religious journey greatly shaped the contours of his anti-slavery thought. In particular, Nicolls emerged from this period of his life with a tremendous regard for black humanity, not to mention military ability, after witnessing blacks fight

FIGURE 3. This 1809 lithograph depicts a meeting at the Philanthropic Society Chapel in London. Unnumbered plate from William Combe and William Henry Pyne, *The Microcosm of London or London in Miniature*, vol. 2 (London: Methune, 1904).

so brutally in pursuit of their freedom and the loftiest ideals of the Age of Revolution. This realization further convinced Nicolls of slavery being an evil institution that could justly be attacked through violence as well as ideas and activism. Ten years later in Florida, Nicolls made it clear that he had vivid memories of the lessons he had learned in the Caribbean and that his anti-slavery beliefs had continued to grow and flourish.

After his service in the Caribbean, Nicolls continued to distinguish himself in the Napoleonic Wars, this time in the Middle East and Europe. In 1807 he served in the Dardanelles, Corfu, and Egypt before returning to Britain to get married in 1808. There was little time for a honeymoon and by 1809 Nicolls had returned to the front lines, where he led the successful defense of the island of Anholt in Denmark. This resulted in his becoming a minor celebrity and the governor of Anholt. From 1813 to 1815 Nicolls would serve in the Caribbean and Gulf South. Ultimately he devoted nearly twenty years, or what amounted to all of his adult life, to fighting in extreme conditions on three continents in defense of the British Empire. Few people would have had a deeper understanding of what the British Empire represented ideologically and practically than Edward Nicolls at the end of the Napoleonic Wars. By this point he had become a member of the Philanthropic Society, where he would have discussed such topics while becoming increasingly involved with the organized anti-slavery movement.[46]

That Nicolls was an opponent of slavery and the slave trade was unusual, given his vocation and origins. However, what was truly unique was exactly how he sought to assault slavery: through combining direct action with what might broadly be termed activism—the traditional avenues such as petitions, correspondences, publications, and membership in leading anti-slavery societies. In particular during the War of 1812 and then as the governor of Fernando Po, Nicolls forcefully liberated thousands of slaves and then organized them as settlers and soldiers. Furthermore, Nicolls's actions were matched by public proclamations of the evils of slavery, a tendency to exceed his orders, and an exceptional fervor, all of which defined his actions during the War of 1812.

To reiterate the threads coming together here: Nicolls's anti-slavery beliefs were the product of his devoutly Protestant northern Irish upbringing, which had instilled in him a stern and unbending morality. Equally important was his understanding of his place as an ethnically peripheral figure within the British Empire, which he conceptualized as an entity of progress and liberalism during the Age of Revolution. Finally, Nicolls's recognition of the power of violence, sacrifice, and service as equalizers within this imperial framework shaped his anti-slavery beliefs. To most onlookers, his actions appeared to be the work of a reckless fanatic. While this was not entirely the case, it is certainly safe to say that Nicolls was a radical opponent of slavery whose efforts to destroy the institution ideologically, intellectually, and physically across the Atlantic world had few equals.

This anti-slavery ideology is succinctly captured in an 1842 letter to the editor of the *Times* that Nicolls wrote after the rebellion of the slaves aboard the *Creole*.[47] In the first half of the letter he recounted an incident at Fernando Po when hundreds of Portuguese slaves, including a number belonging to the Portuguese governor's wife, escaped to British protection from nearby Prince's Island. When the governor asked for the slaves to be returned, Nicolls forcefully responded, "I knew of no such disgrace as that of having a slave under the British flag, that all persons in [Fernando Po] were free, and must be so whilst they obeyed the law." When pressed more aggressively for the return of the slaves, Nicolls responded in kind by insisting "it was more than my commission was worth, as a British officer, or my character as a magistrate, or a friend of Africa, to be found guilty of so infamous an act as that of depriving a fellow-creature of his liberty." In the midst of this standoff, much to Nicolls's delight, word spread among the slaves on Prince's Island and St. Thomas that freedom could be found with the British on Fernando Po. Hundreds of slaves fled, which made an already combustible situation explode. The furious Portuguese governor accused Nicolls of encouraging slaves to flee and harboring "murderers and . . . stolen goods," before promising to report Nicolls to the British government in what threatened to be a serious diplomatic incident. Far from being deterred, Nicolls met the governor's threats with the radical boast that "it would be contrary to British law to give up a slave under any circumstances, particularly such as that of killing any one during a scuffle to obtain his liberty, which the law of God and England justified, and nobly acknowledged to be no murder." The governor's shock deepened when Nicolls claimed that "it was his duty as a Christian man and a governor to discourage crime of every description . . . [but it was a] . . . gross and unmerited insult, by even supposing or hinting that a British officer could possibly descend to become a slave-driver to a slave-dealer." The governor never pursued the matter with either the British or Portuguese government.

The second half of the letter elaborated on these ideas in relation to the case of the *Creole*.[48] In the midst of a deeply emotional and sensational trial that was having global repercussions, Nicolls wrote:

> I am sorry to hear that the 18 men who had the spirit to free themselves and their less courageous fellow-sufferers should be put in prison by our Government at the Bahamas; the killing they have been forced to commit is no murder, but only justifiable homicide in self-defence, and their taking away a short time the vessels that their oppressors had destined to carry their victims farther into the God-abandoned and infamous regions of republican slavery, for the purpose of conveying themselves into a land of constitutional liberty, was no piracy. I therefore earnestly contend that the brave men, who, by God's help and their own courage, have thus set themselves at liberty, have committed no fault, but on the contrary, that they have done that which is lawful and right, and that I believe they have, and ought to have, the good wishes, and that they are entitled to the protection, of our most gracious Sovereign and all her subjects, accompanied with those of all Christian free men in the states of America.

This letter vividly conveys Nicolls's profound hatred of slavery as an affront to his Christian faith; his conviction that slavery could not be reconciled with his understanding of the British Empire and the modern world; his belief that Africans were fully human and could enjoy full equality in a "land of constitutional liberty" (the British Empire); and his acceptance of violence as an entirely appropriate means with which to combat the institution. In other words, this letter captured Nicolls's radicalism. This same radicalism and ideology informed his thoughts and actions at Prospect Bluff and would provide the maroon community with its identity. Indeed, Nicolls began the letter to the *Times* by noting that "having had several similar affairs to manage, when in command of the British, Spanish, and Indian forces in the Floridas during the late war with the United States in the years 1814 and 1815 . . . if you think the manner in which I managed those matters can be of any benefit or consequence to the cause of the long and cruelly-oppressed Africans, the annexed description is at your service." Nicolls was both making it clear that he had already fully developed his unique ideology of anti-slavery while serving on the Gulf Coast and that he had acted on these ideas during the War of 1812.

With profound consequences, Nicolls's understanding of Cochrane's proclamation was rooted in his unique anti-slavery beliefs. Nicolls believed that the proclamation was a legally binding agreement between the British military (and ultimately the British state) and the former slaves who "enlisted in the British forces on the faith of the . . . Proclamation."[49] This offer was not limited to potential soldiers but extended also to women, children, and former slaves incapable of military service. Equally important was Nicolls's firm belief that when slaves "volunteered their services . . . we of course were obliged to accept."[50] The careful choice of the word "obliged" is significant. This sense of obligation applied to all slaves and was one of the defining elements of Nicolls's actions in North America. The guiding principle of his actions in the war, contrary to the intentions of Cochrane's proclamation, was recruiting slave soldiers and their families, who would be rewarded by being made full subjects of the British Empire, possessing the same rights as free white Britons. As I later demonstrate in detail, Nicolls carefully explained to his slave recruits the rights and privileges that came with full membership of the British Empire. These lessons were filtered through the prism of his radical anti-slavery ideology. This combination of political message and radical anti-slavery ideology is essential for understanding both Nicolls's thoughts and actions and those of the former slaves at Prospect Buff, for two reasons. First, had Nicolls not been a radical anti-slavery advocate, he would never have been able to conceptualize blacks as innately capable of enjoying such status and equality. In turn, his actions would have been entirely different while in the Southeast and would have been limited to performing his military duties as effectively and efficiently a possible with little personal concern for his black and Indian recruits. Second, without exposure to Nicolls's anti-slavery ideology, the former slave recruits would never have believed themselves so fully and insistently to be capable of enjoying full rights and equality within the British Empire—given the stifling racism and elaborate arguments against black equality, rights, and political inclusion that were common in early nineteenth-century North America and indeed formed much of the intellectual and ideological foundation on which the United State had been built. Ultimately Nicolls used his commission in the Southeast to undertake a radical anti-slavery experiment, with the enthusiastic participation of hundreds of former slaves, who quickly realized the benefits that might arise from working with Nicolls.

Nicolls's Ability to Radicalize

In August 1814, while waiting anxiously in the Bahamas to be deployed to the Southeast, Nicolls started to plan how he could most successfully recruit American slaves. He reported that the Second West India Regiment had requested he inform Cochrane "how happy they would be to serve with me under your orders in Florida." Nicolls welcomed the opportunity to work with the regiment: "I think if I had that Regiment there with me, or a corps or detachments of several Black Regiments . . . it would have a very good effect. Blacks I think would the more readily join us if they saw men of their own color in a state of discipline."[51]

Nicolls clearly spent much of his time in the Bahamas with members of the Second West India Regiment and later crossed paths with a detachment of its soldiers in Florida.[52] Likewise Nicolls felt at ease with blacks (which could not have been said of all anti-slavery advocates) and had tremendous faith in their fighting ability. His remarks also demonstrate that members of the Second West India Regiment were developing opinions about the War of 1812, which they would have discussed with free and enslaved blacks in the bustling port city of Nassau.[53] The members of the Second West India Regiment appear to have shared a sense of racial and African-diaspora-wide solidarity with enslaved Americans that was not reciprocal.[54]

Shortly after returning to the Bahamas, where the Second West India Regiment was stationed from 1809 with the exception of the mission to Florida, "a spirit of dissatisfaction" arose among the soldiers, "which but for the prompt measures adopted to allay it might possibly have led to dangerous excesses on the part of some of the soldiery which may still lead to the same consequences if the causes of the same be not removed."[55] This anxiety grew over the course of 1816 and reached near hysteria with the outbreak of Bussa's Rebellion in Barbados on April 14, 1816.[56] In May, George Chalmers, the colonial agent for the Bahamas, reported that "in consequence of the discontent of the soldiers" of the Second West India Regiment, "the Commander of the Forces in

Jamaica has thought proper to withdraw five companies (including the flank companies) of that regiment from this station, and to replace them with an equal number of companies of the 5th which is also a *black regiment*."[57] The fact that Chalmers was willing to accept companies of the Fifth West India Regiment illustrates that he was not frightened of black soldiers in general but of the Second West India Regiment in particular. Chalmers concluded by making it clear that an imminent slave rebellion was his greatest fear and that the Second West India Regiment was "the instrument from which the very danger itself is but justly apprehended."[58] By the end of the year Chalmers reported that because of the "present state of [the Second West India Regiment] . . . the domestic Negroes were not so calm, and obedient as they used to be."[59] In early 1817 Chalmers captured the general opinion of whites in the Caribbean when he forcefully proclaimed that "it has become the clear opinion of the most intelligent of the West India body that now is the proper time to get rid of the black troops, altogether. They are distrusted; they form a balance to the efficient power of the white troops . . . [and] . . . the principle and precedent of having black troops offensive and inefficient."[60]

At first glance it may appear highly speculative to argue that Nicolls had influenced the behavior of the Second West India Regiment. However, when a number of factors and two other events are considered, it becomes clear that their relationship with Nicolls had a major impact on their unrest. Nicolls had spent a tremendous amount of time with the regiment analyzing the war. Their conversations would have turned to slavery and freedom if for no other reason than his impending mission and that he possessed Cochrane's proclamation. Moreover, Nicolls believed that blacks should enjoy the rights and privileges of white British subjects, and he was intent on liberating as many slaves as possible. Given his passions and personality, he must have made a strong impression on free and enslaved blacks.

More concrete evidence is found in the actions of the Jamaican George Woodbine in 1817, when he was trying to raise a black army to conquer Spanish Florida. As a member of Gregor MacGregor's Venezuelan revolutionary army of filibusters, which Woodbine had joined after the War of 1812, he went to New Providence to "enlist some disbanded people of the West India Regiment."[61] These soldiers included members of the Second West India Regiment who remembered Nicolls's message and his second in command, Woodbine. Thus in 1817 members of the Second West India Regiment were still so committed to Nicolls's message that they volunteered to fight once again in North America.

Nicolls's more general ability to radicalize is strongly supported by a report Agent Chalmers made in May 1816. The report concerned the case of

Boatswain, Sally, and their children as well as a number of other former slaves who had recently arrived in the Bahamas from Spanish Florida as a result of Nicolls's recruitment efforts.[62] Chalmers complained that this was yet "another device of the Abolitionists to harass the West Indies . . . [that these were] . . . slaves *unlawfully imported* with a view to obtain a decree which will make them free."[63] Clearly Nicolls was numbered among the "Abolitionists," and the "decree" was his interpretation of Cochrane's proclamation. Chalmers objected to this because of his understanding of the Abolition Laws and feared that if it continued, the Bahamas would become a "festering Asylum for everything that is to be detested and feared in the Negro Character throughout the Western World." He also argued that these refugees were "poor wretches who have had the misfortune to fall under the humane protection of the Abolition system . . . [and] . . . suffered infinitely beyond all the horrors of the middle passage, awaiting the decision of their cause." However, Chalmers's deepest fear was "negroes of this description in freedom among us; increasing to a highly alarming degree this most unwelcome and dangerous class of our coloured population." He complained that because "every black fugitive from justice is encouraged to seek an asylum among us and his liberty as the legal reward of his crimes it is easy to foresee what must belong to the fate of the Bahamas." The problem had become so severe that it was serving as a "temporary respite from our apprehensions . . . on the subject of the Black Regiments."[64] Chalmers directly referred to the actions of Nicolls and felt that he had unleashed on the Bahamas a wave of dangerous freedom-seeking refugees who were convinced that they were British subjects with full rights as a result of their relationship with the Royal Marines, while also inciting the Second West India Regiment to the verge of rebellion.

A final fascinating piece of evidence of what Nicolls had wrought on the islands involves the former advocate general Wylly, who defended the refugee slaves in court.[65] Wylly and Nicolls met in the Bahamas, and it is virtually certain that in 1817 when Wylly confessed to having engaged in "correspondence with the Abolitionists," he meant Nicolls (among others).[66] It is equally clear that Wylly's hugely unpopular legal defense of the refugee slaves meant that he admired Nicolls's actions. Much more important, however, Wylly's own actions in late 1816 and early 1817 were likely inspired by Nicolls and grew out of the conditions that the Royal Marine had created. In February 1817, Commissioner Chalmers reported that remarkably, Wylly was "an honorary Governor for life of the African Institute," and in 1815 he had been quoted in James Stephen's abolitionist pamphlet *A Second Letter to Mr. Wilberforce.* Officials in the Bahamas were outraged by the publication of "W[ylly]'s testimony to Parliament in 1815 about the Registration Bill [which had been] unfairly taken." As a result he was charged with "misrepresentation of the House," and a warrant for his arrest was issued. But Wylly "forcibly resisted, and in a manner which we committed with a little pain, at this critical season of alarm and dismay throughout the colonies. For he retired to his plantation, and there armed his own slaves, with firearms and bayonets, to resist . . . the highest Civil authority of the country." During the standoff Wylly hid in an outhouse while his plantation was "defended by the Negroes in military arrangement." Wylly "boasted" that the blacks were "equal if not superior to . . . the militia of the colony, and even H.M.'s West India Regiment." He was captured while visiting a government building. During his subsequent trial Wylly "addressed himself, at least, indirectly, to a number of Blacks, then among the numerous bystanders declaring them an oppressed people and himself their protector."[67] In the midst of a turbulent time marked by a flood of freedom-seeking American refugee slaves and a deeply unhappy black regiment, a highly privileged associate of Nicolls revealed his anti-slavery connections and proceeded to resist the island's government by arming his slaves.

The War of 1812 began at a moment when American slavery faced a number of domestic and international challenges while expanding into new and difficult physical terrain. A war against the world's foremost power, set to the backdrop of the Age of Revolution, was guaranteed to heighten tension and make Americans of all races and classes ask difficult questions and confront many of their darkest fears or greatest hopes about slavery, freedom, the status of the young nation, and violence. Edward Nicolls and his anti-slavery ideas and actions, which he quickly made public and sought to instill in his former slave recruits, greatly exacerbated all these emotions. This fundamentally shaped the dynamics of the War of 1812 in the Deep South and would eventually provide the maroon community at Prospect Bluff with its guiding principles and identity.

2 ⇛ War Comes to the Southeast

BRITAIN'S GRAND MILITARY DESIGN in the Deep South revolved around a multipronged attack on New Orleans.[1] British military planners rightly believed that if their force could take New Orleans, they would deal the United States a severe if not decisive blow. The city's great wealth (cotton worth 3.5 million pounds sterling sat blockaded there) enhanced the appeal of New Orleans, as did the British perception that the local population, which was multiethnic and had relatively recently become part of the United States, would quickly turn away from the upstart nation.[2] Much of the attack on New Orleans was to be carried out in a straightforward assault by the Royal Navy. However, it was planned that smaller British land forces were to converge on the city from the east and north at the same time. In the buildup up to the attack British military planners decided that some of these forces would launch raids across the Deep South at strategically important locations to distract American forces from the defense of New Orleans. The most important of these missions was led by Edward Nicolls and George Woodbine from a base in Spanish Florida.

The British, even more than had been the case in the Chesapeake and Lowcountry, sought to recruit local whites, slaves, and Indians in the Deep South and the Gulf Coast for this purpose. Consequently the war in the Deep South would become "an elaborate example of British peripheral warfare and the use of irregular troops," reminiscent of the British military's campaigns in the revolutionary Caribbean.[3] As a result both the British and Americans perceived the war in the Gulf South as a fundamentally different conflict than what was occurring in the Lowcountry and Chesapeake. This was because of the region's polyglot population, whose history, culture, international connections, and ethnic and racial composition frequently evoked images of the Caribbean and Latin America as much as of the Chesapeake or Lowcountry. Consequently both belligerents designed tailor-made strategies for the region. Lt. John Smith's doomsday prediction vividly reflected these realities. With "astonishment and chagrin," Smith lamented, "If the English have landed on the coast, or if they do in superior force to Gen. Jackson's regular troops the country will fall." In Smith's opinion, this was because "there is a rottinness in the people. If the country is invaded they will be divided. The timid will fly to Tennessee and Kentucky—the perfidious to the enemy and many of the faithful will perish." The lieutenant went on to bemoan that "the militia of this state [Louisiana] cannot be relied on. Two thirds of the people are English or Spanish in heart and many openly avow it . . . [and that from Florida] the Spaniards will coalesce with the creeks, chocktaws, negros and English in offensive war. Of all our country this part is the most vulnerable."[4]

Centuries of Mounting Tensions in the Southeast

The Southeast in which Edward Nicolls and George Woodbine were soon to begin their radical anti-slavery plan had a deeply complicated and violent history that had reached a new low on the eve of the War of 1812. The origins of this instability lay many years in the past, rooted in the fact that the Southeast had been home to two extreme and starkly contrasting manifestations of the English (and later American—together referred to as Anglo America) and Spanish Atlantic empires. A large and balanced white population that craved land defined Anglo America, especially in the South, where planters imported large numbers of slaves to work their agricultural holdings.[5] Conversely, Spanish Florida was thinly populated by soldiers, missionaries, and various settlers who struggled to survive on the periphery of Spain's Atlantic Empire.[6] The area had a small and dispersed Native population because of a rapid decline that had begun with European contact. The region lacked valuable minerals and offered little potential for large-scale agriculture. However, the peninsula was strategically important because it commanded the entrance to the Caribbean, through which lucrative Spanish shipping passed, forcing Spain to cling precariously to Florida.

On the surface the immediate proximity of two deeply divergent imperial systems in such a volatile region meant that tension and conflict were a highly probable geopolitical reality. The greatest source of stress to emerge out of these conditions derived from two very different sets of racial sensibilities that became starker over time and defined the rivalry between Spain and Anglo America in the Southeast.[7] People of color were active participants in this rivalry and were motivated by an array of individual and group goals. Nowhere did Anglo and Spanish racial attitudes and practices manifest themselves in more extreme forms than in southeastern North America.

From its inception Spanish Florida became a multiracial society that required interracial cooperation to resist the encroachments of Anglo America. Blacks, Indians, and mixed race people benefited in spatial, political, military, cultural, and economic terms from this situation in a manner that would have been unusual in most other parts of the Iberian Atlantic world. Conditions in Spanish Florida were highly public and closely watched by whites, blacks, and Indians to the north. Conversely, as the white population of Anglo America grew over the seventeenth and eighteenth centuries and after Independence, it did so by pressing on Native Americans, by appropriating the Indian slave trade, and then by escalating African slavery. All of this led to the creation of a settler society that embraced a deeply conservative understanding of race. The founding of Carolina in 1670 and the decision of Georgia (1750) to legalize slavery were perhaps the two most important developments in the geopolitics of the colonial Southeast. As these racial attitudes hardened over time with the growing Anglo-American commitment to slavery, people of color gained increasingly elevated status in Spanish Florida. This was because black and Indian help was required to keep Anglo America at bay as its inhabitants frequently sought to end the threat of racial disorder that they perceived as emanating from Spanish Florida. This created a destabilizing cycle of violence.

The powerful forces of the Age of Revolution and the shifting weight of American slavery meant that the threat of racial disorder posed by the example of the Spanish Floridas on the eve of the War of 1812 appeared as an overt call to large-scale rebellion in the Southeast—a call that was within plain sight of many American slaves. For both blacks and whites, the Florida Peninsula appeared to be a geographical and intellectual bridge between the revolutionary Caribbean and the postrevolutionary United States that was grappling with the expansion of slavery. To the north of Florida, the political revolution had been largely successful for white male property owners but had left Indians, women, and slaves aware of the ironical hierarchies in the new republic. To the south of Florida, people of color had boldly and violently attempted to claim the inheritance of the Age of Revolution as their own, but at the price of incredible violence and upheaval, the legacy of which was only beginning to be absorbed. At this moment, the greatest significance of the Caribbean and Latin American slave rebellions and Wars of Independence was that they showed the full extent of freedom that lay at the intersection of local conditions and international patterns of revolution. For their part, some North American slaves had recognized the language and ideas of Republicanism and revolution and appropriated it to their condition. The actions of tens of thousands of slaves during the American Revolution as well as the slave conspirators in Charleston in 1793 and Gabriel in 1800 clearly demonstrate this.[8] Despite their defeat, these rebellions illustrated an understanding of the potential power of combining ideas taken from the Age of Revolution with violent action in a North American context. Slaves in the Deep South witnessed these traditions firsthand at a moment when tensions had reached critical mass on both sides of the border. This occurred because local, international, and historical pressures intermixed in a highly combustible combination that was primarily driven by issues relating to race.

The Atlantic Borderlands

Further clarity is added to our understanding of what occurred in the Southeast during the Age of Revolution if we recognize the area as a quintessential "Atlantic-borderland" region.[9] Many places at many times in North American history could best be described as being both borderlands and part of the Atlantic world or as borderlands within the Atlantic world. Such regions were defined by their proximity to the Atlantic Ocean and corresponding political systems, economies, intellectual currents, material culture, biology, flora and fauna, cultures, and societies that exposed people formally or informally to large-scale and international forces. At the same time, due to environment, demographics, and location (proximity to or distance from the Atlantic Ocean or stable colonial settlements and competing empires), these regions also exhibited exceptional economies, cultures, societies, and political and military power structures that resembled the borderlands. The convergence of the Atlantic world and borderlands meant that life within such a region was demonstrably different than in either of its constituent parts. As was the case in other borderlands, the inhabitants of the Atlantic borderlands, particularly people of color and of lower social standing, enjoyed elevated status and freedom of movement that allowed them to shape events and society in unusually strong ways. Colonial, state, or tribal officials grudgingly accepted this as a reality of local conditions while attempting to manipulate people and events in favor of their ends. Again as in other borderlands, imperial competition, physical environment, and geography were common ingredients in creating the conditions of the Atlantic borderlands—much more so than in "frontier regions" or in center vs. periphery models.[10] However, unlike in more traditional borderlands and resembling instead the Atlantic world, these regions were more integrated into or clearly affected by large-scale economies, and the presence of imperial, state, or tribal officials was more evident, as was the power of the interests that they represented. Consequently people in these regions were more exposed to ideas, cultures, developments, and trends on a large scale and were subjected to such forces more than were residents of purely borderlands regions. Thus in the simplest sense, Atlantic borderlands were regions in which many people and groups simultaneously enjoyed enhanced mobility and status while being exposed and subjected to large-scale forces.

The Southeast was a borderland that was in equal measures an intimate part of the North American mainland, the circum-Caribbean, and ultimately the Atlantic world. At the very edge of the Anglo–United States and Spanish Atlantic empires lay a region that was populated by various Europeans, Indians, blacks, and mixed race people who crossed borders freely, traded across the Western Hemisphere, maintained political and military links with Spanish and British colonial holdings as well as the United States, carefully followed world developments, and reflected a culture that was influenced by Europe, Africa, other parts of the Americas, and Native American societies. Not only did free and enslaved blacks and Native Americans enjoy enhanced mobility and elevated status in this setting; they were aware of the revolutionary ideas that were sweeping the globe, ideas that would scarcely have been known to residents of more remote regions.[11] Because of the intersection of the Atlantic world and borderlands, the black population of the Southeast enjoyed great potential for both physical and intellectual agency that compared starkly with what the majority of blacks elsewhere in North America possessed. This was a particularly fertile and explosive setting for Nicolls's unveiling of his radical anti-slavery ideology.

The Patriot Invasion and Creek War

Two regional wars heightened white anxiety to near fever pitch. The first conflagration began in 1812 with the Patriot Invasion of East Florida.[12] The former governor of Georgia, George Matthews, and John Houston McIntosh led the plot, which was inspired by nationalism, greed, and racial anxiety. The Patriots, as they called themselves, conquered Fernandina and Amelia Islands and declared a Republic of Florida before unsuccessfully besieging St. Augustine. Because of a crippling lack of manpower, the Spanish were forced to rely on diplomacy and recently arrived companies of the Cuban Black Militia. The latter deeply offended American racial sensibilities. Speaking on behalf of the governor of East Florida, José Hibberson made it clear that when it came to the use of black soldiers, "the inhabitants of Florida have the same interest as those of Georgia, and it is only from necessity that the Government detained the three companies of Havanna coloured troops in this province."[13] The Spanish were acutely aware of how provocative this black presence was to the United States. For example, the governor of East Florida refused to place a black militia unit on Amelia Island, which desperately needed an armed contingent, because he believed a black outfit would give the Georgians the impression that he was attempting to incite a slave rebellion.[14]

Seminoles and their black allies as well as maroons and a flood of fugitive American slaves joined the black companies that collectively formed the backbone of the Floridas' defense. As a result of wartime chaos, many black soldiers who fought on behalf of the Spanish came from the ranks of former slaves of the American insurgents. In the summer of 1812, for example, a number of former slaves belonging to the American insurgents joined a militia company and worked on the defenses of St. Augustine.[15] White Americans closely followed these developments, fearing that each new event might lead to slave rebellions across the South. At the beginning of the war the Floridian Enrique Yonge reported that the American invasion stemmed from a fear that a Haitian-style revolution would soon begin in Florida and spread to Georgia.[16] East Florida's Jorge Clarke echoed these sentiments when he noted that the Spanish reliance on black and Indian troops, combined with the outbreak of the War of 1812, had the potential to escalate the Patriot Invasion into a "Second Saint Domingue."[17] From St. Augustine, McIntosh warned: "Our slaves are excited to rebel." McIntosh went on to warn that if such a rebellion occurred, "the whole province [of Florida] will be the refuge of fugitive slaves; and from thence emissaries . . . will be detached to bring about a revolt of the black population in the United States."[18] Out of desperation the Spanish occasionally exploited these fears. For example, Hibberson reminded a district attorney in Savannah that "if it is suffered by the State of Georgia to continue [the invasion], I need not inform you that in all probability one half of the negroes of your sea coast would be over the St. Mary's river in less than one month if a system of retaliation was adopted by our Government and assurances of protection to them."[19]

The Patriot Invasion eventually devolved into a savagely contested series of back and forth border raids. The bulk of the American invaders were effectively beaten by the middle of 1813, sending shock waves across the slave-owning South. The Patriot leaders accepted the offer of amnesty put forth on behalf of Fernando VII in May of that year. Some Patriots remained in East Florida for another year and caused immeasurable damage to the province, burning and destroying much in their wake. East Florida had gone from relative stability to almost complete anarchy in only a few years. The province's political and military systems collapsed into disarray, hunger threatened, and the economy fell into ruin. The Spanish government's inability to help both compounded and caused these problems. The inability to aid the Floridas was caused by the Peninsular War and the series of rebellions that were rocking the Spanish Empire.[20] To white Americans it appeared that racialized anarchy had broken out in the Spanish Floridas at a highly critical moment and threatened to spread into the Deep South. Few Americans would have disagreed with Georgia's Col. Daniel Newman that Florida was the "bosom of a wild and savage country, surrounded by prowling and butchering barbarians."[21]

To people of color, Spanish Florida provided a haven from the oppressively racialized society of the United States, a haven that was worth fighting to defend. Each of the groups of people involved realized that a Spanish-controlled Florida offered an appealing alternative to life within the rapidly expanding American plantation complex. However, among Americans the dominant impression left by the Patriot Invasion was unease over the actions of blacks and Indians in the Southeast. As an editor at the *Niles Weekly Register* noted anxiously, "nor are the black troops in Florida very pleasant neighbours to the people of the South."[22] Benjamin Hawkins, the American agent to the Creek Indians, nervously observed shortly after the proclamation of amnesty that "we have [?] our Negro business in inextricable difficulties.... If the Governor of St. Augustine possesses the disposition he has not the power to put an end to this very serious evil to the citizens of Georgia."[23] The Georgian William Ashley wrote to Governor David Mitchell that "the Black Troops are getting very bad and oppressive on the inhabitants of East Florida and from their enmity towards the people of this state, we have no doubt, but they will shortly begin to exercise their influence over our slaves."[24]

In numerous depositions filed by former American residents of East Florida the picture became even gloomier for the United States. One testified that in 1813 he had witnessed the arrival of two fugitive slaves from Georgia who sold their canoe and were given passes to St. Augustine by a Spanish commandant. He went on to swear that black troops under Don Justo Lopas "range . . . between St. Mary's River and the St. John's Rivers," which meant they were active far into Georgia. He continued by stating that the black troops "hand out a General Protection to all negroes that may join them . . . also said Troops are hostile to the people of the United States and treat the inhabitants who have taken the Oath of Allegiance with every kind of indignity and . . . say they will rule the country."[25] A second deposition confirmed that Lopas's troops were providing sanctuary for fugitive slaves but went on to add that all Americans who had taken the oath and remained in Florida were to be "governed by the Negroes . . . [and the blacks] would slap any white man's jaws who would dare to say anything not pleasing to them." The same deposition noted that the black troops "are hostile to the Government and people of the United States and are using all means in their power to induce the slaves of the people of Georgia to join them . . . [and worse still] Negro Troops are in no wise under the direction of the Spanish officer for whatever they wish to do they do it."[26]

In 1813 a civil war began within the Creek Nation in the Deep South that represented another highly racialized regional war, overlapping in real and imaginary ways with the Patriot Invasion and the War of 1812.[27] This overlap can be seen clearly in Thomas Flournoy's panicked request that his Louisiana militia unit be reinforced by companies from Tennessee and Georgia in order to "put a speedy end to the war with the Creeks, and prepare in time for a more powerful enemy; from whom we expect a visit during the fall or winter."[28] At the heart of the civil war were growing economic, cultural, political, ethnic/racial, and power issues as well as the pan-Indian prophetic movement of Tecumseh that tore at Creek society. The conflict pitted the dissident Red Stick faction, who had taken up Tecumseh's call, against the wealthier and more accommodationist leadership of the Creeks, who were allied with the United States. The red stick symbolized both justice and Tecumseh's prophetic movement, having assumed this symbolic importance when the prophetic leader Little Warrior was murdered by the Creeks in 1813. Because of Tecumseh's alliance with Great Britain, many Americans believed that the Red Sticks were "deluded by . . . agents of the British government" who were instigating the hostilities.[29]

By the middle of 1813 the Red Sticks had begun to win numerous allies among the Upper Creek towns. The escalating war was brutal and consisted of skirmishes and raids across the Southeast, in which American military morale was often extremely low because of hunger, disease, lack of supplies, and poor leadership.[30] In July 1813 the Red Stick leader Peter McQueen arrived in Pensacola to request arms and supplies from the governor of West Florida. McQueen made it clear that the constant encroachments of Americans into their territory forced the Spanish to side either with the Red Sticks or the Americans. The Red Sticks openly expressed their plans to attack white Americans.[31]

The bloodiest and most symbolically important battle of the war came in August 1813 when Red Sticks attacked Fort Mims in Alabama.[32] As many as 250 American settlers were killed, including many women and children. Blacks had given the Red Sticks reports on the state of the fort's defenses, helped them get in, and urged them on during the fighting. Many blacks went with the Red Sticks to Eccanachaca, near present day Mobile, and fought alongside them until the very end of the conflict.[33]

The end came in the five months between November 1813 and March 1814, when the U.S. Army destroyed Upper Creek towns across the Southeast, culminating with the Battle of Horseshoe Bend. On August 9, 1814, the Treaty of Fort Jackson officially ended hostilities between the United States and the Creek Nation and ceded 23 million acres of land to the United States. The Creeks who were allied to the United States were the only Indians to sign the treaty. The Red Sticks were vehemently opposed to the treaty and fled to Spanish West Florida with their black allies. They grew more resolute in their opposition to the United States and the Creeks than ever before. Accordingly, the Red Sticks would see in the British a way to seek justice against the United States and the Creeks as well as viewing the British as the surest route to slowing the encroaching American plantation complex.

Most people in the region saw that racial order had essentially broken down in the Spanish Floridas. Whites, blacks, and Indians understood the implications of the conditions that were created by the peripheral remnants of a dying empire. The Seminole chief Alexander Durant demonstrated this outlook when he begged the British for military aid, imploring the officials to realize the "distress that our country is in at this present time and likewise the horrid situation that the Spanish government our friends is in at the present they can neither help themselves or us."[34] Andrew Jackson correlated conditions in Spanish Florida with racial disorder when he thundered that "permanent peace [would be brought] to our Southern frontier" if the Red Sticks were "destroyed" and "we . . . [took] possession of Pensacola."[35] Likewise an anonymous American veteran of the First Seminole War noted that during this period "Florida was peculiar; its vicinity to the four southern tribes of Indians, and its extensive forests, beyond the control of the Spanish authorities, affording all times an asylum to fugitives from justice, to the disaffected restless savage, as well as to a more dangerous population, absconding from the southern states, were circumstances demanding vigilance on the frontier."[36]

The Arrival of the British

To the British this state of affairs presented distinct military advantages. In 1813 Governor Cameron of the Bahamas laid out a ten-point plan for a mission to the Gulf Coast based on intelligence that had been collected earlier that year by British officials.[37] Cameron argued that Pensacola, and West Florida more generally, was an ideal place for the British to make contact with the Red Sticks and Seminoles because it was nominally under the control of their Spanish allies. Furthermore, the British merchant house of Panton, Leslie and Company had extensive ties to the city, and as a result of the Creek War, thousands of Indians and blacks were heading to its proximity to request aid from the Spanish government. In the spring of 1814 Alexander Cochrane, acting on Bathurst's orders, dispatched an expedition to the Apalachicola River with instructions from Governor Cameron. Capt. Hugh Pigot, commander of the *Orpheus*, was placed in charge of the mission, and George Woodbine was its translator. Pigot received a map of the Apalachicola River and surrounding area from Alexander Gordon, a Bahamian merchant who was familiar with the region. Gordon advised Pigot to take on board blankets, clothing, and various other items to give as presents to the chiefs from Governor Cameron.[38] The *Orpheus* set sail on April 28 on "a very special mission of the utmost importance to our Indian allies in the Southern states" and landed at Apalachicola Bay on May 10.[39]

Almost immediately after the British expedition landed at Apalachicola Bay, Woodbine was promoted to the rank of brevet captain of the Royal Marines, which for the moment placed him in charge of the British expedition. Woodbine's first assignment was to proceed up the Apalachicola River, and to procure at all costs an interview with the Seminole and Red Stick chiefs. Woodbine's orders were to inform the Indians that anchored at the mouth of the Apalachicola River was the *Orpheus*, which contained two thousand muskets and ammunition for their use. He was to inquire where the arms might best be landed, whether the Indians required more, and where was the best location for future communications in order to furnish the Indians with all the supplies they needed. Woodbine was further instructed to gather information about the neighboring Indian nations and to ascertain whether the cavalry would be useful.

Woodbine's background was ideal preparation for his mission to the Southeast. A young white Jamaican who was "an intelligent man that had traded with the Indians and is known to many of the chiefs," he had lived in Florida before while working as an Indian trader.[40] His career as a Jamaican merchant had brought him into daily contact with people from across the Atlantic world, and he himself had traveled extensively across the Caribbean, North America, and Africa. Woodbine came of age in the revolutionary Caribbean. Accordingly he knew intimately the dynamics of the Atlantic world during this period: multiracial wars, slave resistance, and imperial struggles that had convulsed the region since his childhood. Consequently he fully understood the complexities that would arise from the arming of slaves in enemy country. Like Cochrane and the majority of the architects of Britain's military plans in the South, Woodbine deeply understood the delicate power dynamics of race relations across the Greater Caribbean and the Gulf Coast. At the same time Woodbine was aggressive, confrontational, manipulative, and extraordinarily ambitious. He eagerly provoked his Gulf Coast adversaries by embracing blacks and Natives. However, Woodbine does not appear to have shared Nicolls's radical anti-slavery beliefs on a personal or intellectual level. In 1811, using the alias "Jorge Madresilva," Woodbine was detained by the Royal Navy off the coast of Africa while serving as "Super Cargo" onboard the illegal slaver *Gallicia*.[41] In 1815 the directors of the African Institution offered a hundred-guinea reward for the capture of Woodbine, who had failed to appear in court to answer these charges. It appears that Nicolls did not know about these activities while serving in Florida with the Jamaican. Even more remarkable evidence of Woodbine's pro-slavery feelings appeared many years after his mission in the Southeast. After the conclusion of the War of 1812 Woodbine joined Sir Gregor MacGregor's filibustering army commissioned by the Venezuelan revolutionaries.[42] As a result of this service Woodbine would ultimately settle near Cartagena, raise a family, and become a slave owner. This irony would end with tragic consequences when Woodbine and his entire family were murdered by his slaves in 1833.[43] Nonetheless, while on the mission to the Southeast, Woodbine treated people of color as equals and would join Nicolls in publicly promoting a radical emancipatory message that they followed with an equally radical anti-slavery experiment. Indeed, the fact that the Jamaican was not a radical anti-slavery advocate did not limit his effectiveness in the Southeast, nor did it hinder his ability to work with Nicolls, who regarded Woodbine as an invaluable aid. This made Woodbine's ultimate fate all the more remarkable. In the end the most accurate way to describe Woodbine would be as a "radical filibuster" whose life symbolized the tumult and complexity of the Greater Caribbean during the Age of Revolution, especially when it came to issues relating to race.[44]

On May 20, 1814, Woodbine had assembled ten principal chiefs, their interpreters, and a number of lesser chiefs aboard the British vessels.[45] The majority of these were Seminoles, and they included Thomas Perryman and Cappachamico, head of the Miccosukee. Woodbine nominated Perryman and Cappachamico to the rank of general, to both men's satisfaction. After his meeting with the two chiefs Woodbine noted that "I know I can twist [Perryman and Cappachamico] around my finger and induce them to think as I do, particularly the latter."[46] From an Indian perspective, a strong and wealthy ally had been acquired in the British, who might prove invaluable in their struggle against the United States and the Creeks. Both sides were happy with this arrangement. Tellingly, the one specific request made by the chiefs was for war paint. This deeply pleased the British.[47] The next day Sergeant Smith and Corporal Denny volunteered to "instruct the Creek Nation in the use of small arms and to assist them against their common enemy the

Americans."[48] These initial recruits marked the official beginning of Nicolls's multiracial army and would be joined by thousands more over the coming months.

Soon Woodbine oversaw the construction of a base approximately fifteen miles up the Apalachicola River at an easily defensible point called Prospect Bluff, where Indians frequently gathered for trade.[49] By May 25 a large storehouse and a powder magazine that probably measured 40 by 24 feet were complete. The location, from which word of the British presence rapidly spread, proved to be ideal, and within days Prospect Bluff was so overwhelmed by the flood of Native Americans that Woodbine was left to exclaim "for god sake land the canoes with [supplies] as I have more than 1200 men waiting here and 7 or 8 hundred tomorrow or next day."[50] The estimate appears to have been an exaggeration to emphasize urgency but was nonetheless indicative of a substantial number of people heading to Prospect Bluff. Included in this wave of refugees were Hillis Hadjo (Josiah Francis) and Peter McQueen: the two most powerful and anti-American Red Stick leaders, who had recently been reduced to requesting carbines or fusils from the British because muskets were too heavy for children.[51]

On May 28 Woodbine delivered a "Talk to the Chiefs of the Creek Nation," which covered many of the same points as a proclamation he had issued earlier on Cochrane's behalf.[52] Claims of British strength, the hopelessness of the American cause, and promises to aid the Indians filled the talk and proclamation. The talk and proclamation pleased the chiefs, who unanimously proclaimed Woodbine to be "Chief of all."[53] British plans were coming together more quickly and easily than even the most optimistic official could have predicted.

Slavery and the British Mission to the Southeast

While Woodbine was enjoying tremendous success in gaining the allegiance of the Red Sticks and Seminoles, the recruitment of American slaves was equally important to the British mission, if not more so. Indeed, many officials referred to the purpose of the mission as being to raise "a Regiment of Colonial Marines from the American Blacks" with no mention of the Indians in official correspondence.[54] From this perspective the purpose of the British mission was to recruit as many "Negroes . . . as may be induced to desert from the territory of the United States, to whom you are to hold out every encouragement," and to then supply and train a corps of five hundred (and more if possible) blacks who were to be organized into the Third Battalion of Royal Colonial Marines.[55]

Just before embarking on the initial mission for the Apalachicola River, Captain Pigot received a number of the earliest copies of Cochrane's proclamation to "be promulgated on that part of the United States that you are about to go to."[56] Woodbine wasted no time in taking steps to ensure the circulation of the proclamation. Even as he was busy with the construction of the fort he had already forwarded the proclamation to "Georgia, Tennessee and New Orleans [presumably meaning Louisiana, Alabama, and Mississippi] by trusty Indians who have been appointed at a general meeting of the Chiefs, for such purposes, and I have no doubt of several hundred American slaves joining our standard."[57] Few images were more apocalyptic to white southerners and slave-owning Creeks than hostile Native Americans attempting to stir slaves to acts of rebellion at the instigation of the British. The citizens of Greene County, Georgia, captured this fear when they lamented that from their base in Florida, the British would soon be able to encourage "the merciless and unrelenting Savages, immediately bordering upon us; from a history of the revolutionary war, have we not much to fear from the seductive overtures to our black population, exciting them to abandon their owners, and perhaps to rise in rebellion against them[?]"[58] Even more darkly, Georgia's Assembly reported that if British forces were able to garrison the fortress at St. Augustine (which would place them in command of East Florida), "assylum and protection to all of the outcasts of society [would be offered] . . . pouring out its ruffian bands, and exciting merciless savages, red and black, to their accustomed deeds of murder, rapine, and desolation."[59] The *Niles Weekly Register* invoked the most powerful racialized image in the contemporary southern imagination when it reported that from their base in Florida the British would "excite new assassinations like those at Fort Mims."[60]

The aim of the British military in West Florida was to cause a distraction to aid its assault on New Orleans. Rumors and fear accomplished this by raising southern anxiety and causing a deep psychological distraction.[61] For more than two years the United States constantly overestimated British activity in the Deep South, which meant that the more rampant southern speculation became, the closer the British came to realizing their goals. For example, earlier in 1814, as rumors of British and Indian activity began to spread across the Gulf South, Gen. David Blackshear of the Georgia Militia complained bitterly that the intelligence he was receiving was "ambiguous [and] calculated to keep the army bandied about . . . [and] all the information on the subject was so vague and evasive, and contained so many ambiguities," that it was nearly impossible to know what to believe.[62] Lt. John Smith's account of recently having received intelligence that the British had landed on the Gulf Coast and that "the report would fly through the country and create alarm whether true or false" illustrates the speed at which information passed through the region (whether correct or rumor).[63]

Rumor was inevitable, but it was compounded by the fact that Woodbine fully understood the power of (mis)information and the process by which news spread. For example, shortly after having arrived in West Florida, he realized that "issuing Proclamations calling on all persons, whether natives of the country or residents for a time hostile to the American Government to join me, immediately for the purpose of expelling them from Louisiana and Florida, also that all those who assist me, will have their property protected from the fury of the Indians" would be an effective use of information against the United States. Edmund Doyle's angry assertion that only after having spent a great deal of time working closely with Woodbine did he realize that prior to his arrival at Prospect Bluff "a thousand unheard of reports before his arrival was set afloat to our prejudice, which I now believe was thro' his means," illustrates Woodbine's ability to manipulate and spread information effectively.[64] Another resident of Pensacola accused Woodbine of having "spread a report that he had two thousand or more Indians under his command, whom he armed and disciplined, and with whom he was about to march against the Americans, a piece of intelligence (altho false) that was not unpleasing to the inhabitants and Govt of this place."[65] This use of information had the intended effect, as Americans in the Deep South were thrown into "terrible consternation, and [were removing] their property in the greatest haste," while others were "fleeing precipitately to the interior . . . many leaving nearly all they possess for the merciless savages. Hundreds of inhabitants are now on the road."[66] On occasion rumors circulated that inspired hope among Americans. For example, dozens of newspapers printed versions of a report alleging (falsely) that Woodbine and his force had received a "good drubbing" by General Floyd and the Georgia militia early in 1815.[67]

Before Woodbine had even circulated the proclamation, the first large group of blacks headed toward Prospect Bluff. In May Woodbine recorded—presumably with a degree of exaggeration but nonetheless referring to a large group of people—that "there is also a party of negroes, upwards of 200 men, who have run away from the States, and are on their march for this, in company with Cappachimico's tribe that I look for in a very few days."[68] Only days later Woodbine recorded that "negroes are flocking in from the United States and make no doubt that I shall have occasion for a considerable supply more of musquets."[69] Since the proclamation had not yet been fully circulated, the majority of the blacks en route with the Red Sticks and Seminoles had already joined one of the groups earlier, had begun to flee, or had previously become maroons. Due to the history of Indian-black relations and maroon activity in the Southeast, any attempts to recruit slaves or Indians would doubtless create a very complex web of interrelations. This gave the process of recruitment in the area, and indeed race relations, an extra dynamic that was lacking in the Chesapeake and Lowcountry.

To Indian, Spanish, and American slaves, freedom was the primary motivation for joining the British. The experience of Boatswain and Rose, a married couple, and their children, Sally and Boyer (mentioned in chapter 1) illustrates the powerful lure of freedom that emanated from the British in Florida. The family were slaves from East Florida who belonged to an Anglo-American planter named Gabriel William Perpall.[70] After being arrested in the Bahamas in June 1815, the family testified that they had fled their master's plantation that spring "in consequence of having understood, that all negro slaves joining the British troops in the Floridas or America would be made free . . . [and as a result] traveled to Apalachicola where they joined the expedition of Colonel Nicoll."[71] This example is deeply informative, not merely because it shows that families were capable of successful flight but also because it illustrates how information traveled among slaves and how slaves understood this information. Knowledge of the British "offer" had been acquired through word of mouth. Furthermore this specific rumor would have been understood and become more believable in the context of an array of new rumors appearing on a daily basis alongside the tangible and visible manifestations of war that had engulfed the Southeast. In this case the former slaves had latched onto a simple yet very appealing message that was supported by daily observations: any North American slave could win unconditional freedom with any British force and Nicolls's in particular. This was not the aim of British officials. However, in the black imagination there quickly developed a powerful association between the British military and freedom. The fact that forty other slaves fled Perpall's plantation, never to be recovered, testifies to the power of this message and the chaotic world in which it traveled.[72]

The Arrival of Nicolls

At the beginning of June 1814 Pigot left for Nassau, leaving Woodbine at Prospect Bluff, where he continued in his diplomatic and recruiting efforts. Upon arriving in the Bahamas, Pigot immediately presented to Cochrane a report of the expedition.[73] Included was a list of 3,255 Red Sticks and Seminoles at Pensacola and at Prospect Bluff allied with the British and ready to fight against America.[74] This pleased Cochrane, who quickly ordered that along with a massive supply of military hardware, a detachment of Royal

Marines be sent to Florida to train the Indians.[75] Previously, in Cameron's ten-point report about a British mission to the Southeast, the governor had insisted that the leader of the operation "must be a *mind* of no common stamp to command the whole—his powers in respect to military operations must be unlimited. . . . Perhaps for the first class young man commissioned officers who had seen service and learned to support fatigue would be preferable to others more delicately trained."[76] Cochrane had already recognized that Nicolls fit this description perfectly and, accordingly, had placed him in charge of the mission.

Nicolls's arrival was preceded by a proclamation from Cochrane boldly stating "that so I may know your real wants and the number of your Warriors I send you Colonel Nicolls, with some officers and men to instruct you in the military Exercises." The proclamation continued to note: "In him you may confide, he is an experienced Warrior, and under his guidance you may look for Victory over your foes, but to secure this a strict discipline must be submitted to, and an implicit obedience to orders."[77] Nicolls was instructed that his mission was "intended as the Ground Work of a Corps which you are to endeavor to raise to the numbers of five hundred men . . . upon the Creek and other Indian Nations situated to the Northward of the Floridas . . . and such Negroes and others as may be induced to desert from the territory of the United States, to whom you are to hold out every encouragement."[78] When his corps numbered five hundred, Nicolls was to become colonel commandant.[79] The British marines were to train the force in the use of firearms and to instruct them in "organized" warfare. Cochrane was at pains to stress that Nicolls should at all times remain on the best possible terms with the Indians and "be particularly cautious not to assume more power over them than their Chiefs may think proper."[80] All the intelligence Woodbine had collected was given to Nicolls, who was assured that his mission would be well supplied. Finally Nicolls was instructed to respect Spanish neutrality.[81] In July Cochrane informed London that Nicolls and a detachment of marines had boarded the *Hermes* and the *Carron* and were destined for the Apalachicola River with a large amount of military supplies.[82] Nicolls stopped at Havana to meet with Governor Apodaca and assure him of the peaceful intentions of the British and to offer aid in case of an American invasion.[83] In August Governor Manrique of West Florida wrote to Apodaca informing him that he had allowed the British military to land a number of troops and supplies because of his fear of an American invasion and the poor quality and lack of Spanish troops in West Florida.[84] As a result Nicolls and his detachment arrived at the mouth of the Apalachicola River on August 13. This situation demonstrates the shifting realities that defined life in the Atlantic borderlands. For centuries Spanish Florida had relied on blacks and Indians to defend itself against the aggressive encroachments of the British and the Anglo Americans. Now the Spanish were forced to rely on the British to defend them against the United States in an alliance that would have mystified earlier generations on both sides of the border.

The British had recognized the strategic advantages offered by conditions in the Southeast and fully understood the complexities of race in the region. As a result Woodbine was sent ahead of Nicolls and began to recruit blacks and Indians in what was a promising start from a British perspective and a dangerous and frightening first advance in the minds of whites and Creeks. Nicolls, with all his energy and passions, stepped into a region that for many years had been defined by violence and deeply seated racial tensions. At the moment of his arrival these tensions had intersected with powerful national and global forces in a firestorm of chaotic and cross-border warfare that appeared to offer the distinct possibility of engulfing the expanding plantation complex. Far from deterred, Nicolls embraced these conditions and would waste little time in beginning his radical anti-slavery experiment.

3 ➤ The British Occupation
of Pensacola

UPON ARRIVING AT PROSPECT BLUFF, Edward Nicolls and his men found only a small detachment left behind by George Woodbine, who had recently gone to Pensacola. Woodbine had taken relief supplies to Pensacola at the desperate request of the bulk of the surviving Red Sticks, who were encamped near the city and amounted to nearly two thousand men, women, and children, including Hillis Hadjo and Peter McQueen. At the same time nearly three hundred Seminoles had marched overland from the Apalachicola River toward Pensacola, as part of what Woodbine hoped would result in a Red Stick and Seminole force that would attack Mobile.[1]

At the end of July when Woodbine arrived at the Indian encampment, he found the Red Sticks in desperate shape. Famine and disease were having a crippling effect on the Indians, but they were also being mercilessly hounded and murdered by Col. Joseph Carson and William Weatherford, a Red Stick who had surrendered to Andrew Jackson and become a Red Stick killer.[2] When Woodbine entered Pensacola nearly the entire body of Red Sticks flooded into the city in search of clothing, food, and provisions. The Indians were quickly assembled as part of a multiracial force that was designed to ward off a feared attack by Andrew Jackson.[3] Woodbine had brought a smaller version of such a force from Prospect Bluff to Pensacola and was very pleased with the results, noting: "I assure you the few of my guard that I brought down here have inspired no little proportion of terror in Mobille and New Orleans."[4]

Nicolls arrived at Pensacola on August 14 and was allowed to enter with his detachment of Royal Marines because the governor of West Florida, Mateo González Manrique, deeply feared an attack by Jackson and had minimal faith in his own troops. Nicolls was given command of Fort San Miguel and was permitted to raise both the British and Spanish flags before ordering Captain Percy to retrieve the Royal Marines who had been left at Prospect Bluff. While the Spanish were far from pleased with the situation in Pensacola, for Woodbine and Nicolls the situation was ideal. Official British strategy had grown to favor the occupation of Pensacola and then Mobile as bases for an advance on New Orleans. Mobile was still in American hands, but Pensacola, bloodlessly and with almost no effort, was now in possession of the British. Writing after the war, Daniel Patterson of the U.S. Navy noted what the British presently understood and Americans deeply feared: that Pensacola was an excellent sheltered harbor and that if the British were able to occupy the fort at Mobile Point, the "enemy will then have it in their power to place arms in the hands of the hostile Indians, and to excite the friendly tribes against us at three important points; viz Mobile Point, Pensacola and Apalachicola River." Patterson believed that if this were allowed to happen, many Americans would "perish under the tamohawk, or scalping knife, of the merciless savage; set on by our [?] merciless enemy."[5]

Revolutionary Pensacola

Located on the Gulf Coast, Florida's only deepwater harbor and capital of the increasingly beleaguered West Florida, Pensacola was a garrison town that maintained close ties to Cuba and the rest of the Caribbean. It was populated by various creole whites, diverse Europeans, and a slave and free black population that was African as well as Spanish, French, and Anglo creole.[6] The black population labored as skilled artisans, municipal workers, and domestic help or in light agricultural chores and, in the case of the black militias, were relied on for the town's defense. They were largely responsible for their own provisions and moved about the town freely, conversing with local or visiting blacks, whites, or Native Americans. These were blacks who enjoyed a privileged position in the realm of New World slavery. They had virtually unlimited access to information and could freely discuss any of the disturbances that had plagued the Greater Caribbean during the Age of Revolution.

On an even more localized level, Pensacola underwent its own episode of political upheaval during this era. In 1812 Spain had adopted a liberal constitution that allowed for municipal self-government for any imperial community with a population of one thousand or more subjects, a definition that included Pensacola. The town was thus authorized to elect four *regidores* (councilmen), an *alcalde* (an official who combined the duties of mayor and justice of the peace), and a *sindicaprocurador* (town delegate). Vincent Ordozgoity, a prosperous merchant, was chosen as alcalde. The new form of government caused a great deal of controversy as the governor and the alcalde clashed over who should ultimately be responsible for exercising civil functions in Pensacola.[7] In 1814 the constitution was abrogated, and Pensacola returned to garrison status. However, the black and white inhabitants now had direct and personal experience with revolutionary era political debates in a quintessentially Atlantic-borderland city.

Nicolls Takes Control of Pensacola

Nicolls assumed nearly complete and brutal control of Pensacola shortly after his arrival. While the Spanish were prepared, out of necessity, to yield a considerable amount of authority to Nicolls, his approach was very heavy-handed and served to alienate a great deal of the population. From his headquarters in the middle of the town Nicolls oversaw the physical abuse and intimidation of many of the town's inhabitants, implemented a strict system of passports designed to control the flow of travel in any direction, and jailed anyone who was deemed "suspicious." An American named William Robertson had the misfortune to visit Pensacola, something that he had done frequently in the past, during the British occupation. Robertson was told by the Spanish governor that he was a "suspicious character" and was to leave the town within twenty-four hours. Robertson attempted to comply, but while packing his bags at his lodgings he was seized and taken prisoner by Woodbine. When he asked whether Woodbine had a warrant from the Spanish governor, he received the response, "Damn the governor, my orders are received from Colonel Nichols, and I must obey them, if I go to hell for it."[8] Robertson was incarcerated and interrogated for four days before finally being released. Soon the white population (military, civilians, and politicians) began to suffer under the mistreatment of Nicolls and his men.[9] Nicolls had instituted British military rule in a city in the Atlantic borderlands where the residents were not accustomed to governmental interference in their lives. His actions, which resulted in the "ruin of many and the abhorrence and detestation of all," turned a fair proportion of the town's population into active American spies.[10]

Nobody suffered more, or at the same time caused Nicolls more aggravation, than the employees and associates of the House of Forbes and Company.[11] After the war Nicolls made a number of bitter yet accurate complaints about the trading company's employees. He complained that John Forbes had frequently lied to the British about any number of topics. Nicolls alleged that James Innerarity had ordered the American Customs House in Mobile to stop supplying Pensacola with food. James's brother John was accused of having warned the Americans about the invasion of Mobile and thus bore primary responsibility for the heavy British and Native American casualties suffered there. Nicolls even noted that the town's priest, Father Coleman, who "I am sorry to say is a Native of Ireland . . . [used] his inquisitive disposition endeavouring to worm himself into my secrets (none of which he got) but being the Confessor of the Governor of Pensacola a weak old Man he counteracted every endeavour of mine to get the place into a proper state of defence." Nicolls further lamented that "I solemnly declare . . . that if I have committed any fault whilst I was employed on that Service I do conceive that fault was my preventing the Indian Chiefs from putting to death the members of the iniquitous house of Forbes & Co."[12] The deep hostility between Nicolls and Forbes and Company illustrates the political realities of life in the Atlantic borderlands. The employees of the trading house, at varying points in their lives, were British subjects and were one of the main reasons that Pensacola had been chosen as a base of operations. However, Forbes and Company quickly realized that Nicolls's actions threatened their interests and set about undermining British efforts.

Soon Nicolls began to clash with the governor and threatened to "remove off all of the Indians, and Troops" who were protecting Pensacola if the Spanish did not give the British full control of Fort Barrancas. Moreover, he expected "an answer in one hour."[13] After another disagreement with Manrique, Nicolls sought to demonstrate his "power and prowess, [by parading] his savage force, marched it thro' the town saluting his Excellency with the war whoop, and threatening to scalp the inhabitants . . . end[ing] the strife."[14] Woodbine was subtler but was still described as having "manners and behaviour [that were] insinuating, and he soon ingratiated himself into the general good opinion."[15] Less delicately, Woodbine had been overheard boasting about his "masterly talents in 'tricking the old Governor.'"[16] In a matter of days the British had taken complete control of the capital of Spanish West Florida.

Nicolls's Proclamation to the First Battalion of Royal Colonial Marines

Throughout Nicolls's time in the Southeast he worked tirelessly to free and organize former slaves and their families. While doing this, he sought to instill his radical anti-slavery message into his recruits. Both of these points can be heard clearly in Nicolls's boast in 1818 that during his time in Florida, "by the public orders that I issued to all Colors of Men under me . . . [I] did my best to inspire them by my writings . . . [and] by my Acts."[17] Ultimately Nicolls saw himself as leading both a military expedition and an anti-slavery experiment. Indeed Nicolls's actions and decisions while in the Southeast would have been very different had they not been informed by his radical anti-slavery ideology. Likewise, his former slave recruits would have acted differently had they not come to understand Nicolls's anti-slavery ideology.

Nicolls's belief that he was leading an anti-slavery crusade and a military expedition was clear in his public orders to the First Battalion of Royal Colonial Marines, who were delivered at Pensacola within days of his August arrival in front of 82 Marines, "320 Indians," and "200 spectators of every colour." In the words of one eyewitness, these orders served as a statement of Nicolls's "ultimate intentions" that rang out across the Deep South.[18] The proclamation was indeed a statement of Nicolls's intentions and succinctly captured the essence of his anti-slavery experiment as well as his clearly developed radicalism. Furthermore, the ideas contained in the proclamation would become the foundation of the maroon community's identity and the former slaves' understanding of their place within the British Empire. This was because the orders were a direct product of Nicolls's unique anti-slavery beliefs and conception of the British Empire, a philosophy that warrants citing at length:

> In Europe they [swords] were not drawn for Country alone but for all those who lingered in oppressions bonds, in America they will shine forth in the same cause—the People you are about to aid have had robberies and cruel murders committed on them by the Americans, these atrocities will I know excite honor in the breast of a British soldier, they will urge you to avenge them and you will do so with the British Soldiers valor and humanity. Towards the Indians you will show the most exact discipline, you will be an example to those sons of nature, you will have to drill and instruct them, in doing which you must be patient with and watch their likes and dislikes and be careful to offend them in nothing. Above all things sobriety must be your constant care, one example of drunkeness may ruin this. . . . When the men of colour who are expected to join us arrive you will be strictly careful in your language and manners to them if they do not take your instructions as readily as you wish, or have a right to expect you will make allowances for them, remember they have been oppressed by cruel taskmasters and under slavery man's best faculties are kept dormant, what a glorious prospect for British soldiers to set them free how grateful will they be to you, how ready to mix their Blood with yours in so good a cause, additional lustre will beam on that standard and whose waft no slave can combat, your ranks must be crowded with such auspices.[19]

Nicolls's orders and their tone were exceptional on a number of levels. The introduction, in which a comparison was made between Britain's struggle to "liberate" or "defend" the continent of Europe against Napoleon and Britain's aid of Native Americans and slaves, was remarkable. Nicolls was using the most colorful and timely language which would not have been lost on any of his contemporaries. Nicolls was playing to the triumphalist spirit of Britain as the guarantor of the universal liberties of the people from across the world so as to secure the position of Native Americans and blacks. His call for the protection of the liberties of blacks and Indians was equally remarkable. According to the proclamation, the ideas and mission described in it were worth the lives of white British soldiers. This was a radical statement of racial egalitarianism on the part of Nicolls. Furthermore he had clearly come to view the Native Americans in the classic "noble savage" role; as the glorious "sons of nature," as he put it, who were making an honorable attempt to survive in the face of the constant threat of extermination by the United States. He similarly conceptualized blacks as fully human and potentially equal to whites. In his view they had suffered so horribly under slavery as to have had much of their most basic humanity compromised, but their condition was artificially imposed, was no way inherent or innate, and could be rectified through patience and diligent instruction. Nicolls regarded blacks and Indians as more than potential allies or pawns; they were human beings who required aid in the defense of their liberties, as so recently had the inhabitants of much of Europe. In Nicolls's mind and rhetoric, his conceptualization of the British Empire was perfectly suited to help these people.

In his proclamation to the First Battalion of Royal Colonial Marines, Nicolls included a large section addressed to the former slaves whom he hoped to recruit:

To you Men of Colour I now address myself, you are truly [heroes?] for you have dared to be free[—]exert yourselves to the utmost to become disciplined without Zeal and Bravery will avail you little [for?] you will unrivet the Chains of Thousands of your Colour now lingering in Bonds, you may think (it will be but for a little time) that military life is a hard one, remember that good follows evil and [?] labour, that your Services will be required but for a short time and that a peace taking place you will have the comforts of enjoying rational liberty, solid property with the rights of a British Man, for lands will be given to you in the British Colonies, the ground you will then cultivate will be yours and your childrens for ever, never again will you have to undergo the heartrending misery of seeing the partner of your love or the children of your effection cruelly dragged from your [side?] sold to a foreign oppression and carried beyond your reach for ever. Men of Colour as you have suffered persecutions from them [?] to your Enemies you will then teach them and the world to respect you show yourselves to be Christians by your deeds—mercy will cause the British men to love you, it will be a chief motive for their acknowledging you as brothers, write deep these words on the Tablets of your memory and look at them with serious and charitable resolution, when we in the possessions of your former taskmasters do them no other harm or violence than is necessary to put it out of their power to harm us, [?] inflict an unnecessary wound, when they ask you for quarter, freely give it and bring them as prisoners to me, it is only the coward that will take revenge on a fallen enemy, none such will be tolerated in his ranks, but as long as they resist you fight them valiantly rush on with the Bayonet it is the brave mans weapon, aided by the [?] use of it they must fall before you—pay strict attention to those officers I shall appoint to and command you, they have left their homes and their comforts and have travelled far to aid you, but above all things / and rivetted with your duty to your God, be loyal and true to your King and Country, if you observe these orders you cannot fail of succeeding in, and doing honor to our good cause, that benevolent Providence which has aided the disinterested exertions of our King and Country in Europe will not fail to support us here, and if we arrive at the haven of Peace, may Industry Plenty and Happiness surround your fireside and amply reward your hardships, your sufferings and your wanderings.[20]

Nicolls's promise that black soldiers would be rewarded with "the comforts of enjoying rational liberty, solid property with the rights of a British Man" embodied key Enlightenment ideals like rationality, liberty, individual rights, and property rights and was much more explicit and far reaching than what Cochrane's proclamation had promised. These were the key ingredients in becoming full British subjects. Issuing the promise in such a public manner spoke volumes to both white and black southerners. To slaves, it suggested the possibility of racial equality while challenging the daily ironies that they endured even as slave owners attempted to reconcile the ideals of the American Revolution with the owning of human property. Nicolls boldly situated slaves as heirs to the enlightened inheritance of the Age of Revolution that their masters claimed. He would eventually take a step further when he formally granted the former slaves the status of full British subjects with corresponding rights and liberties. To slave owners and white southerners, his message and the challenge it posed to slavery would have been as frightening as any development in recent times. Because Nicolls's anti-slavery thought emphasized the combination of activism and action, the British were presenting a physical challenge to slavery as well as an intellectual one that attacked racist, religious, and political justifications of slavery; news of both would quickly have passed through the white and black populations of the Deep South.

Perhaps nothing demonstrates Nicolls's profound respect for black humanity more than the fact that he envisioned his soldiers being able to check their vengeful impulses and spare their former masters. He had clearly decided that appealing to the Christian morality of former slaves was the best method for ensuring good behavior. While Nicolls appealed to the blacks' sense of Christian ethics, morality, and humanity, he also appealed to their economic interests and raw emotions. Specifically when he assured slaves who joined him that "lands will be given to you in the British Colonies, the ground you will then cultivate will be yours and your childrens for ever, never again will you have to undergo the heartrending misery of seeing the partner of your love or the children of your effection cruelly dragged from your [side?] sold to a foreign oppression and carried beyond your reach for ever." The fear of separating families would have been certain to elicit strong emotions among slaves; it was generally regarded by slaves and abolitionists as one of the more onerous aspects of slavery. True to the proclamation, Nicolls would go to great lengths to keep his recruits and their families together.

Rhetorically, Nicolls pulled no punches. He used timely and poignant language to attack American slavery, encourage American slaves to flee, and assert these same slaves' humanity. Ultimately, there was an overarching sense that Nicolls viewed himself as the leader of a just and moral crusade, a crusade that pitted a liberated and empowered black army of British subjects, with Christian morality and zeal on its side, against the United States. His combination of morality and black liberation in the form of a crusade made Nicolls's vision a fundamental challenge to racial order in the slaveholding South, a message that spoke to white and black Americans on many levels. To slaves this was an example and call to resistance that emphasized their humanity and potential for racial equality. To white pro-slavery southerners, Nicolls presented not only a physical challenge to slavery but, through his repeated insistence on the humanity and potential Christian virtue of the slaves, a fundamental intellectual challenge to the increasingly racialized defense of slavery that arose from the dehumanization of Africans and their descendants.[21]

Very possibly, Nicolls's most dangerous assault on slavery was his assertion that blacks, as much as whites, were the heirs to the most modern political currents in the revolutionary Atlantic world in terms of liberty, rights, and individual freedoms and were capable of enjoying the status of full and equal British subjects. He made this clear throughout the proclamation in statements such as "your [British] King and Country" or when he took this idea a step further by using the phrase "our King and Country." The pronoun *our*, like his use of the word *brothers*, demonstrates that Nicolls viewed the former slaves as equals who were capable of enjoying the same version of British rights that he did, regardless of their race or status. Accordingly, white Americans who saw themselves as the self-conscious defenders and heirs of the liberal and republican tradition of the Age of Revolution would have been uneasy with Nicolls's ideas. As historian François Furstenberg has shown, such individuals reconciled the existence of slavery in a republican land of liberty through the assertion that freedom was a choice and that the enslaved, through their lack of resistance, acquiesced to their condition.[22] This rationalization would have been greatly threatened at the appearance of a well-ordered Christian former slave army of British subjects led by an officer of the Royal Marines. Furthermore, if Britain and America were locked in a battle to claim the title of "standard bearers of human liberation in the Age of Revolution," a battle that in many ways turned on slavery, then Nicolls's bold experiment was making quite a statement on Britain's behalf.[23] He encouraged slaves to resist; undermined pro-slavery arguments by asserting slaves' humanity, spirituality, and enlightened rights; and undercut efforts to make slavery palatable by showing that slaves were far from happy in their current condition—all while enhancing Britain's credentials as the "Universal Liberator." Only a radical and deeply committed anti-slavery advocate would be capable of conceptualizing slaves and slavery in such a light and then so publically acting on these ideas in a context so combustible. The thoughts contained in this proclamation were one of the first steps in Nicolls's effort to bring his anti-slavery ideology to life in the Southeast. Even at his most zealously optimistic, he could not have predicted the response from the hundreds of slaves who would form a maroon community guided by these ideas. The actions of these former slaves would make it clear that they had fully absorbed Nicolls's anti-slavery rhetoric and clearly understood what they might gain by participating in his mission and experiment.

The proclamation, which was quickly "published and circulated," was so effective that within weeks John Innerarity had filed a memorial claiming it had led to the loss of a number of his slaves and the outbreak of generalized racial disorder.[24] Word and knowledge of the "address to the Indians, negroes, royal marines, and inhabitants of Pensacola" had spread so rapidly across the region that William Robertson casually remarked to a friend in Alabama, "You have no doubt seen [the Proclamation]."[25] C. G. Apodaca, the governor of Cuba, held a copy within less than a month, which would have sent a shiver up the spine of the man who had vivid memories of the recent Aponte Rebellion.[26] For many people, Nicolls's proclamation reinforced Andrew Jackson's opinion that one of Britain's major aims in West Florida was "exciting the black population to insurrection and massacre."[27]

The Expansion of Nicolls's Army

From Pensacola the British were very successful in recruiting blacks and Indians. Soon the British had raised over 500 Indians and 100 blacks in an army that would reach 2,000 warriors by December 1814.[28] The Indians and blacks were provided with uniforms and arms and were organized into military units that were drilled and instructed by British officers. These units patrolled the streets and manned the defenses of Pensacola. The black recruits were provided with "a Kind of uniform and red Caps" in a symbolic and public gesture that conjured up images of the revolutionary Caribbean while further impressing upon the locals and people across the region the full extent to which racial order had broken down in Pensacola.[29] From their first encounter with Nicolls until years after they last saw him, the former slaves made a powerful association between formal military service and their freedom.

To the inhabitants of Pensacola, the black and Indian troops began to be viewed as Nicolls's henchmen. José de Soto was far from alone in complaining about the actions of the Indians and blacks under Nicolls and Woodbine.[30] One resident described the situation as Nicolls having taken military command of the city "not indeed [by assuming] the immediate command of the Spanish troops . . . this he effected by means of a band of about 800 desperate savages that joined his standard, and whom he kept constantly on the scout in every direction."[31] Edmund Doyle recounted a tense encounter with Nicolls and Woodbine in which they were "surrounded by their damned Negro and Redstick Allies" in an effort to intimidate him.[32]

Spanish grievances with Britain's black troops were much deeper and more bitter than their grievances toward the Indian troops. The main problem arose because blacks were recruited from a vast region. Some had arrived with the Red Sticks or Seminoles. Others were from maroon communities. Still others had fled from the United States, but ominously for Pensacola's residents, Woodbine had been overheard saying that he and Nicolls "were to rouse a regiment of Blacks and did not care where they came from."[33] Equally ominous for the town's inhabitants, as well as slave owners across the Southeast,

Nicolls told a British commissioner at the end of October that it was impossible for him to gauge how many slaves he was aiming to recruit because he had been "asked to raise the whole black population [of the region]."[34]

Much to the dismay of Pensacola's white residents, the vast majority of the blacks who were joining the British were their very own slaves. Part of this was the result of slaves flocking to the British standard, which offered freedom. Woodbine made this prospect even more appealing by making it public knowledge that any slave who joined the British forces would have to serve for a maximum of only six months.[35] The slaves of Pensacola were obviously aware of Cochrane's and Nicolls's proclamations, but Woodbine emphasized the temporary nature of the military service. Likewise, it was easy for Pensacola slaves to join the British. If slaves from Pensacola sought to escape to the British they merely had to sail to the other side of the bay in stolen boats. José de Soto noted that the slaves were continually escaping because of the "shelter that they find, be it from our [British] assistants or from the Indians."[36] However, the British had launched an even more aggressive and calculated campaign to "entice" as many of the Spanish slaves to join them as possible:

A few American fugitive slaves that from time to time joined them were by no means sufficient to satisfy their eager appetite, their worthy panders aforementioned assiduously visited the negro Cabins in this town, attended their many meetings and by every means that the genius of seduction could invent endeavoured to entice the slaves of the Spanish Citizens to join them—whenever they succeeded, the evasion of the slave was easy he had but to walk to the fort [San Miguel], at noon day or at night, he was sure of reception—did the Owner complain? He was answered with scurrility—did the weak Government interfere? Its requests, its orders, or its menaces were alike treated with insulting contempt—or if in any instance the least degree of energy was shown, the negro or negroes who were its objects were sent off at night across the bay and thence to the Grand depot at Apalachicola.[37]

If their owners had any inclination toward recovering their slaves they were "frequently treated with the grossest abuse for daring to claim them ... and ... dared scarcely utter a murmur from dread of the Indians whom he [Nicolls] held at his back."[38]

This situation caused slave owners an immense sense of helplessness and bitterness, which was compounded by other calculated efforts to recruit Pensacola's slaves, with Woodbine or one of his agents frequently behind the moves. Woodbine was often seen offering freedom and protection to individual slaves.[39] He had a silver tongue and was capable of enticing even the most reticent of slaves to join the British. For example, a domestic slave of John Innerarity's named Phillis was persuaded by Woodbine to go to Prospect Bluff but was so unsure of her decision that she gave up her freedom and voluntarily returned to her master.[40] Although Phillis ultimately returned to her master, it was remarkable that Woodbine was able to get somebody with such misgivings to leave her home in the first place.

On occasion Woodbine even resorted to paying slaves to join the British. Peter Gilchrist had seen him give cash to a Madame Eslava's slave, Charles, one afternoon. Gilchrist had advised her to pay extra close attention to Charles, but he escaped that night.[41] For a bounty of thirty dollars, Woodbine had employed four "renegades"—Sergeant Dogherty, Colonel Wallace, Colonel Perdu, and Sergeant McGill—to help steal Pensacola slaves.[42] Part of the men's jobs was to encourage the slaves to leave their masters, but they were also employed in transporting slaves around the town. At a trial two years later, a witness named DeLisle was asked whether he knew "that Sergt. McGill was employed in this service under the direction of Capt. Woodbine, and that many Negros were carried off from Pensacola in consequence of this conduct?" The witness answered, "McGill was employed by Woodbine to take away all Negros, that could be got at."[43] Woodbine employed a Mr. Caldwell to ferry blacks across the bay and, because of this relationship, was free from chastisement by the Spanish governor despite frequent sightings of his activities.[44] One witness testified that the ferry service was protected by armed blacks whom Woodbine instructed to shoot anybody who attempted to interfere with the crossing.[45] During a trial after the war Nicolls claimed that he had taken "the most effectual means in his power to prevent the slaves of Spanish Subjects from joining him by requesting the Governor to place an officers Guard of Spanish troops in the Fort with the British." Nicolls went on to claim that he also ordered the governor "to detect any Spanish Slave that came to enlist—the Governor did, and some were sent Back that proved to be the property of Spaniards."[46] Nicolls knew full well that even if he allowed this measure to proceed in earnest, it had no chance of success because there were hardly any "Spanish Troops" other than one company of *pardos* and *morenos* (men of mixed race) who had recently arrived from Cuba and would have been ineffective because of empathy and their fear of the much larger multiracial British force.

The British employed Indians to encourage slaves to join their growing force. For example, DeLisle was an Indian who had first met Woodbine at Prospect Bluff in July 1814 and had traveled with him to Pensacola. In

Pensacola Woodbine employed DeLisle "to enlist Negroes . . . [and] to look after such Negros as would be suitable for the service."[47] Less than a year later DeLisle was tried in a sensational case in St. Augustine on charges that he had attempted to incite a rebellion among Spanish troops on Fernandina Island, making it clear that he was a committed revolutionary.[48] Antonio Collins found a group of Indians stealing his brother's slave and eventually tracked them to Fort San Miguel. When Collins attempted to recover her, twelve to fifteen Indians stopped him.[49] All of James Innerarity's slaves were stolen by Indians.[50] The slaves of Pensacola, and elsewhere in the Deep South, had been witnesses to the close relationship between blacks and Seminoles and Red Sticks, making the decision to join them that much easier. At the same time, the Seminoles and the Red Sticks, as a result of their alliances and experience with blacks, were ideal recruiting agents.

Enlisting blacks to recruit their enslaved brethren further enraged the white population of Pensacola. Free blacks aided Britain's efforts at recruitment. For example, Woodbine had enlisted the help of a free black man named Bennet with whom he was frequently seen talking.[51] More commonly, recently freed slaves encouraged those still in bondage to join the British. From his arrival in the town, Woodbine had frequently been seen talking to a slave named Prince, who belonged to a Don Eugenio Sierra.[52] According to the testimony of a number of witnesses, Prince had been promised wages and a lieutenant's or officer's commission if he were to persuade "all sorts of Negroes whether Freemen or Slaves . . . all the smart young fellows" to join the British corps. There was no better agent to spread the word of the freedom to be found with the British than a slave, particularly a local slave. This was where the image of "visit[ing] the negro Cabins" had originated among the Americans. Slaves could easily and stealthily encourage their enslaved counterparts, through either words or deeds, to join the British. Such encouragement was easy in a small city like Pensacola, where the slave population was intimately linked by kin, social, and economic ties and enjoyed tremendous freedom of movement.

The decision by blacks in West Florida and especially East Florida to join the British provides an excellent example of racial politics in the Atlantic borderlands. For centuries both slaves and free blacks had recognized the relative benevolence of Spanish rule in Florida and had fought fiercely against the encroachments of Anglo America. To varying degrees, the Spanish and allied whites, blacks, and Indians ensured that Florida remained a haven from the harsh and rigid realities of slaveholding Anglo America to the north. If, for nearly a century and a half, life with or near the Spanish had seemed to provide an appealing alternative to life under Anglo-American rule, however, at this moment in time, life with the British appeared to offer even more benefits. The British promised a greater degree of freedom, autonomy, equality, political inclusion, and economic opportunity. The Spanish simply could not match the appeal of the British offer, which became even more alluring after the former slaves had listened to or discussed Nicolls's anti-slavery rhetoric.

The power of Nicolls's message and the contours of freedom that it promised are further illustrated by the fact that free people of color, from Pensacola and St. Augustine especially, were willing to join the British. In the Spanish Floridas free people of color would have enjoyed tremendously elevated status when compared to virtually any other person of African descent in North America. Nonetheless they were still second-class subjects who suffered legal, social, cultural, and economic inequalities based on their race. As a result, they clearly found Nicolls's message of black humanity and equality, military service, and British rights appealing enough to turn their backs on their privileged status and define their freedom in the terms that Nicolls had outlined. This was a huge and informative leap. The fact that the most privileged free blacks in North America chose to join Nicolls is a tremendous statement, demonstrating that the royal marine had clearly, carefully, and successfully explained what he was offering, exactly what rights and privileges a British subject enjoyed, and his anti-slavery ideology. This was a precise and essential combination of ideas, because knowledge of Nicolls's anti-slavery ideology, with its strong emphasis on black equality, would have affected how free people of color understood what he was offering. In particular, such knowledge would have helped them to believe that they were fully capable of enjoying total equality, rights, and privileges within the British Empire. The vision that Nicolls explained to them contrasted sharply with the reality of their lives within the Spanish Empire. If this had not been the case, few if any free Florida blacks would voluntarily have offered to risk their privileged status by joining Nicolls. In this case, "free" people of color realized that life with the Spanish placed a number of formal and informal limits on their freedom. However, life with the British, as explained by Nicolls and viewed through the lens of his anti-slavery ideology, would at the very least increase their political and legal equality. Finally, the decision by many of Florida's free blacks to join the British is strong evidence that the maroon community at Prospect Bluff provides deeper insights into black concepts of freedom than can be gained by studying formal free black communities who lived surrounded by white society. The perspectives emerge from analyzing how, particularly after the departure of the British, previously "free" people of color sought to cultivate a fuller version of freedom after consciously choosing to leave Pensacola.

Race and Service in Nicolls's Army

Within Nicolls's rapidly growing multiracial army there was a complex interplay between issues of race and military service. Three sources provide important insights into this interplay as well as demonstrating the black recruits' understanding of what could be gained through military service. The first document is a "scale of allowances" for Nicolls's army that was proposed by Alexander Cochrane.[53] The two best paid people were Indian "Kings" at $2 per day and "Chief[s] who bring 100 armed men into the field" at $1 per day. "Second" and "third" chiefs received $4 and $3 per week, respectively. "Chief[s] bringing into the field less than 100 men" were to be paid $4 per week, and their "second" and "third" chiefs were to receive $3 and $2 per week, respectively. There was no mention of pay for Indian warriors, because it would have been assumed that the leaders would pay the men from their own salaries. These were substantial wages, especially considering that the Indians were also receiving an immense amount of supplies and provisions as well as numerous presents.

The allowance for black soldiers is more informative. The "Chief of the Negro Slaves employed while actually in the field; or assembled for that purpose" was to receive $4 per week. Nicolls's was a distinctly free army, and the term "slaves" was presumably used as the result of an oversight or out of ignorance on Cochrane's part. These "chiefs" were former slaves whom Nicolls had commissioned as officers. Indian kings and chiefs who brought a hundred or more warriors to the field were the only people who were paid more than these black "chiefs," who were paid the same amount as secondary Indian chiefs and chiefs who brought fewer than a hundred men to the field. Thus they were paid very well, and great importance was attached to their role within the British armed forces. Being placed in charge of their own men in individual units also illustrates a tremendous amount of military responsibility and a respect harbored by the British for the military abilities of the former slaves. Not surprisingly, many of these men would assume leadership positions within the maroon community after the British departure.

Each "Negro" was to be paid 50 cents a week, and the "master of each Negro" was allotted $1 per week. For rank-and-file black soldiers 50 cents a week was a fair wage, drastically exceeding the amount of hard cash that Native warriors were receiving. Furthermore, a weekly wage was yet another mark of freedom and empowerment. Many of the former slaves would previously have been paid for certain types of labor or would have participated in various exchange economies, but they were now being paid a fair and regular wage by the British military for their services as soldiers in keeping with an official agreement, which they had entered of their own volition. Thus their 50 cents a week would have been economically empowering, but it also drove home a sense of being in control of their own destiny and served as a weekly reminder that the British were respecting their obligations and making good on their promises to their fellow subjects. Finally, the $1 a week for the "master of each Negro" was to be paid to Indians who allowed their black slaves to join the British military. Given the fact that Nicolls and Woodbine had sought to instill anti-slavery beliefs within the Native Americans and encouraged them to manumit those few slaves whom the Red Sticks and Seminoles owned (discussed in chapter 4) meant that very few blacks would have served under their Native American masters in Nicolls's army. This conclusion is further supported by the fact that $1 a week was a low wage, suggesting that the British attached little importance to the position.

In December 1814 Cochrane wrote to Nicolls that he was "sorry to hear the Indians have expressed a dislike to being regularly trained."[54] Three months earlier, an American prisoner in Pensacola had recorded in his diary that one night "the Indians refused to obey their chief (Woodbine) and would not stand sentry."[55] On at least occasion Nicolls and Woodbine clearly had difficulties maintaining military discipline among the Red Sticks and Seminoles. Their problems stemmed from a number of causes. Britain's Native American allies had extensive and highly developed military traditions and techniques that were suited to warfare in the Southeast, styles of warfare that frequently contrasted with European notions.[56] Second, both the Red Sticks and Seminoles were reeling from material, territorial, and human losses suffered at the hands of the United States. And finally, a generational rift among the Seminoles and Red Sticks had led young warriors to join the British, contrary to the wishes of their older leaders. In short, the Native Americans took advantage of the opportunity to ally themselves with Great Britain in the hopes of striking a blow against the United States and the Creeks, but they had their own military traditions and were suffering greatly from recent events; all these factors help explain the difficulties in formally training the Indians.

In contrast, Nicolls reported that his black recruits had enlisted "with the strictest good faith and conduct, so much so, that out of 1,500 of them I never had occasion to punish one of them."[57] Likewise, he reported that their work ethic and ability to adjust to military life were impressive and that "the fellows I had in North America, that came over from the States to us; they were good men, rather better than our own, for they would not get drunk."[58] (The abstention from alcohol is informative. Since Nicolls was a temperance advocate, it is further evidence of just how closely the former slaves listened to his message and absorbed his beliefs.) While reflecting about the former slave soldiers he had recruited during the War of 1812 Nicolls fondly noted that "better or braver soldiers I would never wish to serve with."[59] This final assessment is doubly remarkable and telling because it was made after Nicolls had retired from the Royal Marines, having served with thousands of soldiers across the globe.

The former slaves were able to adjust smoothly to military service for a number of reasons. They had the same understanding of military organization and tactics as Europeans or white Americans because they were intimate members of the same societies, so cultural differences would not have hindered their ability to serve. Across the region they had witnessed or heard detailed accounts of the growing use of black fighting forces, most recently including the West India Regiments and Cuban *pardo* and *moreno* units. The best explanation, however, for the different attitudes held by blacks and Indians toward military service and discipline lies in understanding exactly what the two groups were fighting for. The Seminoles and Red Sticks were locked in a simmering and brutal war that pitted them against an encroaching American slave frontier and pro-American Creeks. They faced serious territorial, economic, cultural, and political challenges, but they were still sovereign people largely in control of their own destiny, even if currently involved in yet another conflict in which they sought to manipulate circumstances in their favor. In contrast, prior to joining the British, the slaves were neither free nor sovereign people. Rather, organized military service offered a clear and direct path to reverse both these conditions in a profound political, spatial, spiritual, gendered, and material manner. Such a path became even clearer after listening to Nicolls's anti-slavery rhetoric and thoughts about the British Empire, both of which emphasized the power of military service, honor, and sacrifice as social, cultural, political, and racial equalizers. Finally, an element of urgency was added when the former slaves realized that the offer of military enlistment and the exceptional conditions that made it possible might never again appear. Britain's fleeting offer of military service presented the clearest and most complete route to freedom, but the window might close at any moment.

That service led to freedom became especially clear in the spring of 1815, when the *pardo* and *moreno* troops who had been taken from Pensacola to Prospect Bluff in November 1814 were returned to the Spanish officials. Governor Manrique reported that the fifty-six black troops "find themselves submerged in the most frightful misery, unshod, unclad and forced to excessive labor" at Prospect Bluff.[60] Their suffering was not the result of a lack of supplies at Prospect Bluff during their four-month stay. Rather Nicolls noted that "I was heartily glad to get rid of them, they would neither work or fight, and I was most reluctantly obliged to give them a part of my small provision store."[61] Any soldiers, regardless of race, would have found themselves treated in a similar manner if they had refused to fight or work. The behavior of the *pardo* and *moreno* soldiers contrasted starkly with that of the former slave recruits, whose bravery, willingness to fight, military order, sobriety, and work ethic Nicolls frequently mentioned in the most positive terms.

On the surface it appears deeply ironic that it was the professional soldiers who were reluctant to work. But it must be remembered how the professional soldiers and the former slaves viewed the British. Former slaves were fighting for and protecting their freedom, whereas the Spanish black troops were already free. Furthermore, the Spanish soldiers had been torn from a city in which they had enjoyed elevated status, impressed into a foreign army to fight against a nation with which Spain was at peace, and taken to the Florida wilderness, which would have been an extremely hostile environment for people who originated in Cuba and in all likelihood in Havana. Because of ethnic and class prejudices, many of the professional black soldiers would have been humiliated at the idea of serving with recently liberated Spanish, American, and Indian slaves. Immediately on returning to Pensacola the Spanish black soldiers were ordered back to Cuba over what appeared to be concerns that they had learned dangerous lessons at Prospect Bluff.[62]

Defeat at Mobile

Nicolls and Woodbine had found no shortage of willing recruits. The men had been "armed . . . and put . . . in so imposing an attitude as to cause the Government of the United States" to redirect to the Southeast thousands of troops who were sorely needed elsewhere. But British plans in the region were soon dealt two severe blows.[63] Possibly dizzy with his success and contrary to his orders, Nicolls decided to lead an assault on Mobile in early September 1814.[64] Unfortunately for the British, Andrew Jackson, who was the commander of the Seventh Military District, anticipated the assault and rushed his troops there, arriving on August 22. Jackson's first orders were to repair and reinforce Fort Bowyer, which commanded Mobile Bay. Jackson's was a wise decision, because on September 12 four British ships (the *Hermes, Carron, Sophie,* and *Childers*) arrived at Mobile Bay. On board were Nicolls and between 150 and 250 Indians. A detachment of Royal Marines was marching overland as part of the assault. During the ensuing battle Nicolls, who was desperately ill, was shot in the eye and nearly killed, leading Jackson to remark snidely, "We will have no more proclamations shortly from the Colonel."[65] The assault was a disaster and was thoroughly defeated within three days. The attackers were left to limp back to Pensacola with Britain's Gulf Coast strategy in disarray.

Defeat at Mobile had done nothing to dampen British efforts to recruit slaves. It was reported that upon the return of British forces to Pensacola, they had increased their efforts to raise a black army from local slaves, because as "naturalists say of some of the ferocious prowlers of the forest that when once they have tasted human flesh they disdain all other and hunt their prey with redoubled keenness—So it happened with those heroes." As a result, "the capture of these negroes [taken from West Florida while in retreat] roused their appetites that until then in appearance at least had been nearly dormant—No sooner were they returned, than they began to exert all their faculties of deceit, to set all their traps, to put all their tools to work, to catch negro Slaves."[66]

The next disaster to befall the British on the Gulf Coast was at Pensacola. One of the major effects of Jackson's victory at Fort Bowyer was that he was now convinced British strategy in the South revolved around a major attack on Mobile and that the British force at Pensacola was an integral part of this plan. As a result Jackson spent weeks at Mobile, sorely neglecting the defenses of New Orleans. On October 10, Secretary of War Monroe informed Jackson that he had received information from the American ministers at Ghent that a British expedition was to sail from Ireland in September bound for New Orleans.[67] Jackson would not be moved. He was obsessed with the British in Florida and tenaciously stuck by his earlier observation that "Pensacola is more important to the British than any other point on our South or Southwest."[68] As early as August Jackson had "issued orders to stop all vessels [from New Orleans and Mobile] loaded in whole or part with corn Flour or other provisions . . . and charged the officers commanding the frontier to keep good patroles and apprehend all droves of cattle with their drivers bound for Pensacola," in an increasingly effective blockade of the city that drove up the price of food, causing considerable suffering.[69] Jackson, contrary to the government's direct orders, began to prepare for an invasion of Pensacola, a city that was deep in the heart of neutral Spanish territory. Much of Jackson's decision to invade Pensacola was based on his honest understanding of the strategic issues at stake. At the same time Jackson was eager to teach the British and Spanish a lesson for their collective breach of neutrality. Furthermore, Jackson believed that he was dealing with a dangerous threat to the United States and so much the better if his actions resulted in the long desired acquisition of part or all of the Floridas.

Fear Grips the Southeast

A deeper and much darker concern that weighed heavily on the thinking of Jackson and other southerners was related to the idea of protecting American safety. For centuries Spanish Florida's reliance on blacks and Indians for defense and the enhanced role that both groups had played in the region's culture and society had deeply troubled Anglo America. Part of Anglo America's continuing desire to acquire Florida was as a means of permanently stomping out this threat to racial order in the South. Anglo-American anxiety had been greatly heightened by the expansion of slavery into the immediate proximity of Spanish Florida, the destruction and chaos caused by the Pan-Indian Nativist wars in the interior from Canada to the Gulf Coast, and the shadow of Haiti and the Age of Revolution. The recent Patriot Invasion and Creek War had served to emphasize the extent to which blacks and Indians had carved out their own thriving niche in the Floridas. Jackson, as a southern slave owner who had fought many wars against Indians, was certainly sympathetic to the notion that racial order must always be maintained, and he saw the recent arrival of the British and the Red Sticks in the area as an urgent call to action.[70] Jackson felt that British actions in the Deep South posed a real threat of widespread slave insurrections and Indian massacres, especially after receiving vivid and concrete details of black and Indian trained military units patrolling the streets and ruling over the white inhabitants, prompting him to write to his wife: "It is an old adage how true I cannot say in the present instance that the darkest hour of all night is Just before day."[71]

Jackson was far from alone in such beliefs. In July Daniel Patterson of the U.S. Navy suggested "every arrival from Pensacola" corroborated a report that "the enemy have in contemplation an attack on this country from the . . . Apalachicola, as well as to excite the Indian tribes to hostilities with us, I cannot doubt." Patterson went on to note nervously that the possibility the British would "also endeavour to create an insurrection among the Blacks here, is I think no longer to be doubted, for after enducing the savages to raise the Tomahawk and draw the scalping knife, they will descend to tamper with negroes."[72] It is important to note Patterson's fear and anxiety, but it is equally important to note the volume of information and the speed at which it spread across the Deep South. After poring over a tremendous amount of intelligence, Georgia's governor, Peter Early, wrote to the secretary of war that "you have no doubt been informed of the measures which our enemy is pursuing in Pensacola with the hostile Creek Indians . . . you will discover that the mischief to be apprehended from that quarter is truly serious."[73] Two weeks later Early's mood had worsened; he wrote to the commander of the Georgia Militia, Thomas Pickney, that the British presence in West Florida represented "a storm . . . [that] is gathering in that quarter which if not guarded against in time, may burst with destruction on the lower frontier of this state."[74] It is impossible to blame Early for such sentiments when the intelligence he was receiving contained reports such as one stating that Woodbine was "at Perrymans recently . . . has given out [that] he expects a considerable number negros from Georgia this moon; probably through the aid of such people as mentioned by Maj. Wooten, and the hostile party of Seminoles moving towards us." The report made it clear that this "business must be put a stop to by cutting off the British officer and his adherents in that quarter or the evil will soon become seriously alarming to the citizens throughout your state."[75] Based on the testimony of refugees from Pensacola, Tennessee's governor, William Blount, informed James Monroe that because of British and Spanish actions at Pensacola, the United States was more than justified in invading West Florida in an attack that would permanently pacify the southeastern frontier. However, Blount warned:

> So long as the British are permitted to be there, and to exercise such conduct, so long may the south-western section of the United States expect to be harassed by them, and by straggling parties of hostile Indians, by disaffected white men, and by run away and plundered negroes, who have an asylum there, and who will flock to the British standard by invitation; such choice spirits will hurdle together . . . their schemes and plans, calculated to injure our frontier.[76]

Fear was hardly limited to politicians and military officers. The general public received information about Pensacola and Florida through word of mouth, exhaustive reports in the press about developments in the region, and rumors (such as were contained in the numerous private letters that the U.S. Army intercepted from residents of Pensacola to people in Mobile urging "friends here to secure themselves by removing to Pensacola without delay, as this country will be shortly overwhelmed with numbers, and all who resist are doomed to destruction").[77] One issue of the *Georgia Journal* included three separate articles about the British occupation of Pensacola. One informed the public that the British "increase their numbers by enticing away the negroes from the friendly Indians." Another article noted that Nicolls "spoke freely of great cruelties committed by the troops under General Jackson during his expedition against the Indians; and seemed exasperated against the Americans—He urged that the country belonged to the Indians." The same article finished by stating that a passenger on the *Hermes* "read one of the proclamations signed by colonel Woodbine inviting all classes and descriptions of people to join the British standard for protection and freedom." To make matters worse, each article carefully detailed the immense amount of military supplies that the British had brought to Florida.[78]

The press, politicians, and black, white, and Native American refugees had spread detailed word across the South about British activities in Pensacola, resulting in a deep fear among whites of all nationalities and loyalties and Native Americans on both sides of the border. Most important, in terms of shaping events on the ground, much of the information that Jackson was receiving and/or sending about the area was deeply racially charged, which was hardening his resolve to end the threat posed by the British at Pensacola. Benjamin Hawkins informed Jackson: "I have from other sources which I credit corroborative information of a plan [by the British] to free and prepare for war all of the Blacks in this quarter."[79] Two weeks earlier Hawkins had reported to John Armstrong that the British at Prospect Bluff and Pensacola had begun to clothe and train "the Indians and some negros for purposes hostile to us . . . the Indian training is to fire a swivel, sound the war whoop, fire three or four rounds of small arms."[80] In early November 1814 Col. Robert Butler, in an attempt to convince Jackson to invade Pensacola, accused the Spanish of having "formed a league with our declared enemy Great Britain who has invited every pirate, and robbers to their standard, and has endeavored to arm our slaves against us: nay more." Butler then implored Jackson to "destroy this infernal combination of monsters, who forgetful of the rules of Christian Warfare has assembled a banditti of Pirates, Robbers, and savage murders in support of their cause—to drive them from our shores is the task assigned to you."[81]

The correlation between Pensacola and racial disorder in the mind of Andrew Jackson was brought forth in detail in a report he sent to the secretary of war in early September 1814. In the report Jackson desperately attempted to argue that the British must be expelled from Pensacola and replaced by a garrison of American troops who would remain there, and then "all resistance in this quarter would cease." Jackson signed off with the line "I beg you to glance at the situation in Pensacola." He enclosed an attachment recounting the events of the previous night, when a party of Indians had come within nine miles of Fort Jackson and attacked a house with one white man and three slaves in it. One of the blacks escaped with the Indians, whom Jackson was at pains to stress had come from Pensacola.[82] In one of his last letters prior to the invasion of Pensacola, Jackson assured John Coffee—in a highly self-conscious reversal of the rhetoric found in Nicolls's proclamation—that "the tyrants of England will be taught soon to know that he may conquer slaves in Europe but in America they are determined to live free or die and will expel tyranny from the continent."[83] Building on this language, Jackson aggressively made his case to Secretary of War Armstrong that the British garrison at Pensacola threatened the entire South and that had he been allowed to invade, "the American Eagle would now have soared above the fangs of the British Lyon."[84]

The depths of Jackson's anxieties are made clear in his "Proclamation to the People of Louisiana," issued in September. The proclamation drew clear connections between the actions of the British and racial disorder across the region.[85] For example, Jackson proclaimed that the British had assaulted Fort Bowyer with a "horde of Indian and Negro assassins . . . [but] they seemed to have forgotten that this Fort was defended by freeman. . . . [The commander of the Fort] taught them what they can do, when fighting for their liberty when contending against Slaves." The rest of the proclamation was devoted to attempting to assure the loyalty of Louisiana's Francophone population by reminding them of their traditional hostility to Great Britain and by emphasizing the extensive freedoms that they enjoyed as American citizens. Jackson followed with a proclamation "To the Free Coloured Inhabitants of Louisiana" that was addressed to "my brave fellow Citizens . . . sons of freedom," who were "now called upon to defend our most estimable blessing [freedom]." A day earlier Jackson had told Governor Claiborne of his plan to use free black soldiers and made it clear that he understood how objectionable the white population of New Orleans would find this.[86] Jackson argued that using free black soldiers was an absolute military necessity and that the black unit would be carefully controlled by white officers.

In both proclamations Jackson was deeply influenced by the public rhetoric and successes of Nicolls, as was evidenced by the invocation of highly nationalistic language fueled by images of freedom, citizenship, and violence, not to mention the frequent references to Nicolls himself. Jackson was seeking to assure the loyalty and service of both the non-Anglo white population and the free black population—and even the slave population, who as Jackson well knew, would be encouraged to rebel violently if the white and free black population fought among themselves during a time of war. The fact that Jackson was at least in part willing to embrace both populations so publicly and in such specific terms in hope of undermining Nicolls's message illustrates the extent to which he felt the British threatened racial order.

Britain's relationship with blacks and Indians and the rising fears of racial disorder were of primary importance in Jackson's decision to invade Pensacola and West Florida. Long- and short-term strategic concerns certainly figured into his decision to invade. After all, Jackson fully believed his "promise" that if he was allowed to invade West Florida, "the war in the South . . . [will have] a speedy termination and British influence forever ends . . . [with] the Indians in that Quarter."[87] Further, there was a strong lobby within the United States that deeply wanted to acquire the Floridas for economic and territorial reasons.[88] Still, the British were providing a fundamental and extremely public challenge to racial order from a highly sensitive area and, in Jackson's view, had to be stopped before the chaos spread. Driving home the role that the restoration of racial order played in the decision to invade Pensacola, Jackson toyed with the idea of "giv[ing] the Seminoles and refugee Creeks a final blow" after Pensacola had been conquered.[89]

The Invasion Begins

Given Jackson's personal convictions and the depths of regional white and Indian anxiety that had been caused by Britain's occupation of Pensacola, he felt more than justified in leading an invasion of neutral West Florida. Jackson left Mobile on October 25 with what grew into a force of more than four thousand hardened white and Indian frontier warriors, who vastly outnumbered Pensacola's defenders. Four days earlier James Monroe had penned a letter to Jackson on behalf of the president, approving of the "tone with which you have assisted the rights of your country" in his correspondences with the governor of Pensacola. But the letter said: "At present you should take no measures which would involve this government in a contest with Spain" and suggested that complaints against "the indolent and unjustifiable conduct of the Governor of Pensacola should be made through the ordinary channels of communication."[90]

Undeterred, Jackson never made any pretenses of having government approval for the invasion and even went so far as to send a letter to the secretary of war that began: "As I act without the orders of the government, I deem it important to state to you my reasons for the measure I am about to adopt."[91] On November 6, 1814, Jackson and his force, which had been preceded by Indian raiding parties, arrived at Pensacola. Jackson had earlier issued what amounted to an ultimatum to Governor Manrique to expel any hostile Indians from Spanish territory and to remove the British from Pensacola.[92] Never having received a satisfactory response to any of his ultimatums, Jackson began the American invasion the next day. Before the assault, however, "the inhabitants were thrown into the greatest consternation and alarm" over a rumor spreading throughout the town that Jackson had been able to raise his force only by "promising to give up the Town to 24 hours of pillage, to which he had been obliged reluctantly to submit." The effects of his promise were "infinitely increased by the threats of the B[ritish] Commodore that so soon as the Spanish flag was lowered the Town would be leveled."[93] The population of Pensacola was thrown into a frenzy.

Recognizing that they were hugely outnumbered, the British, with their black and Indian army, had occupied Fort Barrancas, which was at the mouth of the harbor and was the one sound fortification in Pensacola. Meeting with virtually no resistance, the American and Indian force entered the city from the east and launched "a first onset [that] was dreadful," leaving the "inhabitants terror struck, flying some to the Shipping, some to the woods," in a desperate effort in which "every one thought only of their personal safety."[94]

Nobody had more to fear from the invasion than free and enslaved blacks who had yet to join the British. As a result, the "negro slaves who dreaded the ["Chactaw Indians and Militia"] as much as did their masters, very generally fled for security to the East side of the Bay."[95] "Observe the blacks," wrote one witness, "in Canoes, Boats . . . flying to the opposite shore, and there see Col. Nicolls like a demon riding in the storm, sweeping down, and driving them before him, even in view of their distracted owners, who are petrified with astonishment at the action."[96] Virtually the entire black population of Pensacola fled across the bay in the chaos caused by the American invasion in any and every vessel that held water including "negro women and their infant children" in a process that was "publick and notorious."[97] No doubt their flight was in part the result of Nicolls's immediate actions during the American invasion, but it was equally the result of fear at the potential consequences of an American occupation of Pensacola, which might well have resulted in enslavement for the free or a more dire form of bondage for the enslaved. More important, those who remained enslaved realized that the British were evacuating Pensacola and that with their departure the window for freedom was closing, perhaps permanently. Their decision was made even easier by the fact that for more than three months, slaves in Pensacola had listened to Nicolls's fiery rhetoric and watched as hundreds of blacks joined the British standard. Thus more accurately "when the Americans took possession of Pensacola the Slaves fled . . . and claimed our [British] protection in [view] of Sir A Cochranes proclamation."[98]

Pensacola slaves did not merely want freedom in spatial and physical terms, which they had as soon as they left their masters and would have been more than capable of cultivating in the wilds of Florida by themselves. Rather, by so consciously choosing to follow and join the British, they wanted to claim the version of freedom that Nicolls had laid out in his proclamation and had then preached for three months. The fact that slaves self-consciously wanted to join the British in hopes of acquiring freedom is further supported by the fact that many of the slaves presented "themselves as having come from the

United States, all speaking good English—it was a long time before he knew of their having come from Pensacola"; they were aiming to trick Nicolls in case he decided to stop accepting slaves from West Florida.[99]

When the situation became hopeless, the decision was made to board the British fleet that was anchored in the bay, blow up Fort Barrancas, and retreat to Prospect Bluff. In the ensuing chaos the British forces departed with all of their men, their Indian and black army, nearly the entire slave population of Pensacola, and fifty-six *pardo* and *moreno* troops from Havana. As the dust settled it emerged that "nothing now remains of the Town or Forts . . . but piles of ashes," a destruction entirely the result of British actions during the evacuation and not those of Jackson's forces who, after the terrifying initial siege, "have obtained for themselves a lasting name for their humanity and good order. . . . not a single excess was committed . . . [and the Americans are now held in] the most favorable opinion among the inhabitants."[100] A witness remarked that although the conduct of the enemy had been such as to warrant "revenge in its most malignant form . . . yet private property and persons were religiously respected."[101]

Notwithstanding Jackson's overwhelming success and his forces' admirable behavior, his occupation of Pensacola lasted only four days. Immediately upon receiving Jackson's letter advising that he was going to invade Pensacola with or without the government's approval, James Monroe penned a sternly worded letter that, while recognizing "that the conduct of the Spanish authorities . . . may justify the measure," also said "the President desires that it may be avoided," in hopes of finding a diplomatic solution. Monroe continued, "Should you have made the proposed attack you will on the receipt of this letter withdraw your troops from the Spanish Territory, declaring that you had entered it for the sole purpose of freeing it from British violation."[102] Monroe's was an extraordinarily flimsy excuse for leaving, and nobody in the Southeast would have doubted that Jackson had invaded West Florida to root out the British and their black and Indian allies, but he quickly obeyed the order and Spain's territorial sovereignty was temporarily restored.

In a little less than three months at Pensacola, Nicolls and the British had made major inroads with the region's Indians and slaves. Nicolls's radical anti-slavery stance had stirred deeply seated racialized tensions and brought new ones to the fore. This tension became so acute that Andrew Jackson felt compelled to defy his orders and invade neutral country. Word of Nicolls's message had spread across the Southeast, while the effects of his military actions and the broader war were taking a further toll on regional geopolitics. The uproar would continue from Prospect Bluff, where Nicolls's military mission and radical anti-slavery experiment was soon to enter into a new phase.

4 ⇒ Edward Nicolls and the Indians of the Southeast

As a result of Andrew Jackson's invasion of Pensacola, the British modified their plans to invade New Orleans in favor of a direct assault on the city. According to the new plans, Edward Nicolls and George Woodbine were to launch raids across the interior of Georgia as a means to distract American forces from their new base at Prospect Bluff, which was now the center of British, Indian, and black activity in the region.[1] Nicolls's forces were to attack the interior of Georgia in concert with raids by the British Navy along the coasts of South Carolina and Georgia. Cochrane detailed these plans in a letter to Nicolls that began by severely criticizing him for the decision to attack Mobile. Cochrane then informed Nicolls:

> The first [priority is] to draw off the Negroes from Georgia and South Carolina, and secondly to make a diversion in favor of the projected attack upon New Orleans. You will have two strong well appointed companies of one of the West India Regt sent you from hence. This will make good recruiting parties. You will therefore encourage the Negroes to enter into them in preference to any corps originally raised . . . as Ministers are particularly anxious to recruit West India Regts. . . . Suspect much from your exertions in the Georgia frontier where you must lay all waste. . . . [Get] all the Negroes that you can to come over. Those that are not willing to be soldiers shall be provided for as the families of all you expect.[2]

The recruitment of black soldiers and their families was now more central to British strategy in the Gulf Coast than at any other point in the war. This strategy doubtless served to raise the fear and anxiety among white southerners as a means to divert American forces. As a result of this modified strategy and the British expulsion from Pensacola, Prospect Bluff quickly became home to thousands of Indians and fugitive slaves as Nicolls and Woodbine continued their mission in earnest across a region that was increasingly unstable and volatile.

The War of 1812 officially ended in February 1815, but from their fortified base at Prospect Bluff, Nicolls and Woodbine continued in what they perceived as their mission until May. During these months Nicolls took it upon himself to become an advocate for the Seminoles and Red Sticks in the Indians' ongoing struggles with the United States. In particular, Nicolls petitioned American officials on behalf of the Red Sticks over the Treaty of Ghent and argued that Americans needed to stop encroaching on the territory of both groups of Indians. When diplomacy failed, Nicolls signed a treaty of alliance with the Indians, armed them heavily, and then encouraged them to resist American encroachments violently. When Nicolls left Prospect Bluff the Seminoles and Red Sticks were convinced that they were formal allies of Great Britain and could rely on British military aid in future conflicts with the United States. These actions were in direct defiance of Nicolls's orders and had powerful repercussions that lasted for years to come.

Recruitment Continues in Earnest

From Prospect Bluff, Nicolls and Woodbine aggressively continued to recruit slaves from the United States, East and West Florida, Indian Territory, and maroon communities, who joined former slaves from Pensacola and across the Southeast, or a West India Regiment, or the Cuban *pardo* and *moreno* regiment. At the same time Cochrane's proclamation and word of mouth led hundreds of slaves to join the British. For example, it was reported that "thro' the means of Woodbine Seventy Negroes of both sexes arrived at the Bluff from St. Augustine, St. Johns and Lachua."[3] In December it was alleged that Woodbine's primary motive in journeying to St. Augustine was not merely to meet with Governor Kindelán but rather to engage in "his old trade of seducing negroes . . . during the few days he was permitted to remain [in St. Augustine], many negroes deserted from their masters and many complaints were made about him and soon after his departure, no less than eighty followed him . . . and . . . in passing thro' Indian towns within the Jurisdiction of Florida he picked up a few more."[4] The accusation was fair, and while Woodbine remained in St. Augustine, a number of the town's inhabitants came to him and claimed that many of his force of forty former slaves, who sat in plain view in the middle of the town for days, were their property.[5] Woodbine "told them they could take them, that he would not oppose it in any way but that [they] could not use force for he did not have any [of their slaves]."[6] Woodbine was well aware that the former slaves valued the freedom they had found with the British and would undoubtedly refuse to return to former masters who were not in a position to use force. As Kindelán lamented, "What slave, when it is left to his own choice, will voluntarily return to slavery?"[7] Woodbine's actions in St. Augustine, which had been so public that an American military official had enquired about the visit within days, illustrated the powerlessness of East Florida's white population.[8] The fact that free blacks were joining Woodbine's force, as had been the case in Pensacola, further illustrates how highly blacks from across the region regarded the British anti-slavery experiment and the extent to which they believed that their freedom and material prospects could be enhanced by joining the British.

Prior to Jackson's invasion of Pensacola, Woodbine was seen arriving into town with "betwixt thirty and forty negroes principally men, with bundles on their backs—they made no secret of having come from East Florida ... [there was] a Black Corporal belonging to the Garrison of St. Augustine who spoke nothing but Spanish who was amongst them."[9] Later Woodbine's presence in the area caused ninety slaves from the Mosquito River on the east coast of Florida to flee to Prospect Bluff.[10] Governor Kindelán wrote to Woodbine that he had commissioned two men, Fernando Arredando and Juan Huertas, to return former slaves or freemen from St. Augustine who had joined Woodbine, but to no avail.[11] Edmund Doyle was able to speak to a number of these former slaves, and when he "asked them where they came from, they told me from Lachua." This implied that they had been living either with the Seminoles or in maroon communities. "I asked if any came from St. Augustine, I was told not one, those fellows of course received their Lesson along the way."[12] The "Lesson" they were learning consisted of Nicolls's anti-slavery rhetoric and promises as well as the fact that freedom was to found with the British at Prospect Bluff and that, in the meantime, it was a wise idea to lie about their origins. Such actions by the former slaves clearly demonstrate their willful participation in Nicolls's plans based on their recognition that these provided them with a direct path to an expansive version of freedom.

Kindelán, regardless of these weaknesses, was now pushed past his limits. The governor presented Woodbine with an official complaint that forbade him from communicating with British vessels on the east coast of Florida. Woodbine was then asked to "discharge your escort of colored people," and Kindelán carefully defined the borders of Florida, stating that "all the Indians inhabiting the country South of this line are under the domain of the Spanish Nation." He finished by warning Woodbine that any further British activity within the Floridas against the United States would be treated as an act of aggression against Spain.[13] Yet both Kindelán and Woodbine knew that the remonstrance was completely hollow. The governor was soon forced to swallow Woodbine's snide and absurd assurance that "I have never used any endeavors to induce the colored people . . . of the province to desert; on the contrary, my instructions . . . have been to give every aid (as far as requisite) to the cause of our good and faithful ally, the Spanish nation."[14] Ultimately the best that Kindelán could do was to send a detailed report to Luis de Onis, the Spanish minister to the United States in Philadelphia, before writing a panicked letter to Mateo González Manrique, the governor of West Florida, informing him that Woodbine was returning to his province with many slaves and free people of color from East Florida and that his help in recovering them was imperative.[15] Manrique, who had just witnessed the removal of nearly the entire slave population of Pensacola and was in the midst of his own futile efforts to retrieve these slaves, was of little help and meekly forwarded this request to Cochrane.[16] Kindelán soon wrote another letter directly to the governor of Cuba, in which he expressed his growing concern that so many free and enslaved blacks were leaving East Florida to join the British that the area's stability and the continuance of Spanish rule were under threat.[17]

Residents of West Florida outside Pensacola also had their slaves stolen. Upon returning from the failed attack on Mobile, Woodbine, Lieutenant Cassel, and their force came upon a number of slaves belonging to Forbes and Company at Bayou la Lanche on the west side of the Perdido River and took these slaves with them.[18] Later eleven slaves were taken from Forbes and Company's trading factory on the Apalachicola River by the British.[19] John Innerarity testified that late in 1814 Nicolls had "carried or caused to be carried to a Fort" twenty-three of his slaves from West Florida.[20]

Before and after the assault on New Orleans, the British had taken American slaves from across the Deep South on their return to Prospect Bluff, including a number from Alabama.[21] A British deserter estimated that of the three to four hundred former slaves at Prospect Bluff, all were "taken from the United States, principally Louisiana."[22] While the composition of this estimate was obviously incorrect, it still suggests that many slaves from the United States were fleeing to Spanish Florida to join the British. In the spring of 1815 the Spanish surveyor general reported that while at Prospect Bluff he had witnessed Nicolls's return to the fort with "many negroes, immigrated or brought from the American possessions," who joined many more slaves from the United States who were already there.[23]

Britain's Indian allies aggressively recruited slaves from across the Southeast. In his proclamation introducing Nicolls to the Red Sticks and Seminoles, Cochrane urged the Indians to "encourage . . . by every means the

Emigration of Negroes from Georgia and the Carolinas. . . . [Nicolls will] organize, cloth and arm as many as can be got to engage in the common cause."[24] Agent Hawkins reported in October 1814 that on the evening of the previous Saturday, "the sound of cannon was distinctly heard at the agency. . . . Mr. Wigginton informs me it was southwardly of that place, continued for four hours and he counted distinctly 180. It appears some signal of this sort has been agreed on between the Seminoles, the negros and the British." As a result of the signal, five of Hawkins's "negros run off or were stolen on Sunday and 5 of Mr. Barnards and I have heard of four running from Capt. Smith below this line."[25]

Many of the slaves belonging to the Creek Indians joined the British. For example, the Creek chief Stedham had slaves stolen by the British forces from Georgia.[26] The disappearance of Stedham's slaves serves to emphasize the role that blacks played in recruiting their enslaved brethren. It was reported that "there was one negro March and one of Stedhams runaway and went down, come here stole Hardridges two negro woman and 14 of J. Stedhams negros and went to the British."[27] Edmund Doyle noted that among Britain's greatest aids in recruiting slaves were "their agents and black spies, [who] corrupted the Negroes of their Indian friends and Spanish allies."[28] James Perryman, another wealthy Creek, had his slaves stolen as well.[29] To white and Indian observers on both sides of the Florida border, the fact that the Indians were now losing their slaves appeared to mark a further disintegration of racial order. A surprised John Innerarity noted: "It is known that even the Indians have Suffered equal oppressions from Capt Woodbine and his other agents, who have despoiled them of their slaves."[30] The decision by the Creeks' slaves to join the British further illustrates the powerful lure of freedom emanating from Prospect Bluff and the full extent to which it appealed to slaves of numerous backgrounds.

Southeastern Indians, Race, and the British Message

British actions with slaves greatly affected the Indians of the Southeast, regardless of tribe or allegiances. Many Creeks allied to the United States agreed with white southerners that racial order was threatened by the British presence in West Florida, a belief that reveals a great deal about their evolving racial consciousness.[31] During this period Creek racial consciousness was increasingly based on the ever more prevalent opinion that different groups of humans were innately or, in modern parlance, biologically different. These differences were not to be embraced but rather led to a distinct hierarchy of races, in which blacks were more often than not at or near the bottom. Preying on the opinion that the British presented Creek society with a racialized threat, Hawkins encouraged the Indians to

> attack and take or destroy all the white and black people you find in arms [at Pensacola]. Take such white people as you see encouraging the black to mischief . . . fire on them and compell them . . . [they are stealing your slaves and cattle]. . . . Take him [Woodbine] and all white people with him by force and send him and them to me. . . . The negroes you take who have no masters will be your property, and those who have white masters shall pay you 50 dollars a head. The Red people who will not listen to the terms of peace offered by Gen'l Pinckney are our enemies, those who have been doing mischief in Georgia must be shot.[32]

That the Creeks agreed with such talk and sentiments is evidenced in a letter written by Big Warrior in response to Hawkins, focusing on the impact of British actions with the Indians' slaves.[33] Big Warrior's letter recounted the futile efforts of Mad Bear to "have a talk with the Lower towns" about their British-influenced actions. Big Warrior noted:

> The British officer [Woodbine] who came on here promised them soldiers, but they got none they have 300 negros of the Nation under arms at Forbes's store [they are starting to steal our slaves]. The British came on here and said they were the Indians friend but they came not for that they came for Negros and they think it is a second Bowles. . . . [The British have large supplies of arms and ammunition] and our youngers want to go and get it from them. We want to know your opinion on the subject. McIntosh will head the party if you will say the word. McIntosh wants to go and see what the British mean by arming the Negros. it is not the Indians they are fooling, but the negros, we ant at war as yet but we want to go and see, and if they fire on us we will return fire.

Big Warrior was demonstrating a deep-seated fear over British intrigues with the Creek slaves. He was clearly bothered by the loss of so many slaves, but he was more worried about the implications of the arming and training of the Creek slaves—worried to the point of offering to start another ill-advised war, for which he provided not a single justification other than British intrigues with Creek slaves. Big Warrior's fear of "fooling" was an intellectual fear of the radical anti-slavery message that the British were instilling in the Creek slaves and spreading across the Southeast. In Big Warrior's mind, arming, training, and radicalizing slaves had the potential to escalate into further acts of violent slave resistance. Big Warrior's fears would have been different if the British had been meddling with any other race of people and were very similar to those harbored by white southerners.

William McIntosh, a powerful Creek slave owner whose long-term animosity toward the maroons at Prospect Bluff was rivaled only by that of Andrew Jackson, immediately acted on Creek fear of growing racial disorder. With a heavily armed detachment he traveled to the Seminole town of Eufaula, where he learned that Woodbine, who had recently returned to Pensacola, had been traveling across "Seminole country" with "runaway and stolen negros," spreading his message and recruiting blacks and Indians. An increasingly nervous McIntosh and his force then traveled to "Perrymans square, where all the Seminole Chiefs were convened. They seemed much surprised at his appearance in arms among them, assured him of their pacific disposition and determination to hunt up and send all runaway negros in their country to their owners." McIntosh had so little faith in what he was told by the Seminole chiefs that "he left two Chiefs to have an eye to their conduct and see whether they will comply with their promise or not."[34]

McIntosh was correct not to trust the Seminole chiefs. Only weeks later it was reported that Woodbine and Perryman (who had just promised McIntosh his aid in retrieving fugitive slaves) had visited the "King of the Miccasookies ['Caupichau Micco']" and "urged him to go to war with the warriors offering him one hundred dollars for every trader cow buyer or other American found in their country and the like sum for every captured negro."[35] McIntosh's sense of betrayal by Perryman intensified when he learned that "the head quarters of the encouragers of mischief is Perrymans."[36] In a politicized effort to avoid committing his people to a war they could ill afford, Cappachamico told McIntosh, "Begin you first the war, and you will then see what the Red People will do."[37] But already many of Cappachamico's warriors were stealing Creek- and white-owned slaves. The chief went on to inform McIntosh that he "does what he can to restrain his young people but they are independent and eager for mischief."[38]

Elsewhere it was reported that "Caupichau Micco (Chief of the Miccosoooce and the Seminoles) is not unfriendly [to the Creek and American cause]; but he says 'his young men are rude, impudent and ungovernable.' Some of them are out in thieving parties, they are ready to join any party of the British or Indians, in their predatory warfare against us. They give encouragement to negros to run to them."[39] The very detailed report continued to note the towns that were allied or likely to be allied with the British (Alachua, Hitchiti or Fowltown, and Oketeyoconne), which "must be chastised speedily and the party and their doings there crushed or there will be no peace in Georgia."

The report then reiterated the scale of the British rewards for plunder including slaves, noting that "there is one British officer . . . [at Prospect Bluff] and a few British and the assemblage of Blacks" and that three "parties for predatory warfare" had recently been sent out: "The first plundered negros from the [Creek] half breeds. The second time they plundered two citizens of Georgia . . . of two horses and their loads of homespun, Mr. Barnard . . . of six horses and Col. Hawkins of four horses and five negros [the third party had yet to be heard from]."[40] McIntosh's findings and concerns echoed those of Big Warrior. The British and their Indian allies were stealing Creek slaves or encouraging these slaves to flee their masters. The flight of the slaves was deeply destabilizing to Creek and white society and had the potential to escalate into larger-scale acts of slave resistance. The Creeks needed to take immediate steps to stop the British and their message before it infected anymore slaves. Like Big Warrior, McIntosh had made it clear that he was willing to enter into a war in which British actions with Creek slaves was the primary, if not sole, justification.

That the Creeks' racial sensibilities were threatened by these developments was made even clearer by Hawkins's assertion that he could raise a thousand Creek warriors "to move at half a days notice" to fight a "war which is necessary to the safety of this frontier [that] will be entered into heartily by them, as they deem it equally necessary to their own safety."[41] Little Prince, who was the "Speaker of the Lower Creeks," expressed a similar sentiment. He reported that his "man of truth" had recently witnessed the arrival of British reinforcements at Prospect Bluff, including a "number . . . of . . . troops [who] are negros. . . . All the Red Sticks have arrived there and all runaway negros have gone to the British." As a result of this intelligence, Little Prince assured Hawkins that even though the "friendly Indians are . . . in great distress for clothing and for food," as soon as the warriors were paid, they would "fight when and where required."[42] Little Prince's promise meant that Hawkins was correct when he claimed it had only become necessary to "enroll Indians into the service of the United States . . . after the negros of Marshall, Stedham, and Kinnard, three half breeds, were taken from them, by force or stratagem."[43] Thus the main reason the Creeks entered a war they could barely afford against the British was over fears of British-instigated slave resistance.

From a Creek perspective, not only were the British encouraging the Red Sticks and Seminoles to acts of violence against them and urging their slaves to flee or rebel, both of which challenged racial order, but the British threatened to destroy all the progress they had made through their embrace of accommodation. This embrace of accommodation, which was especially common amongst mixed race and wealthy Creeks, most notably involved the adoption of plantation slavery worked by blacks and greatly contributed to the Creeks' evolving racial consciousness. Hawkins lamented that prior to British arrival at Pensacola the Creeks had been "a happy and contented people, cultivating their *farms* and *manufacturing*, until the *British*, like the devil in *Eden*, tempted them to evil. They have already paid a dreadful penalty for their folly and weakness—but the end is not yet. They still listen to the deceiver." Hawkins concluded by imploring the "Inhuman *Englishman*! [to] let the poor savage have peace. Wretched *murderers*! permit us in safety to spare the remnant of the *Creeks*! Monsters, let them return to that progressive state of civilization we fostered with so much charity, justice and good faith."[44] To American-allied Creeks, the British not only challenged the racial foundation of their society but imperiled the fabric of this society and threatened its existence.

Like those of white southerners, the Creeks' fears of "strategem[s]," "corruption," "spies," and "fooling" were fears over ideas and their implications rather than actions and their obvious consequences. The Creeks were scared of both the British message and how their slaves might act on it. This was a deeper fear than merely that of losing their human property, and it reflected a fuller conceptualization of the differences between themselves and people of African descent. The deep fear of the message and corresponding slave revolts was so intensely felt because the Creeks were coming to view their slaves, and blacks more generally, as being fundamentally different from themselves and capable of large-scale violence against the "master class" in a way that other people might not be. The Creeks also demonstrated the centrality of slavery to their society and economy by so willingly defending the institution at such an inopportune time in their history. The nature of these fears strongly suggests that the Creeks were developing a racial consciousness increasingly similar to that of contemporary white Americans and largely the product of slavery and, ultimately, accommodation.[45] In sum the Indians' response to and understanding of the threat posed by the British to their slaves was virtually indistinguishable from that of a white southerner. Both the Creeks and white slave owners felt it was dangerous to expose blacks to such radical ideas, because as a race of people lower down the racial hierarchy, their slaves might well respond with uncontrollable violence if given such provocations. The Creeks would not have responded in such a particular manner if the British were recruiting a different race of people.

Creek and white racial anxiety was further compounded by a frightening event: the Seminoles and Red Sticks were experiencing a violent generational rift that was being exacerbated by the British and that contributed to Seminole and Red Stick willingness to recruit American and Creek slaves through virtually any means possible. The inability of Perryman and Cappachamico to control their young warriors, who were spoiling for war and had readily embraced the British offer of alliance, illustrates this generational divide. The rift had grown so deep and intense that in November 1814 a group of young Seminole warriors (who if not immediately "chastised . . . will begin to destroy our frontiers") accused Perryman "of being tardy and unfit for command and advised the warriors to appoint a more energetic commander."[46]

The origins of the rift were manifold: a youthful belief in the adventure and glory of war versus the cynical realism of age; a rapidly changing economy and society that placed extra strains on the young; an increasingly desperate awareness that the American slave frontier was swallowing their lands; an enhanced affinity with their black allies, born of the realization that they were joined in a common cause enhanced by their dual inexperience as slave owners and their dislike for slavery as an American and accommodationist institution; and a simple hatred of the United States and their Creek allies, forged in war. To the British, all these factors made the young warriors ideal recruits who required minimal persuasion to join their forces. To whites and Creek Indians it often appeared that bands of uncontrollable rogue warriors were preying on the frontier in frenzied attacks, spurred on by a radical anti-slavery advocate in a process that had deeply unsettling racial implications.

The reception by the Seminoles and Red Sticks of some of Nicolls's anti-slavery message provides insight into both groups' evolving racial consciousness, which was related to what was occurring within the Creek nation. When Nicolls left Prospect Bluff in the spring of 1815 he instructed his Red Stick and Seminole allies "to suffer no Indian to have a slave."[47] It is hardly surprising that Nicolls sought to instill this simple yet powerful anti-slavery message among his Native allies. His message would have been doubly appealing to Red Sticks and Seminoles because of the small number of slaves they owned; their military, political, and social alliances with blacks; and the association between slave owning and accommodation. Nonetheless both Nicolls and Woodbine had gone much further in attempting to instill an anti-slavery ideology in their Native allies and spur them to like action. In October, Woodbine had excitedly informed Nicolls that "from my residence in the Creek Nation and knowledge of the Indian character, I feel fully convinced, that the desirable object which we have often and were this morning canvassing, may be carried into effect viz *The liberation of the poor unfortunate Africans, taken prisoners by the Inds."* On a practical level, Woodbine was pleased that the Red Sticks and Seminoles were turning over the slaves they had stolen from Americans and Creeks, but he was even more pleased "that the lessons of humanity, inculcated in the minds of our aggrieved red brethren, have not been thrown away . . . [which] makes me feel not a bit proud, in having been the first instrument of inducing them to lay aside the Tamahawk and scalping knifes [and return their captive slaves]." Later in this report it becomes even clearer that Woodbine and Nicolls had sown the seeds of an intellectual anti-slavery ideology in their Native allies. Woodbine concluded that "the Indians will also liberate their slaves, tho. they were to lose what they cost them. To prevent these poor Indians suffering their all, without compensation induces me to request your permission, to purchase such slaves as the Indians may be at present possessed of, and also that they may capture in war, with the inten-tion of giving them their liberty, and enlisting them in the corps." Woodbine believed that "they will I am convinced each have their chains struck off for a very low sum," for which he set aside one hundred guineas.[48]

These efforts were provided with sharper official teeth when Captain Henry, one of Nicolls's subordinate officers, issued a declaration that "the English are sent by their great father and King to restore his Indian people to their lands, and we are desired by him not to take away their negroes, un-less they freely give them to us, or sell them for money."[49] On the surface, the intention of this declaration was to gain black military recruits for the sake of the war effort. Nicolls and Woodbine understood it, however, as further encouragement as well as official sanction to continue their anti-slavery proj-ect. While the number of slaves owned by the Seminoles and Red Sticks was small, their commitment, at least in some cases, voluntarily to purge them-selves of slavery was nonetheless remarkable and reflects at least a partial un-derstanding of Woodbine and Nicolls's anti-slavery rhetoric, which both men had gone to lengths to instill in the Indians. Interestingly, at this same point in time, Peter McQueen and Josiah Francis sent a talk to Alexander Cochrane thanking him for sending British forces to West Florida and agreeing to serve under Nicolls. The talk began with the unusually worded line "Our breasts are filled with the Glorious love of liberty and protected by our great and good Father, we will live or die free, of which we have given a hard proof by choosing to abandon our Country rather than live in it as Slaves."[50] This lan-guage of slavery and freedom was clearly inspired by Nicolls's proclamations and his rhetoric. Again, none of this behavior meant that the Indians had become anti-slavery ideologues or that their ideas about slavery and blacks had radically changed. Rather, exposure to Nicolls's anti-slavery ideas had brought to the surface one aspect of the Indians' ever-evolving understanding of race.

If one combines the Seminole and Red Stick embrace of Nicolls's anti-slavery ideology with the racialized anxiety felt by American-allied Creek Indians, then one can conclude that by this point each group had developed or was developing a sense of modern racial consciousness hinging on a belief that people were divided into distinct and innately different groups. Furthermore, these differences were often negative and led to these groups or races of people falling into a rough hierarchy. The Creeks' fears resembled those of a contemporary white slave owner, whereas the Seminoles' and Red Sticks' at least partial embrace of anti-slavery ideas and actions also demonstrated a racial consciousness similar to that of Nicolls and others who shared his beliefs. Neither of these responses was identical to that of contemporary whites, especially not that of the Seminoles and Red Sticks, but the responses nonetheless illustrated a growing awareness that slavery was a defining institution in their world, in which a different and distinct race of people could provoke fear or merit help that was unique to their race. By choosing to fear or help the slaves in a manner that would not have been extended to other races, both groups of Indians demonstrated that they believed themselves to be fundamentally different from people of African descent and thus demonstrated a discernible understanding of race and a hierarchy of race. Both these understandings of race were brought to light by Nicolls's anti-slavery ideas and actions.

Growing Regional Instability

As a result of the continuing war in general and Nicolls's and Woodbine's actions in particular, an already unstable area was now becoming increasingly chaotic. This played to British strategy and aided potential fugitive slaves. In January 1815 Thomas Havente wrote to the governor of East Florida that the local population was living in fear of the British and their black and Native allies and needed protection immediately.[51] Havente expressed disappointment at and remained unconvinced by the governor's hollow assurance that the Indians and "your blacks" would not harm the residents of East Florida.[52] The Spanish, now more than ever, believed that British activities at Prospect Bluff threatened the very continuance of their possession of the Floridas. A month later Kindelán wrote a deeply pessimistic letter to Governor Apodaca of Cuba detailing how the free blacks and slaves belonging to Native Americans had joined Woodbine's multiracial force on his recent "diplomatic" mission to East Florida. Kindelán believed that these developments directly and immediately compromised the provinces' security.[53] This was two weeks after Kindelán had informed Ruiz that the British presence at Prospect Bluff was having the same effect on West Florida.[54]

Americans fully shared these fears with the Spanish. By the spring, the *Milledgeville Journal* had replaced "black troops" with "***** troops" when reporting on British troop levels at Prospect Bluff in a desperate effort to alleviate public fears.[55] During this period Georgia's Governor Early, wishfully if unconvincingly, wrote to a resident of the Georgia backcountry that he hoped the time was "at hand when your Indian frontier will be relieved forever" as a result of the state militia's planned expedition against the British. However, the more realistic portion of the letter was its first line: "The exposed condition of Camden County is felt by me with deep interest."[56] The Georgia slave owner John Sawyer reported that "his [neighbor's] negroes exhibited signs of rebellion. . . . You can have no idea of the distress of the low country—every one moving their negroes that can, and many leaving them behind." In Sawyer's mind, "the idea of Woodbine was more alarming than the British, if possible."[57] Lt. Col. William Scott of the Georgia militia echoed this sentiment when he wrote: "I never experienced so much alarm. The inhabitants are flying in all directions. If we do not get reinforced, there will be scarce a family left in the county. The inhabitants dread Colonel Woodbine and his Indians, more than the British."[58]

Disaster at New Orleans, the End of the War of 1812, and Evacuation

In December, as had been planned, Nicolls's force launched a number of raids against the Georgia frontier that, while not on the scale that Cochrane had envisioned, created a considerable physical and psychological distraction. Nicolls described the raids as highly effective "small parties . . . that distract[ed] and annoy[ed] the Enemy on his Georgian Frontiers, which caused the United States a great loss of lives and property as well as cutting off his convoys which very much distressed his Garrisons on the Mobille, Coosa, and Amibama Rivers."[59] In the middle of January, as near hysteria had spread across the Deep South over the fear of a full invasion, Governor Early reported that Major Blackshear and a large portion of the Georgia militia were occupied on a mission "for the special purpose of chastising and destroying the hostile settlements of Indians, and also for the purpose of breaking up the British establishment at the River Appalachicola."[60] A week earlier the governor had written a surprisingly diplomatically worded letter to the governor of East Florida that both nations "have obligations to keep Indians within limits under control," but since the Indians of East Florida were being "instigated by the British at Apalachicola" and the Spanish military was incapable of dealing with the issue, "you ought not to take it amiss, should we send a force and destroy the towns. . . . [which is justified] by the great principle of self preservation."[61] Four days earlier a furious Blackshear—who had already sent a number of letters complaining savagely about the contradictory intelligence he was daily receiving about the activities of Nicolls and the size of his force—reported that "a great number of my men are sick . . . [many] have died. . . . More like to die . . . [and] a number have deserted." Even though his forces were in such poor shape, he continued: "I have about seven hundred effectives to guard my places of deposit which [I] must necessarily establish, to destroy all the hostile Indians, all the negroes, and all the British at the mouth of this river, and at the same time keep an artful commander and seven hundred warriors in check."[62] Blackshear faced an immense task in defending the frontier against Nicolls and his multiracial army, and the difficulty was compounded by fear, rumor, desertion, and sickness.

As a result of these factors, a further 2,500 American soldiers under Maj. Uriah Blue were diverted to the area to fend off possible British incursions.[63] All totaled, thousands of American and Indian troops were diverted to the Southeast to defend against Nicolls's army, which meant that Cochrane's plans had worked to near perfection. In the end Nicolls and a number of his Indian troops traveled with the British Navy to New Orleans, where his request to lead the marines in the "general attack" was denied by Cochrane. The admiral refused Nicolls's request because he feared that "if any accident happened to [Nicolls] he would have all the difficulty of getting another officer acquainted with the Indians to go through again."[64] It is virtually certain that this decision saved Nicolls's life. Nicolls and his troops were passive witnesses to the British defeat before retreating overland to Prospect Bluff.

The British defeat at New Orleans was by any standards a disaster. However, Cochrane was not finished in his efforts to win the war in the South, and a new British plan emerged that was essentially the same as the original plan for the taking of New Orleans. This included the role of Nicolls's army. By this point Nicolls's black troops had proved themselves well organized and numbered between three and four hundred. They also received reinforcements from the Fifth West India Regiment.[65] The image of hundreds of armed and uniformed black soldiers marching in unison was deeply disturbing to white southerners. Equally disturbing was Nicolls's boast, prior to the invasion, that he was "to march towards Charleston, where he soon expected to hear of the arrival of Lord Hill, with a powerful force. He is to free negros and compel the Americans to restore back the lands to the Indians, and make every thing submit to him as he marches along."[66] This threat to carry his mission deep into the heart of the slaveholding South was a frightening one that ultimately led to "many families [having] quitted their Houses upon the Sea Board and fled to the Northward . . . [because] so great was the dread of an invasion from the back of Georgia and South Carolina."[67] As it turned out this operation was so brief and the closing stages of the war were so chaotic that Nicolls's force was never given a realistic chance to execute its orders. In February 1815 John Lambert successfully captured Fort Bowyer at the mouth of Mobile Bay, while the forces under Nicolls were left to launch a handful of uncoordinated raids. Lambert's capture of Fort Bowyer marked the first British success in the Deep South for some time, but it was followed almost immediately by the announcement that the War of 1812 was over.

Official British Policy toward the Seminoles and Red Sticks

In the same month that the war officially ended, Alexander Cochrane expressed an opinion shared by many British politicians and military leaders when he wrote that Britain must take active measures "for relieving West Florida from the usurped authority of the American Government (being a colony belonging to Spain) and at the same time to afford to the Indian Nations an opportunity of recovering territories of which they have been so unjustly deprived by the United States."[68] The British feared an American Florida and wanted their Red Stick allies to recover the lands taken from them by the Treaty of Fort Jackson. These two goals were intertwined with the realization that a strong and well-armed Red Stick and Seminole presence in the Southeast represented the most realistic hope for Spain to maintain possession of the Floridas. With this in mind, the British encouraged the Red Sticks to endorse the Treaty of Ghent because of the inclusion of Article 9, calling for the restoration of Indian lands to their 1811 boundaries. Accordingly, Cochrane instructed Nicolls to "tell our Indian Allies that they have been included [in the treaty] and that they are placed as to territory as they were in 1811[.] If the peace shall not be ratified, you will have a large reinforcement sent to you at Apalachicola."[69]

The United States was equally fearful that the Floridas might fall into British hands. This longstanding anxiety had been exacerbated by the British assault on Mobile in October 1814 and the "previous conduct [by the British] in Pensacola [which] give some cause to apprehend that there may have been some arrangement between the British and the Spanish governments respecting the occupation of West Florida." The belief that Nicolls was part of a conspiracy to acquire the Floridas was taken so seriously that just weeks after Congress ratified the peace treaty, Secretary of State Monroe instructed Jackson that if "British forces have obtained possession of any part of that country formerly claimed as part of W. Florida . . . and refuse to deliver it up [as stipulated in the Treaty of Ghent] you will make use of the force under . . . [your]

command to expel them from it."[70] That same week Monroe informed Jackson that in case the "British forces tak[e] possession of the Floridas . . . you should draw all the regular forces under your command to some convenient position adjacent to East Florida" and wait for further instructions.[71]

The British saw the continued presence of Nicolls and his army in West Florida as an important bargaining chip as well as a powerful contingency plan should the treaty negotiations fail. However, in early March, when it had become clear that the Treaty of Ghent would soon be ratified, Nicolls received a series of clearly worded orders concerning his evacuation:

> you will do your utmost to persuade the Indian Nations to accept . . . the Treaty as independent Nations—ceasing from all kinds of hostilities against the U.S. who are to restore to them all the territory of which they were in possession in 1811. You will endeavour to impress upon them the risk they will run by continuing to war with the U.S. in which they cannot be assisted by G.B.; that by Peace a free commerce with the British nation by the River Apalachicola they will grow rich, and being free from war become populous so as to be able to defend themselves from the future encroachments of the U.S. You will leave them such cannon and military stores as they may require for their Fort at Apalachicola, and have distributed among them such presents as you may think requisite for those which I shall forward to you in a Transport Brig . . . you will also give them a supply of Indian corn.[72]

The British valued their commitments to their Native American allies as much as they feared an American-controlled Florida. However, when formal negotiations ultimately failed, the British were not prepared to risk more bloodshed and decided to arm and supply their Native allies heavily in the hopes that they could fend off the encroachments of the United States and keep Florida in Spanish hands. The British also made it clear that they intended to continue their formal economic alliances, from the Caribbean, combined with a subtler and less official political alliance with the Native Americans. Nicolls was far from content with this outcome and took it upon himself to see the Seminoles and Red Sticks righted.

Nicolls's Rogue and Unofficial Advocacy on Behalf of His Indian Allies

Since Nicolls's arrival in North America some in the British military had grumbled about his willingness to ignore orders and make bold decisions in the field that circumvented the chain of command and "disgusted all the army as well as the navy."[73] However, by the winter and spring of 1815 it had become clear that Nicolls was now waging an unsanctioned war on behalf of the Red Sticks and Seminoles against the United States, a war with which the British foreign secretary, Lord Bathurst, was "altogether unacquainted."[74] Bathurst, who was joined in both his claims of ignorance and official disavowal by Lords Liverpool and Castlereagh, among other prominent officials, later told his secretary Henry Baker to produce his correspondence with Nicolls in order "to convince the Americans of the total ignorance in which this government was respecting the conduct of this officer, and of its disapprobation, when informed of it." Bathurst hoped "these documents will satisfy the Government of the United States, that the interference of Major Nicholls may have been occasioned by an ill judged zeal in the prosecution of the military duties with which he was entrusted, but was in no way sanctioned by H.M.'s Government."[75] Later, in a tense encounter with John Quincy Adams, Bathurst added that Nicolls was a "man of activity and spirit, but a very wild fellow."[76] American officials believed their British counterparts' claims in part because they had intercepted a copy of Nicolls's orders from London in mid-March and thus knew he was exceeding his orders.[77]

Long after other British officials had given up on this point, Nicolls doggedly insisted that the ninth article of the Treaty of Ghent rendered the Treaty of Fort Jackson null and void and returned the Indians' lands to their 1811 boundaries.[78] Nicolls added a further twist in his denial of the legality of the Treaty of Fort Jackson when he stated that "no such treaty was made with the Creek Indians. They were always in Camp or Quarters with me or an officer left by me in command . . . until two months after the Peace."[79] He further maintained that "General Jackson . . . did trump up a sort of Treaty with about two hundred fugitive Indians who had deserted to him from the nations," which Jackson attempted to pass off as the Treaty of Fort Jackson. However, Nicolls argued that this was doubly ridiculous because on the date when Jackson's treaty was signed "most, if not all, of the Chiefs were in the vicinity of Apalachicola, preparing to invade the back part of Georgia." Furthermore, he wrote, "it is not to be supposed that so great a proportion of the Indian population [estimated at over 4,000 individuals] could have been ignorant of the conclusion of a Treaty that would have rendered unnecessary any further actions or hostility against the United States." Robert Spencer of the Royal Navy, who had little patience with Nicolls's tendency to ignore orders, added that while at Prospect Bluff in March 1815, he had met the "major part of the Creek Chiefs . . . [and] none of them had signed the Treaty with the United States."[80] These Red Stick leaders spoke of the Treaty of Fort Jackson with contempt as "being done by those who had no real power or authority to negotiate for the Creek Nation . . . therefore it is not likely that they should have formed any separate treaty with the U.S. prior to this date."[81]

Nicolls aggressively defended the Red Stick position that the Treaty of Fort Jackson was null and void because it predated the Treaty of Ghent, and only a handful of Creek leaders allied to the United States had signed it. The Creeks lacked any authority to sign a treaty on behalf of the Red Sticks, their mortal enemies. To the ire of the United States and their Creek allies, Nicolls, on behalf of the British, recognized the militant Red Sticks Hepoeth Micco and Hopoy Micco and the Seminole Cappachamico (whom they referred to collectively as the "Chiefs of the Muscogee nation") as the supreme leaders of the Creeks. Nicolls then argued that the treaty these three men signed on April 2 at Prospect Bluff (discussed in the next section) was legally binding and lent further legal support to the proposition that their lands must be returned to their 1811 boundaries.[82]

American officials strenuously objected to this and accused Nicolls of negotiating a farcical treaty with the "Creek nation . . . [based solely on] the authority created by yourself for the purpose, [which] must be a novelty."[83] U.S. leaders insisted that none of the three chiefs whom Nicolls recognized "has ever attended the national councils of the Creeks, or is in any way a part of their Executive Government," and that one was a Seminole.[84] Government officials further alleged that Nicolls and the three chiefs were "attempt[ing] to usurp the Government of the Creeks as well as the rights of our fellow citizens within their territory."[85]

Nicolls's Indian allies, meanwhile, celebrated his message. They felt fully "assured . . . that, according to the treaty of Ghent, all the lands ceded by the Creeks, in treaty with General Jackson, were to be restored; otherwise, the Indians must fight for those lands, and that the British would in short time assist them."[86] Edmund Gaines believed that "so industriously have these impressions been circulated by the British and Spanish agents among the Indians, that, so far as I can learn, not only the chiefs, but the common warriors, are in the habit of saying that the British treaty with the Americans gives the Indians their lands taken by the treaty with General Jackson." If this failed, "a war must ensue; and that their friends, the British will re-establish them in the possession of these lands."[87]

Nicolls's treaty with the Red Sticks and Seminoles called for the Indians to "desist from hostilities of every kind against the citizens and subjects of the United States," but it also insisted that, in the case of the Red Sticks, their lands be returned to their 1811 boundaries.[88] Soon a number of Indians reported that "Col. Nicolls has advised them to use force to stop [the] running of the Line of Creek Limits and promised to return in six months from his departure with orders and force to stop it and to compel the United States to conform their conduct to his construction of the treaty of Ghent."[89] The Indians would remain absolutely steadfast in these beliefs for years to come. Furthermore Nicolls made it clear that "he considers the territories of the Creeks to be as they stood before the war; and arrogating to himself the entire control of the Indians, warns the citizens of the United States from entering the Creek territory, or holding any communication with the inhabitants thereof."[90] Nicolls's actions virtually guaranteed that bloodshed would continue to destabilize the Southeast.

Adding to the growing list of American grievances against Nicolls was the fact that he had come to style himself the "Col. Commanding His Britannic Majesty's forces in the Creek Nation." Hawkins sarcastically told him "being a stranger is an apology for not knowing the Geography of the country where you are. You have never been in the Creek Nation, nor within fifty miles of it, nor has His B.M. had any forces there since 1783."[91] In this self-appointed capacity Nicolls relentlessly petitioned American officials when he felt that his Indian allies were suffering at the hands of American citizens. For example, when the Seminole chief Bowlegs reported that "a party of Americans . . . have made an incursion into his towns, killed one man, wounded another, and stole some of his cattle," Nicolls requested that Hawkins "enquire into this affair and cause justice to be done."[92] Hawkins ignored Nicolls's request but had no doubt that a recent robbery in Camden County, Georgia, was only the beginning of Seminole "revenge . . . on the unoffending citizens of the frontiers."[93]

Hawkins believed that Nicolls's actions amounted to an effort to "gratify their revenge [on] the good and innocent citizens of our frontiers [who] are to be the victims of such barbarity. Suppose a banditti of white people were to commit a violent outrage such as that of 17 April are we to charge it to the unoffending people on the frontiers? and kill them without mercy, if we could not find the guilty?"[94] Hawkins had carefully chosen his hypothetical scenario to underscore the racialized violence that Nicolls was encouraging. Hawkins's concerns were correct: Nicolls was overtly preying upon American and Creek fears of racialized violence as a tool in his advocacy for the Red Sticks and Seminoles. The Creeks in particular were experiencing an "anxious leaning . . . towards the expected fulfillment of the promises made them by Col. Nicolls."[95]

Nicolls made this clear in his warning that if the U.S. government did not immediately address the crimes against Bowlegs, settlers could expect retribution. His Indian allies had "given their consent to wait your answer before they take revenge, but, Sir, they are impatient for it, and well armed, as the whole nation now is. . . . Picture to yourself, Sir, the miseries that may be suffered by good and innocent Citizens on your Frontiers, and I am sure you lend me your best aid in keeping the bad spirits in subjection."[96] Similarly, Nicolls played to the fears of American and Spanish slave owners when he admitted awareness that both believed the "Indians are supported by the British Government in encouraging the desertion, or stealing or harbouring Negroes, I can assure that I have given most positive orders to the contrary"—a lie nobody would have believed. Nicolls signed off by assuring that "I trust Governor Early will put a stop to those Robbers who call themselves Patriots for they will cause much mischief if they are not suppressed."[97]

His point would have been clear to all parties: American and Spanish slaves were being targeted in a tit-for-tat border war that the Americans had the power to stop. Hawkins's frustration deepened when it became clear that Nicolls's influence was beginning to "derange the peaceful desires of my red charge [the American-allied Creeks]. . . . Some of our Chiefs begin to be lukewarm to us. . . . our young lads are secretly going to the British establishments to be and are accommodated in all their wants. Our Chiefs will follow soon."[98] In this case Nicolls was taking advantage of the Indians' financial problems while trying, once again, to exacerbate a generational rift. Nicolls's advocacy on behalf of his Indian allies so frustrated American and Spanish officials that in one of his very first letters as the governor of Georgia, David Mitchell insisted: "We wish nothing more than to be at peace with the Indians within or without our territory, and those who have taken refuge in Florida. . . . But we can never rest contented and see a British officer (especially of Colonel Nicolls's Stamp) acting as their superintendent."[99] From his base at Prospect Bluff, Nicolls's unofficial war continued seriously undermining the stability of the Southeast long after the final shot of the War of 1812 had been fired.

An Unsanctioned Treaty and the Arming and Supplying of the Indians

Prior to leaving Prospect Bluff, Nicolls took an even more drastic step with far reaching consequences that provoked anger on both sides of the Atlantic. On behalf of Great Britain, he signed an "offensive and defensive . . . [treaty of] alliance . . . as well as one of commerce and navigation" with the Red Sticks and Seminoles.[100] Even though official British policy was merely to encourage an economic alliance with the Red Sticks and Seminoles and he had absolutely no authority to create such a treaty on behalf of his government, Nicolls firmly believed that it would be ratified. The Indians believed so thoroughly in this treaty and Nicolls's other promises that years later they petitioned British officials in the Bahamas for aid against the United States because "we consider ourselves allies of Great Britain entitled to the full benefit of that . . . when the British evacuated the Floridas . . . we were expressly informed so by . . . Nicolls."[101] Nicolls backed up his promises by leaving the Indians and blacks in charge of the fort at Prospect Bluff upon his departure in May. The Indians soon returned to their villages, but for a time a black and Indian alliance commanded an imposing and well-positioned fort. To bolster this claim to the fort, Nicolls left his allies an immense amount of military hardware and tools along with items vital on a daily basis, such as pots, pans, utensils, and storage vessels. All these materials became the property of Nicolls's black allies in May 1815, making Prospect Bluff home to one of the hemisphere's wealthiest maroon communities.

The Journey to England

In May of 1815, at the request of his Indian allies, Nicolls took Hillis Hadjo, whom he presented as the "King of the Four Nations," and his son to England to meet the prince regent and to ratify the treaty.[102] The delegation arrived in Britain in February 1816. The prince regent not only unceremoniously rejected the treaty but also refused to meet with Hillis Hadjo or even accept the "Calumet of Peace." Nicolls was ordered to return the Indians to North America immediately. In a desperate effort to gain at least some concessions, he pleaded that "I have seen them brought in wounded, and the Balls and Buckshot cut out of them, I have had 4, 8 and 13 of them killed in different affairs in all of which they fought one against three."[103] Nicolls then requested that a trading post be established at the mouth of the Apalachicola River and that twice a year the governor of the Bahamas send representatives to meet with the Indians.[104] He further requested that Hadjo's son remain in "England to learn to read and write so they won't be cheated again like when they got the Governor of Canada's letter to commence the War with nobody to read it to them."[105] Clearly the Indians understood that acquiring the power of literacy would undercut a great advantage enjoyed by whites and their Creek enemies.[106] British officials denied all these requests, and as a consequence, over three years later Perryman admitted that among the "Moskogi Tribes" there were "no Papers, as no one amongst themselves could *write* they did not like to employ 'White Men' to write for them, as they were fearful of being betrayed by the Americans."[107] Hadjo received a brace of pistols as a "present from His Majesty's Government" before brusquely being ordered to return to Florida.[108] The next spring Hadjo received two hundred pounds sterling worth of "presents exclusively confined to clothing and agricultural implements."[109] Government officials chastised Nicolls for bringing the Indians to Britain; the stunt "had been productive of great Inconvenience and Expence, and entirely unauthorized."[110] However, despite these failures, the Indians would vehemently persist for years to come in the belief that they were formal allies of Great Britain based on the treaty they had signed with Nicolls, whose return to Florida they continued to expect. Likewise, the Red Sticks never ceased in their belief that the Treaty of Fort Jackson was illegal.

American Anger and the British Officially Distance Themselves from the Indians

The British decision to distance themselves from the Indians was made easier when officials in London realized that Nicolls's rogue actions in the Southeast had led the Americans to begin preparing for war. Secretary of War Alexander Dallas had ordered Edmund Gaines to prepare cautiously for military action against "the Indians, or with the remnant of British Troops under Colonel Nichols" if diplomatic efforts should fail, because Nicolls was "violating the neutral territory of Spain for the obvious purpose of exciting the Indians to war upon the citizens of the United States." While Dallas maintained that "the incompetence of the Spanish authorities to prevent or punish the evil, would certainly justify any use of our arms for self-defense," he exercised restraint. Gaines's orders stated that any actions "should be limited to the single object of defeating and dispersing the Indians and negroes who are in arms against us."[111] In the letter to Gaines, Dallas wrote that the president's object was "to preserve peace by conciliatory [means], then by forcible means; but at all events the people and the country must be protected from savage violence . . . we hope [that the "extravagant" conduct of Nicolls] . . . is unauthorized by his Government."[112] The *Niles Weekly Register* made the case to the nation that "being guilty of a flagrant violation of the late treaty of peace, colonel Nicolls and his *banditti* should instantly [be] driven off at the point of the bayonet. . . . The British officers at Appalachicola . . . make no secret of the determination of their government to occupy Florida in the course of the ensuing summer." According to the paper, Florida should be occupied "peaceably if they can—*forcibly*, if they must. . . . If Spain be disposed to part with Florida, the United States ought to possess it, cost what it may. . . . At all events . . . it should not be suffered to pass into the hands of the British."[113]

Nicolls's actions led to the most serious diplomatic row between the United States and Great Britain since the official end of the war. Secretary of State Monroe sent a fiercely worded letter to the British ambassador, Anthony St.

John Baker, complaining about Nicolls's "extraordinary and unjustifiable interference" with the southern Indians from neutral Spanish territory, where he was "endeavouring to impress that opinion on them [that the Treaty of Ghent was null and void], and to excite them to hostility in support of it: that he has supplied them with arms and munitions of war, and had actually formed a Treaty of Alliance offensive and defensive with certain Indians whom he calls the Creek Nation." Monroe then summarized "that in short he had made Appalachicola a military station, at which he had collected a large body of Indians, and fugitive slaves from the U.S., evidently for hostile purposes against the U.S. The conduct of this officer is of too marked a character, to require any comment. His proceedings are utterly, and evidently incompatible with the late treaty with Great Britain."[114] Monroe finished the letter by firmly explaining that Article 9 did not apply to the "Creeks," because the Treaty of Fort Jackson had been signed prior to the Treaty of Ghent, and that Nicolls's actions, which the President "cannot doubt . . . [are] unauthorized by your government," were totally "improper and unjustifiable" and brazenly defied the Treaty of Ghent.[115] On the other side of the Atlantic the American ambassador to Great Britain, John Quincy Adams, informed Westminster that the "unfriendly and unwarranted tampering of Col. Nicholls and others to instigate Indian hostilities against the United States . . . is an eminent degree injurious to the United States and having been in direct contravention to the orders of the British Government," this, along with British interference with American fisherman in the Northeast and the British occupation of a fort at Michilimackinac, was the single biggest threat to the continuance of peace between the two nations.[116]

In the end Nicolls failed to find official support for his Native allies. However, through the end of the First Seminole War in 1818, he and various proxies maintained close contact with the Indians, who never failed to believe that they were full allies of Great Britain until at least the formal American annexation of the Floridas in 1821. In the process of defending their interests, Nicolls spread fear, anger, and violence across the Southeast and caused a serious diplomatic rift between the United States and Great Britain while strengthening the resolve of the Red Sticks and Seminoles. After having spent months radicalizing the former slaves and Indians and antagonizing white Americans and their Creek allies by exploiting their darkest fears of racial disorder, Nicolls left his Indian and black allies in charge of a heavily armed fort. When he departed, Nicolls could take solace in the fact that he had left his allies so well fortified that "the whole Peace Establishment of America could not take their lands."[117]

5 ⟿ Edward Nicolls and His Black Allies

DURING THE WINTER AND SPRING of 1815 Edward Nicolls's anti-slavery plans entered a new and more radical phase at the same time that he was advocating on behalf of the Red Sticks and Seminoles. Remarkably, Nicolls's actions with his black recruits were bolder than his actions with his Indian allies and would have repercussions for years to come. Each step in Nicolls's anti-slavery plan was to be executed carefully and in close cooperation with his black allies. In a clear testament to their agency, the former slaves, who were astute observers, correctly came to believe that Nicolls offered the surest route to the fullest version of freedom and thus willingly participated in his anti-slavery plans.

Prior to departing Nicolls had already displayed his determination to keep his black recruits from being returned to their masters but was unable to comply with Alexander Cochrane's orders to evacuate the former slaves due to the amount of space available on British ships. Instead, he established at Prospect Bluff a heavily armed and well-supplied free black community. Long before this step Nicolls had sought to instill his radical anti-slavery ideology in the minds of his former slave recruits, beginning with his arrival in August 1814. However, during the months between the evacuation of Pensacola and the British departure in May 1815, Nicolls took further measures to radicalize the former slaves. They proved a receptive audience. The final step in Nicolls's anti-slavery plan (prior to turning the fort over to the former slaves) came when he formally granted his black recruits the status of British subjects with full and equal rights to those enjoyed by white Britons. The former slaves became profoundly committed to this idea, in part because they viewed their status through the lens of Nicolls's anti-slavery ideology and his understanding of the British Empire. Faith in their status as full British subjects and their corresponding rights guided the maroons at Prospect Bluff and provided the community with its core principles and identity. Thus, when Nicolls departed Florida in May, he left behind one of the most unusual maroon communities in the history of the hemisphere at the crossroads of the revolutionary Caribbean and the American slave frontier.

Beginning with this chapter, the settlement at Prospect Bluff is compared extensively with maroon communities from across the Western Hemisphere. This comparative approach is designed to accomplish a number of goals. First, it demonstrates that the community at Prospect Bluff was indeed an unusual variation of marronage regardless of its origins, relationship with the British, or duration. Second, and more important, the comparative data, when combined with evidence from Prospect Bluff, illustrate the extent to which former slaves desired their freedom and how shrewdly and intelligently they would act to achieve the fullest version of freedom allowed by their particular circumstances. As is demonstrated, the Prospect Bluff maroons were able to achieve a more cutting-edge, sophisticated, and complete version of freedom than had most other maroon communities, not because of some innate ability or skill but rather due to the unique conditions that had been presented to them. Analyzing how other maroon communities were able to maximize their freedom when presented with less advantageous conditions emphasizes both former slaves' desire to achieve the fullest version of freedom possible and the process by which this was achieved or attempted. The process of comparing Prospect Bluff with other maroon settlements provides a rare glimpse into how a community of successful North American slave rebels might chose to live, when entirely on their own terms. The comparative method demonstrates how full and remarkable a version of freedom had been achieved at Prospect Bluff.

The Unfolding of Nicolls's Radical Anti-Slavery Plan

The first step in Nicolls's plan centered on assuring that his black recruits were not returned to their masters. This was easy when the former slaves fled from the United States or its allies, since his orders were to recruit exactly such people. However, it became much more complicated when the former slaves belonged to non-enemy residents of the Spanish Floridas or Native Americans. When this was the case, Nicolls frequently lied about the origins of his recruits. For example, he argued that many of the slaves from Pensacola had "report[ed] themselves as having come from the united states, all speaking good English—it was a long time before [I] knew of their having come from Pensacola." And yet in the same letter he admitted that "he Enlisted or rather protected the Black Men who fled from Pensacola" with the provision that they not be fully enlisted until returning to Prospect Bluff.[1] In other words, Nicolls knew full well the origins of all of his black recruits.

When not lying outright, Nicolls could be highly technical in defending the origins of his recruits. In October 1814 he met Governor Mateo González Manrique's accusations that he recruited two slaves belonging to a Spanish subject by arguing "that they were . . . [in fact] Property of an American Magistrate taken out of the Territory of the U.S., and *that my orders being to take all such men into our service, they must remain so.*"[2] On other occasions Nicolls argued that he was fully justified in taking the slaves belonging to residents of the Spanish Floridas who were enemies of Britain when he snarled that if John Innerarity "wants security for his property, from a British officer, let him keep it out of an enemy's territory, he is there sitting in defiance . . . I wish that six times as much damage had been done to him, and his double faced concern *as to the Negroes.*"[3] John's brother James also had his slaves taken from well within Spanish territory by the British during their retreat from Fort Bowyer, but Nicolls swiftly dismissed claims to recover them because "they were the slaves of James Innerarity the commandant of Mobille."[4]

Nicolls justified his recruitment of Creek slaves by arguing that they were allies of the United States. Benjamin Hawkins found this argument "an erroneous one; as there is not one Creek who has negroes so situated."[5] Hawkins's argument fell on deaf ears. For his part, Woodbine used Nicolls's methods to great success; he skillfully "evade[d] all evidence except what answered his wicked purposes" when asked to explain the origins of his black recruits.[6] For example, at the end of 1814, after dozens of former slaves from Indian Territory, the United States, and Spanish Florida, left their masters in plain sight to join Woodbine, he assured the governor of East Florida that "I have never used any endeavors to induce the colored people (*los morenos*) of the province to desert; on the contrary my instructions . . . have been to give every aid (as far as requisite) to the cause of our good and faithful ally, the Spanish nation." Woodbine then told the governor that "I am only authorized, in case any deserters should come in from the United States of America, to protect and recruit them for the service of His Britannic Majesty."[7]

In the end the most insurmountable stumbling block in recovering the former slaves was revealed by Nicolls's sincere boast at a trial in England after the war that "neither myself nor the Government of that day ever gave, or thought of giving, up a slave."[8] Nicolls went on to testify that "it may be natural for a Slave owner to think that a British Officer ought to persuade a man who had born arms under the British colors to return to Slavery: . . . [I] would consider that British officer as infamous who did so."[9] Indeed, the British were "determined to keep the negros."[10] And the whole "villainous affair was so ably managed" as to make their return impossible.[11] Nicolls's bold actions left nothing to the imagination. He freed, armed, and trained hundreds of former slaves and, try as he might to justify and rationalize not returning them to their masters, they remained at Prospect Bluff as part of his anti-slavery experiment.

In a comparative perspective, the wartime origin of the maroon community at Prospect Bluff was hardly unique.[12] The disruption caused by warfare provided slaves with increased opportunities for resistance or flight that frequently resulted in the formation or dramatic growth of maroon communities. For example, in Brazil beginning in the early seventeenth century small bands of fugitive slaves had begun to settle in Pernambuco and Alagoas around the area that would become Palmares. However, the *quilombo*'s population really began to explode in the 1630s as a result of the conditions created by the Dutch invasion of northeastern Brazil.[13] The origins of Jamaica's tradition of *grand marronage* lay in England's 1655 invasion of the then Spanish island. During the invasion many free and enslaved blacks aided the Spanish defensive effort, while many more slaves fled to the mountainous interior. When defeat was imminent, the Spanish encouraged hundreds of slaves and free blacks to join those already in the mountains in the hope that the former slaves would slow and hinder England's settlement of the island.[14] With the outbreak of the slave rebellion in Saint Domingue, thousands of slaves fled their plantations and joined swelling maroon groups.[15] Just like at Prospect Bluff, in each of these cases slaves took advantage of warfare to flee and establish maroon communities.

What was unusual about the origins of the maroon community at Prospect Bluff was both the direct role that Nicolls played in its formation and the nature of the community's relationship with the British officer and the British state. Plenty of maroon communities negotiated formal treaties with white colonial officials, and an equal amount of maroons carried on illicit trade with whites. Many of these treaties required that the maroons agree to regular visits by white colonial officials or that they serve in white-led militias. A few intrepid missionaries or priests paid visits to maroon communities. However, most maroon communities were settlements of slave rebels and did everything in their power to remove themselves from white society and, with few exceptions, owed their freedom to their own daring or that of maroon raiders who liberated them. Furthermore, those who entered into treaties did so long after communities were founded and usually regarded colonial officials and missionaries as obtrusive representatives of the society they rejected. They interacted with whites out of necessity, not choice. At the same time, whites regarded the pacification of maroons as their primary responsibility. Few, if any, whites in Atlantic history sought to help create a maroon community.

Nicolls took another path entirely. He directly or indirectly liberated hundreds of the former slaves at Prospect Bluff, and he went to great lengths to make sure that they remained free before placing them in charge of a heavily armed and well-supplied fort. Moreover, Nicolls instilled his radical anti-slavery beliefs in the former slaves before granting them the status of British subjects. No maroons in Atlantic history developed even a vaguely similar relationship with whites. From its inception to its destruction, the maroon community at Prospect Bluff was a carefully orchestrated anti-slavery experiment driven by the combination of Nicolls's beliefs and actions and the former slaves' desire for freedom. This intense relationship with Nicolls and his ideas as well as their reliance on the British for much of their material wealth was not a betrayal of the impulse to live in an independent free black community. Nor did the maroons' relationship with Nicolls undermine the former slaves' agency or make the community at Prospect Bluff any less of an example of slave rebelliousness or marronage. Rather the maroons' relationship with Nicolls was testament to their shrewd realism in determining how best to achieve their freedom. The Prospect Bluff settlement, especially after the British departed, was an independent community of former slaves who had escaped their bondage and were living outside the plantation complex in the midst of Spanish territory which, by any definition, made the former slaves maroons.

As a result of their relationship with the British the Prospect Bluff maroons also possessed formal military skills rarely found among other maroons. Royal Marines officers trained the former slave soldiers into a highly efficient fighting force whose order and prowess Nicolls frequently praised. Long after the British departure the community maintained its formal military organization and trained on a daily basis. Most maroons relied solely on guerilla tactics. If any of their members had formal military training, it would in all probability have been acquired in Africa and therefore would not have been shared by all or even the majority of a community.[16] Across the hemisphere these guerilla tactics, which the community at Prospect Bluff used skillfully and brutally when necessary, were highly effective. But the maroons at Prospect Bluff had an additional tool for defending the community: a formal, uniformed, and trained army. This skilled military organization contributed to the community's confidence and belief that it was a sovereign enclave of British subjects capable of meeting American, Spanish, or Indian forces as equals on the battlefield. It was also a calculated and symbolic statement of the community's status.

Urcullo's Mission to Prospect Bluff and Cochrane's Changing Opinion

In early December 1814 Cochrane penned a long letter to Governor Manrique of West Florida addressing the Spaniard's complaints about slaves taken from Pensacola by Nicolls. Cochrane admitted that a number of slaves had likely "deserted from Pensacola under a supposition that the encouragement held out for the emigration of American negroes has been intended to extend to them." However, he stressed that he felt sure any such slaves had tricked Nicolls by "calling themselves Americans" and that Nicolls had "not knowingly received any [Spanish] deserters." Cochrane counseled Governor Manrique that he could best ensure their return by adopting a "marked lenity that may enable the Lt. Colonel to persuade others who hereafter offer themselves to return voluntarily to their masters." Cochrane then assured the governor that it was not Britain's intention to enlist slaves belonging to "subjects of Spain and France" but only those belonging to "American citizens: unless indeed it shall be found that individuals . . . in hostility to us shall forfeit their neutral character, in which case they will be identified as Enemies." Cochrane closed by reiterating his faith in Nicolls and suggested that any missing slaves from Pensacola had probably "gone over to the opposite side of Pensacola [Bay] with the Body of Indians that quitted the Town upon the entry of the American Troops" and remained there.[17]

However, it soon became clear that Cochrane knew he was lying to the Spanish governor in an attempt to cover for Nicolls, whom he berated in a series of testy letters. In one letter Cochrane expressed his displeasure with Nicolls because "although your instructions permitted your enlisting Negroes from the U.S. they could never convey you an authority to interfere with the slaves of persons in alliance with Great Britain and as their further detention may be productive of the most consequences I have to direct your causing them to immediately be secured and sent back."[18] Within days both Cochrane and Manrique commissioned the first of a number of expeditions to Prospect Bluff to recover Spanish slaves. The Spanish expedition was led by Lt. José Urcullo of Pensacola. Cochrane immediately notified Nicolls that Urcullo was traveling to Prospect Bluff "for the express purpose of bringing back the slaves that have joined [you] from Pensacola. . . . [and] it is my positive directions that you cause them to be delivered in safe custody and that you do not again upon any account enlist slaves that are the property of Spanish subjects."[19] However, four months later, a deeply frustrated Capt. Robert Spencer reported that the "great and primary cause of grievance and discontent at our Government, the loss of [Spanish and Indian] Negroes

... [continues since] all persuasive means of getting them back have been tried and have failed."[20] The difficulties encountered by Urcullo and the leaders of subsequent expeditions to retrieve slaves illustrate what went wrong despite official British and Spanish orders. These difficulties illustrate how well-organized Nicolls's anti-slavery plan was and how actively and skillfully his black recruits were participating in this plan.

Urcullo's expedition arrived at Prospect Bluff on December 27. The Spanish official brought a long list of slaves allegedly stolen from Pensacola as well as stern orders from the governor of West Florida to recover the "slaves whence the English carried off." Urcullo's charge echoed Cochrane's orders to Nicolls.[21] When Urcullo arrived he learned that Nicolls was away meeting with Cochrane and that Capt. Robert Henry was temporarily in charge of the British forces at Prospect Bluff. Henry, a close confidant of Nicolls, had traveled with him from England and been intimately involved in the recruitment and training of the former slaves. While retreating from the assault on Fort Bowyer, Henry reported that he took "ten Black Men who *volunteered* their services" [emphasis added] from Bon Secour.[22] That Henry was at pains to stress the voluntary nature of their recruitment showed that he understood the sensitivity of the mission and the importance of using carefully chosen language in official correspondences. Furthermore Henry was the same officer who had been charged with encouraging the Red Sticks and Seminoles to give up their slaves voluntarily. And he issued the (hollow) declaration that encouraged American-allied Creeks to come to Prospect Bluff to retrieve their slaves (discussed later). In other words, Henry was an active participant in Nicolls's anti-slavery experiment.

Totally unaware of this, Urcullo presented Henry with his orders as well as the list of slaves from Pensacola.[23] Henry acknowledged that the letter "contain[ed] a most positive order, that all those slaves who had joined us from Pensacola should be immediately secured and delivered in safe custody." But he added that because of "particular circumstances ... I found it impracticable at this moment to put his orders in execution."[24] According to Henry, an initial problem arose because without Nicolls, he was "unable to discover these Negroes who may be the property of the inhabitants of Pensacola, as I find there are not any to answer to the Names contained in the list given me by Lieut. Urcullo."[25] The former slaves clearly understood the purpose of Urcullo's mission and remained silent to protect their freedom.

On December 31 Henry deemed that he had enough authority to send an "offer to all persons in the Creek nation owning any negros who had run or were taken into East Florida to receive the same" in Nicolls's absence.[26] The offer to the Indians was a hollow subterfuge. But at the same time it made clear that his claim of being unable to act without Nicolls present was a lie. The British officer and the former slaves worked together to frustrate Urcullo's designs.

Henry then raised a second alleged concern: "It would be dangerous and imprudent to force these People into a Vessel without a strong Guard, as the moment that Lieut Urcullo's mission became public they expressed their sentiments of disapprobation in strong terms, such as to convince me of the danger which might attend those who would attempt to take them in a vessel unarmed."[27] Urcullo concurred that the "Negros under [Henry's] command amount to 500 men all armed and he feared a meeting of them, in which case the white troops were not sufficient to repress them being only 60 men."[28] Henry later testified that he "could not if he would comply with the order [to return the Pensacola slaves forcefully because] there was 5 Black men to 1 white Man under his command at the time. They declared they would die before they would go back—it is well known how bravely they kept their word."[29] This force, when combined with the Fifth West India Regiment and the *pardo* and *moreno* soldiers, comprised one of the largest black military units in the Western Hemisphere. The force was clearly flaunting its strength.[30] The display of strength underscored a clear message: the former slave soldiers intended to protect their freedom to the death. Their freedom derived from a solemn agreement between themselves and Nicolls/Great Britain that was bound by an intense sense of honor. The black soldiers used the language of equals, of men who had earned their status by keeping up their part of a legally binding agreement, not that of desperate outliers trying anything to avoid being returned to their masters. Urcullo eventually conceded to Henry's argument and accepted the British officer's assurance that "those [slaves] who may belong to Pensacola shall be sent there without further delay or Expence to their owners" as soon as Nicolls returned.[31]

Days turned to weeks with no sign of Nicolls, leaving Urcullo finally to lose all patience and demand permission from the British to leave on January 12, 1815. While preparing to depart, Urcullo received a shock when out of the blue and after weeks of contrary actions and denials, Henry ordered the "slaves of Pensacola to be formed in line. . . . [where he informed them] that such as chose to voluntarily return to their masters might be shipped [with Urcullo]."[32] One hundred and thirty three Pensacola slaves of various ages, origins, and occupations and both sexes were formed into lines in front of Urcullo. Twenty-five of the former slaves "voluntarily choose to embark" with the Spanish.[33] This stunning reversal after weeks of stalling only confirmed that Henry and the slaves had been playing a game with the Spanish. Reasoning that twenty-five slaves were better than none, Urcullo, satisfied, agreed that it was too late in the day to begin the journey to Pensacola and retired for the night. The next morning the Spanish officer was bitterly disappointed when "at the time ... [for] them to go on board the greater part told me that ... they were free" and refused to return with him.[34] Henry knew that the former slaves fully understood the advantages of life at Prospect Bluff and were deeply committed to their freedom. Publicly parading the former slaves in front of Urcullo and offering them the option to return to Pensacola was powerful, yet utterly hollow, theater designed to impress upon the Spaniards that the British were cooperating with their efforts to retrieve their slaves in what amounted to "various [and] frivolous pretexts to comply with the order."[35]

The former Pensacola slaves happily participated in the exercise with a wink and nod because they knew that the Spanish were powerless to return them by force and that the British were committed to helping them maintain their freedom. Nonetheless, the former slaves must have been surprised when twenty-five of their number volunteered to return. Not surprisingly all of the slaves who volunteered to return to Pensacola were single mothers and their children.[36] Families eventually flourished at Prospect Bluff, but at this early stage, as the war continued to rage across the region, mothers calculated that the safest option for their children might be to return voluntarily to bondage in Pensacola. Apparently that night a number of the former slaves and their British allies persuaded the would-be returnees that their poor decision would cost them and their children their freedom. Urcullo's translator, William McPherson, a slave driver for Forbes and Company, captured the type of persuasion that occurred that night when he angrily recounted that "all of the artifices and underhand dealing[s] [were] made use of to prevent the return of the Negroes."[37] Nothing more clearly illustrates two of the biggest stumbling blocks in retrieving the former slaves (Spanish powerlessness and the former slaves' confidence in their freedom and their desire to protect this status) than the fact that McPherson's own slave, Jerry, refused, to his owner's face, to return to Pensacola.[38] McPherson, as a slave driver, was by definition capable of extreme brutality, yet Jerry felt secure enough simply to turn his back on his powerless master and choose freedom with the British. The rest of the former slaves shared Jerry's confidence and desires, as was evidenced by Edmund Doyle's lament that "we all Know, by common report, and every Negroe I saw says they were seduced from their Masters ... [yet it will be so difficult to prove this that the only possible way to retrieve a former slave will be] by the Black people who voluntarily return."[39] The former slaves felt so secure in their current position that they taunted their former masters with their freedom.

Urcullo concluded that the former slaves stayed at Prospect Bluff because they "have been seduced by the English. . . . and carried to the river Appalachicola in the promises of having their liberty granted them—of this I have not any doubt the negroes themselves having [been] informed."[40] Urcullo recognized that the former slaves at Prospect Bluff had joined the British to achieve their freedom and that they fully understood the contours of this freedom. This particular understanding was the product both of months of experience and of having been carefully informed of the rights British subjects possessed. Carefully informing the former slaves about the nature of their freedom constituted a key ingredient in Nicolls's plan that began with his proclamation in August and continued until he departed. This information, based on his anti-slavery ideas, gave the former slaves a distinct ideological commitment to their freedom as well as an extra doggedness in protecting it. Indeed without knowledge of Nicolls's anti-slavery ideology and understanding of the British Empire, the former slaves would never have been able to conceptualize themselves as being capable of such equality and status so soon after escaping slavery. In Urcullo's mind these intellectual obstacles made retrieving the former slaves as difficult as the lack of cooperation he received from British officers and the threat of violence if he attempted to remove people forcibly. The next day a dejected Urcullo, along with ten slaves, began his journey back to Pensacola to inform the governor that his mission had failed.

On January 25, upon receiving Urcullo's report, Governor Manrique penned a letter to Cochrane.[41] The governor began by reminding Cochrane of the British officer's letter from December 5 of the previous year in which he promised to order Nicolls to return all the slaves taken from Pensacola. He continued to explain his surprise not only that the slaves refused to return with Urcullo but also that the black soldiers from the garrison at Barrancas remained at Prospect Bluff. Manrique informed Cochrane that he was assigning one of West Florida's most prominent residents and officials, Surveyor General Vicente Sebastián Pintado, to lead a second mission to retrieve the slaves and black soldiers at Prospect Bluff. However, Manrique's confidence had been dealt a serious blow by Urcullo's failure, and so he forced himself to "supplicate your Excellency to interpose your superior authority" that the slaves and soldiers be returned as soon as possible.

Cochrane's response promptly finished off what was left of Manrique's fragile confidence.[42] The letter was written in "evasive terms . . . very different from his former language" and ignored Cochrane's "former promises in the most jesuitical language."[43] Cochrane, anchored off Mobile, expressed "extreme regret" that Urcullo's mission had failed before admitting that events in the last two months made it impossible for him to send a "vessel from the fleet to bring back these troops but in a few days I will dedicate a ship of War solely to that purpose." Cochrane continued to inform Manrique that he had "no sort of controul over any of those actually taken by the British marines; for such as thought proper to join the Indians your Excellency must make application to their Chiefs." This was because "situated as I am with so few white troops at Apalachicola it would be attended with much hazard the making use of forcible measures, which accordingly I must entirely decline." Cochrane, the commander of the North American Station, claimed to have no control over the former slave soldiers at Prospect Bluff and insisted that he could not forcefully impose his will. Whether or not this was true, he certainly had no intention of trying to return Nicolls's recruits.

The best explanation for Cochrane's new stance was that he had been "influenced by Lieut Coll Nicoll's misrepresentations" and that "some Sinister information that has been given [by Nicolls] to His Excellency or that by some influence [Nicolls] has altered his first and just decision."[44] Indeed Cochrane had spent a good deal of time with Nicolls, listening closely to his radical ideas. Edward Codrington, the captain of Cochrane's ship the *Tonnant*, felt that Nicolls held strong sway over Cochrane.[45] Codrington, an intimate witness to their discussions, felt that Cochrane "places a most injurious confidence" in Nicolls, whom he characterized as a "mischievous lying booster." When Codrington attempted to address his concerns about Nicolls to Cochrane, the commander immediately "let out in great anger, that he 'did not care what he said.'" Nicolls certainly did not turn Cochrane into an anti-slavery advocate, but he used all his powers of persuasion to assure Cochrane's acquiescence in not forcing any of his black recruits to return to their masters, a vital step in protecting the community of former slaves.

Pintado's Mission and the Flaunting of Nicolls's Radicalism

Between Urcullo's and Pintado's missions, William Hardridge, a wealthy Creek slave owner, traveled to Prospect Bluff with two other "half breeds."[46] They were responding to Henry's public declaration from December 31 that the Creeks were welcome to claim any of their slaves who had joined the British. This was a substantial number, estimated at two hundred former slaves "belonging to Indians friendly to . . . [the US and to American] citizens."[47] When Hardridge arrived on February 26, 1815, he presented Captain Ross with a number of letters and informed him of his intentions.[48] Ross told him that Nicolls was away, that he could not act until Nicolls returned, and that "he knew nothing about the negros run away from the Indians and white people."[49] In fact the British never had any intention of honoring Henry's offer, and they never expected that a delegation of pro-American Creeks would travel to Prospect Bluff. After days of waiting Hardridge eventually realized this and left after seeing "nearly all the runaway negros . . . the British were determined to keep . . . [having] given them their freedom."[50] Now it was the turn of the former Creek slaves to demonstrate their commitment to their freedom in the face of their powerless masters. The actions of the Creek slaves, which replicated those of Spanish and Anglo slaves presented with the possibility of returning to their masters, testified to the universal nature of Nicolls's message and the freedom enjoyed at Prospect Bluff. It also deepened the Creeks' hostility toward the community and reconfirmed their belief that they were the victims of British-inspired slave resistance.

On February 28 Pintado presented himself to Cochrane, who was anchored in Havana Bay. Pintado informed Cochrane of his orders to recover the slaves and property taken from the residents of Pensacola.[51] Under pressure from Pintado as well as the captain general of Cuba, Cochrane issued "preemptory orders for the restoration of the Negroes."[52] At Prospect Bluff the Spanish expected to be aided by Capt. Robert Spencer of the Royal Navy, who had recently been placed in charge of investigating the garrison's debts and providing it with needed supplies.[53] On the surface, it appeared that Cochrane had reversed his position yet again and that Pintado's mission stood a good chance of success. However, the orders contained a fatal caveat that doomed the mission to failure: neither the Spanish nor the British could use force to compel the former slaves to return; both had to rely solely on persuasion.[54]

After a lengthy and difficult voyage, Pintado, Dr. Eugenio Sierra, and once again William McPherson arrived at Prospect Bluff on April 7.[55] They quickly presented themselves to Spencer, who had arrived earlier with a "commission to enquire into and regulate the claims of the Spanish inhabitants at Pensacola and Apalachicola. . . . I [Admiral Malcolm] have no doubt that the strictest enquiry will be made into the conduct of Col. Nicolls and Cpt. Woodbine, and that the losses sustained by the Spanish inhabitants at Pensacola will be remunerated by the British Government if the slaves don't return voluntarily."[56] Pintado was met by Nicolls, who had just returned from the field with a force of "Indians, and many negroes, immigrated or brought from American possessions and from Indian lands, and among them some of the slaves of the settlers of [Pensacola]."[57]

While Nicolls would temporarily feign that "there was no opposition on his part," Spencer, having spent weeks meticulously reviewing Spanish claims, took his orders very seriously and "pledged himself . . . to do everything that lay in his power to bring back the negroes; that he would make use of every art of *persuasion* to induce them to return."[58] Spencer did not share Nicolls's anti-slavery values and was sincerely attempting to do his job. To this end the former slaves alleged to have come from Pensacola were sent to nearby St. Vincent Island so as not to be influenced by other blacks or the British while being interrogated by Spencer and Pintado. Spencer took each former slave aside and "expostulated with, encouraged, threatened, advised and did every thing short of what ought to have been done, as a dernier resort,—the application of force."[59] Furthermore he sought to "mak[e] them see the horrible and miserable state which they would be in after the evacuation of the place by the English troops . . . and explaining to them the danger in which they were in of being caught by the Indians and delivered to their masters in hope of receiving a reward from them."[60] On the surface at least, Nicolls assisted Spencer in talking to each former slave and informed them that "they were now going to be left by the British; that as soon as they were gone they would quarrel among themselves, become odious to the Indians, a prey to the Americans which they seemed as much to fear, and that their situation would soon be most desperate and forlorn." Nicolls concluded by warning "that they would forfeit the forgiveness of their masters who would inflict on them the punishment which they would bring upon themselves by this obstinate refusal."[61]

Despite this strong message and the apparent cooperation of Nicolls, Pintado succeeded in convincing only 28 out of 128 former slaves to return, and 16 "disappear[ed]" before the Spanish left.[62] One of the best explanations for this refusal was that the former slaves were exercising their free will. According to the testimony of a former slave eyewitness, when offered a choice between "remain[ing] with the Indians as freemen, or to return to their masters . . . few had agreed to return."[63] Once again the vast majority of the former slaves chose freedom at Prospect Bluff over the option to return to their masters. This was underscored on a few occasions when the former slaves received the impression that Pintado and Spencer might attempt to return them to their masters by force. When this happened they simply vanished into the forest or threatened violence.[64]

An equally important reason that the former slaves remained at Prospect Bluff was because of Nicolls's reiteration to them of his anti-slavery rhetoric. Nicolls's critics justly alleged he intentionally undermined Spencer's efforts to convince the slaves to return to their masters: "They had all previously received their lessons. . . . By his audaciousness, hypocrisy, address and all his battery of imposing arts, wiles and intrigues he even blinded Spencer. . . . This apostle of liberty and worthy member of the philanthropic society held them spell bound."[65] The former slaves knew that his cooperation with Spencer was a well-calculated sham. The audience for Nicolls's anti-slavery "lessons" of "liberty" and tales of the "philanthropic society" so absorbed his message that they became "spell bound." His success illustrates the extent to which Nicolls sought to instill his anti-slavery message into the former slaves as well as his skills as an orator, advocate, and educator. At the same time that he was pretending to cooperate with Spencer and Pintado, Nicolls took "infinite pains . . . to persuade [former slaves], that having enlisted into the British Service the British Government would set them free . . . [and] Coll Nicolls by himself and his agents made use of all the influence that he had acquired over them to persuade them not to return."[66] Pintado, Sierra, and McPherson all witnessed Nicolls promising the former slaves "perpetual freedom; lands in Canada or Trinidad; the assurance that the British Gov. would pay their masters for their value; his return; an abundance of provisions to support them and a well constructed fort to defend them in the interim." He even insisted that if the British government refused to reimburse their masters, "he was sure the Philanthropic Society of which he had the honor of being a member would."[67] In both cases Nicolls reminded the former slaves that they had earned their freedom through their service in the British military and that they were well on their way to becoming established as free land-owning farmers within the British Empire. In the meantime they needed to wait at Prospect Bluff, where they were heavily armed and in command of an excellent fort. Once again he evoked the concept of free will, their rights, and the organized anti-slavery movement as he carefully instructed them in these anti-slavery lessons.

Time and again Nicolls flaunted his anti-slavery credentials and rhetoric so publicly and made it so clear that he was working to further these interests that one of the slave owners lamented: "I fear that the far famed . . . humanity of the African Association, Abolition Society and others of a like stamp will prove an inseparable bar to your Success [in recovering runaway slaves]—In the eyes of these Right Reverend, Right Honorable, Right Worshipful and Right Honest Gentry, Negro stealing is no crime, but rather the chief of virtues—of course they will protect their slaves."[68] Nicolls's anti-slavery message and the promise of freedom and land within the British Empire found a receptive audience. However, his effectiveness was enhanced by the fact that he instilled his beliefs in "many officers [who] . . . espoused the cause of the slaves" and in his "agents and black spies [who] corrupted the Negroes of their Indian friends and Spanish allies."[69] The ranks of Nicolls's followers grew daily due to his passions, activity, and message. Among their number were "black spies" who had come to understand deeply Nicolls's anti-slavery ideology and were now instilling the ideas in other blacks. The former masters of Nicolls's ex-slave allies faced an uncommon and clearly insurmountable intellectual challenge in getting the former slaves to return because of their commitment to their freedom, shaped by the adoption of his anti-slavery ideas. The former slaves understood that they had earned their freedom and fully intended to defend it. Their masters, meanwhile, had complained that they had been infected with dangerous and absurd ideas by an out of control radical.

Historians have long sought to understand the extent to which slaves knew about various Atlantic anti-slavery and abolitionist movements. In this process historians have asked a series of questions: If slaves were aware of such movements, to what extent did they fully understand the movements' ideas and messages? If they understood such ideas, were they capable of acting on their understanding of these ideas? And what might such action entail? In the case of the former slaves at Prospect Bluff, the answer to the first two questions is a resounding yes. The answer to the third question is detailed in chapters 6–9. The former slaves at Prospect Bluff became aware of the anti-slavery movement and its ideas directly from the mouth of a radical practitioner. As a result, the former slaves at Prospect Bluff developed a nuanced ideological understanding of freedom, grounded in a very particular and radical strand of anti-slavery thought, which guided the maroon community after the British departure.

The Prospect Bluff maroon community's detailed and intimate knowledge of Nicolls's anti-slavery thought compared starkly with that of other communities and people of color more broadly from across the Americas. Accordingly, this knowledge was the primary reason that the Prospect Bluff maroons believed themselves to be capable of enjoying full political and legal rights within the British Empire and was, in turn, a key ingredient in the version of freedom that they created. Indeed knowledge of Nicolls's radical anti-slavery ideology allowed the Prospect Bluff maroons to construct their freedom in more dimensions than was possible for other maroons who were unaware of such ideas.

The comparative material serves to underscore this important point. Many maroon communities, such as Palmares or the original Nanny Town in Jamaica, simply vanished long before the era of abolitionism and anti-slavery. In other cases not enough documentary evidence remains to speculate about any given community's understanding of such ideas. More realistically, maroon communities were survivalist and generally conservative restorationist communities who lived on the periphery of colonial societies that militantly sought to censor such ideas.[70] Thus many maroons simply did not have access to or interest in detailed information about abolitionist or anti-slavery ideas. When maroons encountered such ideas, as was the case with many slaves across the hemisphere, it was usually through rumor or word of mouth and so was understood in fairly general or hazy terms.[71] At the same time, many maroon communities entered into treaties or other formal alliances with colonial governments and, whether or not they understood these ideas, protected their freedom by minimizing contact with outsiders and frequently returned fugitives, owned slaves, and even fought in defense of colonial regimes. Such maroon communities were essentially pro-slavery entities. None of this was the case at Prospect Bluff: there, for what had to be the only time in history, a maroon community had been founded by and enjoyed a close relationship with a radical anti-slavery advocate who clearly explained his ideology to the community. At face value, this is a remarkable revelation that makes the Prospect Bluff maroon community a valuable tool for understanding the minds of slaves. The usefulness of Prospect Bluff as a tool for understanding slave consciousness is compounded by the fact that the former slaves continued to be strongly influenced by Nicolls's ideas on their own terms for years after they last saw him. Thus the example of Prospect Bluff allows us to see not only whether slaves understood these ideas but exactly how they might apply such ideas directly to their lives when left totally to their own devices.

A number of examples serve to illustrate the distinctiveness of the maroon community at Prospect Bluff in regard to anti-slavery thought and, by extension, the extent to which knowledge of Nicolls's ideas allowed the former slaves to cultivate their version of freedom. In 1795, set against the backdrop of the slave rebellion in Saint Domingue and global war with France, a series of armed rebellions that involved maroons rocked the British Caribbean. British officials and planters largely blamed abolitionists, French saboteurs, the example of Saint Domingue, and wartime chaos. These uprisings included Fedon's deeply ideological rebellion in Grenada, which was fought in close coordination with black and white French Republicans from Guadeloupe and began with the insurgents wearing tricolor cockades and waving a battle flag that read "Liberté, Egalité, ou la Mort."[72] The purpose of the rebellion was to deliver the island to French forces, at which point slavery would be formally abolished and Grenada's black inhabitants would become citizens of the French Republic. As Fedon's Rebellion dragged on, many of these ideologically anti-slavery rebels organized themselves in imitation of maroons.[73] However, they were few in number, desperate, and fleeting. More important, none of these groups of Fedon's followers sought to create a long-term community. These settlements were brief military expediencies. Just to the north of Grenada, the Black Caribs of St. Vincent waged a war against the British that clearly took its cue from global turmoil and was aided by French forces, but it did not appear to be driven by any clear understanding of anti-slavery ideology.[74] Jamaica's Second Maroon War also began in 1795. Rumors circulated that black French agents promising "Liberty and Equality" and material support encouraged the Jamaican maroons to rebel.[75] Bryan Edwards blamed "abolitionists for distributing pamphlets and medals to incite rebellion."[76] A much more likely and less ideological explanation is that the maroons (who owned slaves and policed the island's slaves with brutal efficiency) rose in rebellion because of deep-seated grievances over land and resources. Their timing is largely explained by Britain's disastrous invasion of Saint Domingue and a belief that their treaty with the British had been violated.

Saint Domingue had a long tradition of marronage in its mountains that, though smaller scale than in Jamaica or Cuba, was still significant. Prior to the Haitian Revolution, the island's highly organized maroons closely studied the plantation society and broader world, which they discussed along an extensive communication network. This was most evident in the 1750s under the leadership of Makandal, who preached the destruction of the island's white population, and in 1785 when a small group of maroons negotiated a treaty with the governments of both France and Spain.[77] Likewise during the Haitian Revolution preexisting maroons—who though certainly not directly responsible for the outbreak of the revolution became involved in the fighting—accepted new members and watched as many more maroon communities were formed.[78] All of this occurred, apparently, without any significant knowledge of anti-slavery ideas or conscious ideological commitments, but rather as the result of overwhelmingly powerful politico-military forces intruding into the maroons' world.[79]

In 1796 Cuban authorities passed the first anti-*palenque* legislation in response to the Morales Conspiracy of the previous year (which did not involve the maroon communities known as *palenques*) because of anxiety over the growing population of Haitian refugees and their slaves exacerbating slave flight. In 1820 Madrid passed further anti-*palenque* legislation based on the fear that the communities might receive assistance from Haiti. But this simply was not the case; the island's *palenques* remained largely isolated and disinterested in the ideas embodied by Haiti and anti-slavery concepts. Nearly fifty years later, in the midst of the National Liberation War, the leaders of the resistance had to approach the aloof *palenques* and assure them that anti-slavery lay at the heart of the rebel cause and explain that they would be free in an independent Cuba.[80]

Across the hemisphere maroon communities had a complicated relationship with anti-slavery thought and action. Many treaty maroon communities supported slave regimes by capturing fugitives and fighting against rebels. Furthermore, individuals within some of these same communities owned slaves, who were usually of African descent. All these practices can broadly be described as pro-slavery and are evidence of people who had rejected enslavement for themselves but had no major qualms with the institution more broadly. At the same time maroons exerted a tremendous impact on anti-slavery thought and actions across the globe. Their existence and struggles became a favorite topic of anti-slavery advocates, who used maroon communities to highlight black desire for freedom and the cruelty of slavery.[81] Likewise maroons served as a powerful affront to slavery that threatened the stability of the plantation complex. More profoundly, they reminded the enslaved of their condition and fueled their desire for freedom, which sometimes ended in flight or violent resistance. All this was true even of treaty communities regardless of their behavior toward the enslaved and fugitives. Nonetheless, the vast majority of maroons did not have extensive knowledge of formal anti-slavery ideas—certainly not when compared with the people at Prospect Bluff. In each of these examples the various maroons understood the geopolitical implications of the wars of empire and the Haitian Revolution and recognized that slavery was being challenged intellectually and physically by both blacks and whites. However, taking advantage of wartime disruption to rise behind longstanding grievances or to understand the forces of anti-slavery vaguely based on rumor or speculation was not what occurred at Prospect Bluff. There, the former slaves explicitly understood an anti-slavery ideology, connected it to their lives, and acted on it. In particular, knowledge of Nicolls's anti-slavery beliefs would soon make it possible for the former slaves to believe that they were capable of claiming full rights and equality within the British Empire. Accordingly, the Prospect Bluff maroons would build a community on the foundation of radical anti-slavery thought and their corresponding understanding of their British status. This in no way diminishes the quest for freedom by thousands of other maroons. Rather—by emphasizing the notable degrees of freedom that were achieved by maroon communities from across the hemisphere without knowledge of radical anti-slavery thought or the British Empire—it illustrates the full extent to which the Prospect Bluff maroons were able to achieve their freedom in political and intellectual terms. In turn, this extra intellectual dimension enjoyed by the Prospect Bluff maroons suggests what an unusual opportunity this case provides to understand slave consciousness.

All this was overwhelming for Pintado, whose shock and disbelief at what he witnessed deepened when he inspected one of the former slaves' license of decommission, which read:

> By Lt. Colonel Edward Nicolls commanding his Britannic Majesty's First Battalion of Colonial Marines—Certifies José Hambroso Private in the Battalion aforesaid and in the Third of Lt. Tool's Company has served honestly and faithfully for 4 months and 26 days discharged because of "Preliminaries of Peace with the U.S.," having first received a full and true account of all his clothing pay arrears of pay, and all demands whatsoever from the time of his Enlisting, to the present day of his discharge, as further appears by this receipt on the other side hereof.
>
> Given under my hand and seal at Prospect Bluff River of Apalachicola this thirty first day of March 1815.
>
> Edward Nicolls
>
> I José Hambroso do acknowledge that I have received all my clothing pay arrears of Pay all demand of Pay whatsoever, from the time of my enlisting in the Battalion and Company mentioned on the other side to this present day of my discharge as witness my hand 31 March 1815.[82]

Pintado noted that the license of decommission contained "no mention of their color or state of slavery . . . that each one of the licenses was a letter of freedom for only free men were admitted to the armed service and that they would pass as such in whatever place that they presented themselves with this document."[83] Perhaps no single comment captures the essence of Nicolls's experiment better than Pintado's observation. The soldiers who volunteered for this army had the terms of their service legally defined, and accordingly they received honorable discharges when they completed these terms, as a white British man would have. As Hambroso's license of decommission and Pintado's observation testify, Nicolls conceptualized his army as one of equals because his anti-slavery beliefs hinged on the limitless potential for black equality within the framework of the British Empire. Accordingly Nicolls constructed an army of free soldiers in which their race or former status meant nothing. This was so clear that, as one observer noted, with these papers the former slaves could "pass for free throughout the United States, or wherever they went."[84] Building on this foundation, Nicolls soon extended these ideas to their logical conclusion, at least in his mind: full British rights and liberties for the former slaves.

While Pintado tried to comprehend the full implications of this, Nicolls shocked the Spanish officer once more when he promised that the slave owners would be reimbursed by the British government, "or lacking that, the philanthropic society, would satisfy the worthy masters for the price of the slaves who did not wish to return to the service of their masters, so that afterwards they might be considered entirely free."[85] Nicolls was not sure whether the British government or his Philanthropic Society (the very name of which would have made Pintado uneasy as he was attempting to retrieve hundreds of heavily armed former slaves) would end up paying for the former slaves. However, Nicolls made it explicitly clear that he intended to see the former slaves recognized as being "entirely free." Given Nicolls's conceptualization of the British Empire as a universalist entity and his anti-slavery beliefs, "entirely free" had a broad and deep meaning. It was interesting that he shared this with Pintado. However, much more important was the fact that he had instilled this message in the former slaves themselves, who never ceased to doubt that they were indeed "entirely free" by virtue of their dealings with Nicolls.

A bewildered Pintado remained at Prospect Bluff for a few more days, conducting interviews and taking care of other official business, before returning to Pensacola with twelve former slaves who volunteered to join him. Before leaving, Pintado, who also brought a number of petitions from residents of St. Augustine hoping to see their slaves returned, was disappointed one more time when Woodbine showed him "78 negroes [who] had come with him from East Florida, but that these were negroes that were found among the Indians for several years and none came directly from St. Augustine."[86] Pintado seriously doubted this claim and began his dejected march back to Pensacola.

Evacuation

During Pintado's stay the British garrison began its official evacuation from Prospect Bluff. The Royal Marines were directed to return to England if possible and to either Bermuda or Halifax if not. The members of the Fifth West India Regiment were to return to Jamaica. Cochrane, presumably tired of the topic by this point, ordered that the "Negroes who have taken refuge with the fleet, you will endeavour to persuade to go back to their former Masters, should they determine however not to return, you will suffer those who choose to adopt a Military life, to enlist into any of the West India Regiments now here, where they and their Families will be received . . . those who are not so inclined will be sent to the Island of Trinidad."[87] Spencer was to lead a flotilla of seven ships to evacuate "as many of the Black Corps as they can conveniently stowe. . . . The *Mars* Transport is to be appropriated to receive

Major Nicolls and as many of his officers and men as she can *conveniently* stowe."[88] Nicolls's superiors had every intention of honoring the promises to the former slaves and planned to organize them as units of the West India Regiments or to establish them as free landowners in Trinidad.

However, only weeks later, a defensive Nicolls informed Benjamin Hawkins that "according to orders I have sent . . . [the former slaves] to the British Colonies where they are received as free settlers and Land given them. The newspaper [which suggested that the former slaves were still at Prospect Bluff] you were so obliging to send me is, I rather think, incorrect, but at all events an American newspaper cannot be authority for a British Officer."[89] Nicolls was defensive because he was *lying*. In reality only a handful of the former slaves were *ever* evacuated from Prospect Bluff by British forces. Furthermore, all the former slaves who were evacuated had originated in Bon Secours, and when asked in Bermuda "whether they were willing to return to their previous owners . . . unanimously declared that they would not return but by force."[90] Months later a confused Maj. Alexander Kinsman, the Royal Marines officer responsible for organizing former American slave soldiers and their families at a rendezvous point in Bermuda, noted that Cochrane "has mistaken our numbers from an expectation that between two and three hundred men [this estimate did not include their families and men not organized as soldiers] would have joined us from Major Nicolls, but he enlisted his men to serve during the American War *only* with a *promise of land and protection* at its termination, and they are all discharged."[91]

Eventually Nicolls admitted that "on my leaving the post at the Bluff, in June 1815, I had not transport sufficient to take away 350 men, women, and children the former of whom had enlisted in the British forces on the faith of the enclosed Proclamation [Cochrane's] and my instructions [Nicolls's proclamation], but they agreed to keep together, under protection of Indian Chiefs, until we had an opportunity of sending for them."[92] Here Nicolls told the *truth*. He indeed lacked sufficient space to evacuate hundreds of former slaves, but he clearly intended to keep his promise and transport them elsewhere in the British Empire to begin their lives as free soldiers or farmers.[93] According to a "good Indian authority," Nicolls vowed "to return in six months" to recover the former slaves.[94] This was as part of the same promise he had made to the Indians. Regardless of his sincere intentions, the Royal Navy would never be sent to retrieve the former slaves. Not for a second did the British government entertain the idea of sending a mission to recover hundreds of former slaves from North America long after peace had been negotiated with the United States.

True British Subjects

If Nicolls intended to help the former slaves become "entirely free," then he did anything but betray them as his plan reached its final stage and he prepared to leave Prospect Bluff. He "left with each soldier or head of family a written discharge from the service, and a certificate that the bearer and family, by virtue of the commander-in-chief's proclamation and their acknowledged faithful services to Great Britain, were entitled to all the rights and privileges of true British subjects … [with] a perfect right to their liberty as British subjects."[95] Nicolls provided the former slaves with documentation that declared them not only free but also "true British subjects," who possessed corresponding "rights," "libert[ies]," and "privileges." Prior to this point, physical freedom, military service, and Nicolls's anti-slavery message had left the former slaves with a strong sense of the contours of their newly achieved and multi-dimensional status. These documents, which they would have interpreted through the lens of Nicolls's rhetoric, unmistakably and unambiguously made the *"British Blacks"* British subjects with full rights and served as the cornerstone of their freedom until the last of them died nearly fifty years later.[96]

Mary Ashley and her husband, who had served as one of Nicolls's soldiers, understood the documents as being "free papers" that fully entitled them to all of the rights and privileges that came with belonging to the British state and empire.[97] Susan Christopher also received her "free papers," but in her own right and not on behalf of a husband, demonstrating that Nicolls was willing to extend the offer to single women and not just men and families.[98] Nearly thirty years later both women illustrated the extent to which they believed that their "free papers" entitled them to the rights of British subjects after they were illegally reenslaved in Cuba. The two women petitioned the British Embassy on the island, demanding that the diplomatic officials take immediate action to correct this injustice and secure their freedom.[99] The British consul general in Cuba took the women's claims, as well as his government's obligation to them, so seriously that he immediately ordered an international investigation to make sure that "their freedom and restoration may be demanded and secured." The matter caused a major diplomatic incident between Spain and Britain.[100] The fact that this case occurred more than twenty-five years after the women last saw Nicolls should not call into question its value as historical evidence. Indeed, the fact that the women were still so insistent on their rights so many years later and were able to articulate them so clearly to the officials at the British Embassy, without any physical proof, is strong evidence of just how deeply they had absorbed Nicolls's ideas and message. Having been reenslaved in Cuba, the women would have had minimal exposure to anti-slavery thought or ideas about British rights. While their thinking might have evolved on these topics because of the effects of time, it seems clear that much of their thinking, even twenty-five years later, was largely influenced by Nicolls. Likewise it is unmistakably clear that—twenty-five years later—both women felt they were full British subjects because of what had occurred at Prospect Bluff. For his part, Nicolls had not forgotten Mary Ashley or Susan Christopher. After having become aware of their plight, Nicolls urged the Foreign Office to "use all possible means to obtain the liberty of the persons in question; such praiseworthy exertions will not fail to have a powerful effect among the very intelligent useful coloured population of Cuba, the southern States of North America." Nicolls went on to argue that the admiration of the Cuban and American slaves would be useful "when, if ever the need should come, we can fully depend on their joining us to a man; and better or braver soldiers I would never wish to serve with, which I am able, and ready and willing to do at a moments notice."[101]

Even clearer examples of the documents' legal power and the significance attached to them by the former slaves came from the Bahamas. In 1828 when refugees from the community were first detected on Andros Island, where they had fled after the First Seminole War in the early 1820s, they presented the British with "their discharges from His Majesty's service" as proof of their status as full British subjects. The fact that the former residents of Prospect Bluff had spent nearly a decade on Andros Island in isolation, with little to no exposure to ideas about the British Empire or anti-slavery thought, makes it clear that their thinking was still strongly influenced by Nicolls and that their belief in their British status was a direct product of his actions. Thus the passage of time, rather than calling the evidence into question, is further proof of just how deep an intellectual and ideological impression Nicolls had made on them and how fully the former slaves believed themselves to be full British subjects. The officials agreed with the former slaves' interpretation and proclaimed "that these negroes are as much under the protection of the British Government as any other free person. . . . [No] doubt can be supposed to exist either in the minds of the negroes themselves or . . . any . . . planter . . . as to these people being considered as Free British Subject[s]."[102] The former slaves clearly understood this, or they would not have presented the documents to the British officials. The former residents of Prospect Bluff were so quickly and fully recognized to be British subjects that a number of them drew up and signed a petition against the removal of governor James Carmichael Smith in 1832.[103] Twelve years later, during a hotly contested election, the *Nassau Guardian* reported that about a dozen of one candidate's supporters were "Americans" or their children who "had served as soldiers in the

British Army, under Edward Nicolls in Florida. . . . These persons possessing the other requisite qualifications were considered [to be] British subjects."[104] The documents allowed the holders to participate fully in the political system of the British Empire. These papers and the ideas embedded within them had the most far-reaching and profound consequences of any of the actions that Nicolls took while at Prospect Bluff. The fact that in each of these cases, the former slaves were able to convince British officials, who stood to gain little from helping them, that they were British subjects—years after their time at Prospect Bluff, and in a number of cases with no physical evidence, since their "free papers" were long since lost—demonstrates how deeply they understood these ideas. Finally, the extent to which knowledge of Nicolls's radical anti-slavery ideology shaped the former slaves' understanding of their British status must be borne in mind. Without these recently acquired or clarified ideas about black humanity and equality, rights, the power of military service, and Christian ethics, the former slaves would have struggled to believe that they were capable of achieving the status of full British subjects. Thus Nicolls's radical anti-slavery ideology, conceptualization of the British Empire, and promises were all deeply intertwined. As a result Prospect Bluff was the only maroon community in history that claimed such a clearly defined vision of imperial political rights emphasizing full equality.

Over the centuries many maroons from across the hemisphere entered into formal treaties or alliances with colonial powers. Indeed the Spanish signed treaties with maroons in Santo Domingo and Panama as early as the middle of the sixteenth century and in Colombia by 1619.[105] Such treaties occurred when colonial governments realized that they could not destroy a maroon community and that peace was less dangerous than war. Treaties generally granted maroon communities freedom, defined their territory, and promised to arrange for their economic needs while requiring, in return, an end to hostilities against whites and plantations, a refusal to accept new members, and aid in tracking down fugitives and putting down rebellions.[106] Sometimes these treaties lasted for decades, and sometimes they fell apart in a matter of months. Some garnered respect from both sides, while others meant little to either party involved. But in every case, maroons entered into these treaties as a means to protect their hard-won freedom through formal recognition. Whites grudgingly regarded this as an unfortunate necessity.

Due to geographic, demographic, and politico-military realities, the governments of Jamaica and Suriname had, by some distance, the two greatest traditions of entering into treaties with maroons. In Suriname the Dutch made peace with small maroon groups as early as 1686 and then with larger and more powerful groups in 1760, 1762, and 1767, after failed attempts in the

1730s and 1740s. The treaties were sealed when the maroon leaders agreed to give a son or other close relative as a hostage, and representatives of both sides performed a ritualized blood oath. The treaties guaranteed the maroons' territory and freedom of movement but forbade any travel closer than "two days or 10 hours journey" from the nearest plantation without permission. Under strictly regulated conditions, small parties of maroons could trade with individuals in the plantation complex. Presents from the government supplemented this meager trade. One of the central points of the treaties was the requirement that the maroons stop accepting new members and return captured runaways. Much to the dismay of officials and planters, the maroons of Suriname frequently ignored this responsibility. White civil servants known as "postholders" were charged with checking in on the maroons and making sure that they complied with the treaties. Deep in the jungles of Suriname, in the midst of hundreds of armed maroons, most postholders found their effectiveness limited at best. Ultimately the maroons of Suriname formed a "state within a state," and the best that white officials could hope for was to isolate them from the plantation complex. The maroons of Suriname did not define their freedom in relationship to the Dutch or seek to become Dutch subjects; they had their own political system and identity. Rather, from the maroons' perspective, they voluntarily entered into treaties from a position of strength as a means to withdraw into the hinterland to enjoy their freedom.[107]

After years of protracted and highly destructive warfare, the Leeward and Windward maroons of Jamaica entered into two separate treaties with British officials in 1739. At the time of these treaties, the maroons of Jamaica were under greater military and economic pressure than those in Suriname had been when signing their treaties. Consequently the maroons felt relieved while the British treated them as a largely defeated power. The leaders of the Leeward maroons, Captain Cudjoe and Captain Accompong, and the leader of the Windward maroons, Captain Quao, consulting with the religious leader Nanny, took a solemn and elaborate blood oath with Col. John Guthrie, who represented the British state.[108] Through to the present day the Leeward and Windward maroons regarded these treaties and the oaths that sealed them as "sacred agreements," (ideally) rigidly adhered to by all parties and central to their identity and status.[109] These treaties declared peace between the British and the maroons, defined the territorial boundaries, allowed for self-government under their chiefs, called for official supervision by white superintendents, required future runaways to be returned, and mandated that the maroons contribute to the defense of Jamaica, including quashing slave rebellions.[110] The maroons formed a highly effective police force that regularly returned runaways and intimidated the enslaved population.

Most important for the sake of comparison was the maroons' legal status. The British regarded the treaties as having a "particular place in English law, establishing a relationship between the Crown and a people who had thereby agreed to become a special class of subjects" who were free but not a sovereign nation.[111] The treaties gave the maroons "limited rights as British subjects," which exceeded those of the enslaved but fell well short of those enjoyed by whites.[112] The resulting relationship was one of "patronage" between the whites and the maroons, in which the maroons had a "special status as black British subjects of the king, privileged vassals" who had a "special if ambiguous position in the island society."[113] Both sides described the relationship in parent-child metaphors with the British assuming the role of the father. Through the interference of colonial officials, superintendents, and militia captains, whites shaped the maroons' political, military, economic, and social development.[114] The Jamaican maroons' understanding of the British king was important. Many maroons and indeed slaves developed a strong attachment to far away European monarchs, who they believed were on their side in their struggle against local whites. Accordingly many maroons could be described as "royalists" because of their strong attachment to European kings. This was a conservative and traditionalist means of relating to a European state, an attitude that was largely the product of their African origins in monarchical societies. The opposite was occurring at Prospect Bluff, where the maroons were attached to the more modern ingredients in belonging to the British state, such as individual rights, personal sovereignty, and liberty. Their attachment to their British status did not make them royalists. The Jamaican maroons and those at Prospect Bluff had fundamentally different understandings of the British state. In the Jamaican case, nobody on either side considered the maroons to have anything close to legal and political equality with white Britons. Nor did the maroons, who developed distinct ethnic and cultural identities over the course of the eighteenth century, aspire to the status of full British subjects.

What occurred between Nicolls and the maroons at Prospect Bluff shared some similarities with but had far more differences from the treaties Britain negotiated with the Leeward and Windward maroons. In each case a British military officer entered into an agreement with the maroons that carefully defined their British status. In Jamaica, Guthrie acted on the orders of the island's officials as part of a broader strategy to pacify the maroons. Conversely, Nicolls had no official authority to act as he did and was not seeking to pacify former slaves in the middle of a British possession. Indeed Nicolls was trying to do the opposite: empower the maroons in another empire's territory. In each case the maroons were utterly unrelenting in the significance they attached to the agreements that became defining aspects of their identity and freedom. In Jamaica the maroons viewed the bond as paternal and spiritual, or even sacred, while they were essentially royalists who placed great emphasis on the role of the king, whereas the community at Prospect Bluff regarded their relationship with Great Britain as being secular, legal, and between equals. Accordingly, the Prospect Bluff maroons deemphasized the role of the king and demonstrated a more modern attachment to the revolutionary era British state and arising rights, privileges, and liberties. This difference is explained in part by the fact that the Jamaican maroons were much more conservative and African in their outlook, whereas the vast majority of the former slaves at Prospect Bluff were creole and modern in their worldview. The particularities under which each maroon community entered into its relationship with Great Britain, and the timing, also help to explain these differences. Nicolls's careful instruction about the former slaves' status, filtered through the prism of his anti-slavery ideology and understanding of the British Empire, made it highly improbable that the Prospect Bluff maroons would be conservative royalists. The opposite was true of hundreds of Africans entering into a treaty in 1739 in the mountains of Jamaica. In essence the maroon community at Prospect Bluff developed a more sophisticated and modern understanding of their relationship to Great Britain than did the Jamaican maroons, who held a more traditional, conservative, and spiritual view. However, both were equally fanatical in the importance that they attached to this bond because the maroons knew there were distinct advantages deriving from their relationship with the British.

This issue of status was an important difference between the experience of the Jamaican maroons and those at Prospect Bluff. In both cases the arrangements with the British were cornerstones of the group's freedom and elevated members well beyond the status of the enslaved and, certainly in the case of Prospect Bluff, that of many free blacks. However, the Jamaican maroons were treated as conquered and second-class subjects with limited territorial, legal, military, and political rights and whose internal affairs British officials frequently disrupted. The constant presence of meddling British officials served to remind the maroons that they were second-class subjects of the British Empire. In short, all parties understood that the maroons were not full members of the British Empire. On the other hand, Nicolls declared that the former slaves at Prospect Bluff were "entitled to all the rights and privileges of true British subjects." It was not a coincidence that the only familial metaphor Nicolls used was the word "brothers." Combined with their knowledge of his anti-slavery ideology that stressed black humanity and their potential for equality as well as the universal nature of the British Empire (concepts that would have been largely uncommon among the Jamaican maroons), the former slaves at Prospect Bluff had claimed the status of full British subjects. The power of the "free papers," therefore, was very real and not a mere product of Nicolls's radical imagination. The former slaves felt deeply empowered by their self-identification as a sovereign enclave of British subjects who would soon be left largely to their own devices to cultivate this notion. The Jamaican treaties controlled the maroons within the broader context of the island's slave society, while Nicolls's "free papers" and other actions empowered former slaves in the midst of non-British territory. Finally, because of these differences it is fair to regard the Prospect Bluff community as an anti-slavery institution that ideologically and intellectually challenged slavery, whereas the Jamaican maroon communities were pro-slavery.

Ultimately the comparative material draws out a fundamental and profound truth: the Jamaican and Prospect Bluff maroons sought to achieve the most complete version of freedom available to them based on the opportunities presented to them and on their members' prior experiences. In the case of Jamaica hundreds of mostly African former slaves entered into a political arrangement with the British during the early modern period after a long and grueling series of wars. At Prospect Bluff, during the Age of Revolution, an array of largely creole former slaves entered into a political arrangement with the British Empire as understood by a radical anti-slavery advocate. Thus two very different versions of freedom occurred in Jamaica and at Prospect Bluff. As the examples combine to illustrate, there were few limits to how far slaves would go to achieve the fullest version of freedom available to them.

The Final Days at Prospect Bluff

Nicolls's plans entered their final stage in April and May 1815. He began by presenting to his black and Indian allies a series of orders he felt so confident would be rigidly adhered to that he later boasted he could at any time "raise a black regiment of 1,000 strong" from the former slaves he left behind at Prospect Bluff.[115] The first order was that the freed and decommissioned black soldiers and their families would "keep together, under the protection of the Indian Chiefs, until we had an opportunity of sending for them."[116] He then ordered the Indian chiefs, and by direct extension the former slaves, to

> not . . . commit an act of hostility against either . . . [the Spanish or United States] without written orders from His Majesty's Government accompanied by a token only known to the chiefs and myself, to have little communication with American citizens as possible being the best mode of

preserving peace and to suffer no spirituous liquors to be imported into their country or even listen to any one that urged them to destroy or quarrel one with the other to faithfully protect the black soldiers that were with me and to permit all black men that fell into their hands to join those at the bluff. To pay attention to farming and agriculture and rearing cattle of all descriptions and to suffer no Indian to have a slave.[117]

The inclusion of a temperance clause and the encouragement for Indians to abandon slavery show the full extent to which Nicolls's beliefs shaped these orders. The rest of the message contained here and elsewhere was very clear. The former slaves were now totally free British subjects who enjoyed specific rights. They should remain armed, trained, and organized. They should become independent farmers at Prospect Bluff. They were to avoid contact with whites and defend their land from encroachments. In fact Hawkins learned through an informant that Nicolls had ordered the blacks to "take every American or Spaniard to be found in their territory" and that the black army has "orders . . . from Col. Nicolls to attack the Commissioners if they attempt to press the line [of the Treaty of Fort Jackson]."[118] Nicolls also instructed the maroons to go to great lengths to increase their numbers. The last two orders increased the probability of bloodshed in the Southeast. All totaled, the former slaves were to receive all that had been promised to them not in Trinidad or Nova Scotia (where the majority of American slaves who had joined the British during the War of 1812 were settled) but rather at Prospect Bluff.[119] Shortly after Nicolls's departure, William Hambly, a British employee of Forbes and Company who had been instructed to oversee the community, and nearly all the Native Americans left Prospect Bluff—meaning that the "post at Apalachicola [and all of its resources] is now under command of negros."[120]

Nearly thirty years later Nicolls remained so satisfied with these results that he wrote in the *Times* that "at this hour [it is] a pleasant reflection to me that I was the cause of upwards of 1,500 persons receiving their liberty."[121] A much darker yet equally insightful concern about this situation was reflected in a lament by one of the aggrieved slave owners when he complained that the former slaves lived "as completely out of . . . [our control] as if they had been carried to Trinidad."[122] The slave owner was correct. The former slaves at Prospect Bluff enjoyed more freedom than former slaves who had been spread across the British Empire because they constructed an all-black British polity driven by the lessons they learned from Nicolls. The behavior of the maroons over the course of the next fifteen months and beyond provides an unrivaled insight into the workings of a completely autonomous community of former slaves. Ironically the slaves at Prospect Bluff, because of Nicolls's rhetoric and their "free papers," developed a stronger sense of being British subjects than did the former slaves in Canada or Trinidad—who, unlike their counterparts at Prospect Bluff, were daily reminded of their second-class status. Indeed the Prospect Bluff residents possessed a stronger attachment to the British state and richer knowledge of anti-slavery ideas than any maroon community in Atlantic history, which further deepened their sense of freedom. And yet the former slaves at Prospect Bluff, men and women who embodied the last generation of revolution, war, and slave resistance, were living on the doorstep of the expanding American slave frontier, on the edge of a crumbling empire, and in the aftermath of a highly racialized regional war with roots that lay two hundred years in the past.

6 ⇒ Land, Ecology, and Size

WILLIAM HAMBLY of Forbes and Company swiftly departed Prospect Bluff because he no longer "wished to stay . . . at the head of a band of uppity rogues like the negros."[1] Soon he was joined by the Seminoles and Red Sticks, who returned to their villages, leaving hundreds of "negros [who] are saucy and insolent, and say they are all free" in charge of the fort at Prospect Bluff and its immense store of supplies.[2] During the better part of the next year and a half, with "The English union jack" flying above the fort, the "uppity," "saucy," and "insolent" former slaves, with their "free papers" in hand and Edward Nicolls's radical anti-slavery rhetoric at the fore of their consciousness, welcomed many more escaped slaves from across the Southeast.[3] The former slaves continued with Nicolls's radical anti-slavery experiment that centered on the cultivation of the rights possessed by British subjects. Indeed the maroons' belief in Nicolls's rhetoric and message flourished long after the British left and provided the community with its guiding principles and identity. The former slaves' sense of purpose was so self-conscious that over two years later a discharged British officer met with refugees from the community and reported to Nicolls that "our Bluff People. . . . have stuck to the cause . . . and will always believe in the faith of you [Nicolls]."[4] The "cause" was Nicolls's radical anti-slavery experiment and their belief in British rights.

For all of their conviction and pride, the maroons at Prospect Bluff did not seek to gain their freedom through a violent frontal assault on the institution of slavery, like Gabriel, (perhaps) Denmark Vesey, or Nat Turner.[5] Nor was the community at Prospect Bluff a desperate band of outliers barely surviving on the fringe of a plantation society, as could be found across North America. Rather the former slaves had achieved their freedom and, as their actions demonstrated, intended to distance themselves as far as they could from their prior condition of enslavement. Accordingly, the maroons cultivated a version of freedom that combined their own understanding of the concept with

Nicolls's ideology and their newly acquired identity as British subjects. The former slaves' understanding of their British status centered on the belief by the "British Blacks" at the "Anglo-Negro Fort" that they were entitled to a series of rights, including personal freedom, liberty, political participation and military service for men, protection by laws, the ownership of private property, and control of their labor and the fruits of it. While many of the inhabitants of Prospect Bluff would have had a prior understanding of topics such as political and legal status, inclusion, liberty, and rights, during their time with Nicolls these ideas would have come into much clearer focus. This applied especially regarding what exactly constituted the "rights" and "liberties" of a "true" British subject. Likewise, exposure to Nicolls's anti-slavery ideology and understanding of the British Empire allowed the former slaves to believe that they were fully capable of enjoying such status and rights. Without a detailed understanding of Nicolls's ideas, it is difficult to believe that the former slaves would have been so insistent or knowledgeable about their British status or rights.

Ultimately the maroon community at Prospect Bluff reached a stage that other slave rebel leaders and their followers never achieved in North America: physical, spatial, and intellectual freedom to run an all-black polity, entirely on their own terms. As I demonstrate, at Prospect Bluff an independent community of former slaves occupied a discrete physical space, carefully defined membership, were bound by laws, owned property and participated in an economy, were governed by a political system, and were defended by a militia. Thus the settlement, by accepted definitions, qualified as a both a maroon community and a polity.

The community at Prospect Bluff, even if only temporarily, was an example of successful communal slave resistance. As such the community at Prospect Bluff offers a rare yet revealing example of an autonomous free black community in the era of slavery. Accordingly, a close examination of the maroon community's actions provides insight into how slaves understood and practiced freedom as well as their more general consciousness when entirely free and on their own terms. The picture that emerges may well have been similar to if not the same as how hundreds of thousands of other slaves and slave rebels envisioned freedom and life when totally left to their own devices.

The comparative data serve to emphasize that former slaves sought to create the fullest version of freedom available given their particular conditions. What emerges from the comparative data is the telling revelation that the maroon community at Prospect Bluff was, on one hand, utterly typical in that its members sought to achieve and protect as full a version of freedom as circumstances allowed, but on the other hand it was atypical in the conditions presented to them. As a result of these conditions the maroons at Prospect Bluff were able to create an unusually modern and sophisticated version of freedom.

Naming the Community

The community of former slaves at Prospect Bluff was referred to by many names during and long after its existence, names that revealed as much about the observer as about the maroons.[6] The blacks living at Prospect Bluff used a number of related names to describe their community. For example, in testimony provided in 1843 Mary Ashley referred to "Prospect Bluffs ... [as a] post."[7] In the middle of the nineteenth century, a survivor living in the Bahamas told the *Bahama Herald* that he had been "stationed during the American War, at a fort called Prospect Bluff."[8] In the face of the final American assault on Prospect Bluff, one of the community's leaders, Garçon, warned the attackers that he was in "command of the fort."[9] The attackers had already been warned by the defenders that they were besieging "their fort."[10] In each case the inhabitants described a structure in purely technical and/or geographic terms. The defenders who described it as "their fort" chose the possessive pronoun carefully to illustrate ownership and sovereignty. Thus the closest that the residents had to a proper name for the community was "The Post" or "The Fort," while they correctly identified themselves as living at Prospect Bluff. They simply, but powerfully, thought of the structure and area as their home and felt no need to rely on overly elaborate or loaded names. Tellingly, the only time any of the former slaves provided their home with a proper name was when a group of survivors fled to the Bahamas and founded Nicholls Town, named in honor of the man who both liberated and inspired them.[11] The name Nicholls Town is tremendous evidence of the intellectual and ideological impression that Nicolls had made on the former slaves as well as of their long-term commitment to these ideas that transcended location.

Blacks who were not permanent residents at Prospect Bluff most frequently used geography to describe the community. This was the case when a number of "negro men" from Mobile gave testimony that they had stayed at "Appalachicola" before returning to their masters, and a "very intelligent negro man" also used the name of the river to describe the community.[12] Native Americans used varying terminology to describe the community, depending on the nature of their relationship with the maroons and the British. For example, Seminoles and Red Sticks who were British allies and enjoyed generally positive relations with the community used labels such as the "Fort built by the British."[13] This demonstrated its military nature, origins, recognition of the community's relationship with Great Britain, and the Indians' belief and hope that the British would soon return to make good on their promises and treaties. Importantly, "British" was the only ethnic or racial label that the Red Sticks or Seminoles appear to have used to describe the community. Conversely, the American-allied Creeks, who numbered among the maroon community's most bitter enemies, used racially charged language similar to that used by white Americans, such as the "Fort of the Blacks," to describe the community.[14]

The British nearly always called the actual structure the "post" and then emphasized its location as "Prospect Bluffs" or the "Bluff."[15] Nicolls himself generally referred to the "post at the Bluff" or the "*British* post on the Apalachicola."[16] The community was a British creation that did not cause them any anxiety or fear, making them capable of denoting it with a racially and functionally neutral label. This was similar to the language used by its inhabitants.

Spaniards tended to take a practical and descriptive tack when describing the community. For example, José de Soto described the "black fugitives and refugees living in the Fort that had been built by the British on the Apalachicola River" in an 1815 letter to the governor of Cuba in language that was virtually identical to that used by his successor a year later ("the Fort of Apalachicola, occupied by the negroes").[17] The Spanish described the community's racial composition, location, and the type of dwelling as well as its British origins in what was straightforward bureaucratic language and not a proper name. Nor were Spanish descriptions designed to elicit strong emotions. Spanish word choice derived from the sense of powerlessness and frustration that the Spaniards felt about events at Prospect Bluff.

Not surprisingly, white Americans provided the community with its most loaded name and the one that has persisted across time: the "Negro Fort." For example, while justifying American actions in the First Seminole War, John Quincy Adams noted that when the British evacuated Prospect Bluff, Nicolls "left the fort, amply supplied with military stores and ammunition, to the negro department of his allies. It afterwards became known by the name of Negro Fort."[18] Virtually every American military, diplomatic, and political correspondence used this label, as did the press. Indeed when the government finally allowed for the publication of the official report of the community's destruction, dozens of newspapers across the country ran the same article with the bold-faced and italicized heading "*Negro Fort on the Apalachicola.*"[19] This two-word proper name spoke volumes about the fears of white Americans as well as their most basic conceptualization of the community. The sense of threat derived from the combination of race ("Negro") and organized military violence ("Fort"). Together, these forces threatened to spread violence and bloodshed in organized warfare or, more darkly, to serve as a spur to large-scale slave resistance. By providing the community with a proper name and the article "the," which was much more common than without an article, white Americans tied the community to a distinct location and explicitly defined the threat that it posed with a succinct yet highly emotional label. Pro-American Creeks also frequently used the name Negro Fort, because as among white Americans, the community stirred racialized anxieties within them.[20] The next most common name used by white Americans, although much less so than Negro Fort, was the "British establishment."[21] In this case American observers were emphasizing the connection between the British state and the maroons at Prospect Bluff. Both names reveal much about white American and Creek fears and concerns.

Many of the community's various names bore similarities with the names of maroon settlements elsewhere. However, the specific name Negro Fort stood out. Across the hemisphere proper names were generally reserved and remembered for the largest, strongest, and/or longest-lived maroon communities in a tradition that includes the Negro Fort. Such settlements, to insiders and outsiders, had become true communities that required formal names, many of which are still used today. In itself this affirmed the significance of the community at Prospect Bluff. However, briefly comparing its name with those of other maroon communities provides a number of important insights.

After Palmares, Brazil's most famous *mocambo* was Bahia's Buraco de Tatú.[22] The *mocambo*'s name translates as "Armadillo's Hole" in an apparent reference to its tight and organized streets that were very well defended by hidden paths, palisades, and pits. The *mocambo* was small (it never had more than one hundred members) but lasted for over twenty years on the outskirts of Salvador.[23] The community's fame or notoriety was due to the fact that the Buraco de Tatú supported itself by violently stealing from both whites and blacks. Like the Negro Fort, Buraco de Tatú had a colorful name, in this case emphasizing both defense and predation.

Interesting insights about naming Palmares come from an examination of the etymology of the word *quilombo*.[24] While *quilombo* eventually came to be a synonym for *mocambo*, *quilombo* was initially used solely to describe Palmares. Stuart Schwartz has argued convincingly that the origin of the word *quilombo* was the contemporary Angolan word and concept of *ki-lombo*.[25] In Angola, whence the majority of the founders of Palmares came, a ki-lombo was an all-male initiation society for men who had no familial or social ties.

Life in a ki-lombo prepared its members to become fearsome warriors.[26] At the same time, many members of Palmares referred to the community as "Little Angola," which further illustrates the influence of Angola.[27] If a ki-lombo was indeed the model that the Palmarinos were pursuing and one of two Angolan-derived names they were using, then the inhabitants were making a strong statement about their backgrounds and the community's organization. Furthermore, if the inhabitants of Palmares were essentially calling their community "the war camp," this was similar to the decision of the maroon community at Prospect Bluff to call itself the Fort or the Post. In each case the name emphasized the military nature of the community and contrasted starkly with what outsiders called either community.

Jamaica's maroon communities were divided broadly into the Leewards and Windwards. These divisions simply reflected the area of the island that groups inhabited. In both regions the maroon villages were usually named after their leaders or prominent individuals: Cudjoe's Town, Accompong Town, Crawford Town, Nanny Town, and Moore Town are examples of this pattern. The invariable use of "Town" in the names is deeply informative and illustrates how two sides (whites and maroons) can see different meaning in the same word.[28] To the maroons "Town" was included to establish a sense of permanence and community that was rooted to a particular location.[29] To whites "Town" was a term that suggested control or subordination within the island's hierarchy. Something similar had occurred at Prospect Bluff. The maroon community's inhabitants had chosen names that emphasized permanence, possession, and sovereignty (for example, "their fort"), which the Jamaican maroons had accomplished with the word *town*. At the same time, whites and Creeks gave the community a name that was racially charged but also desperately attempted to tie it to a particular place as a way of making it seem less fearsome. This mirrored the intentions of white Jamaicans' use of the word *town*.

The Prospect Bluff maroons' choice to call their community the Fort or the Post while many observers used geography and the military nature of the community in its name replicated practices from across the hemisphere. At the same time, the use of the term the Negro Fort or labels that incorporated "British" were unusual and informative. No other community was given such an explicitly racialized name. Nor was any community so frequently, if ever, referred to by names that included that of a European nation. In both cases the names demonstrated white and Indian anxiety as well as the prominence of the community's relationship with Great Britain in the midst of a region where whites, blacks, and Indians were being introduced to *grand marronage* at a particularly unsettling time.

Prospect Bluff

The natural environment in which Prospect Bluff was situated compared favorably to that in which most maroon communities from across the hemisphere were located. This is borne out by a careful comparison between the Prospect Bluff region and the physical environments in which other prominent maroon communities were situated. The Apalachicola River slowly meanders and curves along its 110-mile southwesterly course from its origins at the confluence of the Flint and Chattahoochee Rivers near the modern border of Georgia and Florida, draining nearly 20,000 square miles on its way to the Gulf of Mexico. Most of the Apalachicola's banks are steep ravines or bluffs that have been carved from the sandy and clay soil over the last 30 million years. The river, which is marked by dangerous sandbars and occasional rapids, feeds numerous swamps and tributaries along its course. During the spring and summer the river rises to its highest point. In the early nineteenth century the Apalachicola River formed the boundary between Spanish East and West Florida and represented one of the most important waterways in the Southeast.

Because of its climate (the area averages 55 inches of rain a year, with temperatures that range between 80 and 95 degrees between March and October, and with humidity frequently in excess of 90 percent) and fertile soil, the Apalachicola River region is home to an immense and highly diverse array of plant and animal species. Some of these plants and animals are distinctive to regions of Florida including the thirty miles closest to the Gulf of Mexico, where Prospect Bluff is located. The region's terrain is dotted by lakes, limestone sinks, and caverns and supports pine flatwoods, savannas, hammocks, wetlands, swamps, and forests that extend to the river's banks. In pine flatwoods and hammocks one finds various deciduous trees, while the region's swamps are vast and inhospitable aquatic worlds in which the water level rises and falls with the season. In the forests grow cypresses, oaks, and pines that can reach a hundred feet or more in height and create a thick canopy with shade intensified by a great deal of hanging moss. Smaller trees include palmettos, red cedars, scrub oaks, dogwoods, and black gums. The forest floors are covered by underbrush of shrubs, thickets, bushes, and vines and blanketed in places with wild flowers, ferns, and smaller plants. Many of the area's trees and bushes yield edible berries or nuts, while a number of other plants can be eaten. The sandy but well-irrigated soil is suitable for agriculture. The banks of the river close to Prospect Bluff are particularly fertile.

The Apalachicola River, its tributaries, forests, local swamps, and surrounding lakes teem with life. Trout, sturgeon, bass, crappie, sunfish, and catfish are just a few of the hundreds of species of fish that can be caught locally. The area's abundant shellfish, which can easily be trapped or harvested, include crawfish, mussels, crabs, and oysters. Alligators, water moccasins, and snapping turtles constitute the most dangerous of the edible animals in or near the water. Other reptiles and amphibians that live across the region include numerous species of snakes, frogs, toads, salamanders, and turtles. Large mammals such as deer, black bears, wild hogs, and bobcats roam the area, as do smaller ones such as foxes, raccoons, opossums, squirrels, rabbits, skunks, beavers, coyotes, and armadillos. The region's birds range from great predators, such as bald eagles and hawks, to rare woodpeckers, ducks, quail, and wild turkeys. Because of the area's climate and environment, it is home to voracious mosquitoes and other annoying insects. For the skilled hunter, trapper, or fisherman, the land around Prospect Bluff offers a rich supply of good high-protein food. When this is combined with gathering and farming, the surrounding country can provide its inhabitants with a wealth of food making up a diverse and quality diet.

The physical location of Prospect Bluff was ideal for establishing a maroon community. Prospect Bluff is located on the eastern bank of the Apalachicola River, approximately 15 miles from the Gulf of Mexico, 50 miles south of the then border of the United States, and 150 miles east of Pensacola, in what is presently the Apalachicola National Forest along a gentle curve in the river.[30] This was squarely within a contested and dynamic Atlantic borderland populated by a scattering of Indians, who occasionally visited for trade; merchants from Forbes and Company, which owned a store in the area; a weak Spanish garrison that was miles away in Apalachee; and the encroaching American slave frontier. Woodbine had chosen this location upon his arrival in May 1814 because of the fact that Indians periodically gathered there for trade or diplomatic meetings and it was easily defensible. It was a happy coincidence that the region had fertile soil and abounded in edible plants and animals enhanced its appeal. Located at the top of a steep hill, Prospect Bluff afforded excellent views across the half-mile-wide river and over many more miles of terrain. According to a report filed by an American army officer, Prospect Bluff "was situated on a beautiful and commanding bluff," which was why the Spanish called the spot Loma de Buenavista or "good view."[31]

Prospect Bluff is flat with sandy soil and covered with grass and small plants. The spot is situated on the edge of major forests of tall long-leaf pines and sandy flatwoods that extend for miles inland. A large swamp behind Prospect Bluff protected its flank and greatly aided in its defense. With deep frustration, Edmund Gaines noted that Prospect Bluff "is rendered inaccessible by land, excepting a narrow pass up near the margin of the river, by reason of an impenetrable swamp in the rear and extending to the river above."[32] Contemporary reports record a "large creek just below" and a "small creek just above," which were further defensive attributes.[33] Finally, a rare cypress dome can be found at Prospect Bluff.[34]

The greatest drawback to the location was that the river was shallow and small vessels had to be used to land supplies. However, this was a minor disadvantage, and command of Prospect Bluff virtually guaranteed control of one of the Southeast's most important waterways and greatly facilitated transportation across the region from a nearly impenetrable position. Writing with hindsight, the American army engineer James Gadsden assessed the strategic advantages offered by the location. Gadsden's report noted:

> Thus strongly posted, with complete command of the ocean, and consequently of a water communication to such points from whence reinforcements and supplies could be drawn . . . it is impossible to divine what inroads might have been made into our country and what strong points might have been brought in opposition. The Creeks though subdued still had restless warriors among them, who if unsuccessful in again rousing their nation to hostilities, would have been valuable as guides to the enemy. . . . These portions maintained [a British-Indian alliance] it would have been an easy task to unite the four Southern Tribes against us. The Western states would have been cut off from all communication with the Gulf of Mexico, and Louisiana would necessarily have fallen an easy conquest . . . oceans of the best blood of our country would have flown before a powerful enemy thus favorably poised could have been expelled.[35]

The surrounding landscape and physical environment of Prospect Bluff had both similarities to and differences from the type of terrain in which successful maroon communities were frequently located. These commonalities were due to the fact that maroon communities could exist only in areas that allowed for escape from slavery, defense, and survival or sustainability. Escaping from slavery was merely the first step in creating a viable maroon community. Would-be maroons then needed to find a location that allowed them both to feed and defend themselves while creating shelter from the available resources. Without locations meeting these essential criteria, marronage was impossible, certainly for an extended period, no matter how large scale or oppressive a slave society became. The specific location (both physically and in terms of distance from the plantation complex) greatly shaped the demographics, political organization, military system, economy, and culture of maroon communities. These locations included mountains, swamps, and dense jungles or forests, which could be situated anywhere from the very edge of the plantation complex to many miles away.

All this is borne out by comparisons with other examples of marronage from elsewhere in the Western Hemisphere. In Jamaica the largest maroon settlements thrived in the island's vast mountainous interior. This consisted of the Blue Mountains in the east (which would become the home of the Windward maroons) and the Cockpit country that extended from the center of the island to the west (which became home to the Leeward maroons).[36] These tropical mountains, which were heavily forested and marked by numerous caves, cliffs, and steep valleys, rose thousands of feet and provided maroons with expansive places to hide and establish communities while their adversaries were faced with the daunting task of pursing them through difficult terrain that the maroons knew intimately. Within this rugged environment, Jamaican maroons settled on hilltops or in the densest jungles for the purposes of defense. The steep and rocky terrain lacked fertile soil, which provided a challenge for maroon farmers. However maroons could offset the agricultural limitations by hunting (wild pigs in particular), gathering fruit and vegetables, raiding plantations, and trading with slaves, free blacks, and even whites. Like Prospect Bluff, the Blue Mountains and Cockpit country were highly defensible. However the Jamaican setting was harsher and provided more daily challenges for its maroon inhabitants. Due to the island's size, Jamaican maroons were located much closer to ever encroaching plantations than was the case at Prospect Bluff. This greatly complicated the lives of Jamaican maroons who, unlike the inhabitants of Prospect Bluff, were never able to disentangle themselves fully from broader Jamaican society. This greatly affected their demographics, political system, military structure, culture, and economy.

Beginning in the middle of the eighteenth century, sizable maroon communities locally called *palenques* formed in the mountains of Cuba, which provided a stiff challenge to the slave regime for the next century.[37] Cuban *palenques*, while never as large as the Jamaican maroon communities, provide a valuable insight into the importance of physical environment and the formation and sustainability of maroon settlements. The mountains of eastern Cuba were the most common place in which *palenques* were found. The steep and soaring mountains in eastern Cuba are covered with dense and rugged forests. As was the case in Jamaica, this mountainous environment provided wide opportunities for fugitive slaves to establish hidden communities that were highly defensible and were supported by a combination of hunting, gathering, farming, raiding, and trading. And yet the slave society of eastern Cuba existed on a much smaller scale than that in western Cuba with its booming sugar plantations.[38] With a larger population of slaves laboring in brutal conditions, on the surface western Cuba should have been home to many more and much larger *palenques* than eastern Cuba. However, the west lacked the rugged mountainous interior of the east, and thus its slaves never developed a tradition of flight and marronage that corresponded to their numbers. Prospect Bluff was situated in a much more hospitable and fertile environment that allowed for higher quality of life than was the case in either Caribbean colony. At the same time, Prospect Bluff's natural defensive advantages rivaled those to be found in Jamaica or Cuba, while its location made it possible to withdraw from the surrounding slave societies. All of this was within reach for many slaves in the Southeast.

Brazil and Suriname had the most significant traditions of marronage on the South American continent and provide further valuable comparative data. After its acquisition by the Dutch in 1667 Suriname in northeastern South America became a thriving and brutal sugar colony that was marked by enormous imports of slaves, absenteeism, and a very high black to white ratio.[39] Over the course of the next two hundred years Suriname developed a major tradition of marronage as numerous maroon communities fought the government in brutal wars, signed treaties with colonial governors, and sought to establish their own communities in isolation. Many of their descendants live in these maroon communities today.[40] The physical environment in which these maroons lived, while making it difficult to apprehend them, was harsh and even more challenging than in Jamaica and Cuba. Sugar plantations dominated a narrow swath along Suriname's coast, while immediately inland the country turns into swamps or swamp-forests that flood to the point of being impassable during the rainy season and for two months afterward.[41] Within these swamps, maroons frequently formed communities along rivers that they used for fishing and transportation. Over hundreds of years Suriname's maroons flourished because they were able to create shelter, grow crops, forage for food, and hunt or fish in an extremely challenging, though nevertheless defensible, swamp environment. Because of this setting, the maroons of Suriname faced a paradox: they were able to withdraw physically from the broader slave society to an extent that was impossible in virtually any other colony in the hemisphere—but were reliant on the very same slave society for a host of essential goods that could not be produced locally. While the Apalachicola River flooded annually and Prospect Bluff lay close to swamps and forests, it was an easier physical environment to tame than in Suriname.

Beginning in the sixteenth century and continuing until emancipation, the *quilombos* or *mocambos,* as maroon communities were called in Brazil, were part of a territory that was roughly the size of the modern United States. The vast Portuguese colony contained an enormous slave population that was disproportionately male, young, single, and African, and the colony's terrain included vast mountains, dense jungles, endless rivers, and virtually impenetrable swamps. These conditions were highly suitable to the formation of maroon communities, which were most common in the jungles and swamps of Bahia, the rugged mining zone of Minas Gerais, and the Amazonian interior. However, all other *mocambos* paled in terms of size, duration, and strength in comparison to Palmares. Spread along a chain of forested mountains that stretched for nearly 60 leagues from between 15 and 60 miles inland along the coasts of modern Alagoas and Pernambuco, Palmares was made up of a series of related *mocambos* or towns.[42] Incredibly, Palmares existed for nearly the entire seventeenth century and, at its peak, was allegedly home to 20,000 people, although this number was probably exaggerated; its population likely peaked at closer to 10,000 inhabitants.[43] The inhabitants of Palmares or their parents or grandparents had escaped or been rescued from coastal sugar plantations and had made their way through dense jungles and swamps on a journey that would have been similar to that undertaken by a slave from the Deep South to Prospect Bluff. The mountains that were home to Palmares were not nearly as steep, high, or impenetrable as those of Cuba or Jamaica but were nevertheless highly defensible. The soil, climate, flora, and fauna were much richer than those of the Caribbean mountains and provided the associated communities of Palmares with a relative abundance of food.[44] In short, the physical environment in which Palmares was located in (locally, regionally, and colonially) and its proximity to the plantation complex more closely resembled Prospect Bluff and its surroundings than did any of the other maroon communities.

The Fort

Upon his arrival in May 1814, Woodbine wasted no time in fortifying Prospect Bluff. By the end of the month he had overseen the construction of a large storehouse and the near completion of a powder magazine that was reported to have been 40 feet by 24 feet.[45] The fort soon grew into an octagonal earthwork with a parapet that was between 15 and 18 feet thick. It was supported by strong palisades and was surrounded by a dry moat that was ten feet wide and nearly four feet deep.[46] After the evacuation of Pensacola, the British, with the aid of their Indian and black allies, quickly began to build a large and secure fort around the structure that Woodbine had previously constructed. It was completed by December. The fort was made from the area's abundant pine and was surrounded by a moat 4 feet deep and 14 feet wide, which was never filled. Wood and earthen walls 15 feet high and 18 feet thick enclosed nearly two acres and a number of "comfortable barracks and large stone houses."[47] The dwellings, as well as the fort and defenses, were constructed under the guidance of "the superintendences of officers of the Ordinance Department"—that is, by British military engineers.[48] A bustling village soon formed behind the fort, where the majority of the community lived, and dwellings reached north along the river, extending for miles.[49] At the center of the fort was a large powder magazine that stored powder and ammunition for a number of canons, howitzers, and mortars mounted on the ramparts.[50] The fort stood approximately 60 yards steeply uphill from the riverbank, where a barrier and "dock . . . with an embrasure on each side in a position to be able to strike up and down the river" had been constructed.[51] A "stockade" and "parapet of earth" combined to surround the rest of the structure.[52] This system of defense was so effective that when the American armed forces attempted to destroy the fort in 1816, they could build their base no closer than the opposite side of the river, and American soldiers and their Indian allies could approach the fort only under cover of heavy cannon fire launched from hundreds of yards away.[53] This was a tremendously strong and imposing fort. It sat at an ideal and highly defensible position that commanded one of the most important rivers in the Southeast. The remnants of this structure left Gadsden to remark that "from the capacity of this work some idea may be formed of the extent of the Negro and Indian establishment contemplated in that country," while another American observer referred to location and fortification of Prospect Bluff as "almost impregnable."[54]

If the location and physical and environmental setting of Prospect Bluff were equal to or better than those in which most maroons found themselves living, the British-built fort and defenses also afforded major advantages far in excess of what maroons normally relied on for defense and shelter. The fort, defenses, and many of the homes at Prospect Bluff had been built under the guidance of British military engineers, by a large and organized labor force that used high quality tools, and on the edge of a vast forest that provided an easily accessible supply of strong building material. At this point in time the British armed forces amounted to the most technically advanced and efficient military machine in the world. Across the globe, wherever it fought, the British military built similar high quality forts and defenses that were crucial to its success. An American observer rightly recorded that the fort had been built with "all due care, and according to the most approved modern method."[55] Furthermore, Prospect Bluff itself was flat and open, which provided ideal conditions for building, comparing starkly with the challenges presented by rocky, steep, swampy, or enclosed locations. As ingenious and skilled as maroons could be at building their defenses and homes, they were still reliant on materials that they could acquire in often harsh settings and on tools of differing quality. Also individual maroons possessed varying abilities for construction, which were put to the test in rugged settings. These limited building skills were often utilized while guarding against attacks or while engaged in hostilities. When initially establishing shelter and an infrastructure, few if any maroon communities enjoyed such advantageous conditions as those of the community at Prospect Bluff.

Once again Palmares bore the greatest likeness to Prospect Bluff. The villages of Palmares were described as consisting of simple yet organized dwellings that numbered as many as fifteen hundred homes.[56] These villages were bustling scenes of commerce and production, surrounded by farmland. Each of the villages had good defenses that usually consisted of booby traps, walls, and palisades.[57] Palmares's main village had two gates protecting the main entrance to its western side, which was surrounded by a sturdy palisade with crossbeams, according to a 1645 description. Behind this was a deep ditch with a row of sharpened stakes. Its eastern side had a similar defensive system. A swamp protected the northern side, while a number of felled trees protected the southern side. The center of the village, which included governmental buildings, a church, and four smithies, had a further ring of defenses.[58] By the time of its destruction fifty years later Palmares was surrounded by a stockade that was nearly three miles in length. The stockade was supported by trenches and sharpened stakes. An extensive system of ramparts overlooked the stockade.[59] Residents constructed such defenses out of necessity, and their extent reflects the length of the village's existence, its location and bustling economy, and the collected abilities of its thousands of inhabitants. Conversely, Palmares was successful because its people were able to defend themselves so skillfully. As was the case at Prospect Bluff, Palmares could only be destroyed by an enormous standing army.

The maroons of Suriname built impressive and well-defended villages in swampy and isolated settings that provide important comparative material. The maroons constructed breezy rectangular houses with thick walls that occasionally even had balconies from the abundant local wood. While these maroons acquired much of their food by hunting, fishing, and gathering, villages also had extensive fields devoted to crop farming. The maroons practiced shifting cultivation in which each year a portion of the forest was burned to create a highly fertile provision ground.[60] Defense was of the highest priority as the maroons of Suriname remained vigilant militarily to defend themselves from European armies, local whites, Indian tribes, and other maroon settlements. For example, one maroon village in Suriname was built behind palisades on top of a hill. A sunken path led to the village's entrance. If attackers came up the path, the village's defenders rolled logs at the invaders.[61] However, because of the topography and environment, most maroon communities in Suriname proved unable to construct such fortifications. Instead maroons relied on a combination of guerilla warfare and ploys such as false trails and deadly booby traps that, when combined with the treacherous environment, were a formidable challenge to attackers. As efficient as this defensive system was, it required a tremendous amount of ongoing vigilance to maintain. It could also break down if attackers appeared in great numbers or if assailants had identified the location of hidden traps. In short, these defenses were less reliable and more difficult to maintain than the defenses of Prospect Bluff.

Maroons in the mountains of Jamaica and Cuba constructed an impressive array of dwellings and defenses, complemented by highly effective guerilla tactics, camouflage, hidden trails, and booby traps, all of which further enhanced the natural defensive characteristics of the landscape. Cuban *palenques* generally consisted of numerous huts of varying sizes and quality that were surrounded by farmland.[62] The *palenques* were often encircled by steep ditches filled with sharpened spikes.[63] The English translation of *palenque* is "fence" or "palisade," meaning this system of defense was so common that Cubans simply began to use it to refer to maroon communities in general.

The Leeward and Windward maroons of Jamaica lived in collections of villages organized around a central village that served as the economic and political hub of the community.[64] While both groups organized themselves in clusters of villages, the Leeward maroons submitted themselves to leaders with strong centralized authority, whereas the Windward maroons were less centralized in their political organization and gave more autonomy to individual villages.[65] In either case, Jamaican maroon villages consisted of a number of huts and provision grounds that supplemented food acquired through hunting, gathering, fishing; trading with the enslaved, free blacks, and whites; and raiding plantations. Because the Blue Mountains and Cockpit country were steeper and harsher than the mountains of Brazil or Cuba, Jamaican maroons relied more extensively on their environment and various tactics for defense rather than on the building of fortifications. Narrow trails crisscrossed the nearly impenetrable jungles of the Jamaican mountains. These trails, which were littered with booby traps, were all but invisible to anybody other than the maroons who had constructed them and were often designed to lead attackers astray. The Jamaican maroons had designed the trails with a view to ambushes, which they launched with brutal efficiency. The associated villages of Jamaican maroons tended to be located along the faces of hills or mountains, with the less important villages being located farther downhill and the head village being situated at the highest and most naturally defensive position. In the case of an enemy attack, the residents of the outlying villages would retreat uphill as the defenders launched projectiles downhill at the attackers. This was a highly effective system that accepted both the innate limitations and advantages of the Jamaican environment.[66] But as was the case in Suriname, this system of defense and village planning required tremendous vigilance and effort that made it less favorable than the setting and fortification at Prospect Bluff. In the end, the physical setting and manmade defenses and dwellings at Prospect Bluff would have been the envy of most maroons from across the hemisphere. In turn, these advantages, which were largely the result of chance, allowed the maroons more time to focus on economic, cultural, social, and political pursuits.

Size of the Community

Prospect Bluff came to be home to hundreds of former slaves. A close chronological examination of the extant evidence strongly suggests that the community's average population size, between the British departure in May 1815 and its destruction in July 1816, was between 300 and 400 inhabitants, with fugitive slaves joining the community at a steady rate that matched or exceeded the rate of departures. Prior to the British departure, up to 750 former slaves and free people of color may have gathered at Prospect Bluff. Both the average and peak populations of the maroon community at Prospect Bluff were unusually large in comparative perspective. By extension, these numbers were remarkably high in a continent that had virtually no experience with large maroon communities.

Blacks began to flock to Prospect Bluff as soon as Woodbine and the British arrived in the late spring of 1814, but the size of the community's population did not peak until the months between late 1814 and the summer of 1815. The population peaked during these months because all the various means by which the British sought to recruit slaves, including large-scale theft, were fully under way by this point. In 1816 Nicolls claimed that "at any time I can raise a black regiment of 1,000 strong" from the former slaves he had left at Prospect Bluff and those he assumed would have joined them.[67] Years later he boasted that he had freed "upwards of 1,500 persons" at Prospect Bluff.[68] In both cases Nicolls overstated the maroon community's population, but these were still important estimates by an individual with detailed and intimate knowledge of the community. Nicolls's claims, at the very least, suggest that many hundreds of blacks lived at Prospect Bluff both prior to and after the British departure. In early 1815 a less grandiose estimate of the community's population reckoned that the number of former slaves organized as soldiers at Prospect Bluff totaled between 400 and 500 men, if the Fifth West India Regiment and company of *pardos* and *morenos* were included in the estimate.[69] This number included only men who were capable of bearing arms and thus represented only a portion of the community's actual population. The British had accepted slaves of both sexes, various ages, families, and males who were not capable of military service, meaning that an estimate solely of soldiers reflected only a portion of the community's entire population. Considering these factors, the peak population of former slaves and free people of color at Prospect Bluff represented by the 400–500 soldiers probably reached between 600 and 750 people.

At the end of April 1815 the surveyor general of West Florida, Vicente Sebastián Pintado, recorded 250 former slaves belonging to Americans, Indians, and the Spanish at Prospect Bluff. While at Prospect Bluff, Pintado witnessed the arrival of a further 78 former slaves from East Florida.[70] Thus he directly witnessed 328 former slaves. However, this was in all probability an underestimation of the total population of Prospect Bluff. Pintado's numbers were low because he worried especially about the former slaves from Pensacola, many of whom had hidden from him, along with others nervous at the appearance of a white official; he was simply unaware of the presence of yet others who lived on the outskirts of the settlement or were away at that moment. At virtually the exact time as Pintado's mission, Benjamin Hawkins received intelligence that made him "certain" that 100 former slaves belonging to "three half breeds" had "gathered near [Prospect Bluff as well as] . . . 200 belonging to Indians friendly to us and to citizens of the United States."[71] While Hawkins's numbers may have been somewhat inflated, they are nonetheless proof that a substantial number of people had escaped Pintado's attention and did not appear in his report, making it clear that his eyewitness estimates were much lower than reality. The British deserter Samuel Jervais, who spent months at Prospect Bluff, made a more accurate and reliable estimate at this point in time, though he too failed to take into account distant dwellings. Jervais told American officials that the black population of the *fort* numbered between 300 and 400.[72] Captain Rawlins of the Royal Navy informed an acquaintance in Bermuda that there were "upwards of three hundred" former slaves at Prospect Bluff at this time.[73] When the British departed, Edmund Gaines's black informant reported that there were "450 negroes under arms" at Prospect Bluff but made no mention of the community's large civilian population.[74] During the same period a "gentleman on St. Simon's Island" wrote to a friend that he had "authentic" information that the British had left "three hundred—well organized" at Prospect Bluff.[75] The word "organized" means that his estimate applied solely to soldiers and that the total population of Prospect Bluff was higher. Each of these estimates represents a substantial population of at least 500 people or more when adjusted to take into account former slaves who were hiding, female, males incapable of military service, away, or living outside the fort.

The maroon community continued to have a large population after the departure of the British. A close chronological analysis of the evidence demonstrates that a steady average population emerged at Prospect Bluff between May 1815 and July 1816. In August 1815 Hawkins noted that the fort was now under black control and was defended by 100 black soldiers.[76] This was an underestimation of one section of the community's population and did not include women, children, or men not organized as soldiers. Six months later he reported that "from the concurring testimony of white & red people in my confidence the number of blacks [at Prospect Bluff] is 350."[77] At the end of 1815 a free black man named Ned who had recently spent time at Prospect Bluff claimed that the community consisted of 250 blacks.[78] In the spring of 1816 William Crawford nervously reported that the "negroe fort . . . has been strengthened . . . and is now occupied by between two hundred and fifty and three hundred blacks."[79] Three months later Gaines received information that the "number at and near the Fort is stated to be upwards of three hundred men," and he had "reason to believe [it] is acquiring strength and additional numbers."[80] Again, these men were primarily concerned with the former slaves who were organized as soldiers and did not include in their estimates women, children, or men unable to bear arms. Likewise, none of these estimates paid particular attention to settlements outside the Fort or to the number of maroons who might have been away at any given moment.

In July 1816, when the fort was destroyed, American estimates placed the population at approximately 275 men, women, and children.[81] Spanish estimates corroborated this number.[82] However, these numbers are deeply suspect. The American expedition to destroy the fort was slow and proceeded via a series of raids by Creek Indians, both of which allowed much of the Prospect Bluff population to flee and take refuge across the Floridas. Those killed in the blast included only the community's defenders or those unfortunate enough still to be at Prospect Bluff. In all probability no more than a few dozen maroons died in the American destruction of the fort. It is important to note that the community's population—even as late as the summer of 1816, when it was reported only days before the fort's destruction that "their numbers were daily increasing"—remained fairly steady and was never in a state of serious decline prior to the final evacuation, since it was joined by fugitive slaves from across the Deep South who fled to Prospect Bluff at a rate that was described as "frequent."[83] Accordingly, when the appropriate adjustments are made to each of these figures, a more accurate estimate of the community's average population becomes 300 to 400 former slaves during the period between May 1815 and July 1816.

Most scholars agree that the average size of the largest maroon communities ranged between 100 and 300 inhabitants, with few exceeding these numbers.[84] Palmares's 20,000 (probably half that number in reality and divided into numerous villages) was the most notable exception to this rule. Elsewhere in Brazil the Buraco de Tatú never numbered more than 100 people, while few *mocambos* in the colony's history outnumbered a nameless one of approximately 400 residents that was located in Cairu in the 1720s.[85] In eighteenth-century Cuba, a *palenque* known as the Poblado del Cobre reached 1,065 members, although it was divided into a number of villages that essentially made it into a series of much smaller *palenques*.[86] More realistically, one of the biggest single settlements in Cuban history was the *palenque* known as Coba, which was reported to have 320 members in 1819.[87] On the eve of its 1785 treaty with the French and Spanish governments, Hispaniola's Le Maniel numbered only 137 inhabitants.[88] Colombia's largest maroon community numbered 450 inhabitants in the late seventeenth century, while perhaps 300 maroons lived in the mountains of Guatemala during the colony's fleeting "maroon moment" in the first half of the seventeenth century.[89] It was estimated that the entire colony of Suriname had a "few thousand" maroons in 1740 and between 6,000 and 9,000 in 1863.[90] It must be remembered that these thousands of individuals were divided into six frequently hostile tribes that were subdivided into smaller villages.[91] Few if any Surinamese maroon villages would have had a larger population than Prospect Bluff. Prior to the 1739 treaties in Jamaica, the island's most famous maroon village, Nanny Town, was estimated to have 300 warriors, which would have meant a total population between 400 and 500 inhabitants.[92] In 1773 the total maroon population of Jamaica was 1,500, with the largest maroon village having a population of 414. In 1824 the island's entire maroon population was 2,000 and the largest village had 438 residents.[93]

As the comparative data illustrate, the population of the maroon community at Prospect Bluff exceeded the hemispheric average for large maroon communities. Only a few maroon communities in history achieved a larger peak population than at Prospect Bluff. The fact that the settlement would have stood out as a particularly large maroon community in *any* society in the hemisphere is doubly remarkable, given North America's nominal tradition of marronage and the tense timing of its existence. The community at Prospect Bluff was not simply the largest of many maroon villages or autonomous communities that dotted the periphery of a plantation society. Rather it was the only large maroon community on the entire continent. The fact that the community could not escape notice and elicited powerful emotions among an array of observers was reflected in its various names. Furthermore, the community at Prospect Bluff enjoyed a number of environmental and material advantages that would have made most maroons envious. From high atop Prospect Bluff, the maroons were strongly positioned to control their stretch of the Apalachicola River as well as many miles of surrounding territory. Fortunately for the maroons, this landscape teemed with plant and animal life and offered fertile soil. These natural advantages were greatly enhanced by the British-built fort and dwellings that the maroons came to occupy. Equally important were the immense amounts of supplies, tools, and military hardware that the British left with the former slaves at Prospect Bluff. Virtually no maroon community in history enjoyed such an advantageous combination of natural setting, quality infrastructure, and bountiful supplies. Situated squarely within the Southeast on the edge of the expanding American plantation complex, after its very public founding, it was truly an exceptional community.

7 ⇒ Community and Culture

ADVANTAGEOUSLY POSITIONED at Prospect Bluff, hundreds of maroons constructed a vibrant community. The Prospect Bluff community came to display a variation of maroon culture that had both commonalities and differences when compared with examples of marronage from across the hemisphere. The greatest general similarity between Prospect Bluff and other maroon communities was the development of a synthetic or Atlantic culture that largely reflected its members' varying backgrounds. However, the Prospect Bluff maroon community's culture was much more creole and less African in outlook than was the case in most other maroon communities. This was the result of the maroons' unusually diverse yet largely creole backgrounds and their close relationship with Edward Nicolls and the British.

Prior to coming to Prospect Bluff, the maroons had labored in a diverse array of rural and urban slave systems. This work background had left the maroons with a variety of skills that proved valuable in taming the Florida wilderness. At the same time the Prospect Bluff community's relatively balanced demographics, backgrounds, cultural outlook, and material advantages had cultural and gendered implications that warrant examination. All totaled, as a result of material and physical advantages, members' backgrounds, and the circumstances surrounding the settlement's founding, the former slaves at Prospect Bluff formed an unusual maroon community that diverged from hemispheric patterns as often as it conformed to them. Analyzing these differences and similarities from a comparative perspective helps us understand more fully how things such as demographics, gender, previously developed skills, and cultural outlook shaped the contours of freedom within maroon communities across the hemisphere. By extension, this provides even more clarity on how the maroons at Prospect Bluff sought to construct a community and define their freedom when entirely beyond white interference and when endowed with material and intellectual advantages that distinguished this maroon community from most others.

Origins of the Community's Inhabitants

The origins of the maroon community's inhabitants were unusually varied and lay in a number of different Atlantic world societies. The largest number came from the Spanish Floridas. The evacuation of the entire slave population of Pensacola provided the single largest group of slaves from the Spanish Floridas, although others came from elsewhere in West Florida as well as East Florida. The experience indicated in a petition filed by John Forbes and Company, claiming that all eleven of the slaves from its trading factory on the Apalachicola River fled to the British at Prospect Bluff, was typical.[1] Woodbine's frequent journeys across the Floridas resulted in many slaves arriving at Prospect Bluff, such as the seventy-eight former slaves Pintado had noted returning with Woodbine from East Florida or when "thro' the means of Woodbine Seventy Negroes . . . arrived at the Bluff from St. Augustine, St. John's and Lachua."[2] Furthermore, numerous free people of color from St. Augustine traveled to Prospect Bluff with Woodbine at the end of 1814.[3] The mere presence of the British led many Florida slaves, like the "several" who belonged to the Anglo East Florida planter John Perpall, to flee their masters and travel to Prospect Bluff.[4] Once the British had left, the independent maroon community continued to provide the same attraction for Florida slaves, such as "100 blacks, men, women and children from East Florida" who were "expect[ed]" shortly at Prospect Bluff in August 1815.[5]

Residents from the United States, France, England, Scotland, Ireland, Italy, Germany, Denmark, Sweden, Switzerland, Poland, Portugal, Holland, Honduras, and Greece combined to outnumber Spaniards in the Floridas during this period.[6] Like their masters, many Florida slaves originated elsewhere in the Spanish New World, the United States, or in French or British colonies. Thus many slaves from Spanish Florida were Anglo or French creoles or from a different Hispanic culture. Likewise a substantial number of the former slaves would have been conversant in multiple cultures and, most noticeably, bilingual. For example, it can be assumed that Carlos, Agustin, Ainbrosio, and Antonio, all of whom belonged to a Madame Eslava and escaped from Pensacola, were linguistically and culturally influenced primarily by Spain.[7] These "Spanish slaves" had been baptized in the Catholic Church, spoke Spanish, and were culturally Afro-Hispanic. John Innerarity saw his slaves Tomas, Ben, Mary, and Sophie escape to Prospect Bluff from West Florida.[8] These "Anglo slaves," while probably bilingual, were influenced by their owner's heritage and were originally from the United States or the British Caribbean. However, for every person of Iberian or Anglo-American descent who lost a slave with a name culturally similar to the owner's, there was a Peter Philibert who lost a slave named Eduardo or a Don Martín de Madrid who lost a slave named William.[9] It was equally common for Spanish or Anglo-American slave owners to own and lose slaves who were of varying origins, such as Don Antonio Montero, who lost slaves named Feodora and Maria (Spanish) as well as Betsy and Sam (Anglo-American).[10] Spanish Florida's exceptional political, economic, and military circumstances led to a high degree of cultural fluidity among both blacks and whites. Clear evidence of this cultural hybridity can be seen in the fact that many of the former slaves from Pensacola arrived among the British "speaking good English."[11] The large percentage of former Pensacola slaves who were listed as "mulattos" is also informative. For example, Philis and her child, two men named Charles, and Dick, Anthony, Laura, Francisco, and Hilario were all listed as mulattos. Spanish attitudes toward race and the Atlantic-borderlands setting of urban Pensacola both increased the likelihood of racial intermixing. However, the presence of such a sizable number of mulattos is still notable. All the former slaves from Pensacola had been closely involved with whites on a daily basis, but the experience of mulattos was on a different and more intimate level, which affected how they dealt with whites as well as blacks.

It is difficult to pinpoint slaves from other Spanish colonies, Cuba in particular, who were very common across the Floridas and would have been present at Prospect Bluff, but a reasonable frequency of slaves with French names suggests a link to the former Spanish and French province of Louisiana or the French Caribbean. For example, Garçon, who was one of the community's leaders, was a "French" former slave.[12] Many of these former slaves had first- or, at the very least, secondhand knowledge of the major disturbances that were sweeping the Americas during the Age of Revolution and would have been important sources of information and attitudes toward culture.

Spain continued to import slaves from Africa until an 1817 treaty with Great Britain prohibited the slave trade north of the Equator.[13] As a result, African-born slaves constituted a higher percentage of the slave population of the Spanish Floridas than of the United States during this period. This was reflected in the maroon community's population by the presence of a number of Africans such as Congo Tom, Carlos Congo, Carlos Mayamba, Moses, and Samson.[14] While Africans would certainly have contributed to the community's cultural life, military organization, and political structure, they remained a small minority of the overall population and must never have exceeded 10 percent of its total.

Many Anglo-American slaves who arrived at Prospect Bluff had previously been taken to the Spanish Floridas by their American or British masters. Examples include those lost by John Perpall and Forbes and Company or the native English-speaking fugitive slaves from Pensacola. However, the British succeeded in recruiting slaves from the United States to their base at Prospect Bluff, and many more American slaves fled there after the British departed. For example, shortly after arriving at Prospect Bluff, George Woodbine noted that "negroes are flocking in from the states."[15] Samuel Jervais estimated that of the 300 to 400 former slaves at Prospect Bluff, all were "taken from the United States, principally Louisiana."[16] In all probability the group that Jervais described was more diverse than he suggested and included slaves from the Mississippi Territory, Alabama, and West Florida. Nonetheless, Jervais's statement did "correspond," at least numerically, with that of a number of blacks who had left Prospect Bluff.[17] During the war the British took American slaves from Alabama on their way to Prospect Bluff.[18] Vicente Pintado reported that while at Prospect Bluff he had witnessed Nicolls return to the fort with "many negroes, immigrated or brought from the American possessions," who joined many more former slaves already there.[19] Captain Rawlins told his acquaintance in Bermuda that the community consisted "partly [of] deserters from the United States, and partly from the Spanish provinces of East and West Florida."[20]

After the British departure it was reported by American observers that Prospect Bluff continued as a "harbor . . . for all the discontented negroes in the [United States]," where "fugitive slaves from all the Southern Section of the union" made their home.[21] At the end of 1815 John Innerarity noted with great annoyance that "a considerable number of negroes have escaped from Georgia to that occursed hornet's nest at Prospect Bluff."[22] Innerarity's claim was supported by the four Georgia newspapers that ran advertisements for fifteen male and four female fugitive slaves during this period, which was well above average.[23] Moreover, "several letters from Hartford" reported that "runaway negros . . . who have left Georgia and gone to the negro fort . . . amount to 24." Another report, from the winter of 1815–16, maintained that "several slaves from the neighborhood [of Milledgeville] had fled to the Fort." They were joined by "others [who] have lately gone from Tennessee and the Mississippi Territory" in the summer of 1816.[24] For obvious logistical reasons, nearly every American slave who joined the maroon community came from the Deep South or the Floridas. A remarkable exception to this was a former slave named Charles who escaped from a "Gentleman in Virginia" and traveled to Prospect Bluff on the British vessel *Sea Horse*.[25]

The community and its allies took more proactive measures to increase their numbers than merely waiting for fugitives to travel to Prospect Bluff. For example, in the spring of 1816 William Crawford noted with a great deal of concern that the "secret practice to inveigle negroes from the frontiers of Georgia . . . [is] still continued by the negroes and hostile Creeks."[26] During the same period the governor of West Florida admitted that the community had been "reinforced" by many slaves "seduced from the service of their masters, citizens of the U.S."[27] By late spring 1816 Hawkins warned that Prospect Bluff had become such an attractive "asylum for runaway negroes belonging to people of the United States . . . [that] something must be done soon, or Georgia will be despoiled of all their negroes on the frontier."[28] The maroon community was both a powerful lure and a proactive recruiter for American slaves, who arrived at Prospect Bluff at a steady rate until the fort's destruction. Unlike many maroon communities who turned away newcomers, tracked down fugitive slaves, or owned slaves themselves, the Prospect Bluff community appears to have accepted new arrivals and aggressively recruited others. This is an important distinction and speaks to the fact that the Prospect Bluff maroons saw themselves as an anti-slavery community waging a rebellion against slavery as a social system.

The presence of professional black soldiers at Prospect Bluff served both to emphasize the correlation between formal military service and freedom in the minds of the former slaves and to contribute to the community's diversity. The Fifth West India Regiment and the members of the Spanish *pardo* and *moreno* militia began their service in the Anglo and Spanish Caribbean respectively. Based in Jamaica, the Fifth West India Regiment totaled nearly a thousand soldiers, but only a portion of the total force went to Florida.[29] The West India Regiments consisted of creoles (slave or free) as well as Africans intercepted while being transported in the slave trade. The majority of the Spanish black militia had been born in the New World (usually in Cuba). The presence of black soldiers from the Anglo and Spanish Caribbean, even if brief, increased the community's web of Atlantic connections as well as its exposure to different Afro-American cultures.

Blacks who had lived as independent maroons and among Native Americans, either in associated communities or as their slaves, constituted an important part of the community's population. Nicolls claimed that nearly all his black recruits and their families "left the United States when they rebelled against the British Crown [during the American Revolution], and had . . . lived with [the Seminole] Indians well known under the name of King George's men."[30] Woodbine told Pintado that many of the 78 former slaves he brought from St. Augustine had similar origins.[31] As the extant evidence bears out, the percentages in both men's estimations were exaggerations presumably designed to hide the backgrounds of their former slave recruits, but their claims nonetheless indicate that many blacks joined the community after living with the Seminoles or in independent maroon communities. During the Creek War many slaves fled to the Red Sticks from white Americans or Creeks prior to arriving at Prospect Bluff. This was why Woodbine reported that "there is also a party of negroes, upwards of 200 men, who have run away from the States, and are on their march for this, in company with Cappachimico's Tribe."[32] Pintado supported these claims when he observed that many of the former slaves at Prospect Bluff had come "from Indian land."[33] William Crawford warned that slaves were being encouraged to flee from Georgia to Prospect Bluff not only by the maroons and their allies but also from the "Cherokee and Creek nations."[34] Hawkins believed that three wealthy mixed-race Creeks had lost "nearly 100" slaves to Prospect Bluff and that there were many more there who "belong[ed] to Indians friendly to us."[35]

At Prospect Bluff and elsewhere, the populations of maroon communities tended to reflect the ethnic patterns in the broader slave society from which their members escaped. Despite many efforts to the contrary, it simply was not possible for large and/or long-lived maroon communities to consist of people who shared identical ethnic, cultural, or geographic backgrounds. Particularly the earliest maroon communities (in terms of both the broader slave society and the community's development) were heterogeneous conglomerations of Africans, creoles, and sometimes Indians or even whites. As years passed many of the most successful maroon communities entered into treaties or became isolated to protect themselves. Both developments decreased the flow of new members. At the same time the broader slave population in most plantation societies increasingly came to be locally born. Due to this combination of factors, the most successful maroon communities came to be dominated numerically by creoles. As a result of this process many communities developed new and distinct maroon identities that borrowed from the different traditions and cultures in their collective past.[36] A brief examination of the composition of a number of maroon communities both highlights these patterns and illustrates the extent to which the community at Prospect Bluff adhered to these trends. This analysis, in turn, adds an extra level of depth to our understanding of life at Prospect Bluff and underscores the universality of the maroons' goals.

In Brazil the Buraco de Tatú was populated by creoles and Africans of various ethnicities.[37] While the majority of founders at Palmares were Angolans, the great *quilombo* had become a mostly creole community by the second half of the seventeenth century, albeit one deeply influenced by Angolan culture.[38] Many of Colombia's maroon communities replicated this pattern. They were initially founded by African runaways, who attempted with varying degrees of success to cluster in ethnic or tribal enclaves. As later generations of African or creole runaways joined these communities, they contributed to a growing diversification and then creolization of Colombian maroon settlements.[39] The same pattern emerged in the southern Venezuelan maroon community known as Aripao. One of the more diverse settlements in South American history, the community was founded by African and creole slaves in Dutch Guiana before its members began the long and treacherous journey to Venezuela in the eighteenth century. Upon arriving and settling in Venezuela the community was joined by many Spanish creole and African slaves and perhaps a number of Indians.[40] Maroon communities that originated in Suriname repeated this trajectory and tended to reflect the influences of various West African cultures long after creolization.[41]

Maroon communities in the Caribbean exhibited these patterns. Few Cuban *palenques* were dominated by a single ethnic group, with the exception of the Palenque de los Vivis. Normally Cuban *palenques* were a mixture of creoles, Congos, Gangas, Carabalis, Vivis, and other ethnic groups. As was the case with English at Prospect Bluff, a common knowledge of Spanish was key in most *palenques'* ability to find common ground among various cultures and ethnicities.[42] Although Le Maniel was located on the Spanish side of Hispaniola's border, the community's residents were almost entirely from French Saint Domingue. This meant that the population of Le Maniel, like those of maroon communities from across the island, consisted of a combination of varying African ethnicities and creoles.[43]

Jamaica provides the most detailed (and therefore most revealing) data about the composition of Atlantic maroon communities. The first Jamaican maroon communities appeared in the seventeenth century when fugitive Spanish and Malagasy slaves began to join with rapidly declining groups of Taino Indians.[44] With the British acquisition of the island and the rapid expansion of slavery, frequently set to the backdrop of destabilizing colonial wars, many more fugitives joined these early maroon communities. These later fugitives were numerically dominated by Coromantees from the Gold Coast, but their numbers also included non-Coromantee Africans, such as fugitives from the Slave Coast (Congos, Eboes, or Mundingos, for example) or Yoruba (Nagos, for example), and creoles (born slaves or maroons).[45] The vast majority of African fugitives, who comprised a majority of all fugitives, settled with the Leeward maroons who developed a culture and political system dominated by Akan- and Tiwi-speaking Coromantees, while the Windward maroons were more directly influenced by their Spanish and Indian forebears.[46] In both cases the maroons appear to have had elaborate processes by which new members were incorporated into the community as well as a fairly flexible sense of ethnic identity.[47] However, as occurred elsewhere, Jamaican maroons feared that the presence of too many ethnic groups might threaten internal stability. Solutions to this problem included barring members of certain ethnic groups or imposing that "on pain of Death, they are to use no other language but the English and they are not to be found conversing in small companies," as was decreed by the leader of the Leewards, Cudjoe, in the 1730s.[48] Likewise prior to 1739, ethnic divisions led to violent rivalries between communities. The 1739 treaties required the maroons to stop receiving new members and thus forced the communities to reproduce through natural increase if they hoped to survive. This proved to be a turning point that greatly accelerated the creolization of the maroons and fostered the creation of distinct maroon cultures transcending ethnic divisions.[49]

As the comparative data illustrate, on the surface the Prospect Bluff settlement did not stand out as being unusually diverse by hemispheric standards. Yet if one looks more closely, the composition of Prospect Bluff's population becomes more unusual. This is because the diversity that marked most maroon communities elsewhere in the hemisphere resulted from the presence of an array of African ethnicities and a limited number of creoles. But the inhabitants of the maroon community at Prospect Bluff originated in a broad assortment of Atlantic world societies, which, as the comparative data illustrate, had seldom occurred elsewhere. At Prospect Bluff there were Africans; Spanish creoles from both Floridas, Cuba, and elsewhere in Spain's empire; English-speaking former slaves from the United States and Anglo-Caribbean; and people from French colonies. Other members of the community had lived with various southeastern Indians or in independent maroon communities. Furthermore because of the Atlantic-borderlands nature of the Southeast, many of these labels failed to capture fully the cultural complexity involved; for example, that of an individual born in Africa, who lived as a slave in Cuba prior to moving to Saint Augustine and being captured in a raid by Seminole Indians, or that of a slave born in Saint Domingue, who moved to New Orleans with a master in the wake of the Haitian Revolution and then was sold into slavery in Pensacola. Because of its brief existence it is impossible to tell if the community at Prospect Bluff would have gone through similar processes in terms of culture and ethnicity. Nonetheless, in the end, no maroon community would have spoken so many European, Indian, and African languages nor had such detailed knowledge of so many different Atlantic cultures and societies. Prospect Bluff's varied yet largely creole or Indian slave population shaped how the maroons understood freedom, interpreted Nicolls's ideas, organized themselves, practiced their culture, and lived their daily lives in a manner that diverged from the lives of groups consisting of an array of African ethnicities or who had constructed a common maroon identity over many years. Furthermore, the diversity of the community's inhabitants does not appear to have been a liability. Two explanations stand out: the community's inhabitants shared a belief in Nicolls's message, and they shared an awareness of Prospect Bluff offering the rare and potentially fleeting opportunity to claim their freedom, an opportunity that could be undermined by ethnic and cultural rivalries. Finally, since the community at Prospect Bluff consisted of such a broad cross section of former slaves, who came from a range of slave societies and systems, it is doubly likely that other North American slaves—if presented with the same opportunities—would have behaved in a similar manner. In other words, the fact that former slaves from so many different cultures and systems of slavery could coordinate their actions and ideas in pursuit of freedom demonstrates what a universal goal they were seeking to achieve.

Demographics and Former Occupations

From a comparative perspective, the population of the maroon community at Prospect Bluff consisted of a relatively balanced sex and age ratio, while its inhabitants possessed an unusual assortment of skills due to the numerous systems under which they had labored while enslaved. Other than the Fifth West India Regiment and the *pardo* and *moreno* militias, who were all male professional soldiers, the clearest information pertaining to sex, age, family structure, and former occupations relates to 117 of the 150 slaves from Pensacola.[50] Of the former slaves from Pensacola whose gender is known, 76 were male and 31 were female. We know the age of 62 males and 26 females. There were 9 males and 6 females up to the age of 10, the youngest child being 2 years old; 8 males and 8 females between 10 and 20 years old; 24 males and 9 females between 20 and 30 years old; 14 males and 3 females between 30 and 40 years old; 6 men and no women between 40 and 50 years old; and the oldest man was 55. Families were common among the former slaves from Pensacola.[51]

The former slaves who had traveled to Prospect Bluff from across the Spanish Floridas were men (who made up the majority) and women of various ages and numerous occupational backgrounds. For example, this was the case when seventy fugitive slaves "of both sexes . . . from St. Augustine, St. John's and Lachau" and "100 blacks, men, women and children" from East Florida fled to Prospect Bluff in the summer of 1815.[52] Not all groups of fugitive slaves who arrived at Prospect Bluff from East Florida were as demographically balanced, however. The "thirty to forty negroes principally men" and the "large body of Men" who traveled to Prospect Bluff in 1815 and 1816, respectively, support this.[53] The majority of slaves who fled to Prospect Bluff from the United States were male.[54] For example, Commodore Daniel Patterson's assessment that the American slaves at Prospect Bluff were of "very great importance and value" strongly suggests a male majority, since male slaves were generally valued at higher amounts than female slaves.[55] Likewise, all of the American slaves captured after the fort's destruction were male.[56]

All the available evidence points to a male to female sex ratio at Prospect Bluff of somewhere between 4:1 and 3:1. It appears that the majority of the population was between 20 and 40 years of age, with children under 13 representing perhaps 10 to 15 percent. These ratios become striking in comparative perspective and provide important insights that shed light on the dynamics of life at Prospect Bluff. Across the hemisphere there were distinct demographic patterns that differentiated stable maroon communities from those that were desperately attempting to survive by any means necessary and/or those at an earlier stage in their development. In the latter case, younger men hugely outnumbered women, while children were rare.[57] For example, after war with the island's whites, the lack of women and children was the second biggest obstacle to the viability of Jamaica's maroon communities prior to the 1739 treaties. This posed such a problem that despite extensive flight from the plantations, many Jamaican maroon communities' populations fell into steep decline in the 1730s largely due to their near total inability to reproduce naturally.[58] Prior to the treaties in Suriname, roughly 90 percent of fugitives who became maroons were young men.[59] Even Palmares, as the word *quilombo* suggests, struggled and failed to achieve anything close to a balanced sex and age ratio.[60]

A number of reasons lay behind such sex and age imbalances. In many slave societies across the hemisphere, young males predominated; statistically, then, they would likely dominate any community formed by runaways. Furthermore, young men ran away more frequently than any other group, including women.[61] Women desired their freedom as much as men, but they were frequently more tightly bound to the plantations by family ties and physically less able to make the grueling and dangerous journey into the unknown jungle or forest. The case of Prospect Bluff clearly illustrated the extent to which women desired their freedom. Slave women and mothers found in Prospect Bluff an opportunity to escape their bondage and join a maroon community with little fear of being stopped. However, in the case of mothers, a woman would not have remained at Prospect Bluff with her children if she believed that their time there was fleeting or dangerous. Rather she stayed because she believed that the community offered a realistic opportunity for permanent freedom and safety. This fact also suggests that women and mothers, in particular, had more rebellious potential than is often credited to them. Like men, slave women deeply desired their freedom, but they faced extra physical and familial obstacles in obtaining it. However, when conditions arose that made the probability of successful resistance high, women and mothers were quick to strike for their freedom as well as that of their children.

The development of maroon communities was affected by these demographic imbalances. These ratios slowed the process of community formation by creating a dependence on new recruits to increase their numbers or simply to remain viable. The shortage of women also often led to intra-community violence as men fought over wives; the desire for wives was a frequent motivation behind raids on plantations.[62] Thus a severely imbalanced sex ratio threatened stability and presented yet another obstacle that kept maroons from fully withdrawing from slave society. Treaty maroons were most successful at reversing these demographic trends: the negotiated prohibition against receiving runaways forced them to rely on natural reproduction. Jamaica provides the clearest statistical data on this transformation. A decade after the treaties, Trelawny Town had a total population of 276 inhabitants—112 males, 85 females, and 79 children. Twenty-four years later the population of Trelawny Town had grown to 414, consisting of 121 males, 140 females, and 115 children. Across the island, through 1830, the sex and age ratios of other maroon communities replicated the demographics at Trelawny Town principally because of higher birth rates and lower death rates than on the plantations and the refusal to accept new members.[63]

It is likely that the community at Prospect Bluff would eventually have achieved similarly balanced age and sex ratios. But the residents enjoyed a major advantage over most maroon communities by beginning with a sex ratio between 4:1 and 3:1 and a fairly balanced age distribution. While far from perfectly balanced, the sex and age ratios at Prospect Bluff were much more stable than at the inception of virtually any other maroon community. The balanced numbers undercut the need to make raids for women and to fight over wives. Prospect Bluff's demographics laid the foundation for a healthy and forward-looking community that was anything but a bastion of desperate young men seeking simply to survive deep in the wilderness. This meant, certainly from a demographic perspective, that Prospect Bluff was much more of a full community than most other maroon groups at such an early stage.

Accordingly, the Prospect Bluff maroons moved straight to a stage of cultural and community formation that was unusual so soon after establishment. As a result the maroons at Prospect Bluff would have developed a sense of permanence much more quickly than was normally the case. This distinction would have affected Prospect Bluff's identity greatly in terms of daily life, culture, economy, and political outlook.

Few maroon communities had members who came from so many different systems of labor and possessed such an array of skills as the settlement at Prospect Bluff. Generally, most maroon members shared the same work background. More specifically, the vast majority of maroons came from rural plantations, as was the case in Jamaica, Suriname, and Palmares as well as countless smaller communities across the hemisphere.[64] Part of the reason for this was that most slave societies in the Americas were devoted to staple production on large plantations on which the vast majority of a colony's slaves worked. Furthermore, plantations were heavily populated by African males, who had the highest probability of flight.[65] A number of other factors further skewed these demographic probabilities. Often plantations were in closer proximity to interior regions that were suitable for marronage than were urban areas. Likewise it was more difficult to police the plantation districts than the towns and cities. When urban slaves—frequently skilled creoles or assimilated Africans—opted for flight, they tended not to join maroon communities but rather to use their skills and knowledge of local culture to blend into the free black population.[66]

Thus, across the hemisphere, most maroons had labored in brutal conditions on plantations that were devoted to the production of staple crops. This work in and of itself would have been poor preparation for life in a maroon community. However, many slaves would have brought agricultural, hunting, and craft skills with them from Africa.[67] They also would have learned a number of skills and farming techniques on the plantations that would have been used to feed themselves, supplement their meager existence, and tend to their homes.[68] Either way, new maroons needed to learn or perfect a host of basic survival skills in a highly challenging and alien physical environment, while fending off adversaries, navigating internal divisions, and attempting to found a viable community. This was particularly acute for earlier generations, while later generations who were born as maroons possessed a set of skills that went a long way in overcoming their environment and enemies.

A strength of the maroon community at Prospect Bluff was precisely the skills and abilities that its inhabitants brought with them to the wilderness. This unusual diversity of skills arose because the community's inhabitants were both urban and rural former slaves from a number of different systems who had labored in a variety of conditions. For example, the occupations of the former slaves from Pensacola reflected their urban origins, with nearly all of them having been employed in skilled or semi-skilled jobs that required close contact with whites. Their occupations included carpentry (the most commonly listed occupation for males), shoe making, baking, cooking (a job shared by both sexes, but the most common occupation for women), domestic servitude, blacksmithing, locksmithing (a surprisingly common job), construction, groundskeeping, laundressing, and seamstressing.[69] In this system, slaves were allowed to tend their own gardens and make extra money in their free time by performing various jobs.

Not all slaves from the Floridas who escaped to Prospect Bluff had lived and worked in the colonies' towns. The former slaves from St. John's and Lachua, the ninety slaves who traveled to Prospect Bluff from the Mosquito River, and slaves such as those who escaped from John Perpall, had all labored on plantations.[70] Plantation slaves in the Floridas generally labored under the Anglo-Caribbean/Lowcountry task system, which required slaves to provision themselves and tolerated slave mobility as well as free market and feast days. This system allowed slaves a degree of economic independence and the ability to interact with other slaves and free blacks.[71] In this system some of the slaves were trained in specific skills, but the vast majority were agricultural laborers. Plantation slavery in the Spanish Floridas created a society in which slaves were more independent of white authority and were part of a large and extended network of black friends, family, and associates. The slaves were accustomed to growing their own produce and raising their own livestock as well as doing their own hunting, fishing, and gathering. They were also responsible for maintaining their own quarters. All these skills would prove useful at Prospect Bluff. Likewise the relative social, economic, familial, and religious independence that the plantation slaves were allowed in the Floridas prepared them to coexist in a large and diverse maroon community.

Former slaves from the United States who joined the maroon community closely reflected the expanding plantation world of the Deep South. They were agricultural laborers who had worked in the expanding cotton fields, perhaps the Lowcountry's rice plantations, or, in the case of Louisiana, sugar plantations. These years were a formative period in the westward expansion of American slavery, and many of these former slaves had participated in the brutally difficult work of creating farms and plantations in an environment where few had previously existed. In all probability the former slaves would have traveled to the region from elsewhere with their masters, who kept a watchful eye on all human property. As a result they would have suffered limited mobility and felt the full sting of slavery's oppression.

Those inhabitants of Prospect Bluff who had labored as slaves of the Creek Indians brought useful skills to the maroon community. During this era Creek slavery was becoming increasingly driven by modern agricultural practices and was dominated by an elite section of society.[72] Creek slaves largely cultivated cotton, with women doing the bulk of the fieldwork while also being responsible for domestic duties. Male slaves did the heavier work, such as rearing livestock, clearing fields, building houses, and hunting. This division of labor was based on Creek attitudes toward gender and the appropriate jobs for the sexes. Creek slaves grew their own food and were able to acquire private property. This system was harsher than Seminole slavery but less oppressive than Anglo-American slavery.[73] Unlike Seminole slaves, Creek slaves did not live in separate or autonomous villages but rather lived in close contact with their masters. Intermarriage and manumission were less and less common as Creek racial consciousness changed and came to resemble that of white southerners more closely. The Creek slaves who joined the maroon community were shaped by this world. They had work experiences relatively similar to those of plantation slaves from across the South, with the notable exception that some tasks were allotted differently according to gender. Their self-reliance was more in line with that of slaves who labored under the task system in the Spanish Floridas, and they had more freedom of movement and expression than was typical in the United States. With the exception of blacks who had originally lived as maroons, or as the allies of the Seminoles or Red Sticks, the Creek former slaves had the best set of skills and experiences to survive in the Florida wilderness.

Ultimately the inhabitants of Prospect Bluff brought a wide array of skills and work experiences with them to the Florida wilderness. This combination of skills stood out in comparison with those of other maroon communities, especially at such an early stage, providing Prospect Bluff with the necessary talents and abilities to survive in the harsh and remote wilderness. Of course the community's substantial material wealth and the fact that it was located at a well-built British fort also made survival much easier. When the community's demographics, its members' origins, and their skills are all combined, it becomes clear that in a comparative perspective, an unusually full, balanced, and diverse society had been transplanted to Prospect Bluff. The community started at a point that most maroons normally took generations to reach; from the outset Prospect Bluff was a singularly distinctive example of a stable and healthy maroon community. This fact, in turn, would have shaped how the maroons viewed the world and their community.

Family and Gender

It appears that freedom at Prospect Bluff allowed the members of the maroon community to assert their gendered identities on their own terms in an empowering and humanizing process. Families were an important element in the maroons' understanding of gender. Indeed, families were so central in how the British conceptualized the community that the express purpose of the fort at the time of its construction was to provide a safe haven for the families of the black and Indian recruits while the warriors were in the field. This was further reflected in Cochrane's proclamation and Nicolls's proclamation and rhetoric, all of which explicitly addressed the bonds of family. The British understood the importance of families to potential slave soldiers and used familial rhetoric and promises as powerful recruiting tools. The effectiveness of this policy is evident in Edmund Doyle's complaint that when a number of Forbes and Company's slaves enlisted in Nicolls's army, "their wives and children object of course to be removed from them" and escaped to join their husbands and fathers.[74] The scope of families at Prospect Bluff was further suggested by Nicolls's orders that his black recruits and their families stay together at the fort and await his return and by his careful emphasis that the "free papers" he gave the discharged soldiers extended to their families. In both cases Nicolls made clear that family units were common at Prospect Bluff. Woodbine further emphasized this with his assumption that the community would eventually "consist of about 300 families."[75] He clearly believed that the community was well on its way to becoming a balanced and naturally reproducing society based around families.

Across the hemisphere maroons placed great importance on family, but the vast majority of communities found it impossible to establish them at an early stage, if at all. Demographic instability weakened family ties at most maroon communities, sometimes to the point of complete destruction of conjugal bonds. For example, prior to 1739, the maroons of Jamaica had few women and, proportionately, even fewer children and thus by extension virtually no conjugal families.[76] The same was true in Suriname prior to the mid-eighteenth-century treaties.[77] Maroon communities were survivalist entities that drew from societies with massive male majorities. Even the strongest and fittest young men found it difficult to reach and then live in a maroon community, and the ordeal proved insurmountable for most women and children.

When the most stable and longest-lived maroon communities began naturally reproducing they did so in clearly defined family units that were regulated by custom, religion, and/or law. The importance attached to family was designed to avoid intra-maroon fights over women, help establish viable lineages, lay the foundation for stable communities, and encourage fruitful procreation. Even Bahia's parasitic Buraco de Tatú had apparently organized itself into a series of family-headed households by the time of its destruction.[78] The *mocambo* was certainly not naturally reproducing but clearly aspired to build a foundation based on families, illustrating that even the most militant of maroon communities saw families as the foundation of a stable society. The formation of families was complicated by the frequency of polygamy, which was regarded as a right for important men if they could afford to support multiple wives in maroon communities across the hemisphere, including in Jamaica, Suriname, and Palmares.[79] Because of the relatively balanced demographics and creole backgrounds of the vast majority of the Prospect Bluff inhabitants, polygamy was not only an alien concept but also unnecessary. In most maroon communities, even those that practiced polygamy, the penalty for adultery or wife stealing was almost always death.[80] Regardless of different types of marriages, the creation of families was central in the development of a common identity within any successful maroon community as well as for its long-term viability.[81]

Because of their longevity and success, the maroons of Jamaica and Suriname provide the most data on family structure. In the seventeenth and eighteenth centuries the maroons of Suriname were divided into a series of matriclans. Each matriclan consists of a number of matrilineages further divided into several matrisegments.[82] Marriage, which was frequently polygamous, and childrearing are at the heart of this elaborate web of extended family connections determining status, inheritance, and Surinamese maroon government. In Jamaica prior to the treaties the Leeward and Windward maroons took different approaches to the formation of families, both of which were attempts to overcome highly imbalanced sex ratios while avoiding fights over women. The Windward maroons, who tended to grant women greater political and religious importance, militantly guarded against adultery and emphasized that men had exclusive access to their wives and children.[83] Thus the Windwards sought to overcome demographic difficulties by procreation based on traditional monogamous or polygamous families. The Leewards equally regulated interaction between men and women but relied on a different strategy. It appears that in many cases, multiple men shared sexual access to an individual woman, while one man retained primary rights to her and her children.[84] The purpose of this was the same as with the Windwards: to avoid competition over women and to aid natural population growth. Once demographics became balanced by the middle of the eighteenth century both groups of Jamaican maroons settled into carefully regulated monogamous or polygamous marriages in which men and women were bound together by law, custom, and religion.[85] The result was a naturally reproducing society that quickly developed elaborate structures of kin.

Monogamous marriage was the foundation of the nuclear families at Prospect Bluff, and the institution seems to have flourished within the community. This was demonstrated by the numerous husbands and wives who joined the community together (such as Boatswain and Rose) or the tragic fate of "Black Serjeant-Major Wilson's" wife, who was stabbed and beaten to death by American and Creek soldiers after the fort's destruction because she had refused to flee and leave her husband's side.[86] The strength of families, more generally, was illustrated nearly thirty years later, when Mary Ashley claimed, on behalf of herself and her children, that they were all legally entitled to the "free papers" that had been given to her husband by Nicolls.[87] Mary Ashley felt that her legal bond to her husband—which had been established at Prospect Bluff—was so clear that she inherited his status upon his death.

At Prospect Bluff the former slaves seem to have reconfirmed their commitment to patriarchal nuclear families when beyond white control. The relative ease with which this was accomplished would have inspired no small amount of jealousy among maroons from across the hemisphere and was important to the stability and outlook of the community at Prospect Bluff. At Prospect Bluff husbands, wives, and their children lived and worked together. Parents were able to raise their children as they saw fit, in their own homes and on their own land. An observer recorded that there were "no people . . . more fond of their children, and none so indulgent" as a number of maroon parents, many of whom were refugees from the community.[88] This indulgence was presumably in the eye of the beholder, but what is clear is the existence of intense bonds between parent and child that were able to flourish free from slavery.

At Prospect Bluff the maintenance of families, broader demographic patterns, and general experience of living in an enclave of British subjects had major gendered implications. Perhaps the starkest was the reversal of fortunes for men at Prospect Bluff, which was common in maroon communities across the hemisphere.[89] Fathers and husbands were able to assert their authority over their nuclear families and provide material well-being for them in a process that was central to masculinity during this period. Their masculine identity, as well as that of single men, was further enhanced by their ability to perform military service, to participate in the community's government, and to enjoy the other rights that came with their newly acquired British status. This was a remarkable transformation for men who until recently had been property with few rights and little formal power to control so many aspects of their lives.

Across the hemisphere, life as maroons posed unique challenges for women and mothers in particular. This was most intense in early or desperate communities where women were hugely outnumbered members of warrior bands that did whatever was necessary to survive. In more stable settlements, women's lives became defined by family and work. For example, in the matrilineal clans of Suriname, women's lives were devoted to childrearing, maintaining homes, agriculture, and food preparation, with the mother's family serving as the center of her world.[90] Post-treaty Jamaican maroons lived in communities that were essentially extended families in which women were largely responsible for domestic duties, farming, and childcare and men were warriors and hunters.[91] While these patterns held true for nearly all maroon women across the hemisphere, on some rare occasions women achieved elevated status as political or religious leaders. For example, in the Brazilian interior the Portuguese were forced to make peace with a *mocambo* led by a woman named Filippa Maria Aranha. Aranha had achieved and maintained her leadership position through her great spiritual and magical powers.[92] In the maroon communities of Suriname, women played import political and religious roles as tribal mothers, spiritual mediums, and priestesses.[93] Far and away the most famous maroon woman was Nanny of the Windwards. Much of what is known about Nanny is shrouded in myth and is difficult to verify. What is clear is that prior to the treaties, Nanny, who claimed to be a Coromantee, rose to great prominence among the Windwards because of her Obeah skills (see later discussion), which she used to deflect British bullets, to frustrate her enemies, and in other ways. Nanny was never the leader of the Windwards (that position was always reserved for men), but she was an important political, military, and religious figure, who greatly shaped the Windwards at a vital stage in their early existence and is rightfully remembered as Jamaica's national heroine.[94] As interesting as these prominent maroon women were, they were still exceptions to the rule, which was that the vast majority of maroon women lived difficult lives that were defined in the best case scenario by motherhood and work and, in the worst case scenario, by (sexual) violence, fear, want, reenslavement, or death.

Women at Prospect Bluff did not rise to exalted political or religious positions. This would have been unlikely because when maroon women achieved such status it was as a direct result of African cultural traditions, which would have seemed strange among the almost entirely creole population at Prospect Bluff, if they were known at all. At Prospect Bluff, conversely, women could establish a domestic sphere and create their own version of motherhood; if a woman had children, that was the cornerstone of femininity in societies across the Atlantic world. This was due to the community's material wealth, relative stability, and demographics. In the end it appears that the quality of life for women at Prospect Bluff equaled or exceeded that of women among the most successful and long-term maroons, without as many overtly African influences. Because of the stability, material wealth, fairly balanced demographics, and ideas about British rights and anti-slavery, women at Prospect Bluff enjoyed more fulfilling and empowered lives than did their counterparts in most maroon communities elsewhere in the hemisphere.

Previously, slavery had preyed on the inhabitants' gender identity as a means of asserting control through dehumanization.[95] Now, free in the wilderness of Florida, members of the community could construct and assert their own gender identities in a process that made them into full men, women, and most important, humans. This process complimented Nicolls's message about black humanity and added an extra dimension to the maroons' struggle against their prior condition of slavery. It also shaped how the maroons acted and conceptualized their community.

Culture

Maroon culture, in all of its regional and temporal variations, was a dynamic American, Atlantic, and African diaspora phenomenon that synthesized various African, European, Native American, and creole cultures into something new and unique.[96] This creolization shaped attitudes toward marriage, family, and gender, political organization, religious beliefs, military techniques, food, agriculture, and craftworks. The process by which maroon culture was formed was complicated, uneven, and dependent on numerous variables, including community composition, time, and circumstances. Furthermore, the outcome was seldom a conscious choice, as many maroons sought to recreate what they understood as an African world in the wilds of the Americas.[97] This usually proved impossible because nearly all maroon communities consisted of a diversity of members who, even if all originally from Africa, still represented different cultures as well as the powerful imprint of capture, the middle passage, sale, enslavement, and flight to a maroon community.[98] Thus there was no single version of Africa on which all members of a maroon community could agree but only various real and imagined versions of a distant and mourned homeland. Many maroon communities also attracted creoles and Native Americans, which added further diversity of views to a community's cultural outlook. The gradual creolization of the most successful communities yet again affected their cultural outlook as Africa became an increasingly distant memory in communities that developed their own sense of identity and even ethnicity.[99] All this, once again, was complicated by the fact that males dominated most maroon communities, which undermined a sense of permanence and cultural formation. Ultimately maroon communities were highly adaptive and survivalist entities that required flexibility and fluidity to navigate an endless barrage of demographic, cultural, military, economic, and political challenges.[100] The net result: as hard as maroons sought to re-create Africa, successful communities displayed synthetic cultures.[101]

An examination of a number of prominent maroon communities illustrates the complexity of cultural formation in the wilds of the Americas and provides valuable data to compare with Prospect Bluff. In Suriname the process of cultural fusion is most evident in the maroons' elaborate clan-based system of government and family as well as in the Afro-Surinamese religions practiced by the maroons.[102] In both cases the Surinamese maroons built their traditions on West African culture but not that of one particular culture. In Brazil, Palmares was led by Ganga Zumba for much of its existence. Ganga Zumba was in all probability an Angolan religious or political title and not a proper name. Ganga Zumba's extended family ruled Palmares and its associated villages based on a modified model of African kingship.[103] Further melding of cultures at Palmares can be seen in the community's hybrid Afro-Christian faith, the existence of slavery, family structure, military organization, and dress.[104] Thus even the history of the largest maroon community in the hemisphere was only able to approximate a version of Africa and owed as much of its cultural outlook to numerous Atlantic cultures and a pragmatic willingness to borrow.

In frequently divergent ways, both the Leeward and Windward maroons of Jamaica demonstrated a fusion of cultures that was the result of community composition, time, and adaptability. This can be heard in a distinct Jamaican maroon creole language and can be seen in family structure, elaborate performances and music, attitudes toward gender, food and agricultural techniques, and in the maroons' spiritual attachment to the colonial treaties.[105] The nature and importance of Kromanti Play and Obeah within Jamaican maroon communities is deeply informative from a cultural perspective. Kromanti Play began to emerge in the eighteenth century and is a set of beliefs based on the premise that the natural and spiritual worlds are interconnected, and through these connections, maroons, their ancestors, and their descendants interact.[106] While the term is a corruption of "Coromantee," there is no evidence that it was the direct product of any particular African culture, and in fact Kromanti Play was quickly adopted and added to by maroons of various origins in a process that was central in the development of Jamaican maroon identity.[107] Obeah, which like Kromanti Play was not a direct product of any specific African culture, was a system of beliefs in which religiously powerful individuals attempted to involve spirits in daily life and to communicate with ancestors. Practitioners of Obeah frequently played an important role in maroon politics and society. In both these cases, Jamaican maroons created spiritual practices that borrowed heavily from different African cultures but were tailored to and influenced by their particular New World setting.

Because of the unusual circumstances surrounding the formation of the maroon community at Prospect Bluff, its relationship with Nicolls, and the diversity of its members' backgrounds, the community appears to have diverged from these hemispheric trends as often as it conformed to them. Likewise, because of its brief existence it is impossible to tell whether the community would have gone through a process of cultural and ethnic identity formation similar to that which occurred in the longest-lived and most successful of maroon communities. Nonetheless, the community's greatest divergence from maroon culture elsewhere in the hemisphere was in the relatively weak direct or imagined influence of Africa. The community's population was overwhelmingly creole, and there is no evidence that its African members contributed disproportionately to its cultural life. Nor does it appear that members of the community were seeking to re-create an imagined African world. The community's political system and military organization were inspired by the British, and its economy and material culture were directly shaped by the surrounding environment and British contributions. The maroons' attitudes about gender, marriage, and family appear to have been decidedly creole, and their agricultural techniques were learned among various cultures in the Southeast and circum-Caribbean, which of course would themselves have had African influences. Thus, unlike in many restorationist maroon communities, there is no evidence that the maroons at Prospect Bluff, in either real or fictive terms, harked back to Africa for cultural, economic, military, or political inspiration or legitimacy. Instead the community, particularly after having absorbed Nicolls's message, was a distinctly Atlantic construction that sought legitimacy in its British status, organized itself as an enclave of free and landowning British subjects, and sought to survive using methods that had been learned across the Atlantic world. Thus Britishness was central in the maroons' identity. This does not appear to have been a conscious rejection of African practices but rather the product of demographics, time, their experience with Nicolls, and an intimate and highly observant understanding of the forces that shaped the world in which they found themselves living. Nor is this meant to discount any African influence at all. After all, the inhabitants of the maroon community were descendants of Africa whose outlook would have been shaped in numerous subtle and unsubtle ways by their heritage. Like maroons from across the hemisphere, the community at Prospect Bluff was deeply Afro-American or Atlantic in its cultural outlook.

According to the extant evidence, it does not appear that any single culture was able to dominate at Prospect Bluff. Even though former slaves from the Spanish Floridas and Indian territory held a numerical majority, English was the most common language due to a number of factors. Slaves from the United States made up a substantial percentage of the community's population, while many of the former slaves who had fled from the Creeks, arrived with Seminoles or Red Sticks, or been living as maroons spoke English as a first language or were multilingual. Most significant, many of the former slaves from the Spanish Floridas were either bilingual or spoke English as a first language. The community's political and military leaders clearly spoke English because they were selected by the British for both their skills and their potential to work closely with Nicolls and other British officers. A common language that could be understood by the majority of a maroon community's population was a tremendous attribute and something that the most successful communities aggressively fostered. It allowed for discussion and cooperation on issues from the most mundane or trivial to those essential to a community's defense, government, or survival, while decreasing the chances of internal ethnic or cultural divisions. A common language was also an important step in creating a shared identity. In the case of Prospect Bluff, that identity was primarily British.

As was the case across the hemisphere, religion was central in the community's cultural life. It appears that the majority of the former slaves practiced Catholic or Protestant Christianity prior to joining the community and continued in their religious devotions at Prospect Bluff, as was evidenced by the actions of many survivors.[108] For example, an American observer noted that an "excellent house" was built by refugees from the community to "dance in on Christmas."[109] This example is also evidence of music, musical instruments, and dancing, which would have been a vital form of cultural expression at Prospect Bluff. The dancing and music may well have been influenced by African culture. What is not clear is whether these former slaves had been primarily exposed to Catholicism, Protestant Christianity, or both or were a mixed group; whichever was the case, their style of worship offers a good example of "Afro-Christianity." More detailed evidence comes from the Bahamas, where a group of Prospect Bluff refugees "built a place of worship" in which they were as "comfortable as they can be without a [formal white] minister."[110] This strongly suggests that they must previously have had a black minister or religious leader. These religious activities occurred while the former residents of Prospect Bluff were living in total isolation in the

Bahamas, thus strongly suggesting direct continuity with practices begun at Prospect Bluff. After having been detected by the Bahamian authorities, one of the refugees' first requests was to be formally baptized in the Anglican Church.[111] The rector of Christ Church in New Providence happily agreed to this. Reverend McSweeney, an Anglican clergyman appointed by the bishop of Jamaica, was impressed with the religious practices of the refugees and gave "very good accounts of them."[112] In both examples the survivors were clearly demonstrating a strong Christian faith (Protestant in this case) as well as a deep understanding of the religion. The survivors gathered together for formal worship under the guidance of religious leaders in churches that the community had built. All this would most likely have begun at Prospect Bluff.

The maroon settlement was not an entirely Afro-Christian community. A number of its inhabitants exhibited a devotion and understanding of Native American spirituality and ritual due to their connections to various Indian societies. In the winter of 1816 it was reported that the "negros join the [Red Stick] dance" and later, survivors set up a "red pole . . . in their town and danc[ed] the red stick dance."[113] The Red Stick Dance was a ritualized nativist dance that was central in the Pan-Indian movement inspired by Tecumseh. Knowledge and practice of the dance illustrated an understanding of and adherence to Native religious beliefs. This would have been expected from the former slaves of Indians or those who had lived or worked closely with Indians. While there is no direct evidence of African religious practices at Prospect Bluff, the community's various African members would not have forgotten the religion of their homeland and must have been free to practice their beliefs. These different religions were apparently able to coexist and would have provided the maroons with a tremendous sense of spiritual and cultural fulfillment. However, unlike in many long-lived maroon communities, there is no evidence that the maroons at Prospect Bluff developed any new religious traditions, nor do they appear to have relied on African practices to any major degree. Rather the community's religious outlook was similar to that which would have been found in slave quarters across the Southeast and circum-Caribbean, but on their own terms. Few things would have been more emotionally or intellectually liberating or fulfilling than being able to worship and express themselves spiritually on their own terms, free from any form of white or Indian interference.

It seems that the maroons at Prospect Bluff placed a premium on literacy and education, which was highly unusual from a comparative perspective, as most maroon communities were nonliterate societies in which education was practical and not academic. For example, observers were quick to point out that one of the community's leaders, Cyrus, was literate.[114] Cyrus's literacy was one of the major justifications for his elevated position and would have been a useful skill in dealing with outsiders. Prior to discovery in the Bahamas, the refugees from Prospect Bluff had established a village school in which "merely one of themselves" was serving as teacher.[115] This man, who must have been a former privileged urban slave, and others would most likely have performed the same duties at Prospect Bluff, since it is highly improbable that a school would have been formed and teachers would suddenly have appeared while these people were in isolation in the Bahamas without an earlier precedent at Prospect Bluff. This illustrates the presence of educated individuals, a communal respect for education, and a desire to educate children within the community. It also demonstrates the community's sense of permanence, material prosperity, and confidence; its commitment to its children's welfare, as it took the time to educate them; and perhaps an understanding of the correlation between education and full political inclusion. Few other maroon communities viewed themselves in such a manner. These priorities were born from observing and tasting the power of literacy and education around the Atlantic world. Commenting on a group that included many refugees from Prospect Bluff, the traveler William Haynes Simmons noted that "they are . . . much smarter than their [Indian] owners."[116] Simmons was not commenting on any innate intellectual difference; rather he was struck by the remnants of a community that contained a number of educated individuals and a commitment to learning, which would have struck the traveler as unusual in the wilderness of Florida.

Ultimately, a relatively full and balanced society, certainly when considering the stage of the community's development, emerged at Prospect Bluff. From a comparative perspective this society appeared quickly and without the struggles that most maroon communities were forced to endure during their early stages. Furthermore, the demographics and skills of this diverse group of former slaves provided advantages that few maroon communities had ever enjoyed. These factors, combined with Prospect Bluff's advantageous natural setting and the substantial material contribution made by the British, meant the maroon community was very well positioned to thrive. In this setting families flourished, children were raised and educated, and men and women were free to assert their gendered identities on their own terms. At the same time the community at Prospect Bluff created a distinctive maroon culture because of its particular circumstances and composition. Each of its inhabitants brought expectations and understandings of culture that were shaped by their experiences, age, and gender. Their collective cultural life appears to have been vibrant. And the ultimate goal of protecting their freedom and adhering to Nicolls's message transcended differences that might otherwise have arisen when hundreds of diverse people formed a community in such a short time. At the same time the fact that such a diverse set of former slaves from different societies and systems were able to come together in pursuit of the fullest version of freedom possible speaks to the universality of their pursuit and the extent to which it clearly transcended initial differences. In the end, each of the factors discussed in this chapter shaped how the maroons at Prospect Bluff saw themselves as a community and helps explain many of their actions.

DURING THE maroon community's existence, Prospect Bluff was a hotbed of daily activity. The former slaves built and maintained their homes, tended their fields, hunted, and participated in an exchange economy that impacted the region. Establishing a functioning economy was easier for the Prospect Bluff maroons than was the case for many other communities across the hemisphere. This was because of the scale of British contributions, the advantageous location, and the array of skills and experiences that the maroons brought to Prospect Bluff. Indeed, the settlement at Prospect Bluff was one of the best-supplied maroon communities in history. If the immense defensive advantages of the fort are factored into a comparative analysis, then the community at Prospect Bluff stood virtually alone among maroon communities in being well served by homes, buildings, and defenses. The community's economy was built on this strong foundation.

There was much more to the maroons' economic and daily activities than simply assuring their survival. Through farming, trade, and landownership, the community demonstrated that it was a complete society composed of free landowners who met the economic requirements to be full British subjects. This was an important aspect of the struggle that was being waged at Prospect Bluff and further illustrates the extent to which the maroons were aware of the ingredients of modern freedom and demonstrates the maroons' resistance to slavery as a social system. However, because of its size, location, and conspicuous founding as well as the strong emotions that the community elicited, the maroons found it impossible to live a quiet and undisturbed existence at Prospect Bluff. Consequently the community enjoyed an array of relations with various whites, blacks, and Indians from across the region. As was typical of maroon communities elsewhere, these relations ranged from those of close political, military, and economic allies to those of brutal enemies. A close examination of the Prospect Bluff community's daily life provides a rare glimpse of North American maroons in action. In turn, this glimpse, which becomes more informative in comparative perspective, sheds light on exactly how slave rebels and the enslaved envisioned the daily workings of freedom.

Forging an Existence:
Shelter, Subsistence, and Daily Life

Shortly after the British departure a few reports surfaced claiming that provisions at Prospect Bluff were scarce and that the inhabitants were in a state of near starvation. The vast majority of the extant evidence suggests that this was not the case. Rather such reports were designed to ease American and Spanish apprehensions over what was occurring at Prospect Bluff, and reports such as "an Indian woman [at Prospect Bluff] ate her own child" were simply not true.[1] Fugitive slaves continued to flock to Prospect Bluff until its destruction, and there is no reliable evidence of want, making it clear that the community did not suffer from any severe shortages. In fact quite the opposite was the case: evidence shows that the community enjoyed "arms and ammunition of every kind in the greatest abundance . . . and provisions for their subsistence" that were "not only in abundance but in profusion."[2] This abundance continued until the fort was destroyed in July 1816. Even after the fort's destruction, the Americans reported finding a "great deal of provisions" at Prospect Bluff.[3] The traveler William Hayne Simmons, commenting on a group who included a number of refugees from the community, noted that the "negroes here, both men and women, were, as usual, stout, and even gigantic in their persons."[4] He was describing healthy people thriving in the Florida wilderness.

The maroons' greatest material and infrastructure advantages came when the British left the community in possession of the fort and its enormous store of arms, munitions, supplies, and tools. A British deserter testified that the fort was armed with "Canon[s], 4 12 pounders, one howitzer and two cohorns, about 3,000 stand of small arms, and near 3,000 of powder and ball." A number of slaves returned to their masters from Prospect Bluff and corroborated this testimony.[5] Another eyewitness noted that the fort was stocked with "Indian presents" and Indian corn prior to Britain's departure.[6] When the fort was destroyed in July 1816, American estimates of the "property taken and destroyed could not have amounted to less than two hundred thousand dollars . . . [including] about three thousand stand of arms, from five to six hundred barrels of powder, and a great quantity of fixed ammunition, shot, shells, etc."[7] This was a staggering amount of military hardware.

The Americans found 48 shovels, 26 spades, 55 pick axes, 2 hoes, 1 tin scale, 10 saws, 2 corn mills, various belts and shoes, as well as a myriad of smaller items.[8] Archaeological evidence suggests that since no improvised metal materials or other similar artifacts have been found at Prospect Bluff, the community did not take these advantages for granted, carefully protected its great wealth, and never ran low on supplies.[9] This was wise because a bounty of essential supplies that could not be produced in the wilderness allowed the maroon community to avoid the traditional pitfalls of theft, raids, or overreliance on trade with outsiders, which led to the demise of many maroon communities.[10] Likewise, this material wealth greatly influenced the community's economy, eased efforts at survival, and fundamentally shaped people's outlook and identity because it ultimately allowed the community an unrivaled independence from the outside world and time to concentrate on other matters. Most maroons would have been deeply pleased to possess a fraction of the material wealth of the community at Prospect Bluff.

As ingenious as maroons were at overcoming their physical environment and providing for their defense, there was a long list of essential items that simply could not be produced in the wilderness: guns, ammunition, tools, cloth, pots, and utensils and other items essential for defense, hunting, clothing, the cultivation and preparation of food, and the building and maintenance of shelter. An inability to obtain these goods on a regular basis seriously undermined a maroon community's ability to defend and sustain itself. Maroons might suffer without these goods, but it was much more likely that they would attempt to attain them through trading or raiding. In their initial phase, maroons were largely dependent on raiding plantations for food, tools, weapons, and women. Some maroons were never able to move past this stage and persisted as parasites who scared and antagonized their white, black, or Indian neighbors. More successful maroons, and those whose communities lasted the longest, traded their forest produce for manufactured goods while attempting to minimize raiding.[11] While trade with the enslaved, Indians, free blacks, other maroons, or whites was less violent than raiding, it was almost always illicit. Trade was frequently conducted clandestinely in urban areas, at night on plantations, or deep in the wilderness.[12] And since maroon trading was clandestine, it carried with it a number of potential hazards: colonial governments usually imposed harsh punishments for those caught trading with maroons. Likewise the frequency and results of trade were far from reliable.

Whether raiding or trading, nothing was more coveted by maroons than guns and ammunition. Contrary to suggestions made by colonial artists— who invariably portrayed maroon warriors and hunters as being well armed with quality rifles, sharpened steel knives or hatchets, and ample powder and shot—such items were in desperately short supply in most maroon communities. Firearms were typically so scarce in these settlements that only leaders possessed them, if anyone did.[13] Likewise when maroons owned guns, they frequently found themselves without powder or bullets and were forced to use various objects such as nails, buttons, or rocks as shot. Maroons attempted to overcome this serious defensive liability by carefully maintaining the few guns they owned and, much more important, making weapons with the materials available to them; they made bows and arrows, spears, clubs, and, remarkably, fake guns designed to scare their adversaries.[14] There is no doubt that maroon warriors were highly skilled guerilla combatants who made the most of their limited resources. However, there was no substitute for being heavily armed with quality firearms, let alone heavy canons or howitzers, when it came to fighting imperial armies or other brutal adversaries. This unfortunate cycle of dependence, which frequently resulted in detection and violence along with the persistence of the belief that maroons threatened the plantation complex they had fled, meant that most maroons could never fully free themselves from the plantation society they had sought to escape.[15] This dangerous catch-22 affected large communities in Brazil, the Caribbean, Suriname, and elsewhere, middling settlements across the hemisphere, and small bands of outliers.

The maroon community at Prospect Bluff, materially the wealthiest maroon settlement in the history of the Western Hemisphere, was the single great exception to this trend. The community's immense cache of military hardware made it far and away the most heavily armed community in all of the Spanish Floridas and much of the Southeast. This tremendous defensive and economic strength allowed the community at Prospect Bluff to disentangle itself fully from the surrounding slave societies while spending less time struggling to survive and more time cultivating freedom.

Providing shelter was imperative to any maroon community's survival, and building quality dwellings was an important step in the long-term viability of successful settlements. A maroon community's ability to create shelter depended on the physical setting, external pressures, the availability of materials and tools, and the skills of its inhabitants. Since maroon settlements were generally located in challenging terrain, were undersupplied, and faced brutal military adversaries, many communities struggled to construct quality housing and instead ended up living in caves, poorly constructed shacks, or tents. More successful maroons demonstrated an array of skills at constructing and maintaining their homes. For example, in Cuba the vast majority of *palenques* lived in simple huts made out of fan-palm fronds. Depending on wealth and circumstances, these homes became increasingly elaborate and can be divided into four types, the first humble and the final one the most impressive. They were (1) thatched-roof huts with dirt floors, (2) small huts on piles, (3) huts with walls of royal palm fibers and roofs made of palm, and (4) houses.[16] Jamaican maroons lived in dwellings that ranged from simple huts to large buildings.[17] The Buraco de Tatú consisted of thirty-two well-built rectangular homes that were neatly organized into six rows with a main street running down the middle.[18] Palmares was divided into a number of villages, each of which was filled with hundreds of carefully laid out huts.[19] The *quilombo's* main village contained a church, four smithies, and a council house.[20] Surinamese maroons built breezy rectangular houses with thick walls made from local trees. The roofs were covered with leaves from either *pina* or *tas* palm trees. Most of the houses consisted of one floor with the kitchen below the main floor, but occasionally these homes had two floors, and some even had balconies.[21]

The dwellings of the community at Prospect Bluff compared favorably with those of most maroon settlements across the hemisphere. Only a small percentage of the community lived within the actual British-built fort at Prospect Bluff. As earlier noted, the fort was designed not for permanent residence but as a safe haven for the families of the Indian and black recruits when they were in the field fighting against the United States or as a stronghold if threatened by an attacking force. The fort did contain a number of "comfortable" cabins and barracks as well "large stone houses" that were designed for British soldiers, where some members of the community lived.[22] The majority of the maroons resided next to the fort in quality mud huts in a village facing the river and partially defended by a stockade.[23] Many of these huts had been built under the supervision of British engineers. Vicente Pintado was struck by the considerable number of homes, which extended on both sides of the fort along the river and were neatly organized in lines.[24] The quality of dwellings that the former slaves constructed amazed onlookers. James Sprague described a number of related maroon settlements, dotting the Floridas from St. Augustine to the Apalachicola River, and noted that villages consisted of log and palmetto huts.[25] Simmons described a "new and excellent house [that] was constructed in the Indian manner, without nails—the boards and shingles being lashed to the posts and rafts, by strips of oak, which last a long time," where he "enjoyed, upon a bed of deer skin, a night of refreshing rest"; the house was built by a community that included refugees from Prospect Bluff.[26] The American engineer Capt. H. Young referred to a closely related settlement in West Florida when he recorded that the "cabbins were larger and better constructed then those of the Indians."[27]

Carpenters, Indian slaves, maroons, and slaves who had labored under the task system all had extensive experience building and maintaining housing that was suited to the environment of the Southeast. Furthermore, many of the former slaves had gained valuable experience helping the British engineers build huts at Prospect Bluff. As the population grew, members of the community built additional houses in the village as well as dwellings further afield. Ultimately their settlements and plantations extended nearly fifty miles up the Apalachicola River.[28] The Prospect Bluff community possessed a strong infrastructure from the beginning of its existence.

A maroon community's survival required a regular supply of food, which was difficult. Few communities consistently accomplished this, and some existed in a state of near starvation; others relied on unsustainable plunder. However, some maroon communities provided themselves with an adequate, even healthy, diet. Maroon communities seeking to supply themselves with food wasted little time in getting land under cultivation.[29] Using skills learned in Africa, New World plantations, and from Native Americans, maroon communities grew crops such as manioc, yams, sweet potatoes, bananas, rice, maize, squash, beans, sugar, tobacco, cotton, and other various vegetables, using techniques such as intercropping, crop rotation, and shifting cultivation.[30] They supplemented farming by hunting, fishing, gathering, trading, and theft. In many maroon communities, where demographics made it possible, women took primary responsibility for agriculture and exclusive responsibility for food preparation.

Examples of maroon food production abound from across the hemisphere. Each of the Palmares villages contained fields in which corn, manioc, sweet potatoes, and beans were grown. Fruits, nuts, roots, and berries were gathered from the surrounding forests. The *quilombo*'s men regularly fished and hunted, and domesticated chickens roamed through the villages.[31] Women in Cuban *palenques* grew yams, beans, plantains, and other foods, while men hunted wild hogs and large rodents.[32] The most successful Jamaican maroon communities, such as Trelawny Town, cultivated an array of crops that were supplemented by gathering fruits and vegetables as well as by hunting and fishing.[33] The remarkable population growth enjoyed by the post-treaty Jamaican maroons was in no small way driven by a healthy diet. The maroons of Suriname relied on shifting cultivation (biannually burning down a stretch of forest and cultivating the fertile soil left behind) to grow corn, rice, manioc, peas, pineapples, tobacco, plantains, okra, sugar cane, cotton, and sweet potatoes. In early Surinamese maroon communities the gender distribution of agricultural labor was fairly even. However, as the population of Surinamese maroon communities became more balanced demographically, women were increasingly responsible for agricultural labor while men remained responsible for gathering, hunting, and fishing.[34]

The community at Prospect Bluff lived "in a country where they can procure subsistence with facility."[35] Florida's forests provided an abundance of fruits, nuts, and vegetables that members of the community gathered. Before evacuating, the British forces provided their black and Indian allies with a large amount of Indian corn and salt, which laid a good foundation for self-sufficiency.[36] The Indian corn filled an immediate need as both food and seed, but the salt was ultimately more important. A vital ingredient in the preservation of food and as a mineral essential to the human diet, salt was not readily available in the wilderness. Indeed, salt was one of the most common targets for maroon raiding and trading. The British understood that salt was the only food product required by the community that was available only from an outside source.

In line with maroon communities from across the hemisphere, the settlement at Prospect Bluff relied on horticulture as the backbone of its food supply in an environment that was described by an observer as being "covered with fine rich hammocks, which have a great reputation for fertility."[37] In this promising setting the maroons quickly "commenced several plantations on the fertile banks of the Appalachicola . . . [which would soon have] yielded them every article of sustenance."[38] It seems that this witness was describing the summer of 1816, prior to the harvest in Prospect Bluff's second growing season (the first would have been between the spring and fall of 1815). Other reports suggest that the maroons' farms had been flourishing for some time. These riverfront plantations were primarily devoted to corn, which provided the basis of the community's diet.[39] Grown in neat fields, corn was an ideal dietary staple because it was easy to grow, could be prepared in a number of simple ways, and provided a great deal of sustenance. The two British-supplied corn mills made its preparation that much easier. Potatoes, peas, beans, and other regional fruits and vegetables were grown at the plantations and by the villagers to supplement their diets.[40] One of the first measures that American forces took when beginning the assault on the fort was "destroying their provisions, which consisted of green corn, melons, &c."[41] "Green corn" was southeastern Indian corn that was meant to be eaten when green and should not be interpreted as unripe. Its cultivation reflected the knowledge of former slaves who had lived with Indians. The community may well have received help from its Indian allies when establishing farms. At the same time, former slaves who had belonged to Indians, individuals who had lived as maroons, and those who had labored under the task system all had good agricultural skills that could flourish because the British had left the community with shovels, spades, pickaxes, hoes, saws, and other tools. There is no evidence about the gendered distribution of agricultural labor, but it is likely that women participated in the cultivation of food and it is virtually certain that they were primarily responsible for its preparation. Few other maroon agriculturalists enjoyed such a fortunate combination of past skills, fertile environment, and quality tools in their efforts to feed themselves.

Meat provided a substantial portion of the maroon community's diet. It was even claimed, although with a substantial degree of poetic license, that the maroons at Prospect Bluff "possessed large herds of cattle and horses, which roamed in the forests, gathering their food, both in summer and winter, without expense or trouble to their owners."[42] More realistically, and much to the consternation of their owners, many of the region's cattle were stolen and eaten by the Prospect Bluff community.[43] Shortly after the fort's destruction George Perryman reported that a number of refugees from the community were at Fowltown and were bringing "horses, cattle and hogs, that had come immediately from the state of Georgia and they are bringing them away continually."[44] It seems almost certain that this would have begun earlier at Prospect Bluff.

Like most maroon settlements, the community at Prospect Bluff hunted regularly. The total lack of small animal bones found at the site provides strong archaeological evidence that the community was not desperately foraging for meat but rather was well supplied.[45] The former slaves, who were "strong and expert rifle men," hunted in large and well-organized hunting parties for deer, bears, raccoons, possums, wild birds, and the area's other abundant wildlife.[46] Well-supplied with quality firearms and ammunition, the former slaves had ample tools for hunting with as well as a great deal of prior experience. The area surrounding Prospect Bluff abounds in fish, turtles, snakes, and frogs, all of which were also caught and eaten by the community.

From a comparative perspective, the community at Prospect Bluff lived in relative ease because its inhabitants had an array of useful skills that included carpentry, the ability to farm, hunting, and food preparation and because the British had left behind a tremendous amount of essential supplies that the maroons would otherwise have struggled to acquire. As a result of these advantages, the inhabitants were well fed. Much of the population may well have been better fed and healthier than they had been while enslaved. Tellingly, after they had fled to the Bahamas, many of the community's survivors lived "peacefully and quietly, and have supported themselves upon fish, conchs and crabs which are to be met with in abundance and upon indian corn, plantains, yams, potatoes and peas which they have raised."[47] This was a continuation of what they had done at Prospect Bluff but in a more challenging environment and with fewer resources available to them, because it was accomplished in isolation.

In the best case scenario a maroon community was totally self-sufficient in supplying itself with food and essential goods. In the worst case scenario, a maroon community might rely on raiding or theft, which was a surefire way to attract negative attention. In between these two poles, many maroons traded with outsiders in order to acquire essential goods. Trade brought numerous potential hazards, was unreliable, and perpetually undermined maroons' efforts to disentangle fully from the slave society they had tried to escape. Nonetheless, it was essential; and across the hemisphere maroons exchanged their woodland produce and handicrafts or cash with the enslaved, free blacks, Indians, and even whites.[48] More often than not maroons traded to acquire weapons or tools essential to survival but unavailable in the wilderness. Of course, excepting treaty maroons, trade with maroons was illegal. However, plenty of individuals willingly took the risk, and in virtually every society in the hemisphere, maroons participated in trade networks.

The community at Prospect Bluff established trading networks with Seminoles, Red Sticks, and maroons across the region. Many of these networks had long been established and welcomed trade with the Prospect Bluff community. However, because of the community's great material wealth and self-sufficiency, it could choose its partners carefully. Close ties were maintained with Seminole and black settlements along the Suwannee River and along the Gulf Coast south to Tampa, with the large Seminole and black town of Miccosukee being a common destination for community's inhabitants.[49] It appears that the community traded with Indians and other maroons as part of an exchange economy where goods were the primary currency.[50] The Seminoles and Red Sticks were highly reliant on the Prospect Bluff community for their supply of arms and ammunition, which was the maroons' primary good of exchange. For example, the Spanish worried that the *"chiefs of the neighboring tribes* [travel to Prospect Bluff where they are] *supplied . . . with powder and ball, left for them by the English."*[51] The Spanish officer went on to complain that the brisk trade between the Indians and the maroons undermined the entire economy of Spanish West Florida, because the Indians "having thus obtained a large supply of the kind of powder and ball they most esteemed, they set little value on ours; which, in fact, they view with such indifference, that it is only a chance hunter among those who come to the fort [St. Marks] with venison, wild fowl, &c."[52] The maroon community's economic strength led an employee of Forbes and Company to lament: "Our influence over those Indians [is] dead or expiring."[53] The American Captain Amelung noted that it was not just the economy of rural West Florida that was suffering as the result, but "the inhabitants of Pensacola have suffered, and do now suffer, more than our citizens from the existence of the fort and its garrison."[54] Incredibly, the community's economic might was such that it was regarded as undermining the entire economy of Spanish West Florida. Not even Palmares or the treaty maroons of Jamaica or Suriname exerted such a degree of economic influence over such a large area.

Prospect Bluff's economy had numerous practical and material benefits. However, the former slaves were doing much more than merely assuring their survival when they built and maintained homes, farmed, traded, or hunted: the maroons were demonstrating that they possessed the material basis necessary to be British subjects with full rights. When Pintado interviewed the former slaves he learned that "they had hopes that they would be carried to the English colonies and established there as free men, in virtue of the proclamation of Admiral Cochrane."[55] The former slaves were expressing an obvious desire for freedom as well as their goal of obtaining land, property, and the right to pursue a livelihood. These were key ingredients in the proclamations of Cochrane and Nicolls as well as in the former slaves' understanding of the rights of British subjects. Unable to leave North America, the former slaves transformed Prospect Bluff into a lively community with a bustling economy in which its members owned their own property and enjoyed the fruits of their labor. The careful cultivation of crops, the building of well-crafted dwellings, and the creation of an ordered and prosperous society composed of landowners and defended by British soldiers were far from the acts of outliers desperately attempting to protect a two-dimensional version of freedom in physical and spatial terms. Such a version of freedom could have been achieved by hunkering down at Prospect Bluff, exhausting British-left provisions, and then raiding or foraging for food. Rather the community was emphasizing that it possessed the economic requirements to be British subjects.

Nothing illustrates more clearly the former slaves' commitment to affirming their status through their economy than the maroons' sense of ownership of material possessions and land (or private property more generally). For example, after the destruction of "their fort" it was decided by American forces that the "property captured . . . belong[ed] to runaway slaves" and not the British (who had provided it), the Indians (who had a strong claim to it), or the Spanish (in whose territory Prospect Bluff was located).[56] In other words, the American military recognized that the former slaves owned personal property. This observation was reiterated by a number of onlookers. For example, an employee of Forbes and Company raged that "our Lands [are] in possession of the Negroes."[57] In the wake of the American assault, it was reported that many of the former slaves "left their fields."[58] Each of these observations reflects an awareness that the maroons had a developed sense of the ownership of private property and land in particular. This differed starkly from the attitudes of maroons elsewhere in the hemisphere, who had a strong sense of their territory but a less developed understanding of private property and its implications. Through the creation of order, stability, and material prosperity, based on the cultivation of private property and the control of one's own labor and the fruits of this labor, the former slaves were demonstrating that they had a physical stake in a viable society and that they possessed the material basis required to become full British subjects. When Thomas Jesup, an American officer who possessed a great deal of intelligence about the community, snidely yet informatively referred to the maroons as the "black gentry," he was unwittingly testifying to this.[59] On the one hand, the suggestion that the members of the community were something akin to a well-bred class of landowning European lady and gentleman subjects with full rights was sarcastic. On the other hand, this insult was based on the realization that the community had developed a coherent and organized society consisting of what the maroons contended were landowning subjects. This was a remarkable transformation by people who until only recently had themselves been property.

The Prospect Bluff community of free landowning British subjects enjoyed material wealth that met or exceeded that of nearly any maroon community in Atlantic history. The former slaves understood the interplay between economics and political status because they were astute observers of the societies from which they had originated. Likewise the correlation between freedom and material prosperity was further emphasized by Cochrane's promise of land and freedom in exchange for military service, which had enticed many to join the British. Nicolls's rhetoric and promises were another major reason that the former slaves so fully understood these connections. At Prospect Bluff the former slaves clearly understood that property, power, and political status were all intimately intertwined in a process that had formed the boundaries of the enslavement they were now attempting to redress.

Interaction with Whites, Native Americans, and Blacks

Across the hemisphere maroons had varying relations with whites, Indians, and blacks. While these interactions ranged from mutually beneficial to deeply hostile, they were largely inevitable as most maroons found it impossible to remove themselves fully from the society they were attempting to escape. Due to the Prospect Bluff community's relatively balanced sex ratio, the massive supply of arms and goods left by the British, and its members' efforts to assure self-sufficiency, this maroon settlement was frequently able determine where and when to interact with outsiders. This was a tremendous strength. Like most maroons, those at Prospect Bluff realized that the less attention they attracted the better. However, the community's creation had drawn attention from across North America, and it continued to be centered on a conspicuous structure situated squarely in a volatile Atlantic-borderland region.

Indeed, news about the community spread among the region's whites, Indians, and blacks at lightning speed. For example, in a report that made its way to Governor Early by April 1815 the Creek William Hadridge noted shortly after his visit to Prospect Bluff that "the British are determined to keep the negros. They have joined them as soldiers and they have given them their freedom."[60] The British deserter Samuel Jervais testified in May that the immense amounts of supplies left at the fort were for the "use of the Indians and Negroes, for the purposes, as it was understood, of war with the United States."[61] In a postscript this information was corroborated by a "very intelligent negro man" who had left Prospect Bluff. The military threat was further emphasized in a complaint filed by the residents of West Florida. They lamented that the British had "pledged for [the blacks'] freedom, but they *left* them at Prospect Bluff (after having trained them to military discipline) in possession of a well constructed fort with plenty of provisions and with Cannon Arms and ammunition of every description . . . in profusion."[62] (It is interesting to note that each of these reports made it clear that the former slaves had been granted "freedom" by the British.) Within only a few short weeks a "gentleman of respectability at Bermuda" had heard that hundreds of American and Spanish slaves remained at Prospect Bluff, with "much ammunition, and a good many stands of arms, with some pieces of artillery . . . and that the fort constructed by Colonel Nicholls *would not be destroyed*. . . . No time ought to be lost in recommending the adoption of speedy, energetic measures, for the destruction of a thing held so likely to become dangerous to the State of Georgia."[63] Like many maroon communities, the people at Prospect Bluff sought to isolate themselves from outsiders but aroused such anxiety among whites and Indians that they were never able to disappear quietly into obscurity and be left fully to their own devices.

Logic suggests that throughout the Atlantic world, maroon communities and whites would have been innate and intractable enemies. But this was not the case. Maroon-white relations ranged from violently antagonistic to strategically allied. On rare occasions whites even joined maroon communities.[64] Moreover, a maroon community might have varying relations with different groups of whites at the same time. Most commonly this happened when maroons were employed by an imperial power against its enemies or, internally, when a colony's official policy was deeply hostile to maroons but its subjects nevertheless traded with them.[65]

Brazil represented one extreme. There, maroon-white relations were generally marked by violence and antagonism. *Mocambos* such as the Buraco de Tatú existed in perpetual hostility with whites.[66] Between the 1630s and 1654 Palmares faced regular attacks by the Dutch who controlled Pernambuco. From 1654 until the destruction of Palmares in 1694 the armies of Portugal regularly assaulted the *quilombo*. However, at the same time, Palmares carried out a bustling trade with whites. This lucrative trade even led the region's whites to push colonial officials to break with tradition and sign a treaty with Palmares.[67] Hispaniola's Le Maniel took advantage of its border location and traded extensively, forming alliances with Spanish subjects while simultaneously engaging in frequent warfare with the inhabitants of French Saint Domingue.[68] Another dramatic example of maroons and whites working together against common white enemies had taken place in the 1560s when Sir Francis Drake recruited hundreds of Panamanian maroons to fight against the Spanish.[69]

Most Cuban *palenques* sought to isolate themselves as much as possible; when they interacted with whites it was usually during attacks by military units or groups of *rancheadores* (brutal gangs of slave hunters) or during raids on plantations or towns. On other occasions *palenques* might trade with whites or carry on less orthodox relations, as in the case of a community known as Cobas. Incredibly, members of Cobas tricked local whites in a remote region of the island into believing that they had been sent by a colonial official to open a road through the area. This ruse worked; the road was soon opened, and members of Cobas wasted little time using it to travel along while sowing terror among local inhabitants. By 1818 officials from Havana had become so frustrated with Cobas that they offered to enter into a treaty with the community.[70]

The treaty maroons of Jamaica and Suriname had very complicated relationships with whites. In both cases colonial officials agreed to treaties as a means to pacify the maroons after years of brutal but ineffectual warfare. The maroons of Jamaica and Suriname pledged to stop accepting new members and raiding plantations, were restricted to certain areas, and were given permission to trade with whites under regulated circumstances. The maroons were also forced to allow white colonial officials to interfere with their internal and political affairs and, in the case of Jamaica, to organize into white-led militias that were to aid in the island's defense from internal and external enemies. The Jamaican maroons were much more rigid in their adherence to the terms of their treaties than the Surinamese communities were. However, in each case, for the sake of their own well-being, the maroons had entered into arrangements that placed them in an intermediary position between colonial whites and the slave masses.

As throughout the hemisphere, the community at Prospect Bluff cultivated varying relations with different groups of whites. British whites had the most direct contact with the community. Nicolls, Woodbine, and many white officers and soldiers exerted a profound effect on the maroons, who saw themselves not only as British allies but as full British subjects. William Hambly, an employee of Forbes and Company, had been left in charge of the fort by the British upon their departure. Hambly was a weak man and soon fled from Prospect Bluff and ultimately aided in its destruction. But the British influence, which would continue long after their departure, was overwhelmingly positive and was the single most important reason that the community came into existence and was so strongly positioned.

The maroon community's relationship with the British was unusual in comparative perspective. The first major difference was how closely the community had worked with British officials and the extent to which British actions were responsible for its formation. No large maroon community had been created in such a manner, nor did any community voluntarily work so closely with whites. The second major difference came in the community's knowledge of Nicolls's radical anti-slavery rhetoric, which simply had never happened anywhere else. The third major difference arose when Nicolls made the former slaves full British subjects, which far exceeded the status of even the most powerful treaty maroons. No other community of maroons had come to see themselves as the equals of white male members of a European or American nation-state and empire. The final difference came in the unusual combination of time and space that arose when the British carried out these actions squarely in the midst of territory that did not belong to them. The community at Prospect Bluff was not a pacified community that supported the slave regime located in a colony's hinterlands. Instead it was an empowered anti-slavery community located within a combustible Atlantic-borderland area that divided two other nations' territory. The Prospect Bluff community was the hemisphere's only example of an enclave of radicalized maroons who saw themselves as the equals of the colonial power that had also founded the settlement.

The maroon community largely and self-consciously succeeded in avoiding direct contact with non-British whites, whom residents (rightfully) distrusted. When the British departed from Prospect Bluff, Hawkins reported that the "post at Apalachicola is now under command of negroes, who have orders from Col. Nicolls to arrest every American or Spaniard they find on their lands."[71] The *Niles Weekly Register* corroborated that "Nichols only demand[ed] an oath, that they would never permit [a] white man, except an *Englishman*, to approach [their territory], or leave it alive."[72] Three exceptions to this were the official visits of Urcullo, Pintado, and Felipe Prieto, respectively. The first two missions were almost totally unsuccessful efforts to recover former slaves from Pensacola and occurred prior to the British departure. In the third case Prieto traveled to Prospect Bluff in June 1815 to request supplies for the Spanish Fort San Marcos after the British had left. Prieto's visit ended when he was rudely and forcefully dealt with by the former slaves, who told him to leave immediately.[73] His treatment was further evidence of suspicion and fear of whites on the part of the maroons and the desire to avoid contact with whites. It also demonstrated a clear understanding of the power dynamics present. In the current situation the former slaves were able to dismiss a Spanish officer rudely with total confidence that they held the material and military advantage. This was not a meeting of equals.

Many Anglo-Americans living in the Floridas were intractable enemies of the maroon community. For example, John and James Innerarity, Edmund Doyle, and William Hambly—all employees of Forbes and Company, which had been forced to close its store at Prospect Bluff due to recent events—kept a close eye on the community while hoping for its destruction and the return of their property. Just after the British departure John Innerarity sent a report to Forbes that illustrated the regional economic and military power of the community, its ownership of the land around Prospect Bluff, and its "influence" over the Indians. Innerarity wrote: "I have hopes that a good many of our negroes will return from Appala. as soon as they can find an opportunity." Accordingly, he planned to send Doyle "to Appalacha. and will put every engine in movement to bring back with him . . . as many of the negroes as he can persuade to return. He will also try to regain our influence with the Indians, and to pave the way to the reestablishment of our Store there. This however will be impossible to do until this hornets' nest of negroes is broke up."[74] Doyle did travel to Prospect Bluff, but he returned empty-handed after having spoken to a number of the former slaves, who were happy to admit that "they were seduced from their Masters" and that the only ones who might possibly return were those who "voluntarily" chose to do so.[75] According to Doyle, Nicolls and Woodbine had corrupted the minds of the former slaves against their masters and made it unlikely that any would return. As Doyle's visit also illustrates, the maroons continued to be so confident in their freedom and status that they were able to dismiss their powerless owners unceremoniously when standing face to face. In November 1815 John Innerarity, with a twinge of paranoia, noted of the maroons that "such is their hostility to all intercourse with this place [the Forbes and Company trading house] or any one belonging to it, that a death like silence prevails as to what is passing there. . . . [If it is destroyed] order and tranquility will soon be reestablished. It will give new life and vigor to this country."[76] Even while trying to distance themselves from the outside world, the maroons, from a white perspective, had cast a shadow across the region that was sapping West Florida of life. James Innerarity spent much time in the wake of the American invasion in the summer of 1816 clamoring for "any news that you [his brother John] may have from Appalachicola, about the Negroes, the temper of the Indians, the prospects or possibility of forming peaceable settlements."[77] William Hambly, who had the most intimate knowledge of the community's strengthens and weaknesses and "hoped the negroes will be routed out of their nest before long," had been forced by the spring of 1816 to take "refuge from the fury of the Blacks and Lower Towns" in an American camp while trying to encourage the Creeks and Americans to attack the maroon community.[78] The repeated use of the word "nest" by the community's closest white observers was telling. This image suggested a highly organized, industrious, and vibrant community centered on a clearly defined space. It also suggested a frightening military foe able to unleash a deadly and coordinated assault if threatened. The best thing to do in such a situation was to keep a safe distance. The fear was mutual, as the community recognized that the employees of Forbes and Company were its enemies and wisely went to great lengths to protect itself from them.

White Americans similarly clamored for information about events at Prospect Bluff. Benjamin Hawkins, through a steady series of reports based on the testimony of Indians in the vicinity of Prospect Bluff, provided other American officials with a wealth of information about the maroon community. Hawkins also kept up a great deal of pressure on the Creeks and Seminoles to return fugitive slaves or to attack Prospect Bluff.[79] However, the first and only time that white Americans got a close up view of the community came during the final assault on Prospect Bluff. With few exceptions, the nearest that American and Spanish whites got to the community was through rumors or secondhand information. The community was aware of the advantages of avoiding contact with whites (advantages that had been reiterated by Nicolls prior to his departure), and did so effectively.

Across the Americas, maroons and free or enslaved blacks had varying relations that defy easy generalization. For example, many maroons carried on a mutually beneficial trade with the enslaved or free blacks. Likewise, the enslaved and free blacks frequently provided maroons with intelligence and encouragement in their struggle to survive in the wilderness. This often occurred when maroons paid clandestine visits to plantations to visit friends, family, or associates. Yet desperate maroons also violently preyed on free and enslaved blacks in a process that produced a great deal of black animosity toward the communities. Because of this and reasons that included rewards, torture, or personal feelings, many free and enslaved blacks provided white officials with information about maroons.[80] Black cooperation against maroons did not stop with intelligence, as many anti-maroon militias contained black soldiers.[81] One of the most remarkable examples of this comes from Suriname, where units of black loyalists known as Rangers developed a reputation for their anti-maroon hostility and brutal effectiveness in fighting against the communities.[82] Another source of tension involved maroon raids to acquire enslaved or even free black women. At face value, such actions appear to be noble efforts to liberate women from enslavement. In reality maroon men were usually motivated by more practical considerations. To a woman being "liberated," such an experience would have been a frightening kidnapping that ended in a remote and perhaps desperate encampment of warrior men who were culturally or ethnically different from her. Husbands, children, families, and friends left behind felt someone close them had been cruelly abducted by a group of people who now deserved their hatred.

Whites disliked maroons primarily because they feared slave flight and rebellion.[83] While the connection between maroons and large-scale slave rebellions remains hazy, clearly the very existence of maroons inspired hope among the enslaved, many of whom aspired to join existing communities or to form new ones. However, maroons were wary of would-be new members or of new communities. Because of concerns about things such as demographics, ethnic tensions, treaty obligations, limited resources, or fear of attracting attention, few communities accepted new members lightly, and many turned newcomers away. Even when admitting new members, these fears and legitimate concerns over spies led nearly every major maroon community in colonies such as Jamaica, Suriname, Cuba, and Brazil to require new members to serve a probationary period that frequently resembled domestic slavery.[84] Due to the strong influence of African culture, in which slavery was an acceptable institution, some individuals in Palmares and Jamaica's Leeward and Windward communities remained enslaved for much or all of their lives.[85] Many communities that were willing to admit new members still chose to limit the number of new recruits they accepted. For example in Jamaica in 1735, three hundred Windwards sought to join the Leewards but were refused because of fears of losing resources and attracting white attention.[86] This stood in stark contrast to the Leewards' earlier actions, in which they added greatly to their numbers by incorporating other smaller maroon groups.[87] At this particular time the Leewards needed to control carefully the number of newcomers accepted. With their rigid adherence to their treaties, not only did the post-1739 Jamaican maroons refuse new members, but their soldiers worked closely with white colonial officials to hunt fugitives and brutally suppress slave rebellions.[88] This can be seen clearly in the ferocity with which the Jamaican maroons assisted the colonial regime in suppressing the Tacky Revolt in 1760. Such behavior and the treaty maroons' growing ethnic identity—which emphasized the differences between themselves and the enslaved, whom they looked down upon—led to increasing animosity between the maroons and the enslaved, who derisively referred to the maroon communities as "the King's Negroes" and largely considered them enemies.[89] In Saint Domingue a number of maroons aided the French in their war against Toussaint and the slaves during the Haitian Revolution.[90] Such tensions were less developed in Suriname, where the colony's maroons continued to welcome fugitives regardless of the treaty stipulations and generally enjoyed more positive relations with the enslaved.[91] Finally, hostility between different maroon communities was not uncommon. For example, in eighteenth-century Suriname the Boni maroons were violently driven away by a preexisting community, as were the Paramakkaners a century later.[92] Ultimately maroon-black relations were varied and were shaped by local realities more than by blind adherence to racial solidarity.

Because of their material resources, reliable access to food and trade, strong physical position, relatively healthy demographics, heterogeneous population, and intellectual outlook, the community at Prospect Bluff did not seem to suffer from the most common concerns about attracting new members, nor did they look down on the enslaved as somehow different. Consequently the maroon community enjoyed largely positive relations with free and enslaved blacks. This was the case in the community's relations with blacks who did not live at Prospect Bluff, including the handful of its residents who had volunteered to return to their masters or freemen who returned to white society. For example, Ned, a "freeman of color," spent about a month at Prospect Bluff in late 1815. Ned provided the American armed forces with a detailed account of the fort and the political organization of the community, as did Doyle's "Carpenter Tom" after his voluntary return.[93] The community was also betrayed by Louie, a former slave from Mobile, who voluntarily returned to his master in the spring of 1815 after a few months at Prospect Bluff.[94] It was difficult to anticipate who would betray the community, but given the steady flow of diverse free blacks and fugitive slaves who joined the settlement as well as the maroons' aggressive recruitment efforts, it appears that the maroons turned away few if any blacks who made their way to Prospect Bluff. There is no evidence that the community forced newcomers to serve a probationary period, nor does it seem likely that the maroons were overly concerned about demographics, resources, ethnic tensions, or attracting attention, since the community was so unusually well situated and had such uncommon origins. Indeed, the fact that the maroons of Prospect Bluff continually went out of their way to recruit and raid for new members strongly suggests that they had few misgivings about adding people. This attitude about accepting new members draws out an important distinction between the case of Prospect Bluff and maroon communities from elsewhere in the hemisphere. In particular this distinction speaks to the fact that the Prospect Bluff maroons saw themselves as resisting slavery as a social system. Likewise these raids and flight by would-be members make it likely that the community maintained ties with those who remained enslaved. Such people would have been deeply inspired by tales of the maroons at Prospect Bluff, and given from how slaves from far afield had fled to join the community, it is apparent that word of its existence was widespread among the slaves of the Southeast.

The community at Prospect Bluff maintained ties with numerous maroon and Afro-Indian settlements across the Floridas from which some of its residents had originated. Prior to its destruction many of the inhabitants of the community spread out across West Florida and joined maroons near Tampa.[95] Others had "gone to Savannah (alias St. Josephs) River in East Florida."[96] The St. John's River, which the author mistakenly called the "St. Josephs," had been home to numerous maroons for many years. Sometimes these moves were permanent, while at other times they were made by trade or diplomatic delegations. In addition, members of other maroon communities would have traveled to Prospect Bluff for permanent or temporary stays. Ultimately the people of Prospect Bluff enjoyed more uniformly positive relations with blacks of different status than was often the case elsewhere in the Americas.

Not surprisingly, maroon-Indian relations, in all their hemispheric variations, were no less complicated. In fact many long-lived maroon communities owed their origins, to some degree at least, to black and Indian cooperation. For example, many maroon communities in colonies such as Jamaica, Mexico, Cuba, Brazil, and Venezuela were initially formed when fugitive African slaves joined Indian communities.[97] Indeed in one of the first recorded cases of marronage, the governor of Hispaniola complained about slaves escaping to the Taino Indians in 1502.[98] Such communities were generally formed as marriages of convenience as both groups of people realized that there was strength in numbers in their struggle against whites. These interactions frequently led to racial and cultural intermixing, such as in the cases of the Black Caribs of Dominica and St. Vincent, the Moskitos of Honduras, or the Trios of Suriname.[99]

As many colonial populations increasingly became numerically dominated by whites and blacks at the expense of Indians over the course of the seventeenth and eighteenth centuries, maroon-Indian relations became more complicated. Sometimes maroons and Indians continued to live together or at least trade and interact. For example, excavations at Palmares suggest a steady Indian presence. However, this probably came in the form of Indian women who were forced to join the *quilombo* to alleviate the community's demographic imbalance.[100] While this would have angered Indian men, it was common wherever maroons and Indians existed in close proximity to each other. Across the hemisphere a wealth of Indian material goods found at maroon sites illustrates that maroons were trading or raiding for such goods or had Indian residents.[101] Because of land pressure, fights over women, and colonial policies of "divide and rule," many maroons and Indians had hostile relations that frequently turned violent. This was most widespread in Suriname, where for much of the seventeenth and eighteenth centuries the Indians of the interior resented the appearance and behavior of maroons, with whom they frequently warred.[102] Such animosity was harnessed by whites in Suriname, Guyana, Brazil, Mexico, Venezuela, Colombia, and Peru when colonial officials employed Indians to hunt maroons or incorporated Natives into colonial militias.[103] For example, officials in Jamaica imported Indians from Central America to track and fight against maroons prior to 1739. In 1763 the universally despised Buraco de Tatú in Brazil was destroyed by a mostly Indian auxiliary militia, as Palmares had been in 1694.[104] While maroons and Indians both suffered at the hands of white oppression, a host of unique variables shaped their individual community responses. Sometimes these groups found themselves on the same side and coexisting peacefully, while on other occasions they competed for resources and fought in violent rivalries. The community at Prospect Bluff was a microcosm of this array of relations, as it enjoyed excellent relations with some Indians, had fluctuating relations with others, and was locked in a bitter struggle with yet another group of Indians.

Nearly all the Seminoles and Red Sticks left Prospect Bluff in the weeks after the British departure, dispersing to villages across the Floridas and leaving the former slaves in charge.[105] The Seminoles and Red Sticks did so to protect their communities against increasingly aggressive American encroachments. The maroon community continued to maintain close diplomatic, military, social, and economic ties with Seminoles and Red Sticks, and members of both groups frequently visited Prospect Bluff. Andrew Jackson complained about the alliance between "this banditti [the maroons] and the hostile Creeks [Red Sticks]" that sent recruiting parties into Georgian and Creek plantations and threatened the safety of the southern frontier.[106] Even more ominously, Duncan Clinch learned that a Seminole war party, originating near the confluence of the Flint and "Chatahoouche" Rivers, had captured two Americans and was taking them to the "Negroe Fort."[107] Days later it was reported that the community's leader had sent an American scalp to the "Fowl Town, Mickasooka and Seminole Chiefs."[108] Members of the maroon community traveled to Indian villages for stays that ranged from days to permanently, especially in the wake of the final American assault on Prospect Bluff, when it was reported that "many of them . . . [have] gone over to the Seminoles, on hearing of our [American] approach," or in the case of the refugees who ended up at Miccosukee.[109] The maroon community enjoyed equally positive relations with other groups of Native Americans, such as a renegade group of Choctaws who remained at the fort and served as a vital trading link.[110]

Generally the community could count on the fidelity of its Native American allies, such as the Red Sticks Kinache and Peter McQueen, who never ceased to regard the settlement as an invaluable ally and trading partner.[111] The decentralized political culture of southeastern Indians meant that groups were subject to varying pressures and, on occasion, placed their own community interests before those of others. This became more likely when the Indian leaders were subjected to unrelenting pressure by men such as Hawkins, who warned them to "get rid of the negros without delay or their masters will be after them and involve you in difficulties. If they come you will lose more land."[112] Sometimes they relented, such as when the Seminole chief Bowlegs submitted to Spanish pressure (and a reward of 50 pesos for adults and 25 pesos for children) and captured and returned 27 of the 90 former slaves from the Mosquito Coast who had joined the community.[113] Although Bowlegs had black allies and many blacks lived in his community, he came to resent the negative attention that the maroons were generating for the area and was no longer able to resist pressure to act. Bowlegs came to resent this miscalculation bitterly when he became the leader of hundreds of refugees from the maroon community who formed the core of his force in the First Seminole War.[114]

The maroon community at Prospect Bluff was part of a large network of interconnected Indian and black settlements that had dotted the region's landscape for many years. Its members expertly traversed the Florida wilderness along well-worn and busy paths that connected maroon and Indian villages. The traveler Simmons described how on one such path, "owing to the dullness of our horses, night overtook us on the road; and though there were several Negroes going the same way, who had often traveled it, there was no one but my guide, who, after it became dark, seemed to know the route."[115] These paths were so well trodden by the maroon community and their allies that prior to the American assault on the fort, Hambly recommended trails be blocked off by American and Creek soldiers before "the Bluff is attacked for it would require a considerable force to rout them from the Seminoles."[116] Hambly proved prophetic on this point; the First Seminole War was indeed largely an American operation to destroy the refugees from Prospect Bluff who had joined the Seminoles after the destruction of the British-built fort in July 1816. Following the fort's destruction a number of wagons were found at Prospect Bluff, which would have been used for transportation along these paths.[117]

The maroons relied heavily on water transportation, a vital means of movement that allowed them easily to maintain connections with black and Indian settlements many miles away. After the fort's destruction the American inventory of captured goods included one schooner, one cutter boat, one big boat, and three flats.[118] These boats were donated by the British or were left over from the evacuation of Pensacola, when dozens of vessels were stolen by the fleeing British and the fugitive slaves. From Prospect Bluff expert black sailors were "*organised as Pirates,* have Several Small Vessels well armed, and some piracies that lately occurred in the lakes are supposed to have been committed by them."[119] In the summer of 1816 an American officer noted that members of the maroon community who had traveled to the St. Johns River "have a schooner and several large Boats to make good their retreat, if not intercepted by Sea."[120] From the fortified base at Prospect Bluff, the community's reach extended for many miles in every direction along land and water routes.

The maroon community, "by whom, the Indians themselves, were kept in awe," was a bitter enemy of the American-allied Creeks, who never ceased to work for its destruction. Conditions at and around Prospect Bluff were so combustible that James Innerarity speculated: "We must look for another Creek War, which will only end with the extermination of that Nation . . . [and] the recovery of the Negroes . . . might be hastened on this account."[121] In September 1815, only weeks after the British departure, Benjamin Hawkins ordered a raid against the community that was led by the Creek chief William McIntosh and roughly two hundred of his warriors.[122]

The attack was repulsed by the community but was the first major effort to destroy it. The raid, which lacked official sanction but was approved of by American officials when they became aware of it, was deeply informative to both sides. The Creeks and white Americans were made more aware of what a well-prepared and formidable military antagonist awaited them at Prospect Bluff, while the community was now more cognizant than ever of the immediate threat posed by the United States and its Indian allies. At the ceaseless instigation of the Americans, the Creeks continued violently challenging the community and its allies. The Creeks hated the community at Prospect Bluff for the same reasons that white southerners did: it threatened their racial sensibilities while undermining their economy and security.

With the notable exception of its unique ties with the British, the community at Prospect Bluff had varying relations with peoples of all races. At the same time, the maroons at Prospect Bluff were unusually welcoming to new members and more able than was normal to determine with whom they interacted. These maroons and people with whom they interacted came from a world in which race was deeply complicated, and individuals were as often motivated by self-interest or practical considerations as by blind adherence to racial solidarity. Accordingly, as was typical across the hemisphere, the maroons' relations with outsiders varied greatly. This range of relations illustrates that the maroons were shrewd realists who knew how to read people's intentions and then act accordingly. For example, the community created deep anxiety among most whites, and yet their greatest allies and benefactor were white Britons. Likewise members of the community fought and died alongside Seminole and Red Stick allies in their simmering war against the Creeks.

Examination of the Prospect Bluff maroons' cultural and daily lives tells us a great deal about the aims of slave rebels and slave consciousness more generally. How the former slaves chose to live at Prospect Bluff, when totally free and while enjoying material comfort, strongly suggests that such conditions were what slaves conceptualized as normal or even ideal. Likewise, this evidence suggests that other slave rebels may well have aspired to create conditions similar to those at Prospect Bluff. Finally, the example of Prospect Bluff illustrates the extent to which slaves were capable of cultivating their freedom on a daily basis. Thus, the everyday aspects of life at Prospect Bluff were not a mundane aspect of the maroons' quest for complete freedom, less important than their military or political struggle. Rather the maroons' cultural and daily lives were an intimate part of their broader goal of achieving complete freedom based on their understanding of the world in which they lived.

9 ⇒ Political and Military Organization

IN A SENSE the maroons had achieved freedom as soon as they escaped their bondage and certainly by the time they had arrived at Prospect Bluff and begun to form a community. However, the primary goal of the community was much more than achieving freedom by escaping to the Florida wilderness and carving out a simple survivalist existence. Rather the maroons at Prospect Bluff sought to achieve a multi-dimensional version of freedom. Central to this process was claiming their perceived rights as British subjects. As was evidenced by the community's daily activities, the actions of its refugees during the First Seminole War, the case of Mary Ashley and Susan Christopher in Cuba, and the behavior of the refugees in the Bahamas, the "British blacks" at the fort had stuck to the cause of defending their perceived rights as British subjects as promised to them by Edward Nicolls and formalized in their "free papers." As a result, the maroons had claimed their freedom in physical, spatial, economic, gendered, intellectual, and cultural terms in a process that had gone a long way in liberating their bodies and minds. The maroon community's political and military organization made another bold statement of freedom and autonomy that was shaped by Nicolls's anti-slavery ideology and the former slaves' belief in their British status.

The specifics of the community's political and military structure bore some similarities with but more differences from examples from across the hemisphere. The community's perceived British status was far and away the most important difference between the Prospect Bluff community's political freedom and that of other maroons. Knowledge of Nicolls's anti-slavery ideology allowed the maroons to believe that they had achieved full political and legal inclusion and equality within the British Empire. As a result, the community at Prospect Bluff defined its political freedom in distinctly modern and ideological terms, which was unusual in comparative perspective. This claim to the fullest set of rights and highest standards of political and legal inclusion in the contemporary Atlantic world placed these maroons in line with the most advanced liberationist movements of their time and spoke volumes about their desire to wage a rebellion against slavery as a social system. Closely examining the community's government and political outlook provides a valuable window on how slaves understood contemporary definitions of political freedom as well as on their broader political consciousness. What emerges is a clear picture that the maroon community came to view itself as a complete polity of British subjects. In turn this picture is perhaps the single best opportunity to view the political consciousness of North American former slaves in action, free from any restraints, on their own terms. One of the community's leaders, Garçon, testified to the power and centrality of this belief when, with his last words on earth, he told his American and Creek executioners that "he fought under British colors."[1]

Maroon Government in Comparative Perspective

The particulars of maroon government in the Atlantic world varied according to local circumstances, size, stability, cultural influences, and practical considerations, with defense and survival looming the largest. Accordingly, communities might be organized as centralized states, loose or shifting federations, or remote bands if they were not destroyed shortly after their creation.[2] Early maroons feared internal disorder, spies, violent adversaries, and the consequences of failure, but they lacked developed institutions for maintaining social control. As a result, in such communities individual leaders tended to consolidate a tremendous amount of centralized power over a group's government and military, power that could be wielded brutally to assure order.[3] These and later leaders tended to have the best houses, material goods, and diets as well as multiple wives.[4] Many of these early leaders claimed to have been royalty in Africa or were powerful religious figures, using these characteristics to justify their rule. By the eighteenth century most communities came to be governed by creoles, who had frequently been born in the maroon community and styled themselves "captains," "governors," or "colonels."[5] This reflected both demographic changes and a growing maroon belief that the best leaders were those who most fully understood the broader world in which a maroon community was situated. By the time that maroon settlements had reached this stage, most had developed more advanced institutions for governance with less authority concentrated in the hands of a supreme leader.[6] Usually the result was a degree of consultation or power sharing as well as increased potential for upward mobility among particularly skilled and successful individuals.[7] As was the case with so many other aspects of the internal workings of maroon communities, the most successful communities blended African, European, and Indian ideas, in this case about government, with a shrewd realism and knack for survival. This was the case even when communities sought to construct a purely "African" political system.

A number of examples support these generalizations while providing data to compare with Prospect Bluff. Because of the high premium placed on defense, and owing to their difficult environment and relatively small numbers, Cuban *palenques* tended to be led by military commanders who were referred to as "captains."[8] While little is known about the internal dynamics of *palenques*, it appears that these captains were elected or chosen based on their courage, cunning, local knowledge, and most important, military abilities. Captains were skilled warriors whose primary duty was to coordinate a *palenque*'s defense. Once chosen, they had dictatorial powers.[9] Thus it seems that the conditions Cuban *palenques* faced did not favor the development of expansive political systems. Saint Domingue's two most famous examples of marronage, those led by Makandal in the mid-eighteenth century and the border community of Le Maniel, provide two different examples of maroon leadership. While the extant evidence is sketchy, Makandal apparently rose to prominence among a loosely and widely dispersed array of mobile followers through his magical powers and ability to poison, both of which he learned in Africa.[10] While Makandal did not rule a sedentary community, through his excellent skills as a leader, for the better part of two decades he coordinated the actions of people across a large swath of territory while instilling terror in his enemies. An equally scanty amount is known about Le Maniel's internal dynamics, but it is clear that the community had an organized political system capable of providing for its defense, establishing a flourishing yet (prior to 1785) mobile community and, most tellingly, negotiating a treaty with both Spanish and French officials.[11] This demonstrated a high degree of political sophistication and understanding of colonial politics—a hallmark of the most successful maroon communities and their leaders.

The political system of Palmares provides important comparative data, particularly involving maroon "monarchies." The best evidence about Palmares's government pertains to the rule of Ganga Zumba in the second half of the eighteenth century. While it is likely that Ganga Zumba was a religious or political title rather than a proper name, this man ruled over Palmares and its confederated villages as an African-styled king. African-inspired monarchies were common among maroons; other examples include Venezuela's "el Rey Miguel," Colombia's "Rey del Arcabuco," and King Bayano in Panama.[12]

The Palmares monarchy, like those in other maroon communities, was not based solely on an institution from any single African kingdom. Even though a majority of Palmares founders were from Central Africa (Angola in particular), the *quilombo*'s political system was a synthetic approximation of different real and imagined African systems that had also been influenced by European and Indian practices. This was because of the diversity of African cultures represented within the community, the extent of creolization that had occurred within the *quilombo* (for example, it is likely that Ganga Zumba was born at Palmares), and the need for adaptability to overcome internal and external challenges. Nonetheless, Ganga Zumba oversaw an organized and efficient political system in which he was supported by a royal lineage. While he consulted closely with the heads of the confederated villages, Ganga Zumba was not elected by these men, nor was he the leader of a republic, as has been alleged. Palmares's political system is best understood as an Afro-Brazilian creation that had evolved to deal with a litany of challenges and realities.[13]

The maroons of Suriname adopted another variation of maroon government. When fugitive Surinamese slaves began to escape to the colony's forests and swamps in the late seventeenth century and first half of the eighteenth century, they generally did so in groups composed of Africans of various ethnicities. These early maroons had the daunting task of trying to survive in a difficult environment and facing an onslaught of merciless white, Indian, and occasionally black adversaries. As a result Surinamese maroon communities such as Saramaka were led by authoritarian wartime leaders during this early period. Another example of strong centralized leadership was the dictatorship of Boni, who led the Aluku maroons. Boni's taste for brutal discipline was matched by his skill as a war leader.[14] This was acceptable because the early Alukus lived a mobile and precarious existence that necessitated such a system. When these communities became more secure and established they developed more governmental institutions with less power concentrated in the hands of one individual.[15]

Central to the political development of Surinamese maroon communities was the formation of tribes. This occurred around 1730 when four groups of runaways began to form separate tribes that would eventually be followed by two more.[16] This process of political development was hastened by the stability that was ushered in with the treaties of the 1750s and 1760s and led to the formation of similar political systems in each of the six tribes.[17] Surinamese maroon government was based on a system of family lineages. The matriclan is the central unit in this system, in which all members can trace their origins to a common ancestor. Matriclans shared territory as well as a particular relationship to the spiritual world. Matriclans are then divided into matrilineages, which in turn are subdivided into several matrisegments. Villages, which are usually inhabited by members of the same clan, are led by two or three *kabiten* (headmen). Finally each tribe is led by a *gaanman* (paramount chief) whose position is hereditary through the matrilineal line. The *gaanman* consults with a council of elders whose decisions factor prominently into policy. This political system has proved remarkably resilient and is little changed today. While the system is clearly rooted in Africa, it is not a perfect replica of any specific African culture; rather it is borrowed from various West African cultures that have been fused to a small degree with European and Indian practices and then further shaped by the realities of life in Suriname. Thus the government of Suriname's maroons is best regarded as a highly developed and sophisticated familial-based and African-inspired tribal system.

Jamaica provides a final variation of maroon government to compare with that of Prospect Bluff. Due to a host of internal and external challenges, Jamaica's earliest maroons were led by men with dictatorial power who based their rule on their success as warriors and military strategists. Sometimes the power of these men also had a religious dimension, and at other times Obeah men and women came to play a prominent role in a community's government.[18] This continued with the formation of both the Leeward and Windward maroon communities around the turn of the eighteenth century. Differences soon became clear in the political organization of the two groups of maroons. In the west the Leewards lived in a more autocratic and centralized kinship-based polity that was inspired by the Ashanti.[19] To the east the Windwards reflected an outlook that was more Indian in nature and were organized in loosely confederated villages with less rigid leadership structures and a greater political and religious role for women.[20] During the wars of the 1720s and 1730s the Leewards came to be led by Cudjoe.[21] Cudjoe had inherited this position from his father and used a web of family connections and his own forceful personality to cement his rule.[22] Ultimately both groups created political systems that drew from their members' collective heritages and experiences while emphasizing the importance of military preparedness, stability, and order. In both cases multiple African cultural practices were clearly present, but so were European and Indian influences as well as the effects of shrewd realism and practicality. Given the fact that the British government preferred to sign treaties with both groups in 1739, rather than continue to fight them, it is fair to say that each system served its community well.

Life under the treaties greatly altered the Jamaican maroons' political systems. The treaties called for substantial interference in the maroons' political, military, and legal affairs by white colonial officials. Two of the most prominent treaty requirements were, first, that each maroon village was to have a court that was headed by a white superintendent, who also ran the community's administration; and second, maroon soldiers were organized into units that were led and trained by white officers.[23] Within this system, the communities were meant to be led by their own chiefs, but in reality the treaties drastically undermined the maroons' political effectiveness and led to a decline in discipline and centralized authority.[24] Colonial officials were worried about the decline of centralized maroon power because it undermined the communities' ability to police the island's slaves. The colonial response was to push for more white control within the maroon communities, to which the maroons posed little objection.[25] As a result each community continued to have black chiefs and, in principle, an independent political system, but the ability of these men to wield power and authority over a distinct polity was a shadow of what it had been prior to 1739. In the end the Leewards and Windwards had traded political independence for safety and stability. In each of these cases, maroons formed governments that reflected their members' prior experiences and cultural outlook but, more important, practical decisions based on survival and stability.

Government at Prospect Bluff

No maroon community, including the treaty maroons of Suriname and Jamaica, conceptualized themselves as full subjects of a nation state or its empire with corresponding rights, and thus no community built its political system on such a modern and ideological foundation.[26] Indeed few people of color, regardless of their circumstances, would have made such a claim anywhere in North America at this point in time, because very few people of color found themselves exposed to such a unique combination of forces, ideas, and opportunities. The fact that free people of color from Spanish East and West Florida chose to join the British further supports this claim. Because of these opportunities, the Prospect Bluff maroons were able to create a nuanced and sophisticated version of political freedom that simply would have been impossible in other maroon communities or even formal free black communities. This was a fundamental and profound difference between the community at Prospect Bluff and all other maroon communities across time and space and tells us much about the political consciousness of slaves, because there is no reason to believe that other North American slaves would not have behaved in a similar manner if presented with the same opportunities. Building on the foundation of Nicolls's rhetoric (which made it possible for the maroons to believe that they were capable of possessing such rights, status, and equality) and their "free papers," the people at Prospect Bluff regarded themselves as a complete polity and a sovereign enclave of British subjects. This statement is supported by the community's words, actions, symbolic assertions, territorial claims, and jealous life-long attachment to the status of British subjects as well as by its political system, economy, and military. The community was so committed to the ideas symbolized by the British flag that, in the face of the final American and Creek assault on Prospect Bluff, "Mary Ashley, had the courage and sagacity to hoist and pull down the colours morning and evening for four days."[27]

Spanish and American observers grudgingly recognized the community's efforts to establish itself as a sovereign enclave of British subjects that was situated squarely within Spanish Florida. For example, in April 1816, Andrew Jackson speculated that if the community was to be destroyed, the Americans would first have to learn, "Under whose authority has this fort been established? Whose subjects do they profess to be? . . . If they profess to be the subjects of a power with whom we are at peace then their acts are acts of war and ought to be made the subject . . . for redress by our government." Jackson further speculated: "If they are a Banditti assembled in the Territory of Spain or claim to be the subjects of any other [nation] and are stealing and enticing away our negroes, they ought to be [treated] as a band of outlaws . . . and . . . destroyed."[28] These were not typical questions for Andrew Jackson to ask, especially considering his feelings about Nicolls and the fact that he had crossed into Spanish territory before with little regard for international law when he felt that racial order in the South was threatened. Jackson's first two questions, while entirely rhetorical, were answered by the Union Jack flying above the fort at Prospect Bluff and by one of the maroon community's leaders, Garçon, immediately prior to the fort's destruction, when the former slave "heaped much abuse on the Americans, and said that he had been left in command of the fort by the British Government."[29] Despite their rhetorical nature, Jackson's questions illustrated an awareness of the community's formal political relationship with Great Britain and its members' claim of a particular British status. Jackson demonstrated this when he wrote repeatedly about "subjects" and "acts of war." In the case of "subjects," Jackson demonstrated his awareness that the maroons were claiming the status of full members of the British state. When describing "acts of war," Jackson was making a subtler yet informative point. Formal acts of war—as opposed to a slave rebellion, uprising, or other acts of violence—occurred between clearly defined states, empires, or their members. Jackson was not arguing that the maroon community at Prospect Bluff constituted an independent state. Rather he was arguing that the maroons saw themselves as an enclave of British subjects and thus an extension of the British state. Obviously Jackson felt strongly that neither legally nor racially did the former slaves have the ability to claim British status or rights or to establish themselves as a sovereign community at Prospect Bluff. Nonetheless, Jackson made it clear that he understood this not as a band of desperate outliers but rather as an organized community with a complicated status raising numerous international legal and diplomatic questions. Furthermore, if Jackson had perceived Prospect Bluff as a simple slave rebellion, he would have wasted little time in destroying the community. Indeed Jackson was preparing to use the maroons' relationship with Great Britain and their claims to be British subjects as a legal justification for an invasion of Spanish territory.

The Seminole chief Bowlegs offered an Indian perspective that supported Jackson's observations when he told the Spanish that the members of the maroon community had "come here by the persuasion of the British so if you can make good with the English you are welcome to them."[30] By suggesting that the Spanish would have to seek British permission to retrieve the former slaves, Bowlegs was either arguing that the maroons were British subjects or, at the very least, drawing attention to the special relationship the maroons enjoyed with the British. Either way, the chief was clearly expressing his belief that the former slaves had a special status deriving from their relationship with the British state.

Building on these ideas, Daniel Patterson, who possessed a great deal of intelligence relating to Prospect Bluff, argued that the community had sought to defend itself against "their owners and the [American] government ... [under] the English union jack ... against the American flag. . . . It appears very extraordinary, and remains for the British government to explain, the authority for their flag being thus hoisted by a band of outlaws." The American officer also complained bitterly about Nicolls's decision to arm and supply "the negroes and Indians to prosecute offensive operations against the United States, and that too, some time after peace had taken place."[31] While using the word "outlaws," Patterson nonetheless recognized that the community saw itself as an enclave of British subjects who lived and fought under the Union Jack. By arguing that the British government was ultimately responsible for "explain[ing]" events at Prospect Bluff, Patterson drew even more attention to the British character of the maroon community. His describing the community's enemies as the American "government" and the "American flag" make it clear that he felt he was dealing with a formally organized political body representing the British state "after peace had taken place." Patterson had chosen words that emphasized a conflict between representatives of the British state and the United States, which resembled Jackson's assertion that the maroons were engaged in formal "acts of war" against the United States. The *National Intelligencer* echoed these beliefs when it asserted that the community had been created by the "*British!* and a British flag was raised on the fort. The blacks had declared hostility against the Americans."[32] The most important word here is "declared," because it testifies to an organized and formal polity officially engaging in war with another state or entity. Contemporary observers would not have regarded a desperate and unorganized group of former slaves as capable of declaring war against the United States. As far as Patterson was concerned, the maroons represented something much more than a slave rebellion that consisted of a violent frontal assault against the institution or an effort to live a desperate survivalist existence in the wilderness. Rather the maroons at Prospect Bluff had created a political community of fellow subjects that represented a physical and intellectual challenge to the institution of slavery as well as to the interests of the United States.

An American who witnessed the destruction of the fort at Prospect Bluff echoed the ideas of Patterson and Jackson when he recorded that "*Nicolls* and *Woodbine* . . . planted this *virtuous* community."[33] Like most sarcastic comments, when analyzed closely this observation revealed a telling insecurity, rooted in the truth. In this case the witness was testifying that the community of former slaves had achieved, or at the very least sought to achieve, virtue. In the nineteenth century mind, virtue was a series of traits that allowed individuals to become full members of a polity. To contemporaries, virtue was something that needed to be constantly cultivated and defended through action and carefully regulated behavior. Likewise, few people in the nineteenth century believed virtue was a universal concept that could be applied to people of color, women, or those of a lower social standing. Thus the observer was noting both that the former slaves lived in a formal polity and that the maroons were actively attempting to achieve, cultivate, and defend their British status. Ultimately, each of these observers described a coherent community defined by its relationship to Great Britain and raising difficult questions about sovereignty, inclusion, rights, and international law.

The governor of West Florida, Mauricio de Zúñiga, provided more clarity and a Spanish perspective on the status of the maroons when he told an American delegation: "The negroes, although in part belonging to inhabitants of this province, and, as rational beings, may be subjects of the King my master, are deemed by me insurgents or rebels against the authority not only of His Catholic Majesty, but also of the proprietors from whose service they have withdrawn themselves." Zúñiga believed that the former slaves had been "seduced by the English Colonel Edward Nicholls, Major Woodbine, and their agents; and others from their inclination to run off. . . . Said fort . . . [was] built by the orders of the beforenamed Colonel Nicholls." The governor concluded that he assumed Nicolls had not acted "under authority from his Government ... [but] he left orders with the negroes totally contrary to the incontestable right of sovereignty which the King my master exercises from the line of the thirty-first degree north latitude to the south."[34] Much of Zúñiga's letter echoed the sentiments of the Americans and Seminoles, such as drawing connections between the maroons and Great Britain while questioning Nicolls's authority to take such actions, but a number of his points were more clearly developed and radical. In Zúñiga's assessment "rational beings" were waging an insurgency or rebellion against both their masters (who represented the institution of slavery) and the Spanish state and empire (which represented a political and ideological struggle). According to the governor, by attempting to establish a community of British subjects on Spanish soil, the maroon community was challenging the "right of sovereignty" of the Spanish empire. This is not how the Spaniard would have described a straight-forward slave rebellion or a desperate encampment of fugitive slaves. Coming in the midst of the Latin American wars of independence, this was a powerfully worded and pointed observation by the governor. By choosing such language, Zúñiga both admitted that the maroons had formed a political community of British subjects and situated events at Prospect Bluff within the currents of radical political upheaval that had swept the Atlantic world during the Age of Revolution. In the process Zúñiga reluctantly admitted that a very complicated political rebellion was occurring at Prospect Bluff, in which rational beings had used free will to change their allegiances from the Spanish to the British, under whose flag they enjoyed full rights, inclusion, and equality. This rebellion was more intellectual than physical and was based on the maroons' claim to their British status and the former slaves' effort to construct a virtuous community. The many free people of color from the Spanish Floridas who had joined the community would have convinced Zúñiga definitively that his interpretation was correct. This language of formal and ideological rebellion was shared by various American observers, who complained bitterly about "Nichols and his partisans" or the "renegades and malefactors . . . in an open state of rebellion" at Prospect Bluff, where they had achieved "asylum."[35]

These examples (combined with the community's strong attachment to the ownership of property and the existence of law and order at Prospect Bluff, discussed briefly later) illustrate the coherence of the community's political system as well as their communal vision as a sovereign enclave of British subjects. All these observers were deeply fearful of armed slave revolts, which they were easily able to recognize. However, each observer saw the maroon community as much more than a slave revolt; rather it was seen as a complicated and threatening political and military rebellion against the United States and Spain as well as the institution of slavery as a social system. Each of these men, while strongly denying that the maroons had the right or ability to become full British subjects or to establish a sovereign polity, recognized that this was exactly what the former slaves had done. No other Atlantic maroon community achieved this level of political sophistication so quickly, if at all. Thus few if any maroon communities or slave rebels achieved such a deep and nuanced version of intellectual and political freedom so firmly rooted in modern concepts.

The Prospect Bluff community, like most successful maroon settlements from across the hemisphere, created a strong and coherent government that prized order, stability, defense, and ultimately survival. Quality leadership was essential if these goals were to be achieved. The community's leaders, Garçon, Prince, and Cyrus, were commissioned by Nicolls as officers because of their military and intellectual abilities as well as their knowledge of the societies of the Southeast.[36] When the British and their Indian allies departed Prospect Bluff, these three officers took control of the community. They did not justify their rule by having been African royalty, through inheritance, or by their magical or religious powers. Rather, like many maroon leaders, their rule was partially based on their military abilities and understanding of local conditions. However, the single most important justification for their rule was their especially close relationship with Nicolls and the British military titles bestowed on them. Ultimately the three men represented an unusual variation from the model of maroon leader as gifted warrior and strategist who possessed an excellent knowledge of the region's societies, because their authority largely rested in their relationship with Nicolls and the British state.

Garçon, Prince, and Cyrus were possibly the three most exceptional slaves in Pensacola, and their unique backgrounds provided them with the potential to serve as quality maroon leaders. They were products of the Atlantic borderlands of Pensacola, and prior to coming to Prospect Bluff, each of the three men had enjoyed elevated status.[37] Garçon was a thirty-year-old carpenter who was valued at seven hundred pesos. He and four male and three female slaves had been owned by the moderately successful Don Antonio Montero.[38] Garçon was repeatedly referred to as a "French slave," which provided an important link to the revolutionary French Caribbean or Louisiana.[39]

Cyrus was a twenty-six-year-old literate carpenter and one of the three male and two female slaves who had belonged to Don Vincent Ordozgoity, who had briefly served as *alcalde*.[40] The fact that Cyrus was the literate and skilled former slave of the very man who had been embroiled in Pensacola's greatest ever political fracas meant that he was acutely aware of the nuances of revolutionary era political debate and the Machiavellian actions required to maintain political office. Cyrus's understanding of politics would have grown and changed after time spent listening to Nicolls's ideas about anti-slavery and the British Empire. His literacy was also a powerful tool that earned him the esteem of the majority of the former slaves and all their Indian allies.

Prince was a twenty-six-year-old master carpenter who was valued at the huge sum of fifteen hundred pesos and, along with five men and a mother and a daughter, had been the property of Dr. Don Eugenio Sierra, who twice traveled to Prospect Bluff in the hope of recovering his slaves.[41] Prince, by a great margin, was the second most valuable slave in the entire city, and his position would have afforded him numerous privileges.[42] Equally important was the strong probability that Prince was originally from Africa.[43] During the British occupation of Pensacola, Woodbine had employed Prince to recruit "smart young fellows" from the slave population. This was a reflection of the talents and abilities that Prince fostered while working for the town's sole medical doctor as well as of the esteem that Pensacola's slaves would have had for him.[44] It also illustrates the extent to which Prince fully understood Nicolls's message, because he would have explained these ideas carefully to other slaves during his recruitment efforts.

Taken as a group, these three men represented different parts of the African diaspora and Africa itself, which meant that they could appeal to the sensibilities and beliefs of slaves and free people of color from across the Atlantic world. Yet they were also products of the Southeast, where they had been exposed to various peoples and ideas from across the world and were aware of the economic, military, and political forces that shaped the region. None of these men had suffered the extreme brutality of slavery; rather, because of their skilled urban status, they had enjoyed economic and personal freedoms that were rare.

Essential in shaping their rule was the fact that Garçon, Prince, and Cyrus would have spent a tremendous amount of time conversing in English with Nicolls, whose confidence they clearly enjoyed. This fact, combined with their backgrounds and abilities, placed them in an unusually strong position to comprehend fully and absorb Nicolls's anti-slavery rhetoric and to understand the contours of the British status as he explained it to them. This knowledge of Nicolls's ideas and their British status meant that the three men were ideological rebel slave leaders, steeped in notions about anti-slavery, politics, and racial equality. Their actions and attachment to their British status bore this out clearly and placed the three men at the vanguard of contemporary liberationist movements. This becomes even clearer when the three men are compared with typical maroon leaders, who knew little of such ideas. For over a year Garçon, Prince, and Cyrus were able to organize, govern, and coordinate the defense of hundreds of diverse followers deep in the wilderness of Florida in the face of immense external threats. The fact that the community did not disintegrate, but rather flourished, illustrates the quality of their leadership and the existence of a high degree of support from the rest of the community. Normally it took maroon communities years or decades to develop such an organized political system.[45]

As was nearly always the case with maroons, strong rule was required to make sure that fields were sown, the community was defended, spies were detected, or internal conflicts were avoided. Yet Garçon, Prince, and Cyrus hardly ruled as wanton autocrats or dictators. The maroon community's government appears to have maintained checks and limitations on the leaders' authority. This was evidenced shortly after the American assault on Prospect Bluff by the behavior of refugees from the community, who in one instance "nominated" their leader, and in a different instance when a leader of the community's refugees made it clear that "the respect and affections of the negroes were the only security to the continuance of his magistracy."[46] In all probability these were actions that had been developed at Prospect Bluff. Furthermore, Garçon, Prince, and Cyrus consulted with other members of the community and further shared power with an array of individuals who filled official positions, such as Hilario, who was the sergeant of the guard, and "Black Serjeant-Major Wilson," who would ultimately lose his life desperately attempting to defend the fort.[47] As in successful and long-lived maroon settlements elsewhere, the political system of the community at Prospect Bluff combined consultation and power sharing with strong centralized authority by leaders who had distinguished themselves militarily and, in this case, who had been sanctioned by the British.

Commenting on this level of political sophistication, a contemporary American observer lamented that the community was run by "the worst of all conditions . . . a democracy or government of slaves."[48] "Democracy or government of slaves" was intended as an oxymoron designed to elicit strong emotions among readers in the early republic, for whom the word and concept of "democracy" was deeply meaningful and controversial. Nonetheless, use of the term illustrates a belief that the Prospect Bluff community was governed by a sophisticated and modern political system, even if it was not a formal democracy. Likewise, and contrary to the author's intentions, the fact that the observer felt a "democracy or government of slaves" was an oxymoron, because slaves were incapable of political rights or participation, illustrates and highlights just how bold and radical were the maroons' efforts to establish a government and polity that protected the rights of British subjects.

Pintado offered a similar observation, but from a Spanish perspective, when he referred to the community as a "republic of bandits."[49] From extensive firsthand experience Pintado knew full well that the maroons were much more than bandits, and he was attempting to be snide when he used that word. At the same time Pintado was not suggesting that the community had become a fully developed republic; a system of government that he would have held in low regard. Nor was Pintado comparing the community to a republic of Indians, which was common in colonial Latin America. He knew that the community at Prospect Bluff was neither of these things. Rather the Spaniard's use of "republic" was meant to illustrate that the community had a clearly defined government that was run by active citizens, as would have been the case in contemporary or classical republics. As with those observers who used words like "virtuous," "government," "democracy," and "black gentry" to describe the maroon community's political system, Pintado was inadvertently testifying to the existence of the maroons' strong and developed political system.

However, there was even more to Pintado's choice of words. By using the word "republic" he drew a connection between the community at Prospect Bluff and the most radical change that had swept the Atlantic world in the last generation. First, this is because in the contemporary Spanish mind the concept of a "republic" was directly associated not with ancient Rome or Renaissance Venice but rather with nations such as the young United States, Haiti, France, or rebellious colonies across the Spanish empire. Second, and more important, to Pintado the concept of a "republic" would have conjured up the most violently contested ideas of the Age of Revolution, including struggles over rights, liberty, sovereignty, racial equality, and national independence that had challenged the old order. When using this word, Pintado would have pictured events such as the most radical aspects of the French Revolution, the slave rebellion in Haiti, and the independence struggles that were presently tearing at the Spanish Empire. Thus, in Pintado's vocabulary, referring to the maroon community as a "republic" was not meant as a literal observation but was a powerfully loaded tool for situating the maroons' actions within the revolutionary Atlantic world while grudgingly admitting that it was governed by a coherent political system ruling over a discrete space.

The existence of formalized law at Prospect Bluff is further evidence of a high degree of political sophistication. For example, in 1817 a group that included a number of the community's survivors captured William Hambly and, after struggling to contain their rage and desire for swift vigilante justice, placed the individual whom they most fully blamed for the fort's destruction on trial for his decision to provide intelligence to the Americans. Given the incredibly painful emotions involved, this example of the existence and execution of law is truly remarkable and reflects the power and coherence of law at Prospect Bluff. The trial also demonstrates that the maroons saw themselves as a community of British subjects whose status and rights transcended a physical location or any given set of present circumstances: they were British subjects no matter where they were located. Underscoring this sense of belonging to a universal community is the possibility that the maroons may well have charged Hambly formally with treason. After the fort's destruction, Nicolls was informed in a letter by the British merchant Alexander Arbuthnot that Hambly had "turned traitor" when he decided to leave Prospect Bluff and provide the Americans with intelligence.[50] The use of the word "traitor" is informative and reflects Arbuthnot's belief that a British subject had formally betrayed a community of fellow Britons. If the former slaves formally tried a white British subject for treason, this is further strong evidence not just of the existence of law at Prospect Bluff but of the maroons' belief that they were the legal and political equals of any other British subject. Few symbolic or literal actions would have served as a bolder and more radical statement of full equality within the British Empire than organizing and participating in a formal trial involving a white British subject.

Further examples support the existence of law at Prospect Bluff. When Hawkins reported that the community was determined to "arrest every American and Spaniard they find in their lands," it must have been the "sheriffs" that Nicolls had proposed prior to departure who were responsible for these arrests. This illustrates the existence both of a police force and of laws that the police were enforcing, since to be arrested, rather than taken prisoner or captive, one must have broken a law. Not only does this suggest that the community had a coherent body of laws, but it is also an important statement about sovereignty and jurisdiction, since sheriffs or police enforce the laws of a particular polity over a defined geographic area. This suggests that the community at Prospect Bluff saw itself as an entity of law and order that occupied a specific physical place. Likewise the instructions to arrest "American[s]" and "Spaniard[s]" suggests that this was a British polity, and when non-Britons entered this territory they were likely to be arrested. This was echoed in the "oath" that Nicolls demanded of the former slaves never to "permit [a] white man, except an Englishman to approach." The specific mention of "Englishman" (which ironically did not technically include Nicolls) was further evidence that this polity was the realm of British subjects.

A number of other observers supported the idea that the community had come to regard Prospect Bluff and the surrounding land as its sovereign territory. For example, it was noted that the community's dominion extended to the river, and its defenders attacked "any vessel on the river not flying the Union Jack."[51] Daniel Patterson pointed out that the "negroes" held the fort "and the country in its vicinity," while Hawkins believed that Prospect Bluff and the surrounding area had become "their territory."[52] The Creeks agreed that the "negros had taken the land" at and around Prospect Bluff.[53] When an employee of Forbes and Company came to realize fully the extent to which the maroons had come to control and own the land around Prospect Bluff, a situation which he deemed to be next to permanent, he lamented that "a last recourse [exists in which] the lands can be sold to the Americans, who will settle them in spite of Indians Negroes or *English*."[54] As far as this observer was concerned, Prospect Bluff and the surrounding territory was now the realm of the maroon community. Key to any polity's identity was carefully defining the boundaries of its territory over which its laws were valid. Accordingly, the maroons at Prospect Bluff had clearly decided exactly what territory came under their jurisdiction.

Military Organization

The community's military, while certainly a vital tool for defense, was also a statement about its members' self-identified status as British. Garçon, Prince, and Cyrus were in charge of the community's military, but its organization extended well beyond the three leaders. Based on their training by the Royal Marines, the community's military was a well-organized formal unit composed of men of whom Nicolls had declared that "better or braver soldiers I would never wish to serve with." This degree of organization and training was not typical of most maroon communities, which relied on guerilla tactics; this could more accurately be called a formal army. The informer Ned was impressed to see that the community's soldiers "drilled and perform guard duty."[55] West Florida's governor nervously reported "that all are well armed, provision'd and disciplined."[56] A number of refugees from the community fled to a Seminole village just before the fort's destruction and recreated a similar organization, where they "[choose] officers of every description, and endeavour to keep up a regular discipline, and are very strict in punishing violators of their military rule."[57] Furthermore, "an immense quantity of British uniform clothing" was found in the fort after the assault, which emphasized the importance of British uniforms to the maroons.[58] The insistence on uniforms and formal drilling was practical and symbolic. Drilling and parading in uniforms were calculated to provide daily public displays of strength, British status, and ultimately freedom.

The post-treaty Jamaican maroons were formally trained and uniformed, but they were led by whites, and their primary purpose was to police the island's slaves. Thus, rather than emphasizing rights, status, or equality, the Jamaican maroons' military service highlighted their subjugation and awkward intermediary status within the island's society. Unlike in Jamaica, the highly formalized nature of the Prospect Bluff maroon community's military illustrates that the former slaves were acutely aware of the association between official military service and the status of full British subjects as well as being a testament to strong government. This realization had been reinforced by their experience with the Fifth West India Regiment and the companies of *pardos* and *morenos*, who had both gained their freedom through military service. It was also reinforced by Nicolls's anti-slavery ideology and conceptualization of the British Empire, both of which placed great emphasis on the power of military service and sacrifice. The former slaves were aware of this and were doing much more than physically defending their freedom when they served in the armed forces. After all, especially given their massive store of arms and ammunition and the past military experience of many of members in defense of Spanish Florida, the community of maroons could have relied on guerilla tactics for self-defense and dispensed with daily drills. But on a daily basis Prospect Bluff was defended by organized British soldiers rather than survivalist guerillas.

Collectively the community's political, legal, and military system was an elaborate effort to define, protect, and cultivate their rights as British subjects that stood at the heart of the rebellion they were waging against the system of slavery. In the minds of the former slaves, these rights entitled them to control of their bodies, their labor, their movements, and their families; the ownership and cultivation of land and holding of private property, which included their homes and material goods; the ability to participate in an economy; freedom of religion; access to education for their children; and the ability to participate in a clearly defined political system that emphasized law and order as well as the right to serve in the military. By these standards the maroons at Prospect Bluff had indeed become a "virtuous" community and "black gentry." The maroons' commitment to a specific status and set of rights diverged from the situation of other maroon communities, who tended to embrace less abstract ideas in pursuit of goals such as physical freedom, creating internal stability, and defense. Accordingly, most maroon governments modeled themselves on frequently hazy cultural understandings of what constituted a valid political system; leaders justified their rule by a particular African past, magical or religious powers, lineage, or military abilities. In other words, maroon governments were most often conservative and restorationist in their outlook, whereas the community at Prospect Bluff was modern and Atlantic in its political orientation.

Other maroon governments in the hemisphere were highly effective, but unlike at Prospect Bluff, they paid little attention to such modern constructions as rights and political inclusion, let alone radical anti-slavery. Nor did such concepts form the foundation of any other maroon community's entire political system. The community at Prospect Bluff held a distinctly Western and primarily British political outlook. This grew out of its members' unusual relationship with Nicolls and their overwhelmingly creole background. This is not meant to suggest that there were not African or other cultural influences that shaped the community's outlook nor that the maroons did not bring preexisting ideas with them to Prospect Bluff. However, such influences simply do not appear in the extant historical record, and it is clear that Nicolls's ideas and promises greatly influenced people's actions. This is not meant to imply that the community's leaders were consciously rejecting their African heritage. Rather, because of an exceptional series of events, the community at Prospect Bluff found itself in an unusual relationship with a European power, its broader empire, and a set of ideas about status filtered through Nicolls's radical prism. Like all maroons, the people at Prospect Bluff were shrewd realists who, once they began to understand Nicolls's ideas and the implications of his promises, realized the power of these concepts and constructed their government accordingly.

Placed in comparative perspective, the community at Prospect Bluff offers an unusual example of grand marronage. No other maroon community was so sophisticated politically or so insistent that it was a sovereign enclave of particular subjects who enjoyed specific rights and inhabited a distinct space. This fact placed the Prospect Bluff community squarely within the boldest and most modern efforts by people of color to claim rights, privileges, status, and equality within the contemporary Atlantic world. The maroons were able to achieve such a high degree of political sophistication at Prospect Bluff because of their relationship with Nicolls, knowledge of his anti-slavery ideology, having been granted the status of British subjects, and material well-being. Each of these conditions was unusual, and the convergence of all of them was truly unique. Nonetheless, the maroons' government and political outlook tells us much about slave consciousness and political thought. This is because we can see in the conduct of these maroons the extent to which African Americans understood the contours of slavery and freedom and how far they could go to achieve freedom. In particular, this is evident in the maroons' aggressive efforts to protect and cultivate British rights to the fullest extent possible, long after Nicolls and the British had departed Florida. Onlookers agreed, often grudgingly, that the maroons had succeeded in creating a functioning British polity. Given the fact that this polity flourished for over a year and required the active participation of hundreds of diverse slaves, there is no reason to believe that other slaves from across North America or, indeed, the Atlantic world would not have behaved in a similar manner if provided with similar circumstances. Thus, Prospect Bluff, as the prime example of successful communal slave resistance in North American history, clearly demonstrates that slaves were capable of a deep political understanding of contemporary ideas about status, rights, and, ultimately, freedom and, when circumstances allowed it, were able to act on this understanding.

10   ⇛   Destruction

THE MAROON COMMUNITY at Prospect Bluff was a conspicuous example of slave resistance that inspired both hope and fear among the different inhabitants of the Southeast. White Americans, their Creek allies, and the Spanish saw the community as a powerful spur to slave flight and, more frightening, as encouragement, if not overt incitement, for armed slave rebellion. The enslaved clearly took inspiration from the maroon community as evidenced by the steady flow of fugitives to Prospect Bluff. The community was a serious military antagonist, an economic and geopolitical rival, and a major challenge to the expanding American plantation complex. The threat posed by the maroon community was rendered more immediate because of its unusual origins, its members' reception of Edward Nicolls's radical anti-slavery ideas, its wealth and fortified location, and its relationship with the Red Sticks and Seminoles. Furthermore, the community at Prospect Bluff was on a continent with little *grand marronage* and at a particularly combustible time, making it appear that much more threatening.

Prior to the British departure, the community's formation had caused deep anxiety in the Southeast, which only intensified as it became clear to observers that the maroon settlement continued to exist as an independent black polity of British subjects after May 1815. By 1816 this anxiety had spiked, leaving Andrew Jackson to complain bitterly that this "evil of so serious a nature" was "a state of things that cannot fail to produce much injury to the neighbouring settlements and excite Irritations which eventually may endanger the peace of the Nation."[1] He had already claimed that "this fort has been established . . . for the purpose of murder, rapine and plunder."[2] Jackson, while prone to colorful language, was nonetheless arguing sincerely that the maroon community challenged the stability of the Deep South, which had only just been secured at the price of immense bloodshed over the last half dozen years. The governor of Georgia, David Mitchell, reiterated this viewpoint when he promised one of his officers that "[I] shall use my utmost exertions to counteract an evil from which we have to dread such dangerous consequences."[3] Both men saw the maroon community as representing a great "evil" that was casting a shadow across the Southeast from Prospect Bluff. Hundreds of miles away in Bermuda, an observer commented matter-of-factly that "no time ought to be lost in recommending the adoption of speedy, energetic measures, for the destruction of a thing held so likely to become dangerous to the State of Georgia."[4] An American observer saw the maroon community as such a great threat that he thought "vigor beyond the law" ought to be exercised: "Our Southern property will not be worth holding unless most energetic steps are taken to repress the insidious attempts of our most inveterate enemies, the British."[5]

In this type of opinion the maroon community threatened the very existence of the institution of slavery in the United States. The press relayed these sentiments to a national audience who were kept constantly apprised about the Prospect Bluff community through a torrent of articles, editorials, and firsthand accounts of events. For example, the *Savannah Journal* invoked the specter of slave rebellion when it reported that "an establishment so pernicious to the Southern States, hold[s] out to a part of their population temptations to insubordination" and must be destroyed.[6] The *Niles Weekly Register* reported that "it had become a great nuisance, not only as a harbor for the hostile Indians, but for all the discontented negroes in the country, whose desertions were frequent."[7] Anyone with access to a newspaper or word-of-mouth exchanges was aware of what was occurring at Prospect Bluff. Given these fears, it was not going to take long for the community's many enemies to plot its destruction.[8]

The Beginning of Hostilities

The British had left the fort at Prospect Bluff well armed and supplied in order to aid the Seminoles and Red Sticks against the encroachments of the United States and to provide a safe haven for their black allies as part of Nicolls's personal crusade. Nicolls had assured the Red Sticks that the Treaty of Fort Jackson was not legally binding and that the Indians' lands were returned to their 1811 boundaries. To emphasize this, he entered into a defensive alliance with the Indians and instructed them to resist violently any American efforts to survey the boundaries of the Treaty of Fort Jackson. The Seminoles and Red Sticks had taken him at face value and, for years, firmly believed that they were allies of Great Britain by virtue of the treaty with Nicolls, whose return they expected soon. Consequently they continued to deny the legality of the Treaty of Fort Jackson. This stance mirrored the maroon community's conviction that they were British subjects who were protecting their territory and rights, with their lives if need be. Both the Indians and the blacks believed that they had a particular status (as allies of Great Britain and British subjects, respectively) because of Nicolls's promises. As a result they stood in diametric opposition to American, Spanish, and Creek adversaries until the end of the First Seminole War. Of course both the blacks and Indians had many reasons to clash with the United States and Creeks long before encountering Nicolls. However, their relationship with Nicolls added a new and combustible dimension in both groups' struggle with the United States and Creeks. Likewise, Nicolls's material and legal support as well as his promises emboldened the blacks and Indians. In the opinion of white Americans and their Creek allies, Nicolls's promises and actions fell outside any legal standard, stood to impede the expansion of the plantation frontier, and threatened to engulf the Deep South in more racialized violence.

Predictably, it was the surveying of the Treaty of Fort Jackson that led to the first violent encounter with the maroon community. In September 1815 Benjamin Hawkins ordered a raid led by the Creek chief William McIntosh and roughly two hundred of his warriors.[9] McIntosh was a powerful Creek chief who was a large-scale slave and plantation owner as well as a prominent advocate of accommodation.[10] Ultimately McIntosh was executed in 1825 for his role in the Treaty of Indian Springs, which eliminated much of the remaining Creek land in the Southeast. McIntosh personified the racial, cultural, social, and economic transformations that had torn at Creek society in recent years. Accordingly, McIntosh's fears about the community at Prospect Bluff were virtually indistinguishable from those of a prominent white southerner.

McIntosh's force of two hundred battle-hardened warriors was repulsed by Prospect Bluff's well-trained and organized militia of British subjects. The defeated raid made Americans and Creeks fully aware that they were dealing with a serious military antagonist who would not easily be destroyed, if defeated at all. The size of the community's population and its economy became clearer to the United States and its allies after the raid. The Creek raid reiterated to the community the need for defense, strong leadership, and constant vigilance. The raid also set an important precedent in the use of Creek raiding parties rather than U.S. troops against Prospect Bluff. It was symbolic that the first major assault on Prospect Bluff was an American-instigated Creek detachment—few combinations of instigator, attacker, and defender could more fully capture the complexities of race in the early nineteenth-century Southeast.

Shortly after the end of the War of 1812, Brigadier General Edmund Gaines assumed command of the Southern Section of the Southern Military District. Gaines was an aristocratic southerner who had grown up in Virginia and North Carolina in a family of politicians and plantation owners.[11] By 1816 Gaines was in his late thirties and had spent nearly all his adult life as a professional soldier. More important, he had spent much of the 1810s overseeing the surveying of the Mississippi Territory. During the War of 1812 Gaines distinguished himself but almost lost his life when he was shot at the First Battle of Lake Erie in the summer of 1814. This injury ended Gaines's combat career but did nothing to dampen his desire to serve in the U.S. military. Ultimately Gaines was a shrewd and skillful career soldier with a good eye for politics and a deep understanding of the racialized and geopolitical dynamics of the Southeast.

Gaines's primary responsibility was overseeing the surveying of the boundaries of the Treaty of Fort Jackson, which placed him in the position of observing what was happening at Prospect Bluff. It also meant that he was on a collision course with the maroon community and its Indian allies. The brigadier general fully understood that the British-allied Indians denied the legitimacy of the Treaty of Fort Jackson and that they were prepared to resist American efforts to run the lines. Accordingly, Gaines formed a substantial military force to protect the surveyors as they worked. As a cautious man, Gaines became preoccupied by the hostile Red Sticks, Seminoles, and maroons. He requested that Governor Early keep as many as 2,000 militiamen on alert and wrote to the secretary of war that 6,000 troops would be required to maintain the boundaries of the Treaty of Fort Jackson.[12]

By December 1815 the surveyors had established the new Creek boundary. However, Gaines did not believe that the establishment of the boundary had removed the threat emanating from the Floridas. Rather, he was convinced that as long as the maroon community and its Native allies remained in their haven, there would always be endemic hostilities along the southern frontier, which could escalate into widespread racialized violence undermining American interests across the region. As a result Gaines believed that a substantial military presence in southern Georgia and Alabama was the only way to defend the region effectively. Jackson agreed with Gaines and assigned him one thousand troops to patrol the Southeast.[13] Even at a time of official peace, Prospect Bluff cast an unsettling shadow across the Southeast, which prompted heightened vigilance and the reallocation of troops and resources.

American Efforts at Diplomacy with the Indians and Spanish

This state of affairs was deeply troubling to Andrew Jackson, who soon took the first steps to remove permanently the threat posed by the maroon community and its Indian allies. This carefully coordinated diplomatic and military process would take months, and it ended with the destruction of the fort at Prospect Bluff. Jackson began by ordering Gaines to construct a fort inside the lines of the Treaty of Fort Jackson on the Escambia River. This move placed the American military within miles of Prospect Bluff and greatly increased the odds of direct confrontation. Jackson then ordered Gaines to send scouts to investigate activities at Prospect Bluff. Gaines's next orders were to destroy the maroon community immediately if it was continuing to harbor fugitive American slaves.[14] Jackson knew full well that the community welcomed American runaways on a regular basis, and he intended this proviso as a step toward the final showdown. At the time, Jackson still lacked the authority to order Gaines to take such definitive action. For his part, Gaines was too much of a politician to invade Spanish Florida without the formal right to do so. In the meantime, Gaines circulated a dire ultimatum among the Indians of the Southeast that they faced an immediate choice between peace or war with the United States if they did not cease hostilities, concede the validity of the Treaty of Fort Jackson, and turn on their allies at Prospect Bluff. In the face of a rapidly expanding American presence in the area, and with fresh memories of the Battle of Horseshoe Bend and of Jackson's invasion of Pensacola, this message represented an intimidating challenge that required careful consideration.

Central to American planning was a steady stream of valuable intelligence that United States officials received from Edmund Doyle and William Hambly. Hambly was eventually blamed by the Red Sticks, Seminoles, and maroons as "the instrumental cause of the Fort at Prospect Bluff being destroyed by the Americans" because this intelligence was so useful.[15] Upon becoming aware that Hambly was working for the Americans, the Seminoles threatened to kill him, forcing him to take refuge at Fort Gaines, where Doyle soon joined him.[16]

Providing intelligence was not the only way in which Hambly worked against the community. He and Hawkins made sure that the Creeks joined the fight against the maroon community once again. Most important, Little Prince, tribal leader of the Lower Creeks, and numerous Upper Creeks were recruited for the American attack on the community. Little Prince had been instrumental in the execution of Little Warrior, which had begun the Creek

War. During the war he distinguished himself fighting alongside Jackson against the Red Sticks and their black allies. Little Prince later served on the powerful Creek National Council, making him one of the most powerful men among the Creeks. Like McIntosh, Little Prince embodied much of the turmoil that marked the recent history of the Creeks.

In the spring of 1816 the Americans provided three hundred barrels of corn for Little Prince and his sizable force of warriors. They were also promised fifty dollars for every fugitive slave captured.[17] Once again American officials preferred to send the Creeks, who were willing to oblige because of the substantial American reward and their shared hostility against the maroon community. Gaines noted that "Col Hawkins is of the opinion they will succeed, and, although I have little faith in Indian promises, it seems to me proper to encourage the undertaking and wait a reasonable time for the result. . . . Should they fail, I shall then avail myself of the discretionary power . . . best Calculated to Counteract Indian hostility."[18] Gaines was not entirely convinced that the Creeks could launch a successful raid into Florida to destroy the community at Prospect Bluff, but he felt it was worth a try before mobilizing American troops in what had the potential to cause yet another diplomatic rift with the Spanish.

After unrelenting American pressure, the Seminoles made a half-hearted promise to aid in the capture of the blacks at Prospect Bluff, even though the Indians regarded the community as their ally against the United States.[19] Any real chance of turning the Seminoles against the maroons was lost with the construction of Camp Crawford, which was located very close to Seminole territory and was regarded by the Indians as a dangerous encroachment by the United States. Red Stick leaders such as Peter McQueen and Kinache had never wavered in their alliance with the maroon community at Prospect Bluff, realizing that it was a valuable ally in their struggle against the United States and the Creeks. Accordingly, when Little Prince returned from talks with the Red Sticks and Seminoles in May 1816, he reported that "he had done everything that was in his power to induce the Lower Indians to go against the Negro Fort, and to let the white people alone, but they were crazy and would not listen to him . . . they were determined on their own destruction."[20] The Seminoles and Red Sticks had made it clear whose side they were on and began to launch increasingly aggressive raids in American territory against white settlers. Less than three weeks later Gaines reported that a party of Indians had captured two American soldiers and stolen thirty head of cattle near Camp Crawford. This raid was preceded by the murders of two American citizens, soon followed by a report that "certain indications of general hostility [are emerging] such as the war dance and drinking war physic by the Indians from below and above the line."[21] The Seminoles and Red Sticks, who continued to deny the legality of the Treaty of Fort Jackson, felt threatened by the American presence, recognized the maroon community as an ally, and were preparing for war. Gaines's cold, if not angry, response to these reports was that "[I] have little doubt that we shall be compelled to destroy the hostile towns [after the maroon community]."[22]

Diplomacy and Planning

Over the course of 1815 and 1816 a number of American officials were surprisingly diplomatic in their efforts to gain official Spanish approval for an assault on Prospect Bluff. In response to American pressure the Spanish governor of West Florida had previously claimed that Prospect Bluff was not in his jurisdiction.[23] This was an effort to stall for time because the governor was in a difficult position. The maroon community was inhabited by numerous Spanish slaves and posed a major threat to Spanish interests. Furthermore, the Spanish had blamed the British presence along the Apalachicola River and the maroon community for damaging their relations with the area's Indians, which further undermined the stability of the province. The destruction of the community would clearly benefit the Spaniards, but they lacked the military ability to take action themselves as Spain turned its energies to restoring order across its collapsing empire. However, because of the centuries-long history of deeply destabilizing Anglo-American incursions into the Floridas and the American desire to annex the colonies, the Spanish were reluctant to request or accept American aid. Ultimately the Spanish had to decide what frightened them more: the maroons or yet another invading American army that might well never leave.

In the first half of 1815 Peter Early and East Florida's governor Sebastian Kindelán entered into a series of exchanges in which Early demanded that the Spanish destroy the community and put a stop to all Indian and black raids along the American frontier. Early interpreted the tone of Kindelán's correspondence to suggest that the Spanish would not object if the United States launched a strike against Prospect Bluff.[24] The next governor of East Florida, Juan José de Estrada, did not take such an accommodating stance to American interference in Spanish affairs and was quick to remind the Americans of their previous raids into the Floridas. Having lost his patience by the summer of 1815, Estrada informed Early that he had no control over the maroon community and that he must refer the matter to his superiors.[25]

As 1815 passed into 1816 Americans were becoming increasingly determined to destroy the community with or without Spanish approval. Secretary of

War William Crawford, in relaying President Madison's opinions to Jackson, wrote in March 1816 that "the principle of good neighborhood requires the interference of the Spanish authority, to put an end to an evil of so serious a nature. Should he [the governor of West Florida] decline this interference, it will be incumbent on the Executive to determine what course shall be adopted in relation to this banditti." Madison concluded that "should it be determined, that the destruction of the fort does not require the sanction of the legislature, measures will be promptly taken for its reduction."[26] While the secretary of war wrote about executive authority and the sanction of the legislature, he had effectively turned the matter over to Jackson and the military. Given Jackson's recent history of invading Spanish Florida as part of his extended war against various Indians, blacks, and/or the British, this greatly increased the probability that he would attack Prospect Bluff sooner rather than later.

Emboldened, Jackson quickly contacted Mauricio de Zúñiga, the governor of West Florida, and bluntly stated: "I cannot permit myself to indulge a Belief that the governor of Pensacola or the military commander of the place will hesitate a moment in giving orders for this [force?] to be dispersed and the property of the Citizens of the United States forthwith restored to them, and our friendly Indians." Jackson told the governor that this was the case "particularly since I reflect that the conduct of this Banditti is such as will not be tolerated by our government, and if not put down by Spanish Authority compel us in self Defence to destroy them."[27] Jackson had delivered yet another ultimatum, which reflected Madison and Crawford's opinion that if the Spanish did not act, then the United States was justified in taking matters into its own hands out of self-defense. This was the first time this argument appeared so clearly in American-Spanish discussions on the matter.

Mauricio de Zúñiga's response left Jackson feeling conflicted. The governor admitted that the Spanish considered the blacks and Indians at Prospect Bluff to be rebels and that the community was "the root of an Evil" that posed a great threat to American and Spanish interests and consequently needed to be destroyed in order to bring peace and stability to the region. Zúñiga enthusiastically suggested that the Americans might receive Spanish assistance in a joint operation against Prospect Bluff. He could not, however, authorize a strike against the community without permission from the captain general of Cuba, which he promised to request immediately. Zúñiga signed off by requesting that in the meantime, "neither the Government of the U.S.: nor [Jackson] will take any step to the prejudice of the sovereignty of the King, my master, over the district of Apalachicola."[28] Jackson received an attachment with Zúñiga's letter from the American Capt. Ferdinand Amelung, who had held extensive conversations with the governor while visiting Pensacola. Amelung assured Jackson that "the Governor asserts the truth . . . and am convinced that the Inhabitants of Panzacola have suffered and do suffer more than our Citizens from the Fort and its Garrison. . . . The Governor also, on my mentioning in conversation that I was persuaded you would willingly assist in destroying the Fort, said that if the object was sufficiently important to require the presence of General Jackson he would be proud to be commanded by you." Amelung then recounted the governor having said "that if the Captain General of Cuba could not furnish him with the necessary means, he might perhaps apply to you for assistance." Feeling that he had executive approval, Jackson was satisfied with the tone of Zúñiga's letter and ordered Gaines to proceed with operations against Prospect Bluff, which had essentially already begun with the construction of Camp Crawford. The Spanish would ultimately send a small military detachment to consult with the American force during its assault on the maroon community.[29] The Americans, however, proceeded without having received official approval from the captain general of Cuba.

Plans for the Final Invasion Begin

In June 1816 the American and Creek movement against Prospect Bluff entered its final stage, leading one observer to posit that "if the negroes dare to oppose them they will doubtless be destroyed."[30] Gaines was spurred to immediate action by increased Indian and black activity near the limits of the Treaty of Fort Jackson.[31] Weeks earlier Gaines had received detailed intelligence about the dimensions of the fort, its defenses, military organization, population, and food supply.[32] The mission was a joint army and navy operation, coordinated from Camp Crawford, which presently found itself in a vulnerable position. The Spanish had given the Americans permission to supply Camp Crawford by traveling along the Apalachicola River from the Gulf of Mexico. However, Prospect Bluff blocked water access to the camp, thus making it difficult to supply. The inability to supply Camp Crawford caused no small amount of anxiety among American officials. Gaines believed that if this continued, it "will expose us to great inconveniences and hazards in obtaining supplies by land particularly in the event of war. As the road will be bad and the distance from the settlements of Georgia near 150 miles," this problem added an extra dimension to American concerns that the maroon community undermined their ability to control the Southeast effectively from a practical and logistical standpoint.[33] In hope of alleviating the pressure on Camp Crawford, Col. Duncan Clinch of the army proceeded with a detachment of troops down the Apalachicola River from American territory to a spot near Prospect Bluff to await a naval convoy from New Orleans loaded with supplies. Clinch was a southerner and a hardened career soldier who had spent much of his life fighting in the Southeast.[34] He was an ideal candidate to execute Gaines's and Jackson's carefully laid plans. Clinch also understood that from high atop Prospect Bluff, the maroons commanded all the territory for miles around where the two forces were planning to rendezvous and just how strong and formidable the community and its allies were. Accordingly, Clinch did not approach the mission lightly. In May he had privately admitted that "alltho he would rather the Indians would do it themselves . . . if [they] failed entirely that he would send down a detachment to [destroy] the negroes himself."[35] At the moment Clinch's orders made this impossible.

Slowly making its way from New Orleans, the naval convoy consisted of Gunboat 149, under the command of Sailing Master Louis Jarius Loomis, the schooners *Semilante* and *General Pike*, and Gunboat 154, commanded by Sailing Master James Bassett.[36] This was a well-supplied and heavily armed naval flotilla that had the same instructions as Clinch: to destroy the community at Prospect Bluff if it provided any opposition to the convoy's safe passage along the Apalachicola River. These orders were a clever scheme or "experiment" Gaines had hatched in May to allow the Americans to attack the fort while not risking upsetting the Spanish by ignoring Zúñiga's insistence that no actions be taken before he had received instructions from Cuba. Gaines had instructed the navy to prepare the boats for "an attack by small arms from the shore . . . [at which time]. . . . from the information I have received of the Negro Fort . . . should we meet fire from the Fort it shall be destroyed."[37] Based on all the intelligence that Gaines possessed, he was betting that the maroon community's armed forces would launch an attack on the passing American ships. Since the Americans had official Spanish permission to be on the Apalachicola River, Gaines reasoned that if the community attacked the convoy, then the American forces would be able to claim that they were merely acting in self-defense. At the beginning of July the naval convoy reached the mouth of the Apalachicola River, where it was to anchor and establish a blockade of Prospect Bluff until Clinch's detachment joined it. The purpose of the blockade, which had been suggested by Doyle, was to keep the Seminoles from aiding the maroons and to prohibit the members of the community from fleeing to the Indians.[38] The distance of the blockade from Prospect Bluff illustrates the community's maritime abilities and the full reach of its power.

The maroon community was well aware of the American advance. From the thick cover of the banks of the Apalachicola River, black and Indian scouts were following the Americans' every move as the leadership of the community carefully planned a strategy to deal with the threat. Unfortunately for its defense, many of the maroon community's most skilled warriors were away on an extended hunting trip.[39] On July 15 gunboat commander Loomis spotted one of the community's "boats pulling out of the river; and being anxious to ascertain whether we should be permitted peaceably to pass the fort above us, I dispatched a boat with an officer to gain the necessary information."[40] The maroon sailors and soldiers were in no mood to negotiate and immediately opened fire upon the Americans. The fact that the Americans attempted to engage in diplomacy with the Prospect Bluff settlement illustrated their serious regard for the community's military strength and political cohesion. The closer the Americans got to Prospect Bluff, the colder their feet became, as they began to realize fully what a challenge lay ahead of them.

On July 17 four sailors under the leadership of Midshipman Luffborough were sent to collect fresh water and they spotted a black man. Luffborough ordered the ship ashore in pursuit of the man. The Americans had sailed directly into a carefully orchestrated trap. As the vessel pulled to shore it was met with a wall of bullets fired by "more than fifty" blacks and Indians who had carefully stalked the sailors.[41] Luffborough and two sailors were killed, and a third sailor was captured. The fourth sailor managed to swim to safety. In Patterson's words, these two acts of "unprovoked and wanton aggression . . . [and] hostile disposition and conduct . . . evincing the strongest manner their intention to dispute his passage past their fort, rendered it necessary to silence their fire, and capture the fort."[42] Gaines's plan to provoke the community's defenders had worked to near perfection, and the Americans were now free to attack the community behind a claim of self-defense.

At nearly the same time the naval detachment was being ambushed, Clinch and 116 men began the army's advance from Camp Crawford to Prospect Bluff. Clinch and his men met with William McIntosh and 150 warriors who were heading to Prospect Bluff to capture blacks for reward money. McIntosh and his Creek warriors played such a crucial role in the assault that in December, when the chief headed a "Muscogee or Creek" delegation to meet the president in Washington, D.C., he was presented to the public as "McIntosh [who], co-operated with Major-General Jackson during the whole war; and latterly . . . marched against the Negro Fort."[43] The next day McIntosh's men were joined by a large detachment of warriors under Koteha Hadjo and Captain Isaacs, resulting in a Creek force of around 500 warriors.[44] According to Clinch, his "junction with these chiefs was accidental; their expedition having long since projected . . . their object was to capture the negroes within the fort, and restore them to their proper owners."[45] Nonetheless, hundreds of heavily armed and well-supplied American and Creek soldiers were converging near Prospect Bluff, all of whom were deeply committed to attacking the community and reenslaving as many of its inhabitants as possible.

As the Americans and Creeks made their way toward Prospect Bluff, a number of Indian scouting parties fanned out in every direction to avoid ambushes and to capture any blacks or hostile Indians they might encounter. On July 19, when Clinch's men and the majority of their Indian allies camped outside Prospect Bluff on the opposite side of the river with the fort ominously looming above them, a group of scouts returned with a black prisoner. The man had a scalp that he had taken from one of Luffborough's sailors. On an urgent mission to request the aid of the Seminoles against the daily increasing American and Creek force, the prisoner reported that the previous day Garçon and the Choctaw chief had returned to Prospect Bluff from the mouth of the Apalachicola, where they and their men had killed Luffborough and the sailors.[46] As would have been the case elsewhere, the community's leader, Garçon, was in the field carefully coordinating actions against an invading army. Foremost in Garçon's mind would have been time and manpower. Because of simple misfortune, most of the community's defenders were away on a hunting trip, and it was not clear when they would return. Furthermore, it was equally unclear whether the Seminoles had received the request for help. In the meantime Garçon, now solely in charge of the community, had evacuated Prospect Bluff of the majority of the maroons. He would now have to utilize every available set of hands and everything he had been taught by Nicolls and the Royal Marines.

Fearing that the naval detachment might be delayed indefinitely, Clinch began an assault on the fort. Few maroon communities in history had faced such a large and powerful force. At the same time, few if any communities had been so securely positioned, well supplied, and well trained. As a result of the convergence of these two opposing forces, the ensuing battle was one of the most epic confrontations between a maroon community and a colonial or national force. Even though Clinch's combined white and Indian force consisted of hundreds of battle-hardened soldiers, they had little hope of breaching the sturdy walls of the British built fort, which was virtually impenetrable in its position high above the Apalachicola River.

The initial assault consisted of a series of confused volleys from the Indian and American troops as they attempted to conceal themselves in the thick brush along the banks of the river. The attackers were at an immense tactical disadvantage, which was exploited by Prospect Bluff's defenders. The black and Choctaw force, directed by Garçon, met every advance on the fort with orderly musket and cannon fire that struck "terror into the souls of most of our red friends" and reflected British military training, rigid discipline, and organization.[47] The coordination of a cannon assault, consisting of a series of deafening explosions, was particularly impressive, and it is no wonder that this terrified the Creeks and not a few American soldiers.

On July 23, when it had become clear to Clinch that the current assault was no match for Prospect Bluff's defenses and organization, a number of Creek chiefs entered the fort under a flag of truce and demanded its surrender. The delegation included Mad Tiger, "whose finger alone spoke a language that went to the soul," and a number of other chiefs whose collective diplomatic skills were described as allowing them to "baffle the machinations of those who were their superiors in council."[48] Their diplomatic skills were for naught, as Garçon met their overtures with an abusive tirade, insisting that he had been left in charge of the fort by the British and would sink any American vessel that attempted to pass it. Furthermore, Garçon threatened to blow up the fort if it could not be defended and then he raised the red flag of no surrender to join the Union Jack above the fort.[49] The symbolism was unmistakable: Garçon was coordinating the actions of British soldiers who would die in defense of their territory and rights. This was deeply disheartening to both the Americans and the Creeks.

It is tempting to interpret Garçon's determination as a desperate, if not romantic, effort to defend what was left of the community's freedom in the face of overwhelming odds. However, this would be entirely incorrect. The community had successfully repulsed the enemy's attack for days, which made surrender seem totally unnecessary. The fate of the captured American sailor, who was tarred and burned alive, further supports this interpretation.[50] This ritualized act of public violence was a clear statement of how the maroons intended to deal with the adversaries who were invading their territory. This decision also made it clear that the maroons did not expect any quarter. In the community's eyes, the battle was a meeting of military equals, not a skirmish between desperate fugitive slaves and the American armed forces and their Creek allies. It appeared that the community had an equal or better chance of victory against the Americans and Creeks rather than succumbing to defeat. Furthermore, the members of the community acted as British subjects who were defending sovereign territory in resisting the American invasion. The community was so committed to defending itself under the auspices of British sovereignty that during the assault Mary Ashley raised and lowered the Union Jack daily and fired the cannons in hope of alerting the community's absent hunters about the American assault. Ashley's actions, while illustrating the lack of manpower and attitudes toward women, underscored the community's strong resolve to defend itself under the flag of Great Britain. The community's intensity and organization struck one American soldier, who noted: "We were pleased with their spirited opposition to the imbecile measures of our Indians, though they were Indians, negroes, and our enemies. Many circumstances convinced us that most of them determined never to be taken alive."[51] Even a young enlisted man realized what an unrelenting and serious foe the Americans and Creeks had engaged at Prospect Bluff.

The Explosion

By July 25 the naval detachment had sailed to the immediate vicinity of Prospect Bluff. This was where Clinch and Loomis agreed, since everything else had failed, that the boats would be positioned for a cannon bombardment. Early on the morning of July 27 the defenders engaged in a fierce exchange of fire with the American boats. During the battle Gunboat 154, under James Bassett, attempted to ascertain the exact distance of the fort by lobbing a series of cannon shots in its general direction, as was the standard technique. The fifth shot, which had been heated in the boat's galley, ignited the fort's powder magazine and resulted in a horrific explosion that virtually incinerated the fort and nearly all its defenders. Clinch recorded that "the explosion was awful and the scene horrible beyond description . . . the War Yells of the Indians, the cries and lamentations of the wounded, compelled the soldier to pause in the midst of victory, and to drop a tear for the sufferings of his fellow Beings." Clinch further reflected that "the Great Ruler of the Universe must have used us as his instrument in chastising the blood-thirsty and murderous wretches that defended the Fort."[52] A young soldier wrote to his father: "You cannot conceive, nor I describe the horrors of the scene. In an instant, hundreds of lifeless bodies were stretched upon the plain, buried in sand and rubbish, or suspended from the tops of the surrounding pines." According to the soldier, "Here lay an innocent babe, there a helpless mother: on the one side a sturdy warrior, on the other a bleeding squaw. Piles of bodies, large heaps of sand, broken guns, accoutrements, &c. covered the site of the fort. The brave soldier was disarmed of his resentment, and checked his victorious career, to drop a tear on the distressing scene." His postscript read tellingly, "First rate land can be purchased in Florida for fifty cents per acre. What speculations! If it should ever be ours, which, I think, will be the case."[53]

The generally accepted opinion of contemporaries and many historians since then was that the shot that destroyed the fort simply reflected the one-in-millions chance of a direct hit in the powder magazine, which had accidentally been left open.[54] Three years later an American engineer determined that the shot soared 3,090 yards (9,270 feet, or 1.75 miles) and would have required a "long eighteen pounder with an angle and elevation of little more than ten degrees and the ordinary charge of six pounds of powder."[55] The engineer was arguing that the probability of the shot going directly into the powder magazine numbered one in millions. Eventually Clinch admitted the virtual impossibility of this shot, when he reported to John Calhoun that given the engineer's findings and the fact that the fort's walls were at least fourteen feet high, "these circumstances, even admitting that a ball thrown from a nine pounder, would range three thousand and ninety yards, what must have been its degree of elevation, when [it] entered a magazine within the fort [?]"[56] Other explanations have included the one by William Hambly, who maintained that the American armed forces possessed precise details of the fort's design, which meant that the Americans were aiming at the powder magazine.[57] Yet the sheer distance, lack of light, and small target located within the fort meant that even if the gunner had known the exact location of the powder magazine, the odds of making the shot, especially in the first round of trying, were long odds indeed. Another explanation has suggested that Garçon made good on his threat to destroy the fort, as a modern day Masada.[58] It was true that Garçon had threatened to blow up the fort, as was common when forces retreated from lost positions and had happened when the British evacuated Fort Barrancas; but he meant *after* he and his people had escaped. Suicide would have been the farthest thing from the defenders' minds as they had worked so hard to gain and protect their freedom, and more important, they had been easily repulsing the American and Creek assault and had no reason to believe their position was suddenly in jeopardy. The Seminoles were expected and the community would have assumed that their soldiers would soon be returning from the hunting trip.[59] Finally, it would have been easy for the defenders to slip out at the back of Prospect Bluff through the swamp to join the hundreds of refugees who had already evacuated.

The best and most plausible explanation posited that "a red hot shot . . . glanced off a tree, and flew out of its course among some loose powder that some of the women were filling cartridges from at the grand magazine door, and which communicated to 300 five-and-a-half-inch shells, and about 300 barrels of powder." This freak accident then "blew the whole of the battery or citadel, which stood in the centre of the fort, to atoms, destroying all of the men, and several of the women and children."[60] If this explanation is true, the community was the victim of incredibly bad luck.

Remarkably Garçon and the Choctaw chief had survived the blast, though Garçon was blinded by the explosion; they were immediately executed by the

Creeks.[61] Creek and American soldiers then swept the area for any survivors before torching the village. The invading forces had already destroyed the community's fields and outlying dwellings. Hambly collected such Spanish slaves as were captured, and the army officers rounded up the few American former slave survivors. Military supplies estimated to be worth approximately $200,000 were seized by the Americans.[62] In one cruel day Prospect Bluff had gone from being the site of one of the hemisphere's wealthiest and most impressively situated maroon communities to a smoking crater where American and Creek soldiers were wiping the last vestiges of the community's existence from the face of the earth. No maroon community had ever seen its fortunes change so radically in such a short time.

Once again, even when taking Gaines's carefully laid plans into consideration, a large American and Indian force had launched an invasion of questionable legality into the Spanish Floridas during a time of official peace to crush the threat of racial disorder to the Deep South. Nicolls believed that Prospect Bluff had been "treacherously attacked by the lawless slaveholders on the Georgian frontier of Florida, aided by . . . [a Naval detachment] from the slaveholding State of Louisiana. . . . I do not think the . . . [government of the United States] authorized the attack." This was because "it was a manifest breach of the treaty of peace, for I am sure they had not then . . . the power to restrain the white population of their southern States, particularly when the subject of slaves is the question."[63] Indeed the diplomatic and political forces at play were so powerful that the American government attempted to cover up through censorship what had occurred at Prospect Bluff. The primary reason for doing this was to avoid antagonizing the Spanish at a time when American officials were working to acquire the Floridas. For three years Washington suppressed the official accounts of the community's destruction in the hope of keeping the public unaware of what had happened. The official story of the community's destruction became public only in 1819, when the *National Intelligencer* published Clinch's official report. The government was so intent on covering up the destruction of the fort that it happened only after Clinch aggressively pushed to have the report published, forcing the secretary of war to make the official military account of the events open to the public.[64] In late 1819, when the *Niles Weekly Register* finally printed the report, under the boldfaced title "Negro Fort on Appalachicola," it was prefaced with a note indicating that "there was an obvious deficiency of the information necessary to give complete view of the transaction, inasmuch as no notice was taken of the assault on the fort by land. That deficiency we have it now in our power to [rectify]. . . . It has never before met the public eye."[65]

Washington's efforts to suppress information notwithstanding, word of the maroon community's destruction quickly spread, and Americans, Spaniards, and Creeks of all walks of life breathed a palpable sigh of relief. The *Georgia Journal* "congratulate[d] our readers upon the annihilation of an establishment calculated to create discontent . . . among a certain class of our population and offering asylum to the perpetrator of every crime."[66] The secretary of war triumphantly reported to Jackson that "the destruction of the Negro Fort . . . may have removed the necessity of keeping up so large a force, in that quarter."[67] Daniel Patterson noted that "the service rendered by the destruction of this fort, and the band of negroes who held it, and the country in its vicinity, is of great and manifest importance to the United States."[68] Patterson believed that a serious military threat to the southern United States had been destroyed and that the area's slaves "have no longer a place to fly to, and will not be so liable to abscond," thus greatly reducing the likelihood of slave resistance. An employee of Forbes and Company wrote a letter that jubilantly proclaimed, "I rejoice at the prospect of recovering a part of the blacks from Appalachicola."[69] It appeared to everyone across the region that after centuries of attempts, Anglo Americans had finally scored a definitive victory and seriously curbed the threat of racial disorder emanating from the Spanish Floridas. The natural assumption was that the annexation of the Floridas would soon follow as a valuable addition to the expanding slave frontier.[70]

11 ⇒ The Seminole War

THE DESTRUCTION OF THE FORT at Prospect Bluff was a blow to black and Indian resistance in the Southeast and a tremendous victory for Anglo America's centuries-long effort to end the perceived threat of racial disorder originating in Spanish Florida. However, the victory was not nearly as total as many had imagined. Americans and their allies were soon to be bitterly disappointed to learn that "contrary to these expectations, it was discovered that a hostile disposition was still entertained by the Seminole tribe . . . aided by fugitive negroes, and instigated by foreign incendiaries."[1] Most important, as one of the refugees from Prospect Bluff later noted with only a small degree of overstatement, "all of those who had been in the British service" had left Prospect Bluff prior to the explosion and had joined Seminole, Red Stick, or maroon villages and remained deeply committed to protecting their freedom and in their belief that they were British subjects.[2] The depth of this commitment, which would last for years, clearly illustrates how fully the former slaves had absorbed Edward Nicolls's ideas and the extent to which they saw themselves as members of a community bound together by their common status as British subjects, which transcended attachment to a particular place or dwelling. Thus the former slaves constituted an intellectual and political community who had rejected slavery as a social system. The maroons maintained close ties to proxies acting on behalf of Nicolls, which intensified these beliefs.[3] Likewise, as late as the time of official annexation of Florida to the United States in 1821, the Seminoles and Red Sticks remained steadfast that "we consider ourselves allies of Great Britain entitled to full benefit[s] . . . when the British evacuated the Floridas . . . we were expressly informed so by . . . Colonel Nicolls."[4] As a result, the Indians were deeply embittered after having suffered American encroachments, which the Red Sticks in particular regarded as violating Article 9 of the Treaty of Ghent. The views of the Prospect Bluff refugees and the Seminoles and Red Sticks affirmed the analysis of the *Niles Weekly Register* that Nicolls and Woodbine were the "real authors of the [Seminole] war."[5] Similarly, the *Army and Navy Chronicle*'s assessment was that the destruction of the fort at Prospect Bluff was the "first and perhaps one of the most hazardous expeditions of the Seminole War."[6] Nicolls's black and Indian allies would soon become the main anti-American combatants in the Seminole War as well as the primary cause of the conflict.[7] However, the survivors from Prospect Bluff first needed to regroup and rebuild their community.

Angola

For decades many southeastern Indians, along with their black allies or slaves, had spent the winter months hunting in the colony's thinly populated southwestern forests and swamps. During the Patriot War hundreds of Florida's black defenders had removed themselves from the reach of American aggression by setting up permanent settlements at the Braden-Manatee River Junction.[8] The members of the settlement, which came to be known as Angola, hunted and grew crops in lush surroundings and were part of an extended trade network. Angola's most important trade partners were Seminoles and Cuban fishermen, who provided the community with access to the greater Caribbean and Atlantic world.[9] Angola was a maroon community that appears to have had much in common with the one at Prospect Bluff. Unfortunately, given the paucity of sources, it is difficult to discern much more about Angola from the historical record. It is clear that Angola was a large and prosperous agricultural settlement that enjoyed close relations with the Seminoles and Red Sticks. However, there is virtually no surviving evidence about the community's government, culture, or daily activities. It is probable that members of Angola had joined Nicolls and Woodbine's force during the War of 1812. It is equally likely that the community at Prospect Bluff had traded with Angola and that some members had moved there before the fort's destruction. Beyond a doubt is that many refugees from the maroon community fled to Angola after the American-led assault on Prospect Bluff.[10] Presumably they were welcomed as skilled farmers, craftsmen, and warriors who shared with the inhabitants of Angola a common history and the goal of freedom. Thus one stream of refugees from Prospect Bluff began to rebuild their lives at Angola.

The Seminoles and Red Sticks

The largest number of refugees from Prospect Bluff had fled east to a cluster of black and Seminole villages on the Suwannee River under the jurisdiction of the Seminole chief Bowlegs.[11] In 1813 Bowlegs and his people were driven to the Suwannee by an American assault on the Alachua savanna. In the past Bowlegs had worried about the negative attention that the maroon community at Prospect Bluff was directing to the Floridas. After having submitted to immense external pressures from American, Spanish, and Creek officials, Bowlegs even instructed his warriors to capture members of the community and return them to their masters. However, as the Seminoles observed American forces encroach more aggressively, remembered Nicolls's promises, and absorbed many Red Sticks, they were becoming increasingly radicalized and hostile toward the United States and the Spanish, "whom they now considered as American partisans to the last."[12] In the fall of 1816, when a Spanish official pleaded with Bowlegs to help the Spanish recover former slaves who had joined his community, the chief's cold response was: "You think hard of your black people but I did not fetch them here they came here by persuasion of the British so if you can make good with the English you are welcome to them."[13] Bowlegs was rebuffing the Spanish while recognizing that the majority of the blacks who had joined his community were refugees from Prospect Bluff who had a special relationship with the British. In symbolic language that reflected Nicolls's influence (anti-slavery imagery, a strong attachment to their land, and a commitment to violence and military service), Bowlegs told the governor of East Florida that "we cannot submit to their [American] shackles, and will die in defense of our country."[14] With the destruction of the fort at Prospect Bluff the two groups were keenly aware that they had to make common cause to have any chance of resisting the rising tide of American expansion. Their shared history and the fact that both groups believed they had a special relationship with the British made the alliance that much stronger.

While the refugees recognized that they were living in Bowlegs's territory, they quickly sought to replicate the society they had created at Prospect Bluff. The first step was setting up associated villages that extended far along the river and maintained ties with Angola.[15] Within these villages, men, women, and children soon rebuilt a similar economy to the one that had served them so well at Prospect Bluff. Living in large and well-built cabins surrounded by wooden fences, the inhabitants tended gardens of peas, beans, corn, and rice.[16] The destruction of the fort was a devastating and traumatic blow; however, families, friends, neighbors, and associates had begun to rebuild their lives and their community.

The refugees were equally quick to recreate the Prospect Bluff maroon community's political system and military structure at Suwannee. They chose Nero, Bowlegs's chief black advisor, as their leader. Nero was a refugee from

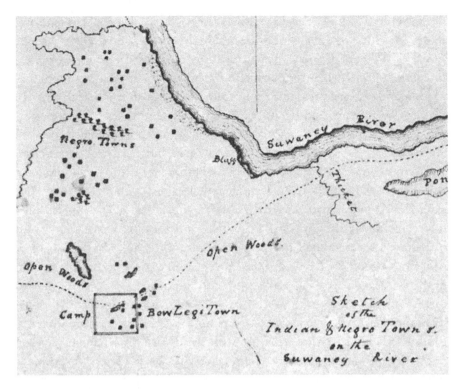

FIGURE 4. Captain Young's Sketch Map. Drawn during the Seminole War, this 1818 map shows Bowlegs' Town and associated black towns in the vicinity of the Suwannee River. (National Archives and Records Administration, Washington, D.C.)

Prospect Bluff who had spent his early life on an East Florida plantation before joining the Seminoles in 1812.[17] Nero was a highly privileged local black and a skilled warrior. This meant that he could be relied on for quality military and political leadership. It also meant that he understood the region's geopolitics. These were the same qualities that had led to the rise of Garçon, Cyrus, and Prince. Nero shared some of his power with "Negro Chiefs," many of whom must have been refugees from Prospect Bluff. Together these men "sat in counsel" with the Seminoles in a process that demonstrated the nature of the union between the Indians and the blacks as well as the workings of their political system.[18]

After the new arrivals had chosen Nero as their leader, a Seminole reported that the refugees "are on parade ... about six hundred that bore arms. They have chosen officers of every description, and endeavour to keep up a regular discipline, and are very strict in punishing violators of their military rules."[19] This was a recreation of the maroon community's military system that had been defined by regular drilling and a clear chain of command at

Prospect Bluff. Word quickly spread to the United States that the "Indians and negroes were collecting in companies west of the Apalachicola."[20] More troubling news came in March 1817, when the Creek Captain Barnard reported what he had learned while on a mission to recover his slaves who had fled to the Seminoles:

> They were all gone off to the mouth of Sawannee . . . [the] runaway blacks were constantly coming from St. Mary's and from other parts of Georgia to the places near the mouth of Sawanne river many of those that were at the Fort . . . are gone on there. . . . There are four hundred [blacks] collected there fit to bear arms exclusive of the women and children and . . . well furnished with arms and ammunition. . . . The Red people say that those blacks have a red pole set up in their town and are dancing the red stick dance. . . . [It] was not only negroes belonging to the white people that are making their escape to that [Suwannee?] Harbour but nearly all that belong to the red people are gone there.[21]

This growing black and Indian force would publicly "speak in the most contemptuous manner of the Americans, and threaten to have satisfaction for what has been done—meaning the destruction of the Negro Fort." Furthermore, the blacks said "they are in a complete fix for fighting, and wish an engagement with the Americans, or McIntosh's troops; they would let them know that they had something more to do than they had at Apalachicola."[22] Another account indicated that those "who were saved from the Negro Fort . . . would revenge themselves for the loss of their friends at that place."[23] This was not the language of a rag-tag assortment of bitter or desperate rebels who were on the run. These were the proclamations of people who felt that their homes, property, and sovereign community had been unfairly attacked by the Americans and Creeks and that many of their fellow British subjects had been murdered during this illegal invasion. They were illustrating a strong sense of community identity and an equally strong attachment to a people, a political institution, and an idea. This was the language of war between two legitimate powers: the British survivors from the maroon community, and the United States and its Creek allies.

Beginning in the spring of 1817 and lasting for over a year, the Indians and their black allies began to launch destructive raids against American frontier settlers. The Indians and blacks were trying to stem the tide of American expansion, demonstrate their continued anger over the Treaty of Fort Jackson, and avenge the destruction of Prospect Bluff. During these months Edmund Doyle described the region as being filled "with outlaws and murderers, runaway Negroes. . . . It would be certain death for a small party of Americans, or

American Indians [to enter the Spanish Floridas]. . . . They daily expect the arrival of a British agent to see them Rited, the Americans and us drove off the land."[24] To American and Creek slave owners, these raids were a return to the darkest days of the Floridas, representing a challenge to racial order in the South and frustrating proof that the 1814 invasion of Pensacola and the destruction of the maroon community had not ended this threat. The appearance of a number of British interlopers among the Indians and refugees from Prospect Bluff soon increased regional tension.

Nicolls's Proxies

Nicolls had not forgotten his black and Indian allies and soon reestablished contact with them through a series of proxies. In 1817 a concerned Governor Cameron of the Bahamas, a man who knew Woodbine well, sent a letter to Lord Bathurst that quickly circulated among British governors in the Caribbean:

> Captain Woodbine of His Majestys late Corps of Colonial Marines and commissary for the Indian Tribes had obtained from Sir Gregor MacGregor a commission as colonel in a corps which Woodbine is to raise . . . and enlist some disbanded people of the West India Regiments. . . . The Creeks [Red Sticks and Seminoles] are much devoted to him and they have always been hostile towards the Spaniards, but there is a large body of American Negroes now among the Indian tribes in the Floridas, they fled their owners in Louisiana and Georgia in consequence of the encouragement offered them by Sir Alexander Cochrane's Proclamation and many of them served some time in the Colonial Marines. These people will at once join Woodbine who is a man of excellent abilities and great activity, and from his knowledge and influence with the Indians and fugitive negroes, will most probably have it in his power to drive the Spaniards out of both Floridas which at the head of the Indian Tribes in 1814 and 1815 Woodbine obtained from the Creek Indians a grant of 40,000 acres of land upon the coast of Florida and this is to be conferred to him by the Spanish insurgents in the event of their conquering that country.[25]

Woodbine had indeed joined MacGregor's revolutionary army and was busy recruiting troops in the Caribbean for a mission to the Floridas. Many of these recruits were West India Regiment veterans of Nicolls's expedition to the Southeast as well as members of the Second West India Regiment. During the War of 1812 many of these men had worked closely with Nicolls and had watched as his anti-slavery experiment unfolded. Although Woodbine would never succeed in conquering any territory or toppling the

Spanish government, his presence had a powerful effect on people across the Southeast. More important, Woodbine had already been to West Florida in late 1816, where he met with the blacks and Indians at Suwannee, whom he informed that "Colonel Nicols would be out here in three months"; he then traveled to Angola and then on to New Providence via Havana.[26] To the refugees from Prospect Bluff, he served as a reminder of their British status and the experiment that had begun under Nicolls. To his Indian allies, his appearance was definitive proof that they might yet hope for British help in resisting the Americans and the boundaries of the Treaty of Fort Jackson. To whites and Creeks, the return of Woodbine, who had been identified as a proxy for Nicolls "of proclamation memory," was frightening. Whites and Creeks justifiably feared that Woodbine had appeared to carry on Nicolls's radical anti-slavery experiment with the "remnant of the slaves who escaped from the Negro Fort."[27] Even if Woodbine was not an ideological opponent of slavery, his actions in Florida served to further Nicolls's anti-slavery experiment by reminding the former slaves of their relationship with Great Britain and Nicolls's message. In the winter of 1817 David Mitchell, the new American agent to the Creek Indians, reported that the "notorious Woodbine has recently made his appearance again at the mouth of the Apalachicola, and that he has an agent now among the Seminolie Indians and Negroes . . . stirring them up to acts of hostility."[28] The *Niles Weekly Register* reported that the "infamous Woodbine" was encouraging the Indians to acts of violence against the United States and hoped that they "may meet the fate of Appalachicola."[29] Driving home the powerful association between Woodbine and the events at Prospect Bluff in the American imagination, William Trimble incorrectly reported "that Woodbine has collected a force of 50 white men, 500 negroes and a large Indian force near the Negro Fort."[30]

Woodbine was aided in his mission by Robert Ambrister. During the War of 1812, Ambrister, a young white Bahamian, had served under Nicolls. Ambrister had become radicalized by Nicolls during this period. After having been decommissioned from the Royal Marines, Ambrister returned to the Bahamas, where Woodbine recruited him to join his revolutionary army. As his first mission, Woodbine sent Ambrister to Tampa to establish a base and to begin training the refugees from the maroon community at Prospect Bluff who were now at Suwannee with the ultimate goal to "see the Negroes righted."[31] It is highly probable that Ambrister and Woodbine had close contacts with Angola, which may even have included overseeing a plantation of two hundred blacks there.[32] What is beyond a doubt is that from his base at Tampa and under the direction of Woodbine, Ambrister energetically and passionately continued the project begun at Prospect Bluff by Nicolls, with whom he regularly corresponded. Ambrister's association with Nicolls and the refugees from Prospect Bluff was so strong that the *Niles Weekly Register* confidently noted he had "served as an engineer under *Nicholls*, and [is] commander of the *negro* allies," and the *Louisiana Gazette* reported that "the commander of the blacks, [is] an Englishman, who served as an engineer under colonel Nichols."[33] Eventually it was reported that Ambrister "had complete command of the Negroes who considered him as their Captain," and at Ambrister's trial a witness testified that he was "a person vested with authority among the Negro leaders, and gave orders for their preparation for war ... and that the leaders came to him for orders."[34]

Militarily, ideologically, and politically, Ambrister was Nicolls's surrogate. Accordingly the refugees from Prospect Bluff respected his authority as a fellow British subject with a high military rank and took great confidence from his presence. Nothing more clearly illustrates the fact that Ambrister was acting as Nicolls's surrogate than a letter he wrote to Nicolls while at Suwannee, stating that "they depend on your promises, and expect you are the way out. They have stuck to the cause, and will always believe in the faith of you."[35] The Americans saw the "cause" as the "savage, servile, exterminating war against the United States."[36] However in reality, the "cause" was the community, freedom, and attachment to British status that had been created by Nicolls and the former slaves at Prospect Bluff. Even after the fort's destruction, "Nicolls's negroes" at both Suwannee and Angola still saw themselves as full British subjects who had been forced by the American and Creek destruction of the fort at Prospect Bluff to relocate and fight brutally in defense of their rights.[37] As was the case when analyzing Nicolls's relationship with the maroons, placing a strong emphasis on the importance of Ambrister's actions in no way undermines the agency of the former slaves. The maroons clearly understood the benefits that came with their relationship with the British and that it provided them with the most likely path to freedom and greatest opportunity to protect their interests.

Alexander Arbuthnot, an aging Scottish merchant who had extensive experience trading with the Natives of the Floridas from his base in the Bahamas, was the third British subject to become conspicuously involved with blacks and Indians in the region. Arbuthnot was a "humanitarian" who had a sincere respect and concern for the Red Sticks and Seminoles, besides being a businessman who hoped to establish a lucrative trade with the Indians. Arbuthnot arrived at Suwannee in the fall of 1817 with a boat packed with Indian supplies, intending to establish a store in West Florida. Forbes and Company, having just begun to rebuild their business, saw his presence as serious economic competition and immediately began to work for his removal.

In a fateful decision, Arbuthnot became the Seminoles' and Red Sticks' tribal advocate. Agreeing with Nicolls, Arbuthnot believed that the Americans were in violation of the Treaty of Ghent and must return the Red Sticks' land to their 1811 boundaries and that the Indians were the formal allies of Great Britain, which was not doing enough to aid them. He petitioned the Americans, Spanish, and British on behalf of the Natives and sought to stop American encroachments on their territory while pushing for the return to the Indians of the land that had been ceded to the United States under the Treaty of Fort Jackson.[38] The British foreign minister had "very little doubt of the justice of the complaints made by these Tribes . . . [but felt that] any interference . . . on behalf of any of the Indians . . . especially those engaged in operations of Colonel Nicolls in 1814, would be viewed with extreme jealousy . . . [that] I should not find myself warranted in provoking."[39] Most offensive to American sensibilities was the fact that Arbuthnot "bitterly complain[ed] in conjunction with the Indians of the destruction of the Negro Fort."[40] To the Americans, Arbuthnot appeared to be yet another dangerous British interloper in the Floridas who had suspicious designs with blacks and Indians. White Americans never doubted that Arbuthnot was the "real successor of Nicholls in the work of stirring up mischief along their borders—It may also be added and of Woodbine too."[41] The reappearance of British instigators who were doing the work of Nicolls was exceptionally provocative to Americans and Creeks. It was also deeply inspiring to the refugees from Prospect Bluff and their Indian allies.

The Outbreak of Hostilities

The United States put in motion plans to end the threat of ongoing black and Indian resistance and British meddling in the Floridas. Gaines had been instructed by his superiors to increase the American military presence along the Escambia River gradually and to rebuild Fort Scott, located just above the Apalachicola River.[42] The increased military presence in the disputed territory was designed by the Americans to quell Indian and black hostilities against the American frontier and to protect growing American settlements in the region. During 1817 Gaines exchanged a number of testy letters with Bowlegs and Kinache demanding that the Seminoles and Red Sticks cease their hostilities against the United States and return fugitive slaves, including the refugees from Prospect Bluff. The Indians responded that they suffered violent American encroachments, that they harbored no blacks, and that if American armed forces attempted to dislodge them, they would respond with force.[43]

Closer to Fort Scott, in what was American territory according to the Treaty of Fort Jackson, stood a large Red Stick and black village known as Fowltown. Many of the refugees from Prospect Bluff had migrated there. At the same time that Gaines was exchanging letters with Bowlegs and Kinache, Maj. David Twiggs, the commander of Fort Scott, received a letter from Neamathla, the Red Stick leader of Fowltown. The letter warned Twiggs "not to cross nor cut a stick of wood in the east side of the Flint. That land is mine. I am directed by the power above and power below to protect and defend it. I shall do so."[44] At virtually the same time, Gaines received intelligence from the "friendly Indians" that the "hostile party [of Indians] and Blacks have been promised a British force to assist them, from New Providence. This promise, though made by Nichols and Woodbine, is nevertheless relied on by these deluded wretches, who, I have no doubt, will sue for peace, as they find their hopes of British aid to be without foundation."[45] The news served to hasten the coming of war because it both made the Americans nervous at the possibility and strengthened the resolve of the Seminoles, Red Sticks, and blacks.

Since Fowltown was located in American territory, Jackson wasted little time ordering Twiggs and a large American force to proceed to the village and arrest Neamathla. The Seminole War officially began on the morning of November 21 when Twigg's force was fired upon by Fowltown's defenders. The Americans returned fire, causing the inhabitants of Fowltown to disperse quickly. Before torching the village the Americans made a discovery that confirmed their suspicion that Indians and blacks were working closely with Nicolls and his proxies. The Americans found "in the house of the Chief . . . a British uniform coat (scarlet), with a pair of gold epaulets, and a certificate, signed by a British Captain of Marines, 'Robert White, in absence of Colonel Nichols,' stating, that the Chief had always been a true and faithful friend to the British."[46]

From the Floridas, the Native and black response was swift and brutal. Days later an American naval vessel commanded by Lt. Robert Scott was ambushed by Indians and blacks on the Apalachicola River near the ruins of the fort at Prospect Bluff. They were seeking to avenge the destruction of Fowltown. Most of the soldiers on board were killed in the attack, but a number of women and children were taken prisoner, then tortured and killed.[47] One white American woman, a Mrs. Stewart, was spared and held as a prisoner by the blacks and Indians until April 1818, when American troops rescued her in an ordeal that was reminiscent of the most dramatic captivity narrative.[48]

In December, as the conflict began to escalate, a number of Fowltown warriors captured Edmund Doyle and William Hambly. The refugees from the maroon community at Prospect Bluff blamed both men for the fort's destruction because of the intelligence that they had given to the Americans. Doyle and Hambly were captured at Forbes and Company's store and transported to the Seminole village of Miccosukee and then to the black towns on the Suwannee, where the two men stood trial for their role in the destruction of the fort and village at Prospect Bluff.[49] That refugees from the community participated in the trial serves as a powerful testament to the maroon community's political system and the guiding principles to which they continued to adhere after Prospect Bluff's destruction. In the end Nero, himself a refugee from Prospect Bluff, intervened and turned the men over to the Spanish garrison at St. Marks.

During Hambly's trial a violent alcoholic kidnapped his wife and children and delivered the family to the Seminoles. The man had "belonged to the Negro Fort previous to its destruction." He went aboard an American ship on the Apalachicola River with Thomas Perryman and informed the Americans that Hambly's family "had been taken by the Indians"; he then requested liquor, which he promptly drank, becoming "much intoxicated . . . [and] outrageous."[50] The next morning, after having sobered up, the man apologized, but he soon began to "show his hostile disposition," which led the Americans to believe "that he would not hesitate to commit any act of villany." Accordingly he was locked up until the boat arrived at Fort Scott. Hambly's wife, who had been rescued from the Indians, explained, without citing specifics, that the kidnapper had become the property of her husband after the fort's destruction. She went on to state that she had feared for her life and that he was "preparing himself to join the hostile Indians and Negroes in November or December 1817. But was at that time prevented from doing so by Mr. Hambly." Hambly's wife recounted: "She has no doubt that he intended doing so as soon as he could possess himself of the money which she was able to save from the wreck of Mr. Hambly's property. Until our arrival at the Bay she was in continual fear of her life. He had the address to get from her all the money amounting to near four hundred dollars, which he refused to return to her." The destruction of the maroon community and his reenslavement had clearly not dampened his desire for freedom or to rejoin the other members of the community and their Indian allies. He wanted so badly to accomplish this that he turned to violence, theft, and kidnapping. However circumstances and his drinking ultimately derailed these efforts.

The ambush of Scott and his detachment had further enlivened American opinion. Consequently, in the winter of 1818 Secretary of War John Calhoun ordered Jackson to raise as many troops as he deemed necessary to bring peace to the Southeast and to proceed to Fort Scott, where he arrived in March. Jackson then traveled to Prospect Bluff, where he ordered the construction of Fort Gadsden. Here he waited for reinforcements from Tennessee and for the arrival of the Creek chief William McIntosh (who had led the Creek assault on the maroon community) and his men. Soon Jackson's combined Indian and American force numbered more than 3,500 men.[51] Many of these men, both white and Indian, were hardened veterans of Jackson's years of wars against the Indians and blacks of the Southeast. Jackson's motives for his 1818 invasion of the Floridas were the same as they had been in 1814 when he invaded Pensacola and in 1816 when he ordered the destruction of the maroon community: to end the threat of British-instigated Indian and black racialized violence that threatened the security of America's expanding slave frontier. However, this time Jackson was in an even stronger position than before. He was a national celebrity because of his role in the Battle of New Orleans; America was not engaged in a war with Great Britain; Spain had virtually lost control of the Floridas; and the American lobby calling for the annexation of the Floridas was nearly deafening.

At the end of March, Jackson's large and well-supplied force began its descent of the Florida peninsula. Led by Nicolls and Woodbine's old ally Kinache, the first target was the Lake Miccosukee Village. After a brief skirmish the vast majority of the Indians and blacks were able to flee. While searching the abandoned village, the Americans made a shocking discovery. They found fifty fresh scalps, which they believed had come from the raid on Scott's party, and more than three hundred older scalps.[52] Americans burned the village. Small detachments of Creeks were sent in every direction to scour the countryside for hostile Indians and blacks. In the following week Jackson boldly seized the Spanish garrison at St. Mark's, claiming the fort was so weakly held that it might fall into the hands of the Indians and blacks. While at St. Marks, Jackson captured the hapless Arbuthnot as well as the Red Stick chief Hillis Hadjo, who had earlier traveled to England with Nicolls.

At this point Jackson's army had met little resistance in its war against the blacks and Indians. However, the main aim of the invasion was Bowlegs's town and the associated black villages under Nero, where the largest number of the refugees from Prospect Bluff had settled. This was now the epicenter of black and Indian activity in the region, where for months Ambrister had been helping train Nero's black army.[53] Numbers had recently grown even further when the black and Indian refugees from the Lake Miccosukee Village arrived at Bowlegs's town.

Prior to his capture Arbuthnot had sent a letter to Ambrister warning blacks and Indians along the Suwannee River that "the main drift of the Americans is to destroy the black population of Swany. Tell my friend Boleck [Bowlegs] that it is throwing away his people to attempt to resist such a powerful force."[54] Arbuthnot was addressing a fundamental truth: the Americans were taking care of unfinished business, but their greatest concern was over black resistance and, more specifically, the refugees from Prospect Bluff. Even more pointedly, at his trial Arbuthnot recalled bluntly telling the Indians that it "was the Negroes, not the Indians, the Americans were principally moving against."[55] A black resident of Suwannee, who was an eyewitness, corroborated Arbuthnot's belief when he later testified that "the Indians have always said that they should not have been attacked at the Suwanee, if they had not had these negroes among them; that the hope of getting possession of them invited the attack and proved the destruction of the town."[56] Gaines too made this clear when he told the Seminoles that "you harbor a great many of my black people among you, at Sahwahnee. If you give me leave to go by you against them, I shall not hurt anything belonging to you."[57] In John Quincy Adams's careful and telling opinion, this was a "Negro-Indian war" and not the other way around.[58] An American soldier's diary echoed this from the field when he carefully described being involved in the planning of an "attack on the Negro and Bowlegs Town."[59] The soldier's choice of word order made it clear that the primary aim of the assault was the black villages. The *Niles Weekly Register* reiterated this to a national audience when it reported that prior to the destruction of the maroon community, "many runaway negroes, who composed part of its garrison ... deserted from it, and after its destruction ... joined the other banditti under Bowlegs, and now compose part of those negroes who, together with the barbarous Seminolians, have been robbing and murdering the frontier inhabitants both of Georgia and Florida indiscriminately ... these are the main enemies of the people of Florida [and the South]."[60] The Seminoles and Red Sticks were dangerous and deeply embittered foes of the United States, but most observers were aware that Indians were a diminishing threat to American interests east of the Mississippi River. Yet with the expansion of slavery, slave resistance had become the gravest internal danger facing the Deep South. Jackson was doggedly pursuing the refugees of one of North America's most conspicuous acts of slave resistance.

Contrary to Arbuthnot's advice and desperate advice from the recently arrived Lake Miccosukee Village refugees, the inhabitants of Suwannee decided to make a stand against the Americans. The defense would have to be mounted without Ambrister, who had left prior to the American assault. Undeterred, Nero's army established its position on the western bank of the river and sent the women and children into the swamps, from which they could easily flee farther afield if need be. For many of these people, this was the second time in two years they had braced themselves for a large American and Creek assault. On April 16 the American attack on the black settlements began. The Battle of Suwannee proved the decisive engagement of the Seminole War. More than three hundred black soldiers fought skillfully and with bravery that reflected their British training and commitment, but they quickly realized the hopelessness of their cause and fled across the river to join the women and children.[61] Their escape was well executed because they had carefully planned to "decamp as soon as the American force enters the Country, where they intend to make a third retreat at Tampa and the Spanish fisheries not far distance from thence."[62]

Only a handful of blacks had been killed, and the majority had successfully fled the Americans. At the same time, however, the destruction of the towns along the Suwannee River was a major military setback for the blacks and Indians. This setback was compounded by Jackson's capture of Ambrister only days later when the British agent, unaware that the Americans had captured the Suwannee towns, "approached our [American] camp believing us to be Indians and Negroes" before unsuccessfully attempting to flee along with his detachment of one white man and a number of blacks.[63] Before the end of April, in a decision that greatly angered both the American and British governments, Jackson had tried and executed Ambrister and Arbuthnot for stirring the blacks and Indians against the United States.[64]

In May Jackson once again occupied Pensacola because he felt that Indian and black hostility from the Floridas would never cease until the United States acquired the territories.[65] The governor of West Florida sent Jackson a letter insisting he had violated Spanish sovereignty by occupying Pensacola and that he must withdraw his forces immediately.[66] In response Jackson penned a vitriolic letter to the Spanish governor that succinctly captured his rationale for invading the Spanish province and engaging in the Seminole War more generally. Jackson thundered:

> The southern frontier of the United States has, for more than 12 months, been exposed to all the horrors of a cruel and savage war. A party of outlaws and refugees from the Creek nation; negroes who have fled from their masters, citizens of the United States, and sought an asylum in Florida, and the Seminole Indians inhabiting the territory of Spain, all uniting, have raised the tomahawk, and in the character of savage warfare, have neither regarded sex nor age. . . . [The United States appealed to your government through normal diplomatic channels to put an end to this while building forts within our boundaries to protect our citizens until we found out that] Spanish authorities had not the power of controlling the Indians in Florida; that their acts of late were viewed as equally hostile to the interests of Spain . . . and that the negro establishments in the Apalachicola

and St. Juan rivers, were founded by British agents, contrary to the will of Spain. These representations determined the President of the United States to adopt effectual measures to restore tranquility to the southern frontier of the American republic; and pursuant to his orders, justifiably by the immutable laws of self-defence, I have penetrated into Florida, reduced to ashes the Seminole villages, destroyed their magazines of provisions, beaten their warriors whenever they hazarded a contest, dispersed some, and expelled others across the river. . . . This is the third time the American troops have been compelled to enter Pensacola from the same causes. . . . This time it must be held until Spain has the power or will to maintain her neutrality. . . . My resolution is fixed: I have strength enough to enforce.[67]

Jackson drew a direct line connecting the events of the War of 1812 with the Seminole War. He argued that for years now he had been fighting a race war that was the result of Spanish weakness and British intrigues with the blacks and Indians of the Southeast (in the form of Nicolls, Woodbine, and their proxies). He felt that the United States was legally, morally, and ethically justified in invading the Floridas for what he insisted would be the last time. Jackson was more confident in his actions than at any previous point in time because of shifting geopolitical realities and the severity of the threat embodied by recent events in Florida. Less than two weeks later President Monroe delivered a speech to Congress in which he agreed with Jackson's argument that Spanish weakness and self-defense had more than justified the American invasion.[68]

With the Battle of Suwannee, the Seminole War was essentially over. The United States and Spain had begun negotiations over the transfer of the Floridas. Yet the issue of the blacks from the Suwannee towns still had to be resolved. Some had been killed in the town's defense. Others had been captured or killed in subsequent sweeps of the area by Creek Indians. And yet others had fled in various directions across the Floridas with their Seminole or Red Stick allies. However, the vast majority had continued their exodus farther south and had joined Angola.[69] Angola, which was now populated by its initial inhabitants as well as refugees from the maroon community at Prospect Bluff who had arrived in both 1816 and 1818, was the last major bastion of meaningful black resistance in the Floridas.

Jackson recognized this and, in his eagerness to finish the job he had begun in 1813, quickly sent Lt. James Gadsden to investigate Angola and its surrounding settlements. Gadsden reported that Angola was indeed the last major bastion of black and Native resistance in the Floridas and that it was growing as a result of American success in the Seminole War. He also reported that the settlement maintained close ties with Nicolls.[70] Although it never came to fruition, Forbes and Company's plan to send a well-supplied Creek war party against the settlement further underscores how many refugees from Prospect Bluff lived at Angola.[71] Jackson wasted little time in asking Secretary of War John C. Calhoun for permission to invade the area but was denied this in light of the international complications that his recent actions had caused with both the Spanish and the British. For the time being at least, the residents of Angola were free to rebuild their lives while requesting aid from the British and Spanish.[72]

Explaining the Seminole War

During the Seminole War, John Quincy Adams, fearing that the latest American invasion of Spanish territory might result in a war or, more realistically, might derail efforts to acquire the Floridas, was charged by the government with providing an official explanation of the war. Over the next year, as Adams collected all of the intelligence relating to the Seminole War, he came to believe firmly that Jackson, for whom he had no love lost, had been justified in invading the Floridas as an effort to end a British-instigated race war led by the refugees from the maroon community. Adams sent a long and detailed letter to the Spanish minister plenipotentiary that amounted to an official defense of the Seminole War. Adams began the letter by stating that Jackson's invasion of the Floridas was not a measure to acquire the territory, nor was it the product of hostility toward Spain. Adams spent the rest of the letter describing the origins and course of the war. Adams's explanation, which began in August 1814 with the arrival of Nicolls in West Florida, centered almost exclusively, and in great detail, on the role of Nicolls and the British in instigating the blacks and Indians to war against the United States. In Adams's estimation, the primary cause of the present war was Nicolls's insistence that the Treaty of Fort Jackson was null, his arming of the maroons at Prospect Bluff, and the recent work of his proxies to continue hostilities. He also believed that the core combatants were blacks and Indians whom Nicolls had recruited and trained while in the Floridas. In uncharacteristically colorful language, Adams described recent events as being part of a "creeping and insidious war, both against Spain and the United States; this mockery of patriotism; these political philters to fugitive slaves and Indian outlaws . . . all in the name of South American liberty, of the rights of Negroes, and the wrongs of savage murderers . . . [a] war [that was] left us by Nicholls, as his legacy, reinstigated by Woodbine, Arbuthnot and Ambrister."[73]

Many white Americans shared Adams's opinion. For example, the *Niles*

Weekly Register reported that Woodbine, Ambrister, and Arbuthnot "assisted, perhaps, by others yet unknown [Nicolls], uselessly caused the deaths of several thousand human beings—by having been the *real* authors, or at least the principal agents, and supporters of the late and present wars with the Creeks and Seminoles."[74] At a trial concerning the execution of Arbuthnot and Ambrister, Mitchell argued that the root cause of the Seminole War was "the fugitives from the Creek War, and those under the influence of Nichols."[75] In justifying Jackson's recent invasion of Florida, John Overton confidently argued that "from the year 1814 down to the termination of the Seminole War, this motley crew of black and red combatants had been uniformly instigated by British incendiaries, Spanish cupidity, and their own ferocity, to carry on a war of depredation and massacre upon the peaceful citizens of our frontier."[76] In early 1819 a congressional committee noted its disapproval of Jackson's handling of the executions of Arbuthnot and Ambrister but chose not to censor the general. The committee agreed that Jackson was forced to invade Spanish Florida in self-defense to protect American citizens from British-instigated hostilities by blacks and Indians and that by permitting these conditions to exist in its territory, the Spanish had forfeited Florida's neutral status.[77]

Annexation

Jackson's recent invasion of the Floridas aided the transfer of the colonies to the United States by vividly illustrating to the Spanish the impossibility of maintaining any meaningful control over the territory's internal and external affairs. Spain's empire in the Western Hemisphere was crumbling, and its fortunes in Europe were equally dire. These factors made expending manpower and resources to hold onto the Floridas seem pointless, especially when faced with nearly constant American aggression. Antagonizing the Anglo plantation society to the north was no longer a viable defensive strategy but rather a dangerous provocation of an awakening regional power. To this end the Adams-Onís Treaty was signed on February 22, 1819, and took effect two years later.

Land greed, the early stirrings of Manifest Destiny, and a strong southern lobby were important factors in the American decision to acquire the Floridas. However, the single most important factor was a burning desire to end the threat that conditions in the Floridas posed to racial order in the United States and the expanding plantation complex. Recent events, beginning with the Patriot Invasion and ending with the Seminole War, had brought these feelings to a head, but nothing had factored more prominently than the actions of Nicolls, Woodbine, their Seminole and Red Stick allies, and the members of the maroon community at Prospect Bluff. To white Americans, their actions vividly drove home the unique national security threat posed by Spain's continued control of the Floridas. In an article about the community's destruction that appeared within days of the explosion, the *Georgia Journal* implored: "We sincerely hope, that at the ensuing session of congress, proper steps be taken for the acquisition of the two Floridas, not on account of any pecuniary advantages . . . but to shut the door through which the English have so often intrigued with such deadly effect, as well as to deprive the abandoned and vindictive of a retreat from whence their depravity might have a delirious and extensive influence over this, and our sister state."[78] In 1816 a southerner wrote a letter to the *Daily National Intelligencer* that vividly reiterated these concerns. The letter was written in response to rumors that the Floridas were being ceded to the British and claimed that "from the practice recently pursued by the British, with regard to negro slaves, it may be feared that their becoming our neighbors . . . will not only reduce the value of that species of property in the Southern Country, but will render even landed property itself hardly worth possessing."[79] The memory of Nicolls and the maroon community made the author believe that a more extensive British presence in the Floridas would threaten the entire institution of slavery in the United States. In the midst of the Seminole War, the same paper ran a widely reprinted editorial calling for the American acquisition of the Floridas. The author began by arguing that the majority of the provinces' population would prefer annexation and that excellent timber and agricultural land was to be found across the Floridas. However, most of the piece was devoted to making the argument that the Floridas threatened racial order in the United States, as was evidenced by the action of Nicolls and the maroons during the War of 1812 and Seminole War.[80] As far as one of the nation's leading newspapers was concerned, Nicolls, Woodbine, and the maroon community trumped economic, territorial, or nationalistic arguments when it came to making a case for the annexation of the Floridas.

Among its initial printings, territorial Florida's first newspaper, the *Floridian*, ran a four-part pro-Jackson series titled "The Next President." The first installment outlined British activities during the War of 1812 with special attention to the maroon community and praised Jackson for his "unparalleled boldness and energy with which . . . the Negro Fort was demolished . . . [and] he subdued the Seminoles and Red Sticks."[81] The second installment lauded Jackson for directing the Seminole War and defeating "these individuals [that] were the hearts blood of a savage war."[82] The final piece in the series boldly proclaimed that "we are now free from apprehension for the lives of our border settlers. Florida is no longer an asylum for our runaway negroes, and refugees from justice. . . . [These] evils are remedied by this accession to our territory, besides securing many positive advantages . . . [for] the people of the United States."[83] For four months the young newspaper ran a series that vividly and passionately described the role of race and Andrew Jackson in the American acquisition of Florida, and tellingly, it mentioned other "positive advantages" only in passing at the very end of the entire series. Lewis Edwards, who was typical of most white southerners, was happy to hear "the news of the cession of the Floridas . . . [because it will] have the effect of disarming the Seminole Indians of their hostility, restoring the fugitive blacks, and giving security to the frontier."[84] Jackson concurred with all these arguments, while watching Congress debate the "Florida question," when he noted that he hoped "that body will take measures to secure our Southern frontier . . . [from] a renewal of all the horrid scenes of massacre . . . that existed before the campaign."[85] Jackson had already been assured by Secretary of War Calhoun that he and the entire administration "concur in the view which you have taken in relation to the importance of Florida to the effectual peace and security of our Southern Frontier."[86]

As the Seminole War vividly illustrates, the maroon community at Prospect Bluff had been a community in a physical sense, but it was also a community in which its members were bound together by a sense of purpose, mission, and identity that transcended place. When the fort and surrounding village were destroyed, the community simply relocated. Even while on the move, the members of the community never wavered in their belief that they were British subjects who possessed particular rights that were under threat by the Americans and Creeks. This very particular sense of identity and community were both the direct product of Nicolls's actions and the single most important determining factor in the nature of the black resistance during the Seminole War. Likewise, Nicolls's actions with the Seminoles and Red Sticks were equally important in determining how the Indians resisted the Americans and Creeks during this period. For nearly two hundred years white Americans had been deeply concerned about the threat of racial disorder posed by conditions in Spanish Florida. This latest challenge, and the specter of Nicolls and the refugees from Prospect Bluff in particular, were definitive proof that these conditions could no longer be tolerated.

➣ Epilogue

THE 1821 TRANSFER of the Floridas to the United States was yet another blow to the blacks and Indians of the region as the advantageous conditions created by Spanish rule became a memory. This major setback was compounded when Andrew Jackson was appointed as Florida's territorial governor. Acting in direct defiance of Secretary of War John C. Calhoun, Jackson's first order of business was to send his Creek allies on a search and destroy mission against Angola.[1] An eyewitness described the raid as having been orchestrated by "some men of influence and fortune residing somewhere in the western country, [who] thought of making a speculation in order to obtain slaves for a trifle." According to the witness, approximately two hundred Coweta Creek Indians proceeded down the west coast of Florida "in the name of the United States" to capture as many blacks as possible and to bring them to a "secret" location. When the party arrived at Angola, the Indians "surprised and captured about 300 of them, plundered their plantations, set fire to their houses, and then proceeding Southerly captured several others." For the residents of Angola who were refugees from Prospect Bluff via Miccosukee, this was the third time they had seen their community destroyed by the United States and its Indian allies.

The Creek raid against the last major bastion of black and Indian resistance in Florida was so successful that the witness described it as a "terror" that

> spread along the western coast of East Florida, [and] broke all the establishments of both blacks and Indians, who fled in great consternation. The blacks principally thought they could not save their lives but by abandoning the country; therefore, they, by small parties and in their Indian canoes doubled Cape Sable and arrived at Key Taviniere, which is the general place of rendezvous for all the English wreckers. . . . An agreement was

soon entered into between them and about 250 of these Negroes were by the wreckers carried to Nassau and clandestinely landed. On the 7th October last, about 40 more were at Key Taviniere, ready to make their departure for Nassau; these were the stragglers who found it difficult to make their escape, and had remained concealed in the forests. . . . [They are all] runaway slaves, from the planters of St. John's River, in Florida, Georgia, Carolina, and a few from Alabama.[2]

After this latest reversal the blacks felt that freedom could only be achieved outside North America. For some this would be possible, for others not. Many of the captives appear to have been reenslaved by Americans or Creeks. However, as was illustrated by Mary Ashley's relentless pursuit of her rights and freedom thirty years later in Cuba, even these unfortunate people never gave up their belief that they were British subjects by virtue of what had happened at Prospect Bluff.

Not all the maroons were captured in the Indian raid. One small group of refugees from Angola fled the raid and merged with a number of Red Sticks. Together they formed a community called Minatti at the Peace River headwaters.[3] Other refugees managed to escape and join scattered bands of their Seminole and Red Stick allies. In twenty years many of these blacks and Indians, along with their children, would fight the United States armed forces once again in the Second Seminole War. However, in the meantime, the blacks and Indians who remained in Florida were dealt yet another blow in 1823 when the Seminoles were coerced into signing the Treaty of Moultrie Creek. The treaty ceded all the Indians' land in northern Florida to the United States in exchange for a cash settlement and the creation of a reservation in central Florida in which they and their black allies were forced to live.

For nearly one hundred and fifty years, blacks and Indians from across the Southeast had sought to resist the harsh realities of Anglo America's plantation society by fleeing to the vast expanses of Florida. Shifting geopolitical dynamics had finally led to the expulsion of the Spanish and the advantageous conditions that their rule created. By the 1820s the strength of the American military and the weight of the plantation complex had consumed Florida, leaving few places to run and resist. The ascendancy of American slavery, aided by the might of the American armed forces, at the expense of black and Indian interests was symbolized in a pair of profound changes to the Florida landscape. At Prospect Bluff where the maroons had once lived was positioned the imposing Fort Gadsden, from which the American armed forces confidently ruled the entire Apalachicola River region, while the remains of Angola lay beneath a flourishing American plantation.

The picture was not so gloomy for one stream of refugees from Angola (many of whom had originated at Prospect Bluff), who managed to escape the grip of the American plantation complex yet again. The stream of refugees who escaped to Andros Island in the Bahamas managed to continue what they had begun at Prospect Bluff and fully realized all that Nicolls had promised them. After their detection by British officials in 1828 the former slaves were immediately recognized as being full British subjects who were allowed to participate in the islands' government. As had been the case at Prospect Bluff, the former slaves owned property and became successful farmers and businessmen who formed an important part of Andros Island's economy. Furthermore, they had deeply fulfilling spiritual and cultural lives and their children were educated at a local state-run school. All these actions were seamless because the refugees did not need an education in their rights as British subjects; they were merely continuing what they had begun at Prospect Bluff. With unmistakable symbolism, the refugees lived in a village they had named Nicholls Town (with an *h*), where their descendants still live today. It is difficult to imagine stronger evidence of Nicolls's impact on the former slaves' lives than the completely independent decision to name their community in his honor.

William Colby's 1871 will neatly captured the full extent to which the Andros Island settlers realized Nicolls's promises.[4] Colby was the last of the Florida refugees to pass away at Andros Island. In his will, which by definition illustrated both his legal and political rights and his understanding of them, he was able to leave money to pay for his debts and the funeral, household furniture for his wife, and a trust as well as a plot of land for each of his five children and one grandchild. Colby had outlived slavery in the British Empire and his native United States. He had lived a long and prosperous life, surrounded by family, and had reaped the benefits of his British status and corresponding rights until the day he died. After an astonishing odyssey, Colby, and all the refugees from Prospect Bluff at Nicholls Town, had achieved everything that Nicolls had promised them in 1814–15, eventually being physically and not just intellectually located within the British Empire.

The residents of Nicholls Town would have been both pleased and unsurprised to learn that Edward Nicolls went on to help tens of thousands of Africans and African Americans in the fifty years after they last saw him at Prospect Bluff. Most notably, between 1829 and 1834 Nicolls was once again able to strike physically at the institution of slavery but on an even larger scale than at Prospect Bluff. This time he was appointed governor of Fernando Po, which was a British-leased base in West Africa from which the Royal Navy attacked the lingering Atlantic slave trade.[5] Nicolls and his men intercepted hundreds of slave ships and attacked numerous slave factories, ultimately freeing thousands of captives. His abilities and energy were so respected by those who served with him in Africa that one of his officers boasted: "If Colonel Nicolls had three Government steamers under his control he would put down the slave traffic on the coast in six months."[6]

As governor of Fernando Po, Nicolls was responsible for resettling liberated Africans within the colony as well as in Sierra Leone.[7] Much of his time was spent traveling across the region, where he observed in minute detail virtually every aspect of local life.[8] Many of Nicolls's conclusions and suggestions concerning the future of Sierra Leone and Fernando Po were cast in relation to his experiences during the War of 1812. For example, Nicolls compared the work ethic of the population of Fernando Po with "the fellows I had in North America [during the War of 1812]."[9] He had lost none of his respect for black humanity or military prowess in Africa and insisted to Parliament that he was "against having European troops [in Africa]," but would rather have working for him "about a hundred men . . . [who were] Hottentots from the Cape."[10] As had been the case at Prospect Bluff, in Africa Nicolls violently freed thousands of victims of slavery and then settled them into organized communities. The greatest difference between Nicolls's actions in Africa and in Florida was that he was now officially sanctioned to attack slavery, whereas at Prospect Bluff he was acting on his own rogue impulses. In both cases, Nicolls was fueled by his anti-slavery beliefs, understanding of the nature of the British Empire, and boundless energy.

In May 1835 Nicolls retired from the Royal Marines on full pay, and in June 1842 he was awarded a good-service pension of 150 pounds per year before being made a Knight Commander of the Bath in 1855.[11] While Nicolls had been active in the organized anti-slavery movement earlier in his life, it was as his career in the Royal Marines began to wind down that he was able to devote most of his time to anti-slavery advocacy. Nicolls embraced this new vocation with all his usual zeal and intensity. In the process he gained a fair amount of celebrity and the respect and admiration of the leading anti-slavery crusaders of the day, with whom he was personally well acquainted. For example, he was a committee member of the Society for the Extinction of the Slave Trade and for the Civilization of Africa.[12] Nicolls was even a founding member of the hugely influential British and Foreign Anti-Slavery Society, regularly attending and speaking at its meetings.[13] At the society's meetings Nicolls debated, opposed, or approved resolutions as an "amature" who "assisted" the "regular anti-slavery people" in the presence of such men as Thomas Foxwell Buxton and Thomas Clarkson.[14] Finally, Nicolls's anti-slavery letters were frequently published in the editorial pages of Britain's leading newspapers.[15]

Nicolls's greatest strength and his credibility in fighting slavery, in his own eyes as well as those of others, came in his vast global experience in helping blacks resist slavery and then rebuild their lives as free people within the British Empire. This can be heard in his words at the Wesleyan-Methodist Society meeting in 1841. While in the process of proposing a resolution at the society's meeting, Nicolls noted that he had frequently observed the positive work of Wesleyan missionaries in Africa. Regarding recently published works by Sir Thomas Fowell Buxton and the Rev. John Beecham, which had been intended to reveal the horrors of the continuing African slave trade and the "evils which afflict African society," Nicolls went on to state that "he could testify, from personal observation, that [both books] fell short of the truth. The case was still worse than they had described it . . . and he could not too earnestly impress on the minds of the Meeting, the importance of giving this subject every possible consideration." Nicolls concluded his remarks by tellingly proclaiming "that he had been commissioned to convey to the Wesleyan-Methodist Society the most grateful thanks of thousands of Negroes, who had received the blessings it been the means of dispensing."[16] Even among the most committed and influential anti-slavery advocates in the world, Nicolls stood out as the truest and most legitimate friend of the victims of slavery because of his immense firsthand experience. Remarkably, considering the length of his extraordinary career fighting slavery both physically and intellectually, Prospect Bluff was the single most radical manifestation of Nicolls's hatred for slavery and compassion for its victims.

In 1865, as American slavery entered its final death throes, the *United Service Magazine and Naval and Military Journal* printed a poem as part of Nicolls's obituary:

Nicolls, where'er he fought
    Put so much of his heart into the act
    That his example had a magnet's force,
    And all were swift to follow whom all lord.

This was a fitting testament to an extraordinary career soldier who had served the British Empire heroically. The obituary continued with the line that his "exploits in his young days made him as great a favorite with the admirers of true gallantry as his persevering efforts in the after life to help the cause of the negro gained him the admiration of the philanthropist."[17] An obituary in the *Gentleman's Magazine and Historical Review* added that "he was a warm and sincere friend of the African race . . . and he was ever ready to urge the cause of that unhappy race."[18]

Long after Nicolls and Colby had passed away, the maroon community at

Prospect Bluff remains integral to the story of North America and the Atlantic world. The settlement of former slaves shaped the history of the Southeast, and the maroons' behavior tells modern observers much about slavery and the lives and thoughts of slaves. At Prospect Bluff, even if only for a brief time, hundreds of former slaves from various cultures in the Atlantic world formed a community that was unusual by North American or hemispheric standards. Here, high above the Apalachicola River, the maroon community's residents were able to construct a remarkable version of freedom. How the former slaves constructed their freedom provides vital insights into slaves' understanding of their enslavement versus freedom as well as their perception of the world in which they lived. These insights have the potential to alter the way in which one views the lives of slaves.

In particular, the maroons' behavior goes a long way toward answering two central questions in the study of slavery: what were slave rebels aiming for? And, related but more important, how did slaves understand freedom? These questions have been central to the study of American slavery because they essentially exist only in theory, since in North America there were no "successful" large-scale slave rebellions (direct frontal assaults on the institution or large and long-lived maroon communities). Thus scholars have been left to speculate over what the exact motives were for Gabriel, Denmark Vesey, Nat Turner, and other slave rebels as well as those who lived as desperate and survivalist maroons. It has been equally difficult to ascertain exactly how nonrebellious slaves conceptualized their status. In each case discussions of freedom strike at the very heart of what it meant to be a slave or, indeed, any member of a slave society. The example of Prospect Bluff demonstrates that slaves were aware of what constituted freedom as well as the boundaries of their enslavement. The maroons also made it clear that slaves wanted to destroy these boundaries as fully as was possible if provided with the proper conditions.

The inhabitants of the maroon community at Prospect Bluff vividly illustrated what slave rebels aspired to accomplish and, by extension, just how fully slaves understood the ingredients of freedom. This was because, if only fleetingly, the members of the community could be described as "successful" slave rebels who had achieved something of which other rebels or the enslaved could only have dreamed: the ability to establish an autonomous and materially prosperous black polity in which members were in charge of their own destiny. Through the construction of this community, its inhabitants achieved tremendous intellectual and physical freedom by any contemporaries' definitions of the concept. It is irrelevant that this freedom was not accomplished through a violent frontal assault on slavery but rather was the result of an elaborate series of events and trends with origins that lay in both the long- and short-term history of the Southeast and the Atlantic world. Nor is it relevant that these conditions were dependent on the convergence of powerful local and international developments in an exceptional physical environment. The bottom line is that the former slaves *did* find themselves presented with a particular opportunity at Prospect Bluff and, in the process, achieved a degree of freedom that was unrivaled in the history of North America and, indeed, much of the hemisphere, certainly on such a large scale. At the same time, I argue it matters little that the community existed for less than two years, because during its relatively brief existence the community lived and fought to protect an expansive freedom.

An examination of the specific contours of the maroons' freedom provides one of the few opportunities to gain concrete insights into the aims of slave rebels and into slaves' understanding of freedom when left totally to their own devices. This examination sheds light on what a broad-based cross section of slave rebels hoped to achieve. The most complex aspect of the maroons' freedom was political. This was based on Nicolls's granting the former slaves the "rights" and "liberties" of "true" British subjects. Becoming British subjects was not a betrayal of an Afro-nationalist movement, nor did it relegate the maroons to a situation similar to that of treaty maroons or free people of color in Spanish Florida or the United States—degrees of freedom that were tempered by social, cultural, and legal limitations. Indeed the case of Prospect Bluff can perhaps tell us more about slave consciousness than an examination of formal free black communities who lived surrounded by white society, with nothing close to full legal or political equality, while suffering the negative effects of racism. Such free black communities were not fully in control of their own destiny, nor were they capable of full political expression, which leaves historians to speculate about the scope of their ambitions and the contours of their thought. Rather, at Prospect Bluff, the maroons' understanding of their British status was both empowering and liberating. Likewise the depth of the former slaves' understanding of their British status was unusual. Most slaves would have had a general understanding of the power of political and legal membership within a nation or empire. However, the maroons at Prospect Bluff had an unusually strong and bold understanding of this concept because Nicolls, through the filter of his anti-slavery ideology, had carefully instructed them in their rights within his vision of the British Empire. Nicolls's lessons meant the former slaves never doubted that they were equals to anyone within the British Empire.

This notion of being true British subjects with full rights and liberties became the foundation of the maroons' government and identity as well as the community's claim to legitimacy as a distinct and sovereign polity. Collectively the community's government, its military, and belief in British status were distinctly Western methods of constructing political belonging and, ultimately, freedom. This was not a rejection of African culture but rather a statement of the former slaves' understanding of the political contours of the various systems to which they had been collectively exposed, their options, and their origins, which were overwhelmingly creole. Of equal importance in shaping the maroons' political consciousness was Nicolls's careful instruction in their rights as British subjects, underscored by his radical anti-slavery ideology and his understanding of the British Empire as a universalist empire in which blacks and Indians could enjoy political, social, military, and economic equality with whites. Indeed knowledge of Nicolls's anti-slavery ideology made the maroons' political assertions possible in the first place. Few things could have resulted in the former slaves having greater political and intellectual freedom than what occurred at Prospect Bluff. In many ways the community is best understood as an extended effort by radicalized and informed free people to rule themselves and their territory as a sovereign enclave of British subjects. Thus it is also useful to conceptualize much of what occurred at Prospect Bluff as a self-conscious effort by the maroons to claim their rights as British subjects. This was starkly different from the conservative and/or restorationist models that most maroons followed.

Nicolls's radical anti-slavery thought was an equally important ingredient in the former slaves' freedom. Historians have argued over the extent to which slaves and slave rebels understood abolitionism and anti-slavery ideas and debates and whether their actions were shaped by such knowledge. In the case of the maroons at Prospect Bluff the former slaves clearly had an acute knowledge of a very particular strand of anti-slavery thought that added to their understanding of freedom. Virtually no slaves or maroons in the Atlantic world at this point in time would have been so familiar with anti-slavery ideology, nor were many people of color in such an advantageous position to act on this knowledge. Nicolls had convinced the former slaves that they were fully human and virtuous Christian subjects who had earned their place within the British Empire through military service and violently resisting an abhorrent institution. After having listened closely to Nicolls's ideas, creating a polity of British subjects would have seemed perfectly logical to the former slaves. Without knowledge of these ideas, the former slaves would not have been able to conceptualize themselves as being capable of political and legal equality with white Britons, nor would they have believed it possible for themselves to be full members of the British state and empire. Had Nicolls not been a fully developed radical anti-slavery advocate, he would never have taken such actions in Florida, nor would he have believed that slaves were capable of such rights and equality.

Placing such emphasis on the role of Nicolls in influencing the actions and ideas of the former slaves does not undermine their agency. Nicolls's actions and ideas were important, but it was up to the former slaves to comprehend the ideas, to accept them, and then to take advantage of what Nicolls offered them. In essence Nicolls had provided a key, but it was up to the former slaves to unlock the door and walk through it. By walking through the door the former slaves demonstrated a critical understanding of the options open to them and decided that Nicolls offered the surest route to the most extensive version of freedom. The maroons would have brought their own concepts of freedom to Prospect Bluff, which would have influenced their behavior. Nothing would have stopped the former slaves from turning their back on Nicolls and carving out a desperate and survivalist existence in the wilderness, totally free from any white interference. However, if they had chosen this path, the former slaves would have enjoyed a version of freedom that paled in comparison to what Nicolls offered. The fact that for over half a century the former slaves never wavered in their belief that they were British subjects clearly demonstrates their deep commitment to and understanding of these ideas, both of which were testaments to their agency.

Ultimately the maroons at Prospect Bluff built a complete society on this foundation of political and intellectual freedom that revolved around claiming their British rights. This society inhabited a distinct space and was bound by law and order. The community had a bustling economy based on agriculture and the trade of surplus materials that the British had left behind, maintaining trade and diplomatic connections with black and Indian settlements. People lived in their own dwellings on their own land, cultivated and pursued private property, and controlled their labor and bodies. When the community's inhabitants were not working, training in its armed forces, or serving in its government, they worshipped, socialized, and otherwise enjoyed the benefits of their freedom on their own terms. Frequently this was done in family units, one of many means by which the former slaves asserted their gendered identities and humanity. Collectively, the maroon community was a sovereign enclave of British subjects, serving the same function as any polity. Prospect Bluff was a place where British subjects could enjoy their rights. Given the remarkable cross section of former slaves at Prospect Bluff, there is no reason to believe that other slaves would not behave in the same manner if presented with similar circumstances. It is fair to reason that other North American slaves had the same potential to understand anti-slavery rhetoric and ideas about rights and status. The most exceptional thing about the former slaves at Prospect Bluff was the opportunity with which they had been presented. Thus it is not contradictory to suggest that the maroon community was both unusual *and* a window into slave behavior and thought that can be used to understand the minds of slaves across North America.

To nearly every white person and many Indians in the region, the maroon community was a frightening and potentially destructive adversary. Built on many years of flight and rivalry, the living embodiment of slave revolution, radical anti-slavery thought, war, and violent disruption had been transported to the expanding American plantation complex at a time when the Spanish had all but lost control of the Floridas. The maroon community forced white Americans and many Indians to confront dark fears about slavery, freedom, race, violence, and expansion. These fears were compounded by the specter of foreign instigators and Indian war as well as by the shadow of Haiti and the Age of Revolution. The United States had a host of motives to annex the Floridas in 1819, but none was more important than concerns over the challenge that the Spanish colonies presented to racial order along the expanding plantation frontier. This had certainly become a much more intensely felt belief after the horrors of the Patriot War, Creek War, and War of 1812 in the region, as Americans and their Creek allies were fully reminded of the threat posed by the conditions in Spanish Florida. However, nothing embodied all these fears and anxieties more fully or acutely than the maroon community and the Seminole War. Whites and Indians could not have designed a more symbolic menace than a fortified and heavily armed community of radicalized former slaves who were convinced that they were British subjects after having been spurred on by foreigners. All these factors made the destruction of the community highly probable. When it became clear that the majority of the maroon community's inhabitants had survived the blast at Prospect Bluff and had joined the Seminoles and Red Sticks, both of whom believed they were British allies, another mission, to finish the business, became equally probable, as did increasingly intense American pressure to acquire Florida.

In the end the maroon community at Prospect Bluff should be remembered and understood as an important event in the history of colonial and nineteenth-century North America and the Atlantic world and as affording a rare opportunity to ascertain how hundreds of former slaves understood the world in which they lived and the extent to which they desired freedom. Accordingly, the maroons should be placed squarely within the broader historical narrative of North America and of the Atlantic world during this era. This positioning will add to the richness of the era's history while providing an excellent opportunity to cast North America's past in a comparative context that reveals the workings of the Atlantic world. Elevating the community's historical standing also reminds modern observers just how fully slaves struggled against their bondage. In this light, the maroon community at Prospect Bluff makes it clear that slaves were intelligent observers of the wider world who wanted to be as free as was possible. These understandings and desires serve as vivid confirmation of the humanity possessed by the enslaved. This humanity was no different than that possessed by millions of other inhabitants of the Atlantic world and is the single most important fact that the example of Prospect Bluff forces modern observers to consider.

Notes

Introduction

1. Prospect Bluff is located in the Apalachicola National Forest. It is the furthest bluff to the south of the river and fronts the river for approximately a mile. To the north the bluff is bounded by Brickyard Creek and to the south the bluff terminates in the swamp bordering Fort Gadsden Creek. The official location of Prospect Bluff is NE quarter of the SW quarter of Section 23, T 6 S, R 8 W, Franklin County. Taken from Griffin, Report of Investigations at Old Fort Gadsden.

2. Higginson, *Memoir of Thomas Wentworth Higginson*, 296.

3. Throughout the book the community of former slaves is called the "maroon community," and its inhabitants are called the "maroons" or "former slaves," as the term "Negro Fort" meant nothing to the community's inhabitants.

4. The maroon community received the most media attention when it appeared to offer the most direct parallels to contemporary events. These include the partisan bickering that emerged during the rise and presidency of Andrew Jackson, always powerfully associated with the community, and the sectional tensions that led to the Civil War. Nonetheless, the press initially had to overcome official efforts to control public memory of the community in the immediate aftermath of its destruction when the federal government attempted to suppress publication of military reports on the destruction. Prior to this point, newspapers printed collections of various official and unofficial letters relating to the community that they acquired in an effort to satisfy the public's demand for information. For example, the *National Register*, on March 6, 1819, printed an assortment of letters from Spanish and American officials that did not include the official account. This worked until late 1819, when after concerted pressure the military's official report was released and widely published. See *Niles Weekly Register*, November 20, 1819, as one example among many. A small sampling of the explosion of relevant published and accessible primary sources during this period includes *Abridgment of the Debates of Congress from 1789 to 1856*; *Memoirs of General Andrew Jackson, Together with the Letter of Mr. Secretary Adams*; *Letters and Writings of James Madison*, vol. 3; and Adams, ed., *Memoirs of John Quincy Adams*.

5. Perkins, *Historical Sketches of the United States*, 91–117.

6. Barber, *Our Whole Country*, 780–82.

7. Hildreth, *History of the United States*, 605–6. During this period reference works regularly featured the maroon community. A good example is Lalor, ed., *Cyclopedia of Political Science*, which contains a long entry on "Slavery." One of its subsections, entitled "Insurrections," begins by positing that the lack of slave insurrections in American history "can hardly be due to the natural cowardice of the race, for its members have made very good soldiers . . . nor to the exceptional gentleness of the system . . . nor wholly to the affection of the negroes for their masters," before going on to list exhaustively examples of American slave rebellions, including that of the maroons and the "Seminole war in Florida" which "partook very much of the character of a negro insurrection" (731–32).

8. Emerson, *A History of the Nineteenth Century*, 627. Another interesting example from this period is Alexander Johnston's *The Slavery Controversy, Civil War and Reconstruction, 1820–1876* (volume 2 of his *American Political History, 1763–1876*), in which he argues that the First Seminole War was "very much of the character of a negro insurrection." According to Johnston, the drive to reclaim the "very many fugitive slaves" who had "taken refuge" in Florida and intermarried with Indians was the source of many of the region's Indian difficulties (21–22). In 1816 American troops blew up the "Negro Fort" on the Apalachicola, the headquarters of the fugitives. Johnston also discusses the Stono Rebellion, the New York City Conspiracy of 1741, Denmark Vesey, and Nat Turner.

9. Montgomery, *Student's American History*, 309.

10. Forbes, *Sketches, Historical and Topographical of the Floridas*, 121. Two years later, in a slightly more romantic tone, Charles Vignoles, in his *Observations upon the Floridas*, wrote of "a large body of refugee slaves [who] took a desperate stand, and were almost wholly annihilated" (61). John Lee Williams's *A View of West Florida* contains a year-by-year

history of Florida in which the longest entries—for 1814, 1816, and 1818—are concerned with Nicolls's actions in the Southeast, in the community and its destruction, and in the First Seminole War (94–103). George Fairbanks, in his 1871 *History of Florida*, places great emphasis on the role of the maroon community in the outbreak of the First Seminole War and the acquisition of Florida by the United States (262–68). Herbert Fuller's *The Purchase of Florida* introduces the maroon community as "one of the most audacious and surprising incidents of American history." Before beginning his fairly standard account of the community's destruction, Fuller describes Nicolls's diplomacy with the Seminoles and Red Sticks and the "thousand or more" blacks who "rapidly degenerated into an army of outlaws and plunderers" and "harried the country, drove off cattle, freed slaves, rescued criminals, murdered those who resisted, fired upon boats . . . and became the terror of the region" (228–31). William Watson takes time in his exhaustive *The Civil War and Reconstruction in Florida* to note that as American plantations spread into the Deep South, Florida became a dangerous haven for fugitive slaves, with the maroon community being the greatest example of this. Watson concludes that because Spain was incapable of dealing with the situation, the United States was justified in annexing the territory (11).

11. Monette, *History of the Discovery and Settlement of the Valley of the Mississippi*, 86–102. Albert Pickett's *History of Alabama, and Incidentally of Georgia and Mississippi*, while confusing Woodbine with Nicolls and making a handful of chronological mistakes, firmly places the blame for the "Seminole War" on the British and a "colony of negro slaves, which had been stolen by the British during the war from the Southern planters." Interestingly, Pickett argues that "notwithstanding these difficulties emigrants continued to boldly push through the Creek nation and to occupy portions of the Alabama Territory," demonstrating his belief that the maroon community and related events threatened the expansion of the United States (379). When James Lynch, the historian of Mississippi, prefaces his discussion of the maroons by referring to "the Negro Fort, so often mentioned," he demonstrates the extent to which the idea and reality of the fort had become commonplace in the academic and popular imagination (*Bench and Bar of Mississippi*, 65). In his fiery southern nationalist *Confederate Military History*, Clement Evans devotes much attention to the maroon community as the "most formidable of these organized bands" of "fugitive Indians, lawless white men and runaway slaves" spurred on by British instigators (194–200). He goes on, in triumphant terms, to describe the maroon community's destruction, the First Seminole War, and the annexation of Florida. According to Lucian Knight in *A Standard History of Georgia and Georgians*, "the whole of upper Florida had become an asylum for lawless characters, runaway slaves, free-booters, murderers and criminals," and "the negro fort was a center of lawlessness" (481).

12. Frost, *Indian Battles, Captivities, and Adventures*, 354–55.

13. Wilson, *History of the Rise and Fall of the Slave Power in America*, chapter 10.

14. Coe, *Red Patriots: The Story of the Seminoles*, 16–28.

15. The first steady wave of Jackson biographies to address prominently the maroon community began to appear in the decade after the First Seminole War, when Jackson was becoming a national political figure. These biographies sought either to attack or defend him based on the authors' partisan leanings. Biographies of Jackson were produced

at an astounding rate during the nineteenth and early twentieth centuries. Among the more notable examples are Philo Goodwin's 1837 biography, which includes a fairly standard and sympathetic treatment of the events surrounding the community (206–16), and James Parton's well-researched and authoritative 1861 biography. Parton's work contains ten chapters on events in Florida, with two exclusively devoted to the maroons. These identify the community as a maroon settlement, placing it squarely within the history of North American *marronage* (see chapters 30–40). Also notable are Oliver Dyer's 1891 *General Andrew Jackson*, which colorfully describes "the negro runaways, who had no friends, either white or Indian, English, Spanish or American" (259), and Alfred Lewis's 1907 *When Men Grew Tall or the Story of Andrew Jackson*. Before discussing the First Seminole War and annexation of Florida, Lewis describes the aftermath of General Jackson's decision to "see about" frontier violence caused by blacks and Seminoles as one where "three crawled from the blazing chaos, to be hilariously knocked on the head. . . . [and] the world is much rejoiced" (228–29).

16. Jay, *A View of the Action of the Federal Government on Behalf of Slavery*, 63–64. A year earlier, after a number of members of the army and navy detachment that had destroyed the community sued to be awarded their prize money in a highly publicized case, the *Philanthropist* of March 8, 1843, published an article titled "Violation of the Constitution for the Support of Slavery." The article asserted that the inhabitants of Prospect Bluff were "murdered in cold blood, for no other crime than that of preferring *liberty to slavery*. A law was passed in February 1838, to pay more than five thousand dollars to the officers and crew, as bounty for the destruction of our fellow beings. Our people of Ohio, and the other free States, were thus involved in the expense of *murdering fugitive slaves*, for the benefit of that institution."

17. *Christian Examiner*, July–November 1858, 452. John Palfrey's 1846 collection of anti-slavery publications that originally appeared in the *Boston Whig* contains a section titled "What has the North to do with it?—Costly and Wicked Wars." The inhabitants of the community were described as living peaceful and unobtrusive lives until the "army and navy of the United States . . . [appeared] . . . on a slave-hunting expedition, and . . . caught and butchered the blacks at the expense of the slavery-hating freemen of the North. The Indians resented the death of some of their friends in the negro fort, and thus began the first Seminole war" (Palfrey, *Papers on the Slave Power* 40).

18. Giddings, *The Exiles of Florida*.

19. There are a number of possible reasons why the maroon community disappeared into the recesses of the scholarly and popular imagination. For much of the twentieth century New England and the Chesapeake received a disproportionate amount of scholarly attention, especially when compared to the Southeast. During this period, studies of the Southeast were frequently relegated to the realm of regional or borderlands history and not given the broader attention that they deserved. Likewise, certainly until the 1960s, most studies of slavery and the South tended to focus on the later Antebellum period. Thus the maroon community did not fit neatly into prevailing geographic or chronological trends. The rise of the field of Atlantic history is ideally suited to reclaim the maroon community from historical obscurity.

20. Modern works that address the community include Covington, "Negro Fort"; Milligan, "Slave Rebelliousness and the Florida Maroons"; Mulroy, *Freedom on the Border*; Owsley and Smith, *Filibusters*; Porter, *The Negro on the Frontier*; Riordan, "Finding Freedom in Florida"; Saunt, *A New Order*; and numerous works by Landers, including *Atlantic Creoles in the Age of Revolutions*; *Black Society in Spanish Florida*; "Africans and Indians on the Spanish Southeastern Frontier," in Restall, ed., *Black and Red*, 53–80; "Black Community and Culture in the Southeastern Borderlands"; "Black-Indian Interactions in Spanish Florida"; "Slave Resistance on the Southern Frontier"; and "Social Control on Spain's Contested Florida Frontier," in De la Teja and Frank, eds., *Choice, Persuasion, and Coercion*, 27–48. On Fort Mose, see Landers, "Gracia Real de Santa Teresa de Mose."

21. Since the 1950s the most able scholars of American slavery have written about maroons but generally in small parts of larger works. Notable examples include Genovese, *Roll, Jordan, Roll*; Berlin, *Many Thousands Gone*; Morgan, *Slave Counterpoint*; and Franklin and Schweninger, *Runaway Slaves*. Works addressing North American marronage in a more sustained manner include Aptheker, "Maroons within the Present Limits of the United States"; Hall, *Africans in Colonial Louisiana*; Leaming, *Hidden Americans*; Milligan, "Slave Rebelliousness and the Florida Maroons"; Mullin, *Flight and Rebellion*; Mulroy, *Freedom on the Border*; and three works by Canter Brown: *Florida's Peace River Frontier*; "The 'Sarrazota, or Runaway Negro Plantations'"; and "Tales of Angola," in Brown and Jackson, eds., *Go Sound the Trumpet*, 1–20. Given the frequency and significance of marronage across the Western Hemisphere, the literature on the subject is voluminous. Notable titles include Agorsah, ed., *Maroon Heritage*; Bilby, *True-Born Maroons*; Campbell, *The Maroons of Jamaica, 1655–1796*; Craton, *Testing the Chains*; Genovese, *Rebellion*; Heuman, ed., *Out of This House of Bondage*; Hoogbergen, *The Boni Maroon Wars in Suriname*; Kopytoff, "Early Political Development of Jamaican Maroon Societies"; La Rosa Corzo, *Runaway Slave Settlements in Cuba*; Schwartz, *Slaves, Peasants, and Rebels*; Price, ed., *Maroon Societies*; and Thompson, *Flight to Freedom*.

22. Interview of Octave Johnson, Louisiana, 1863, in Blassingame, ed., *Slave Testimony*, 395.

23. Governor James Wright to Lt. Governor William Bull, Savannah, November 25, 1765, in Lockley, ed., *Maroon Communities in South Carolina*, 20.

24. Good treatments of the Age of Revolution include Armitage and Subrahmanyam, eds., *Age of Revolution in Global Context*; Hobsbawm, *Age of Revolution*; Klooster, *Revolutions in the Atlantic World*; Langley, *The Americas in the Age of Revolution*; Palmer, *The Age of Democratic Revolution*; and Schama, *Citizens*.

25. For an excellent systematic overview of slave rebellions during the Age of Revolution, see David Geggus, "Slavery, War, and Revolution in the Greater Caribbean, 1789–1815," in Gaspar and Geggus, eds., *A Turbulent Time*.

26. For over thirty years Eugene Genovese's contention in *From Rebellion to Revolution* that the Age of Revolution, and the Haitian Revolution in particular, changed the character of slave resistance—from actions dominated by restorationist Africans and maroons to ideologically driven and creole-led efforts to destroy the entire system of slavery—has greatly influenced the scholarly debate on the subject. Michael Craton (*Testing*

the Chains) and Michael Mullin (*Africa in America*) agree that during this era rebellions were increasingly led by creoles, but they attribute this to shifting demographics and the closing of the frontier. Taking a different perspective in "The Common Wind," Julius Scott argues that resistance inspired by Haiti transcended simple patterns of ethnicity and geography, uniting slaves across boundaries, ethnicities, and occupations in the hope of resisting slavery. Similarly, Robert Paquette contends in "Social History Update" that regardless of their origins, ethnicities, or occupations, slaves had the potential to unify against their common experience of oppression in a process that cannot be attributed to ideological forces. Some of the best works on the contested understandings of slavery and freedom during this era include Blackburn, *The Overthrow of Colonial Slavery*; Childs, *The 1812 Aponte Rebellion in Cuba*; Dubois, *Colony of Citizens*, and *Avengers of the New World*; Egerton, *Death or Liberty*; and Nash, *Forgotten Fifth*.

Chapter 1. Edward Nicolls and the Problem of War and Slavery in the Age of Revolution

1. Good general studies include Coles, *The War of 1812*; Hickey, *The War of 1812*; Horsman, *The War of 1812*; Mahon, *The War of 1812*; and Stagg, *Mr. Madison's War*.

2. The challenges that slavery and slaves faced during the Early Republic are addressed in Davis, *The Problem of Slavery in the Age of Revolution*; Fehrenbacher, *The Slaveholding Republic*; Finkleman, *Slavery and the Founders*; Frehling, *The Reintegration of American History*; Greene, *All Men Are Created Equal*; Jordan, *White over Black*; and Morgan, *American Slavery, American Freedom*.

3. Frey, *Water from the Rock*, 328.

4. Rothman, *Slave Country*, is a good treatment of the physical, economic, and ideological expansion of slavery into the Deep South during the first quarter of the nineteenth century. Also good are Berlin, *Many Thousands Gone*, chapters 11 and 12; Chaplin, "Creating a Cotton South"; Davis, *The Black Experience in Natchez*; Kastor, *The Nation's Crucible*; Klein, *The Unification of a Slave State*; and Moore, *The Emergence of the Cotton Kingdom in the Old Southwest*.

5. Johnson, ed., *The Chattel Principle*; Johnson, *Soul by Soul*; and Tadman, *Speculators and Slaves* combine to provide detailed insights into the frequently inhumane institutions of the internal slave trade and the slave market. For the expanding sugar industry, see Ingersoll, *Mammon and Manon in Early New Orleans*; Follett, *The Sugar Masters*; and Rene LeGardeur Jr., "The Origins of the Sugar Industry in Louisiana," in *Green Fields*, chapter 10.

6. For the often tragic attempts to claim freedom in Haiti, see Blackburn, *The Overthrow of Colonial Slavery*; DuBois, *Avengers of the New World*; Fick, *The Making of Haiti*; Geggus, *Haitian Revolutionary Studies*; and James, *The Black Jacobins*. DuBois, *Colony of Citizens* is a brilliant study of the efforts by slaves in Guadeloupe to claim their freedom. Craton, *Testing the Chains*; Gaspar and Geggus, eds., *A Turbulent Time*; Geggus, ed., *The Impact of the Haitian Revolution*; Genovese, *Rebellion*; Mullin, *Africa in America*; Paquette, "Social History Update"; and Scott, "The Common Wind" all agree that the frequency

and aims of slave rebellions were changing during the era of the Haitian Revolution, even if their explanations differ.

7. Geggus, *Slavery, War and Revolution*, 1–50.

8. For Gabriel, see Sidbury, *Ploughshares into Swords*, and for the German Coast Rebellion, see Paquette, "'A Horde of Brigands?'" and Rodriguez, "Ripe for Revolt."

9. See Blackburn, *The Overthrow of Colonial Slavery*; Davis, *The Problem of Slavery in Western Culture*; Davis, *The Problem of Slavery in the Age of Revolution*; Drescher, *Capitalism and Anti-Slavery*; Drescher, *Econocide*; and Merton, *Slavery Attacked*.

10. Fredrickson, *The Black Image in the White Mind*, and Tise, *Proslavery* are two of many excellent works that consider pro-slavery arguments and thought.

11. *Annals of Congress*, House of Representatives, 12th Cong., 1st sess., 451. Quoted in Rothman, *Slave Country*, 123.

12. John Calhoun, "Speech on the Report of the Foreign Relations Committee," December 12, 1811, in Meriwether, ed., *The Papers of John C. Calhoun: Volume I, 1801–1817*, 80. Given the fact that Calhoun was attempting to alleviate white Southern fears about slave resistance during a potential war with Great Britain, it is curious that he decided to admit that nearly half of all slaves had heard of the French Revolution and, by extension, the Age of Revolution. Calhoun clearly felt that such a ratio should have been calming to Southern nerves. In reality, this ratio would have been deeply unsettling to white Southerners, few of whom would have been reassured by Calhoun.

13. Residents of Lenoir County, N.C., to the North Carolina General Assembly, 1813, General Assembly Session Records, Misc. Petitions, November–December 1813, NC-DAH, reel 5, 0387a, in Schweninger, ed., *Race and Free Blacks*.

14. Mason, *Slavery and Politics in the Early American Republic*, chapters 1 and 2.

15. For the African American role in the War of 1812, see Altoff, *Amongst my Best Men: African-Americans and the War of 1812*; Bullard, *Black Emancipation at Cumberland Island in 1815*; Cassell, "Slaves in the Chesapeake Bay Area and the War of 1812"; and George, "The Mirage of Freedom."

16. Frey, *Water from the Rock*; Egerton, *Death or Liberty*; Nash, *Forgotten Fifth*; and Quarles, *The Negro in the American Revolution* are each important works on slavery and the American Revolution.

17. Mason, "The Battle of the Slaveholding Liberators: Great Britain, the United States, and Slavery in the Early Nineteenth Century," 665. Mason argues that both nations saw themselves as the true defenders of the spirit of the Age of Revolution. Importantly, this debate largely focused on slavery.

18. A general overview is Voelz, *Slave and Soldier*. See Brown and Morgan, eds., *Arming Slaves*, especially Jane Landers, "Transforming Bondsmen into Vassal," 120–45; Hendrik Kraay, "Arming Slaves in Brazil," 146–79; Philip Morgan and Andrew O'Shaughnessy, "Arming Slaves in the American Revolution," 180–208; David Geggus, "The Arming of Slaves in the Haitian Revolution," 233–54; Laurent Dubois, "Citizen Soldiers," 233–55; and Peter Blanchard, "Slave Soldiers of Spanish South America," 255–73.

19. See Geggus, *Slavery, War, and Revolution*; Buckley, *The British Army in the West Indies*; and Duffy, *Soldiers, Sugar, and Seapower*.

20. See Geggus, *Slavery, War, and Revolution*, and Craton, *Testing the Chains*, chapters 15–17.

21. Buckley, *Slaves in Red Coats*, chapter 2. The West India Regiments consisted of Africans and emancipated slaves and were envisioned as being central to the defense of the British Caribbean in light of Britain's immense military obligations across the globe.

22. See the collected essays in Geggus, ed., *The Impact of the Haitian Revolution*, for the various effects of the Haitian Revolution across the Atlantic world. For more specific studies of the human connections between Haiti and the United States, see Dessens, *From Saint Domingue to New Orleans*; Hunt, *Haiti's Influence on Antebellum America*, chapter 2; and White, *Encountering Revolution*.

23. Speech of Frederic Robinson, House of Commons, February 28, 1825, in Brenton, *The Naval History of Great Britain*, 164.

24. Alexander Cochrane to John Croker, February 20, 1815, ADM 1/4359, 197, National Archives of Great Britain, Kew, Richmond, Surrey (hereafter cited as NAGB).

25. Buckley, *The British Army in the West Indies*, chapter 8, deals with disease and the British military.

26. Mahon, *The War of 1812*, 313.

27. Ibid., 312.

28. Ibid., and Edward Codrington to unknown recipient, December 1, 1814, Codrington Papers, COD/7/2, National Maritime Museum, Greenwich, U.K.

29. Edward Codrington to unknown recipient, September 3, 1814, Codrington Papers, COD/7/2, National Maritime Museum, Greenwich, U.K.; Cochrane to Bathurst, July 14, 1814, Lockey Collection, P. K. Yonge Library of Florida History, Gainesville (hereafter cited as PKY).

30. Egerton, *Death or Liberty*, 66–73. On November 7, 1775, Virginia's Royal Governor, Lord Dunmore, issued a proclamation that promised freedom to the slaves of American rebels if the slaves would leave their masters and serve under the British. The proclamation was one of the most important events in the South during the American Revolution; it shocked white Southerners and led to the flight of thousands of slaves.

31. NAGB, ADM 1/508, 579 is one of the many places where the proclamation can be found.

32. Diary of John Quincy Adams, in Ford, ed., *Writings of John Quincy Adams*, vol. 5: *1814–1816*, 113–14.

33. James Madison to Secretary of War, Washington, D.C., May 20, 1814, James Madison Papers, reel 16, Library of Congress, Washington, D.C., online at http://lcweb2.loc.gov/ammem/collections/madison_papers/mjmabout2.html.

34. Sebastián Kindelán to Juan Ruiz de Apodaca, May 5, 1814, East Florida Papers (hereafter cited as EF), reel 12, section 2, PKY. Kindelán believed that the proclamation was designed to cause an "insurreción de los negros de los Estados Unidos."

35. *Morning Chronicle*, July 19, 1814.

36. Peter Early to Thomas Pickney, Milledgeville, Ga., September 16, 1814, Lockey Collection, PKY.

37. See Bardon, *A History of Ulster*; Hechter, *Internal Colonialism*; and Kenny, ed., *Ireland and the British Empire*.

38. Edward Nicolls, June 29, 1830, in *Select Committee on State of Settlements of Sierra Leone and Fernando Po*, 48.

39. Mrs. E. B. Laird, All I Knew of My Mother's Forbears, (manuscript, 1906), Arch 11/13/132, p. 20, Royal Marine Museum, Portsmouth, U.K. See Hill, *Evangelical Protestantism in Ulster Society* for the religious context.

40. Holmes, *The Shaping of Ulster Presbyterian Belief and Practice*, is a superb look at Ulster Presbyterianism and its effects on the society and culture of Northern Ireland.

41. *Dublin Almanac*, 280.

42. Brooks, *The Royal Marines*, is a good general history of the Royal Marines.

43. See Blackburn, *The Overthrow of Colonial Slavery*; Brown, *Moral Capital*; Davis, *The Problem of Slavery in Western Culture*; Davis, *The Problem of Slavery in the Age of Revolution*; Drescher, *Capitalism and Anti-Slavery*; Drescher, *Econocide*; Eltis, *Economic Growth and the Ending of the Transatlantic Slave Trade*; and Miers, *Britain and the Ending of the Slave Trade*.

44. Brown, *Moral Capital*.

45. Nicolls's obituary contains lengthy and detailed accounts of every engagement in which he was involved, including his service in the Caribbean; see *Gentleman's Magazine and Historical Review*, January, 1865, 644–46. Buckley, *The British Army in the West Indies*, and Duffy, *Soldiers, Sugar, and Seapower*, are the best overviews of the British military's experience in the Caribbean during this period.

46. Vicente Sebastián Pintado to José de Soto, April 29, 1815, Vicente Sebastián Pintado Papers, box 3, folder 1, Library of Congress, microfilm, PKY. As discussed in the epilogue to the present volume, from 1829 to 1834 Nicolls served as the governor of Fernando Po, which placed him in charge of British efforts to eradicate the lingering Atlantic slave trade and to resettle the trade's victims in Sierra Leone. Upon retirement from the Royal Marines in 1835 Nicolls became a fulltime anti-slavery advocate who was a prominent and active member of the most important anti-slavery societies of the day.

47. *Times*, February 16, 1842. Nicolls had clearly developed his radical anti-slavery ideology by the time he was deployed to North America during the War of 1812. As is shown later in the present work, Nicolls acted consciously on these ideas during and immediately after the war. Thus, since Nicolls spent his adult life as a radical anti-slavery advocate, it is fair to analyze his later writings for insights into his behavior and ideas during his time in North America. This is because Nicolls was not a late convert to anti-slavery activism, nor did he appear to have become more radical over the years. Thus he was not reenvisioning his past to fit his present beliefs. Instead, an examination of Nicolls's actions and writings over the course of a fifty-year period reveals a great deal of ideological consistency, strongly suggesting that he was recounting events as accurately as was possible.

48. See Sale, *The Slumbering Volcano*, 122–41; Hendrick and Hendrick, *The Creole Mutiny*; and Johnson, "White Lies."

49. Colonel Nicolls to Sir John Barrow, Shooter's Hill, London, September 11, 1843, *Correspondences with Foreign Powers on the Slave Trade, 1844*, 13.

50. Nicolls's rebuttal point 10, in John Forbes and Co. to Lord Castlereagh, Pensacola, May 20, 1815, enclosed in John Croker to William Hamilton, April 7, 1818, PRO, FO 72/219.

51. Nicolls to Cochrane, Nassau, July 27, 1814, Cochrane Papers, MS 2328, 54, PKY. Interestingly, after the war a frustrated Cockburn wrote that American slaves harbored

> "high ideas of superiority which they attach to themselves over the African negroes who chiefly compose these [West Indian] Regiments; with whom I am assured no inducements could probably tempt them to indiscriminately mix and enlist themselves in the same corps—and you will be aware that a most active and excellent officer (2nd Col. Brown) with the advantage of being with them upon service, tried to experiment in vain and at the conclusion of the campaign in the Chesapeake returned to the West Indies without having obtained a man." Cockburn to Major Kinsman, London, August 23, 1815, NAGB, CO 37/73, 52–53.

The British utterly failed to take into account the strong ethnic prejudices harbored by American slaves. Major Kinsman reported that a "great anxiety and some discontent arose" among a number of former American slaves at the prospect of merely being trained by an officer from the Second West India Regiment (Kinsman to Colonial Office, August 18, 1815, Head Quarters 3rd Battalion of Royal Colonial Marines, Ireland Island, Bermuda, NAGB, CO 37/73, 58). And yet they "look up with implicit confidence [in their white British commanding officers and threatened to react violently if a] . . . promise having been made not to separate them from their command [was broken]" (Cockburn to Colonial Office, August 23, 1815, NAGB, CO 37/73, 52). They clearly considered themselves to be different, and North American in particular, as was evidenced by their "dislike to the West Indies and prefer[ence for] settling here [Bermuda] or upon the continent of America" (Cochrane to Melville, *Tonnant* in Bermuda, April 2, 1815, NAGB, CO 37/73, 139). This ethnic chauvinism was the result of the American blacks' belief that their culture was fundamentally different from and superior to that of the soldiers from Africa and the Caribbean. This suggests that they had a strong and clear sense of what it meant to be "American" that easily transcended any understanding of race and racial bonds. Nonetheless the appearance of the West India Regiments had added an extra racial dynamic to the war in the South by further evoking images of the revolutionary Caribbean.

52. Cockburn to Cochrane, Cumberland Island, February 27, 1815, NAGB, ADM 1/509, 180.

53. Craton and Saunders, *Islanders in the Stream*, section 3, is a good overview of Bahamian slavery and society during this era.

54. See note 52.

55. House of Assembly, Nassau, January 9, 1816, NAGB, CO 23/63, 312.

56. See Craton, *Testing the Chains*; Beckles, *Black Rebellion in Barbados*; and Lambert, "Producing/Contesting Whiteness."

57. Chalmers at Meeting of Commissioners of Correspondence, May 2, 1816, in *Correspondence to and from George Chalmers*, 136.

58. Ibid. In Florida Nicolls served with a small detachment of the Fifth West India Regiment that did not include any of the soldiers who were sent from Jamaica to the Bahamas at this point.

59. Chalmers to unknown recipient, December 3, 1816, in *Correspondence to and from George Chalmers*, 19.

60. Chalmers to unknown recipient, February 4 1817, in *Correspondence to and from George Chalmers*, 36.

61. Cameron to Bathurst, Nassau, November 12, 1817, NAGB, CO 23/65.

62. Chalmers at Meeting of Commissioners of Correspondence, May 8, 1816, in *Correspondence to and from George Chalmers*, 144.

63. Ibid.

64. Ibid.

65. Advocate General Wylly's Response, Nassau, March 30, 1816, NAGB, CO 23/63, 188.

66. Chalmers at Meeting of Commissioners of Correspondence, May 8, 1816, in *Correspondence to and from George Chalmers*, 144.

67. Chalmers at Meeting of Commissioners of Correspondence, February 4, 1817, in *Correspondence to and from George Chalmers*, 155.

Chapter 2. War Comes to the Southeast

1. Good accounts of the Battle of New Orleans include Owsley, *Struggle for the Gulf Borderland*; Reilly, *The British at the Gates*; and Remini, *The Battle of New Orleans*.

2. Mahon, *The War of 1812*, 339. See Kastor, *The Nation's Crucible*, chapters 5–7, and Rothman, *Slave Country*, chapter 4.

3. Owsley, "British and Indian Activities in Spanish West Florida during the War of 1812."

4. Lt. John Smith to James Monroe, New Feliciana, August 28, 1814, James Monroe Papers, reel 6, Manuscript Division, Library of Congress, Washington, D.C.

5. See Elliott, *Empires of the Atlantic World*, chapter 2, as well as three edited collections that each contain excellent essays discussing these ideas: Armitage and Braddick, eds., *The British Atlantic World*; Canny, ed., *The Oxford History of the British Empire*; and Mancke and Shammas, eds., *The Creation of the British Atlantic World*.

6. Hoffman, *Florida's Frontiers*, chapters 1–8, and Weber, *The Spanish Frontier in North America*, chapters 3, 4, 6, 7, and 8.

7. For decades historians have debated the differences and similarities between Iberian and Anglo attitudes toward race and the effects that these differences had on the inhabitants of both nations and their empires. This continues to be a contentious subject. However, there is general agreement that these differences—as manifest in law, culture, society,

and the general treatment of people of color—became starker in the Iberian and Anglo empires. Due to a combination of past experiences, demographics, and economic goals, England and its empire embraced a more rigid ideology of race, which rested on the legal and biological separation of different peoples, while Spain and its empire, for the same reasons, was defined by more fluid and dynamic race relations that presented greater advantages for people of color. Both societies made fundamental distinctions based on race (as well as class, gender, and religion) and adhered to rigid racial hierarchies, but there were important differences. These differences became even more apparent after American independence. Much of the work that is explicitly comparative focuses on slavery, such as Tannenbaum, *Slave and Citizen*; Klein, *Slavery in the Americas*; and Degler, *Neither Black nor White*. Chaplin, "Race" (in Armitage and Braddick, eds., *The British Atlantic World*, 154–74), and Lockhart and Schwartz, *Early Latin America*, chapter 1, discuss Anglo and Spanish understandings of race respectively. Also see *Constructing Race*, a thematic issue of *William and Mary Quarterly*.

8. On the American Revolution, see Frey, *Water from the Rock*; for Charleston, see Alderson, "Charleston's Rumored Slave Revolt of 1793," in Geggus, ed., *The Impact of the Haitian Revolution*, 93–111; and on Gabriel, see Sidbury, *Ploughshares into Swords*.

9. For discussions of the theory of Atlantic history, see Armitage and Braddick, eds., *The British Atlantic World*; Bailyn, *Atlantic History*; Games, "Atlantic History: Definitions, Challenges, and Opportunities"; Greene and Morgan, eds., *Atlantic History*; and O'Reilly, "Genealogies of Atlantic History." For borderlands theory, see Adelman and Aron, "From Borderlands to Borders"; Gutiérrez and Young, "Transnationalizing Borderlands History"; Hämäläinen and Truett, "On Borderlands"; Hurtado, "Parkmanizing the Spanish Borderlands"; Jackson, ed., *New Views of Borderlands History*; Johnson and Graybill, "Borders and Their Historians in North America," in Johnson and Graybill, eds., *Bridging National Borders in North America*; Johnson, "Problems and Prospects in North American Borderlands History"; Truett, "Epics of Greater America," in Schmidt-Nowara and Nieto-Phillips, eds., *Interpreting Spanish Colonialism*; Truett and Young, "Making Transnational History," in Truett and Young, eds., *Continental Crossroads*; and Weber, "Turner, the Boltonians, and the Borderlands."

10. For discussion of center versus periphery, see Daniels and Kennedy, eds., *Negotiated Empires*, and Greene, *Peripheries and Center*. For world systems theory, see Wallerstein, *The Modern World-System III*. Alison Games has offered an alternative to the center/core versus periphery model that conceptualizes a web of networks among peoples from various colonial regions. See Games, *The Web of Empire*. Discussions of frontiers can be found in Adelman and Aron, "From Borderlands to Borders"; Cronon, "Revisiting the Vanishing Frontier"; Cronon, Miles, and Gitlin, eds., *Under an Open Sky*; Faragher, "The Frontier Trail"; Limerick, "The Adventures of the Frontier in the Twentieth Century," in Grossman, ed., *The Frontier in American Culture*, 67–102; Limerick, Milner, and Rankin, eds., *Trails towards a New Western History*; and Michael Malone, "Beyond the Last Frontier."

11. On patterns of communication among slaves during this era, see Geggus, "Slavery, War and Revolution in the Greater Caribbean," in Gaspar and Geggus, eds., *A Turbulent*

Time, 1–50; and Scott, "The Common Wind," and "Criss-Crossing Empires," in Engerman and Paquette, eds., *The Lesser Antilles in the Age of European Empires*, 280–301.

12. Cusick's *The Other War of 1812* is an excellent recent study of the Patriot Invasion. An older but interesting account of it is Patrick's, *Florida Fiasco*. Stagg's *Borderlines in Borderlands* is a good new work on American intrigues in both Floridas during this period. Porter's *The Negro on the Frontier* deals with the role of blacks in the defense of Florida during the various American encroachments. Thomas Abernathy's "Florida and the Spanish Frontier, 1811–1819," in Ellsworth, ed., *The Americanization of the Gulf Coast*, 88–120, is a good treatment of the last years of Spain's hold on Florida, as is Crider, "The Borderland Floridas."

13. José Hibberson to Charles Harris, November 9, 1813, Lockey Collection, PKY.

14. Sebastián Kindelán to Juan Ruiz de Apodaca, St. Augustine, September 30, 1813, EF, reel 12, section 2, doc. 295, PKY.

15. Manuel Lopez to Governor of Florida, St. Augustine, August 20, 1812, EF, reel 27, section 15, PKY.

16. Enrique Yonge to John Forbes, St. Augustine, November 11, 1812, EF, reel 42, section 28, PKY.

17. Jorge Clarke to Juan José de Estrada, October 25, 1812, item 1812–65, EF, reel 84, section 45, PKY.

18. John McIntosh to James Monroe, January 1813, qtd. in Saunt, *A New Order*, 245.

19. Hibberson to Charles Harris, November 9, 1813, Lockey Collection, PKY.

20. See Langley, *The Americas in the Age of Revolution*, chapters 7–9, and Elliott, *Empires of the Atlantic World*, chapters 11 and 12.

21. "Report of Colonel Newman about mission against the Seminoles in East Florida," December 3, 1812, Journals, Minutes, and Proceedings, Georgia, 1808–1822, Records of the States of the United States of America, Library of Congress Historical Collections on Microfilm, microfilm 1550, reel 276, 96.

22. *Niles Weekly Register*, May 8, 1813, 159. The same article lamented that Amelia Island would once again become "a mighty scene of smuggling and treasonable intercourse."

23. Benjamin Hawkins to David Mitchell, May 31, 1813, Lockey Collection, PKY.

24. William Ashley to David Mitchell, Camden County, June 11, 1813, Lockey Collection, PKY.

25. "The deposition of Jacob Summerlin in front of B. Harris, J.I.C. in the District of East Florida 16 June 1813," in Hayes, ed., *East and West Florida*, 224.

26. "Deposition of James Black at the Camden Co., Inferior Court June 11, 1813," in Hayes, ed. *East and West Florida*, 222.

27. See Braund, *Deerskins and Duffels*; Dowd, *A Spirited Resistance*; Martin, *Sacred Revolt*; and Saunt, *A New Order*.

28. Thomas Flourney to David Mitchell, Mount Vernon, October 3, 1813, Flournoy File, box 4-2-46, National Archives and Records Administration (hereafter cited as NARA).

29. John Rhea to James Monroe, December, 20, 1813, Washington, D.C., Lockey Collection, PKY.

30. Cpt. Philip Cook to Cpt. Jones, Fort Hawkins, September 6, 1813, William Jones Papers, Georgia Historical Society, Savannah (hereafter cited as GHS).

31. Saunt, *A New Order*, 262.

32. See Waselkov, *A Conquering Spirit*.

33. Saunt, *A New Order*, 270.

34. Alexander Durant to Cameron, September 11, 1813, NAGB, CO 23/60, 111.

35. Andrew Jackson to Governor of Georgia, October 10, 1813, in Hayes, ed., *Creek Indian Letters, Talks, and Treaties*, 832.

36. *A Concise Narrative of the Seminole Campaign*, 9.

37. Cameron to Bathurst, Nassau, November 30, 1813, NAGB, CO 23/60, 132–35.

38. Hugh Pigot to Alexander Cochrane, New Providence, April 13, 1814, Cochrane Papers, MS 2327, 1, PKY. Cameron furnished Pigot with six sergeants' coats, twelve [?], six pieces of linen, seven pieces of fine black cloth, thirty white shirts, and twelve calicos (see Cameron to Bathurst, Nassau, April 17, 1814, NAGB, CO 23/61, 62).

39. Cochrane to John Borlase Warren, March 23, 1814, NAGB, ADM 1/505, 431; Owsley, *Struggle*, 96–98; Sugden, "The Southern Indians," 280–81; Pigot to Cochrane, June 8, 1814, NAGB, ADM 1/506, 394–99.

40. Owsley, *Struggle*, 98; Pigot to Cochrane, HMS *Orpheus*, New Providence, April 13, 1814, Cochrane Papers, MS 2328, 1, reel 1, PKY; Cochrane to Croker, June 16, 1815, London, NAGB, ADM 1/50, 377. These documents confirm that Woodbine was definitely the interpreter. It has been suggested in at least one amateur historical/genealogical forum (see *Caribbean L-Archives*, John Weiss posting "George Woodbine," November 30, 2004) that perhaps Woodbine was a mulatto. This is feasible and would have been common in Jamaica; however, there is no documentary evidence to substantiate it.

41. Reprinted in the *Eastern Argus*, July 19, 1815.

42. See Sinclair, *The Land That Never Was*; Owsley and Smith, *Filibusters*; and Brown, "Gregor MacGregor," in Lambert and Lester, eds., *Colonial Lives across the British Empire*.

43. Brown, *Adventuring through Spanish Colonies*, 148.

44. See Langley, *The Americas in the Age of Revolution*; Gaspar and Geggus, eds., *A Turbulent Time*; and Geggus, ed., *The Impact of the Haitian Revolution*.

45. Pigot to Cochrane, HMS *Orpheus*, New Providence, June 6, 1814, Cochrane Papers, MS 2326, 29, PKY; Owsley claims that the interpreter was Alexander Durant (*Struggle*, 99).

46. Woodbine to Pigot, Prospect Bluff, May 25, 1814, Cochrane Papers, MS 2328, PKY.

47. Ibid.

48. Pigot to Smith and Denny, HMS *Orpheus*, Apalachicola, May 21, 1814, Cochrane Papers, MS 2328, 9, PKY.

49. Saunt notes that the Creeks called the bluff Ackaikwheithle (*A New Order*, 276).

50. Woodbine to Cochrane, Prospect Bluff, May 31, 1814, Cochrane Papers, MS 2328, PKY.

51. Sugden, "The Southern Indians," 282.

52. Copy of a Talk Delivered to the Chiefs of the Creek Nation, May 28, 1814, Cochrane Papers, MS 2328, 8, PKY. Woodbine had earlier delivered Cochrane's general

proclamation to the Indians promising support against the Americans (March 28, 1814, Cochrane Papers, MS 2346, 3, PKY).

53. Woodbine to Pigot, Prospect Bluff, May 25, 1814, Cochrane Papers, MS 2328, PKY.

54. This example is taken from Cochrane to unknown recipient, Bermuda, July 4, 1814, NAGB, CO 23/61.

55. Cochrane to Nicolls, Bermuda, July 23, 1814, NAGB, ADM 1/506, 4. To the great frustration of their superiors, Nicolls and Woodbine did this and much more.

56. Cochrane to Pigot, Bermuda, March 27, 1814, Cochrane Papers, MS 2450, 5, PKY.

57. Woodbine to Cochrane, Prospect Bluff, May 25, 1814, Cochrane Papers, MS 2328, PKY.

58. "From the Citizens of Greene County, Ga., August 13, 1812," in Stagg, ed., *Papers of James Madison*, vol. 5, 154–55.

59. Journal of Georgia, November 9, 1812, 24, Journals, Minutes, and Proceedings, 1808–1822, Records of the States of the United States of America, Library of Congress Historical Collections on Microfilm, microfilm 1550, reel 276.

60. *Niles Weekly Register*, August 6, 1814.

61. Johnson's "Denmark Vesey and His Co-Conspirators" contains an excellent discussion of the power of rumor and a good reading list on the topic. Among other excellent studies of rumor in colonial and nineteenth-century America, see Dowd, "The Panic of 1751"; Davis, *A Rumor of Revolt*; and Riley, "The Specter of a Savage." Rumor was an extraordinarily powerful force in the Southeast during this period and greatly shaped events.

62. David Blackshear to Peter Early, Camp near the Flint River, January 13, 1814, qtd. in *Memoir of General David Blackshear*, 416.

63. Lt. John Smith to James Monroe, New Feliciana, August 28, 1814, in James Monroe Papers, reel 6, Manuscript Division, Library of Congress, Washington, D.C.

64. Woodbine to Cochrane, Summer 1814, Cochrane Papers, MS 2328, 57, PKY. Edmund Doyle to Robert Spencer and Robert Gamble, Prospect Bluff, April 6, 1815, in *Florida Historical Quarterly* (January 1939), 240.

65. "Narrative of the Operations of the British in Florida," 1815, Cruzat Papers, PKY.

66. *Boston Daily Advertiser*, August 31, 1814, and *Petersburg Daily Courier*, January 26, 1815.

67. *Evening Post*, February 15, 1815.

68. Bullard, *Black Emancipation*, 55.

69. Cochrane to Nicolls, Bermuda, July 23, 1814, NAGB, ADM 1/506, 14.

70. Lawsuit brought by John Perpall, June 1815, New Providence, Bahamas, NAGB, CO 23/63, 185.

71. Ibid.

72. Ibid.

73. Pigot's report appears in NAGB, ADM 1/50, 394–400. Sugden, "The Southern Indians," 282, and Owsley, *Struggle*, 100, both address this report.

74. "Pigot's Report," NAGB, ADM 1/506, 399.

75. Cochrane to Coker, Bermuda, June 20, 1814, NAGB, ADM 1/506, 392.

76. Cameron to Bathurst, Nassau, November 30 1813, NAGB, CO 23/60, 135.

77. Cochrane to Nicolls, Bermuda, July 4, 1814, NAGB, ADM 1/506, 480.

78. Ibid.

79. Cochrane to Cameron, Bermuda, July 4, 1814, NAGB, CO 23/61, 81.

80. Cochrane to Nicolls, Bermuda, July 4, 1814, NAGB, ADM 1/506, 481.

81. Ibid., 483–84.

82. Cochrane to Cameron, Bermuda, July 4, 1814, NAGB, CO 23/61, 81.

83. Owsley, *Struggle*, 104–5.

84. Manrique to Ruiz de Apodaca, Pensacola, August 29, 1814, Papeles Procedentes de Cuba (hereafter cited as PC), file 1795, reel 116, 978, PKY.

Chapter 3. The British Occupation of Pensacola

1. Saunt, *A New Order*, 277.

2. Ibid.

3. Ibid., 277–78.

4. George Woodbine to Charles Cameron, Pensacola, August 9, 1814, Cochrane Papers, MS 2328, 38, PKY.

5. Daniel Patterson to Captain Jones, New Orleans, June 24, 1815, NARA, Area File of the Naval Records Collection, 1775–1910, microfilm 625, reel 200 (area 8-1800–1816), 603.

6. William Coker and Susan Parker, "The Second Spanish Period in the Two Floridas," in Gannon, ed., *New History of Florida*, 150–66; Coker and Ingles, *Spanish Censuses of Pensacola*; Holmes, "West Florida, 1779–1821," in George, ed., *Guide to the History of Florida*, 3–76; McAlister, "Pensacola during the Second Spanish Period"; and McGovern, ed., *Colonial Pensacola*.

7. McAlister, "Pensacola during the Second Spanish Period," 314.

8. William Robertson to Willie Blount, Fort Stoddart, October 26, 1814, *United States Territorial Papers (Florida)*, PKY.

9. "Narrative of the Operations of the British in the Floridas," 1815, Cruzat Papers, PKY.

10. John Innerarity to James Innerarity, Pensacola, October 11, 1814, Greenslade Collection, PKY. Remini, *Andrew Jackson*, vol. 1, 237.

11. See Coker and Watson, *Indian Traders of the Southeastern Spanish Borderlands*.

12. Nicolls to Barrow, Woolwich, March 28, 1818, Lockey Collection, PKY. In response to a lawsuit filed by John Forbes, Nicolls described the four men as "enemys of the basest description open rebels to King and Country. Coll. Jas. Innirarity assisted in [driving] the British from Pensacola, being in the Enemys Service, and what was worse his brother John caused the loss of His Majestys Ship H[ermes] and the slaughter of three parts of her crew. John Forbes was doing [all] in his power to keep the Indians from assisting us, and the Reverend Father Coleman was treacherously Collecting information for the Enemy and at the same time professing the warmest friendship for Great Britain." See

Nicolls's rebuttal point 19, in John Forbes and Co. to Lord Castlereagh, Pensacola, May 20, 1815, enclosed in John Croker to William Hamilton, April 7, 1818, NAGB, FO 72/219.

13. Nicolls and James Gordon to Governor of West Florida, November 2, 1814, PC, file 221A, reel 310, 408, PKY.

14. Jackson to Monroe, Mobile, October 10, 1814, in Moser et al., eds., *Papers of Andrew Jackson*, 3:66.

15. "Narrative of the Operations of the British in the Floridas," 1815, Cruzat Papers, PKY.

16. Edmund Doyle to Spencer and Gamble, Prospect Bluff, April 6, 1815, in *Florida Historical Quarterly* (January 1939), 239.

17. Nicolls to John Barrow, Woolwich, March 28, 1818, enclosed in John Croker to William Hamilton, April 7, 1818, NAGB, FO 72/219, 6.

18. "Narrative of the Operations of the British in the Floridas," 1815, Cruzat Papers, PKY.

19. Nicolls, "Orders for the First Battalion of Royal Colonial Marines," 1814, Lockey Collection, PKY.

20. Ibid.

21. See Fredrickson, *The Black Image in the White Mind*; Tise, *Proslavery*; Davis, *The Problem of Slavery in the Age of Revolution*; and Merton, *Slavery Attacked*. These studies help to explain why Nicolls's assertion of slave humanity and spirituality was so dangerous.

22. Furstenberg, "Beyond Freedom and Slavery."

23. Mason, "The Battle of the Slaveholding Liberators," 665. Mason argues that both nations saw themselves as the true defenders of the spirit of the Age of Revolution.

24. Memorial of John Innerarity, September 23, 1814, NAGB, FO 72/219.

25. William Robertson to Harry Foulmin, Fort Stoddart, October 26, 1814, U.S. Territorial Papers (Florida), PKY.

26. José de Soto to C. G. Apodaca, September 10, 1814, PC, file 1795, reel 116, 1080, PKY; Childs, *The 1812 Aponte Rebellion in Cuba*.

27. Jackson to Governor Holmes, Fort Jackson, July 21, 1814, in Bassett, ed., *Correspondences of Andrew Jackson*, 15.

28. Owsley, *Struggle*, 107, and Saunt, *A New Order*, 278. Sugden, "The Southern Indians," 297. These estimates were for warriors; the actual number, including women and children, would have been far greater than 2,000.

29. James Innerarity to the Governor of West Florida, March 1815, Greenslade Papers, PKY.

30. Soto to C. G. Apodaca, Pensacola, October 21, 1814, PC, file 1795, reel 116, 1189, PKY.

31. "Narrative of the Operations of the British in the Floridas," 1815, Cruzat Papers, PKY.

32. Doyle to unknown recipient, 1817, Greenslade Papers, PKY.

33. "File of Witnesses that may be examined by Commissioners in Pensacola in the Suit of Woodbine—Testimony of Peter Gilchrist," 1815, Cruzat Papers, PKY.

34. Nicolls to Commissioners, Pensacola, October, 1814, in *The Papers of Panton, Leslie and Company*, reel 19.

35. "File of Witnesses . . . Testimony of Pedro Suares," 1815, Cruzat Papers, PKY.

36. Saunt, *A New Order*, 278.

37. "Narrative of the Operations of the British in the Floridas," 1815, Cruzat Papers, PKY.

38. John Forbes and Co. to Lord Castlereagh, Pensacola, May 20, 1815, enclosed in John Croker to William Hamilton, April 7, 1818, NAGB, FO 72/219.

39. William Laurence to Forbes, February 1816, Cruzat Papers, PKY.

40. "File of Witnesses . . . Testimony of John Innerarity," 1815, Cruzat Papers, PKY.

41. "File of Witnesses . . . Testimony of Peter Gilchrist," 1815, Cruzat Papers, PKY.

42. Ibid.

43. William Laurence to Forbes, February 1816, Cruzat Papers, PKY.

44. "File of Witnesses . . . Testimony of Peter Gilchrist," 1815, Cruzat Papers, PKY.

45. Ibid.

46. John Forbes and Co. to Lord Castlereagh, Pensacola, May 20, 1815, enclosed in Croker to Hamilton, April 7, 1818, NAGB, FO 72/219.

47. William Laurence to Forbes, February 1816, Cruzat Papers, PKY.

48. Prosecution of Luis Benjamin Delisle, August 15, 1815, St. Augustine, EF, reel 115, section 58, PKY.

49. "File of Witnesses . . . Testimony of Francisco Collins," 1815, Cruzat Papers, PKY.

50. "Extracts from the Journal of William Ellis," September 12, 1814, printed in *Niles Weekly Register*, February 15, 1815.

51. "Indictment of William Augustus Vesey for Perjury," 1816, Cruzat Papers, PKY.

52. "File of Witnesses . . . Testimony of Peter Gilchrist," 1815, Cruzat Papers, PKY. Prince must have exhibited exceptional leadership qualities that Woodbine quickly recognized. Not only did he play a prominent role in the recruitment of slaves in Pensacola and enjoy a great deal of Woodbine's confidence, but he would also become one of the leaders of the maroon community at Prospect Bluff.

53. Cochrane to George Taylor, February 17, 1815, NAGB, ADM 1/508, 575.

54. Cochrane to Nicolls, *Tonnant* off Apalachicola, December 3, 1814, Cochrane Papers MS 2345, reel 5, 16, PKY.

55. "Extracts from the Journal of William Ellis," dated September 14, 1814, printed in *Niles Weekly Register*, February 15, 1815.

56. On different traditions of warfare, see Jennings, *The Invasion of America*, and Starkey, *European and Native American Warfare*.

57. Nicolls to John Barrow, Shooter's Hill, September 11, 1843, in *Correspondences with Foreign Powers on the Slave Trade*, 1844, 13–14.

58. Edward Nicolls, June 29, 1830, in *Select Committee on State of Settlements of Sierra Leone and Fernando Po*, 48.

59. Nicolls to Barrow, Shooter's Hill, September 11, 1843, in *Correspondences with Foreign Powers on the Slave Trade*, 1844, 13–14.

60. Manrique to Cochrane, Pensacola, January 25, 1815, Cruzat Papers, PKY.

61. Nicolls's rebuttal point 23, in Forbes to Castlereagh, Pensacola, May 20, 1815, enclosed in Croker to Hamilton, April 7, 1818, NAGB, FO 72/219.

62. Juan Ruiz de Apodaca to West Florida, Interim Commandant, Pensacola, July 8, 1815, PC, file 158A, reel 15, doc. 297, PKY. West Florida was desperate for manpower and watched urgently as Americans, Indians, the British, and escaped slaves threatened its very existence. However, it is fair to speculate that given their intense familiarity with Nicolls's rhetoric and its effects on people of color, the Spanish authorities could not risk the consequences of these soldiers becoming infected by his radical ideas.

63. Nicolls Memorial to Melville, May 5, 1817, NAGB, War Office (hereafter cited as WO) 1/144. 3.

64. See Coker, "The Last Battle of the War of 1812."

65. Jackson to John Reid, Mobile, September 18, 1814, "Andrew Jackson Information Sketch Letters, 1796–1843," Special Collections, Duke University.

66. "Narrative of the Operations of the British in the Floridas," 1815, Cruzat Papers, PKY.

67. Remini, *Andrew Jackson*, 239.

68. Jackson to Secretary Armstrong, Fort Jackson, July 30, 1814, in Bassett, ed., *Correspondence of Andrew Jackson*, vol. 2, 18.

69. Jackson to Secretary of War, Mobile, August 30, 1814, in Moser et al., eds., *Papers of Andrew Jackson*, 3:33. Nicolls to Commissioners, Pensacola, October 26, 1814, in *The Papers of Panton, Leslie* and *Company*, reel 19. The effects of this blockade were compounded by the efforts of Forbes and Company to stop food supplies from reaching Pensacola.

70. See Remini, *The Legacy of Andrew Jackson*, and Wilentz, *Andrew Jackson*, chapter 7.

71. Jackson to Rachel Jackson, Mobile, August 28, 1814, in Moser et al., eds., *Papers of Andrew Jackson*, 3:32.

72. Patterson to Jones, New Orleans, July 8, 1814, NARA Area File of the Naval Records Collection, 1775–1910, microfilm 625, reel 200, 608.

73. Peter Early to John Armstrong, Milledgeville, Ga., September 2, 1814, Lockey Collection, PKY.

74. Early to Thomas Pickney, Milledgeville, Ga., September 16, 1814, Lockey Collection, PKY.

75. Benjamin Hawkins to Early, District of Fort Hawkins, November 5, 1814, in Grant, ed., *Letters, Journals and Writings of Benjamin Hawkins*, 703.

76. Willie Blount to James Monroe, Nashville, December 18, 1814, James Monroe Papers, reel 6, Manuscript Division, Library of Congress, Washington, D.C.

77. Jackson to Secretary of War, Mobile, August 30, 1814, in Moser et al., eds., *Papers of Andrew Jackson*, 3:33.

78. *Georgia Journal*, September 7, 1814.

79. Hawkins to Jackson, Creek Agency, August 30, 1814, in Grant, ed., *Letters, Journals and Writings of Benjamin Hawkins*, 694.

80. Hawkins to John Armstrong, Creek Agency, August 16, 1814, in Grant, ed., *Letters, Journals and Writings of Benjamin Hawkins*, 693.

81. Butler to Jackson, Headquarters of the 7th Military District, November 6, 1814, NARA, Order Books of the Adjunct General, June 1813–February 1821, RG 98.

82. Jackson to the Secretary of War, James Monroe, Mobile, September 5, 1814, in Bassett, ed., *The Correspondences of Andrew Jackson*, 39.

83. Jackson to John Coffee, Mobile, October 20, 1814, John Coffee Orderbook, September 11, 1814–March 15, 1815, Southern Historical Collection, Wilson Library, University of North Carolina, Chapel Hill (hereafter cited as SHC, UNC).

84. Jackson to Armstrong, Mobile, August 5, 1814, in Moser et al., eds., *Papers of Andrew Jackson*, 3:28.

85. "Proclamation to the People of Louisiana," enclosed in Jackson to Claiborne, Mobile, September 21, 1814, in Bassett, ed., *The Correspondences of Andrew Jackson*, 46–47.

86. Ibid.

87. Jackson to John Armstrong, Headquarters of the 7th Military District, June 17, 1814, NARA, *Territorial Papers of the United States* (U.S. Congress, Senate, December 2, 1806–February 7, 1825), microfilm 721, reel 1.

88. See Cusick, *The Other War of 1812*; Hoffman, *Florida's Frontiers*, chapter 10; Stagg, *Borderlines in Borderlands*; Weber, *The Spanish Frontier in North America*, chapter 10.

89. Jackson to Secretary of War, Headquarters of the 7th Military District, November 15, 1814, in Bassett, ed., *The Correspondences of Andrew Jackson*, 99.

90. Monroe to Jackson, War Department, October 21, 1814, James Monroe Papers, reel 6, Manuscript Division, Library of Congress, Washington, D.C. Considering that southern politicians, military leaders, and civilians were screaming for the removal of the British from West Florida and that southern militias frequently took matters into their own hands, Monroe's tepid order appears somewhat disingenuous.

91. Owsley, *Struggle*, 112.

92. Remini, *Andrew Jackson*, 241. Jackson was entirely willing to overlook the fact that it was indeed his threats and posturing that had led the Spanish to allow the British to enter Pensacola in the first place.

93. John Innerarity to James Innerarity, Pensacola, November 10, 1814, printed in *Florida Historical Quarterly* (January 1931), 127.

94. Ibid., 129; Forbes to Castlereagh, Pensacola, May 20, 1815, enclosed in Croker to Hamilton, April 7, 1818, NAGB, FO 72/219.

95. Forbes to Castlereagh, Pensacola, May 20, 1815, enclosed in Croker to Hamilton, April 7, 1818, NAGB, FO 72/219.

96. Ibid.

97. Residents of West Florida to the Governor, March 1815, Greenslade Papers, PKY.

98. Nicolls's rebuttal point 18, in John Forbes and Co. to Lord Castlereagh, Pensacola, May 20, 1815, enclosed in Croker to Hamilton, April 7, 1818, NAGB, FO/72/219.

99. Nicolls's rebuttal point 19, in John Forbes and Co. to Lord Castlereagh, Pensacola, May 20, 1815, enclosed in Croker to Hamilton, April 7, 1818, NAGB, FO/72/219.

100. John Innerarity to James Innerarity, Pensacola, November 10, 1814, printed in *Florida Historical Quarterly* (January 1931), 129.

101. Robert Butler General Orders, November 14, 1814, Headquarters 7th Military District, "John Coffee Order Book, September 11, 1814–March 15, 1815," SHC, UNC.

102. Monroe to Jackson, Department of War, December 7, 1814, James Monroe Papers, reel 6, Manuscript Division, Library of Congress, Washington, D.C.

Chapter 4. Edward Nicolls and the Indians of the Southeast

1. Prospect Bluff and the British-built fort are discussed in detail in chapter 6.

2. Alexander Cochrane to Edward Nicolls, *Tonnant* at the mouth of the Apalachicola River, December 3, 1814, Cochrane Papers, MS 2345, 16–17, PKY. To ensure the success of the mission, and to underscore its importance, Cochrane sent Nicolls a large supply of arms that included 3,000 muskets, 1,000 pistols, 1,000 carbines, 500 rifles, more than 1,000,000 rounds of ammunition, and 1,000 swords (Owsley, *Struggle* 135).

3. Edmond Doyle to unknown recipient, 1817, Greenslade Papers, PKY.

4. "Narrative of the Operations of the British in the Floridas," 1815, Cruzat Papers, PKY.

5. Vicente Sebastián Pintado to José de Soto, April 29, 1815, Vicente Sebastián Pintado Papers, box 3, folder 1, Library of Congress, microfilm, PKY.

6. Pintado to Soto, April 29, 1815, Vicente Sebastián Pintado Papers, box 3, folder 1, Library of Congress, microfilm, PKY.

7. Sebastián Kindelán to George Cockburn, St. Augustine, February 18, 1815, NAGB, ADM 1/509, 17.

8. Kindelán to Juan Ruiz de Apodaca, St. Augustine, January 12, 1815, EF, reel 13, section 2, doc. 584 5, PKY.

9. "File of Witnesses . . . Testimony of Andres Leno," 1815, Cruzat Papers, PKY.

10. Saunt, *A New Order*, 279.

11. Governor of East Florida to Woodbine, St. Augustine, December 31, 1814, EF, reel 84, section 45, PKY.

12. Doyle to unknown recipient, 1817, Greenslade Papers, PKY.

13. Kindelán to Woodbine, St. Augustine, December 30, 1814, Forbes-Innerarity Papers, reel 2, PKY. Kindelán informed Woodbine of the boundaries that were created by the Treaty of Peace between Britain and Spain in 1783 and the Treaty of St. Eldefanzo between Spain and the United States.

14. Woodbine to Kindelán December 30, 1814, St. Augustine, in *The Papers of Panton, Leslie and Company*, reel 20.

15. Kindelán to Luis de Onis, St. Augustine, January 4, 1815, EF, reel 41, section 26, PKY. Kindelán to Governor of West Florida, February 6, 1815, EF, reel 43, section 29, doc. 1815-2, PKY.

16. Manrique to Kindelán, Pensacola, March 13, 1815, EF, reel 43, section 29, doc. 1815-5, PKY.

17. Kindelán to Juan Ruiz de Apodaca, St. Augustine, January 21, 1815, EF, reel 12, section 2, PKY.

18. John Forbes and Co. to Lord Castlereagh, Pensacola, May 20, 1815, enclosed in John Croker to William Hamilton, April 7, 1818, NAGB, FO 72/219.

19. Forbes to Castlereagh, Pensacola, May 20, 1815, enclosed in Croker to Hamilton, April 7, 1818, NAGB, FO 72/219.

20. "Deposition of Mayor in Relation to Deportation of Slaves," 1814, Pensacola, Greenslade Papers, PKY.

21. Edmund Gaines to Secretary of War, Fort Stoddart, May 22, 1815, U.S. Territorial Papers (Florida), PKY.

22. Gaines to Secretary of War, May 14, 1815, NAGB, FO 5/107.

23. Pintado to Soto, April 29, 1815, Vicente Sebastián Pintado Papers, box 3, folder 1, Library of Congress, microfilm, PKY.

24. "Cochrane to the Great and Illustrious Chiefs of the Indian Nations," Cochrane Papers, MS 2345, 7, PKY.

25. Hawkins to Peter Early, Fort Hawkins, October 26, 1814, in Grant, ed., *Letters, Journals and Writings of Benjamin Hawkins*, 698.

26. Hawkins to Andrew Jackson, Creek Agency, August 30, 1814, in Grant, ed., *Letters, Journals and Writings of Benjamin Hawkins*, 694.

27. Jackson to Secretary of War, Mobile, August 30, 1814, in Moser et al., eds., *Papers of Andrew Jackson*, 3:33.

28. Doyle to unknown recipient, 1817, Greenslade Papers, PKY.

29. Hawkins to the Speakers of the Upper and Lower Creeks, August 1814, in Grant, ed., *Letters, Journals and Writings of Benjamin Hawkins*, 694.

30. James Innerarity to the Governor of West Florida, March, 1815, Greenslade Papers, PKY.

31. See Perdue, "Race and Culture: Writing the Ethnohistory of the Early South," and a reply to it, Saunt et al., "Rethinking Race and Culture in the Early South." Both are good discussions of the evolving racial consciousness of southeastern Indians. Saunt, *Black, White, and Indian* is a superb examination of attitudes about race in one family of mixed race Creeks, with chapters 1 and 2 being particularly useful for the period discussed. In Snyder, *Slavery in Indian Country*, chapters 7 and 8 are valuable. Merrell's "The Racial Education of the Catawba Indians" and Shoemaker's "How Indians Got to Be Red" also discuss evolving racial consciousness among Indians.

32. Hawkins to Tustunnuggee Hopoie, Speaker of the Lower Creeks, and Tustunnuggee Thlucco, Speaker for the Upper Creeks, no date, enclosed in Hawkins to Jackson, Creek Agency, August 30, 1814, in Grant, ed., *Letters, Journals and Writings of Benjamin Hawkins*, 694–95.

33. Big Warrior to Hawkins, August 25, 1814, in Moser et al., eds., *Papers of Andrew Jackson*, 3:33.

34. All taken from Hawkins to Monroe, District of Fort Hawkins, October 12, 1814, in Grant, ed., *Letters, Journals and Writings of Benjamin Hawkins*, 696.

35. Philip Cook to Peter Early, Fort Hawkins, November 16, 1814, in Hayes, ed., *Creek Indian Letters, Talks, and Treaties*, 864.

36. Hawkins to Jackson, Creek Agency, November 11, 1814, in Grant, ed., *Letters, Journals and Writings of Benjamin Hawkins*, 704.

37. Ibid.

38. Cook to Early, Fort Hawkins, November 16, 1814, in Hayes, ed., *Creek Indian Letters, Talks, and Treaties*, 864.

39. Hawkins to McIntosh, Fort Hawkins, November 26, 1814, in Grant, ed., *Letters, Journals and Writings of Benjamin Hawkins*, 706

40. Ibid.

41. Hawkins to McIntosh, Fort Hawkins, November 26, 1814, in Grant, ed., *Letters, Journals and Writings of Benjamin Hawkins*, 707–8

42. Hawkins to James Monroe, Fort Hawkins, December 21, 1814, in Grant, ed., *Letters, Journals and Writings of Benjamin Hawkins*, 709.

43. Hawkins to Nicolls, Creek Agency, May 24, 1815, in Grant, ed., *Letters, Journals and Writings of Benjamin Hawkins*, 728.

44. Hawkins to Early, Creek Agency, August 23, 1814, printed in *Niles Weekly Register*, October 6, 1814.

45. See Braund, *Deerskins and Duffels*; Ethridge, *Creek Country*; Henri, *The Southern Indians and Benjamin Hawkins*; and Saunt, *A New Order*.

46. Hawkins to Jackson, Creek Agency, November 11, 1814, in Grant, ed., *Letters, Journals and Writings of Benjamin Hawkins*, 704–5.

47. Nicolls to Alexander Gordon, Durham Lodge near Eltham, September 24, 1816, Lockey Collection, PKY.

48. Woodbine to Nicolls, Pensacola, October 27, 1814, Cochrane Papers, MS 2328, 99, PKY. Woodbine's personal beliefs do not appear to have affected his ability to instill Nicolls's message in the Indians.

49. The declaration is not dated, but it is contained in Hawkins to Nicolls, Creek Agency, May 24, 1815, in Grant, ed., *Letters, Journals and Writings of Benjamin Hawkins*, 728.

50. John Francis and Peter McQueen to Alexander Cochrane, Pensacola, September 1, 1814, NAGB, FO 5/139.

51. Thomas Havente to Governor of East Florida, January 29, 1815, EF, section 32, reel 62, PKY.

52. Governor to Thomas Havente, St. Augustine, January 31, 1815, EF, section 32, reel 62, doc. 1815–17, PKY.

53. Kindelán to Juan Ruiz de Apodaca, St. Augustine, January 21, 1815, EF, section 2, reel 13, doc. 599, 24, PKY.

54. Kindelán to Juan Ruiz de Apodaca, St. Augustine, January 7, 1815, EF, reel 13, section 2, doc. 578, PKY.

55. Reprinted in the *Times*, August 16, 1815.

56. Early to William Scott, Milledgeville, Ga., January 11, 1815, Lockey Collection, PKY.

57. John Sawyer to Gen. Blackshear, Mr. Shortlong's, January 27, 1815, in *Memoir of General David Blackshear*, 456.

58. William Scott to General Floyd, Jefferson, Ga., January 4, 1815, printed in *Daily National Intelligencer*, January 27, 1815.

59. Nicolls Memorial to Melville, May 5, 1817, NAGB, WO 1/144, 5.

60. Early to Major Elias, January 18, 1815, "Governor's Letter Books, November 1809–October 1829," reel 1196, Georgia Department of Archives and History, Morrow, Georgia (hereafter cited as GDAH).

61. Early to Kindelán, January 11, 1815, "Governor's Letter Books, November 1809–October 1829," reel 1196, GDAH.

62. Blackshear to Early, Camp Ten, South of the Flint River, January 13, 1814, in *Memoir of General David Blackshear*, 416.

63. Owsley, *Struggle*, 135.

64. Nicolls Memorial to Melville, May 5, 1817, NAGB, WO 1/144, 6.

65. Cochrane to Lambert, *Tonnant* off Mobile Bay, February 17, 1815, NAGB, ADM 1/508, 22; Malcolm to Cochrane, *Royal Oak* off Mobile Bay, March 27, 1815, Pultney Malcolm Papers, MAL/106, 189, National Maritime Museum, Greenwich, U.K.

66. Hawkins to Early, Camp 115 Mile, February 20, 1815, in Grant, ed., *Letters, Journals and Writings of Benjamin Hawkins*, 718.

67. Nicolls Memorial to Melville, May 5, 1817, NAGB, WO 1/144.

68. Cochrane to Lambert, *Tonnant* off the Chandeleur Islands, February 3, 1815, Lockey Collection, PKY.

69. Cochrane to Nicolls, *Tonnant* off Mobile Bay, February 18, 1815, Cochrane Papers, MS 2348, reel 5, 277, PKY.

70. Monroe to Jackson, Department of War, March 13, 1815, NARA, Letters Sent by the Secretary of War, Military Affairs, December 27, 1814–April 29, 1816, microfilm 6, reel 8.

71. Monroe to Pinckney, Department of War, March 11, 1815, NARA, Letters Sent by the Secretary of War, Military Affairs, December 27, 1814–April 29, 1816, microfilm 6, reel 8.

72. Malcolm to Nicolls, *Royal Oak* off Mobile Bay, March 5, 1815, Pultney Malcolm Papers MAL/106, 169, National Maritime Museum, Greenwich, U.K.

73. Codrington's Diary, Headquarters near New Orleans, January 13, 1815, Codrington Papers, COD/7/13, National Maritime Museum, Greenwich, U.K.

74. Henry Bunbury to John Barrow, Downing Street, September 7, 1815, NAGB, FO 5/140.

75. Bathurst to Baker, Foreign Office, September 26, 1815, NAGB, FO 115/24, 79.

76. Extract of letter from John Quincy Adams to the Secretary of State, stating the substance of a conversation with Earl Bathurst, London, September 19, 1815, in *The Papers of Panton, Leslie and Company*, reel 20.

77. Hawkins to Andrew Jackson, Creek Agency, March 24, 1815, in Grant, ed., *Letters, Journals and Writings of Benjamin Hawkins*, 723. Conversely, Cochrane took the fact that the Americans had a copy of his orders to Nicolls as further proof that Article 9 of the Treaty of Ghent was a legally binding agreement between the United States and the In-

dians and that no other treaties were valid. Cochrane to Bathurst, 10 Upper Harley St., London, March 12, 1816, NAGB, WO 1/144, 60.

78. Nicolls to Hawkins, British Post, Apalachicola River, May 12, 1815, in Grant, ed., *Letters, Journals and Writings of Benjamin Hawkins*, 730. This belief was so deeply felt by British officials that a year later Cochrane still stuck to this interpretation as he argued with British officials that "[I] as the Person who, under your Lordships' authority, formed the alliance with [the Red Sticks and Seminoles] . . . state to your lordship [that the American argument in favor of the Treaty of Fort Jackson] "is most assuredly without foundation and that it evidently appears fabricated for the purposes of deceiving H. M.'s Government to take their land back." Cochrane to Bathurst, 10 Upper Harley St., London, March 12, 1816, NAGB, WO 1/144, 58.

79. Nicolls to Cochrane, Woolwich, U.K., March 1, 1816, Lockey Collection, PKY.

80. Spencer to Cochrane, Spencer House, U.K., February 17, 1816, NAGB, WO 1/144, 62.

81. Ibid.

82. Contained in Nicolls to Hawkins, British Post, Apalachicola River, April 28, 1815, in Grant, ed., *Letters, Journals and Writings of Benjamin Hawkins*, 730.

83. Hawkins to Nicolls, Creek Agency, May 28, 1815, in Grant, ed., *Letters, Journals and Writings of Benjamin Hawkins*, 732–34.

84. Hawkins to Nicolls, Creek Agency, May 24, 1815, in *The Papers of Panton, Leslie and Company*, reel 20.

85. Hawkins to Jackson, Creek Agency, May 26, 1815, in Grant, ed., *Letters, Journals and Writings of Benjamin Hawkins*, 729.

86. Deposition of Samuel Jervais, Mobile, May 9, 1815, in *The Papers of Panton, Leslie and Company*, reel 20.

87. General Gaines to A. J. Dallas, Acting Secretary at War, Headquarters, Fort Stoddart, Mississippi Territory, May 22, 1815, in *The Papers of Panton, Leslie and Company*, reel 20.

88. Nicolls to Hawkins, British Post, Apalachicola River, April 28, 1815, in Grant, ed., *Letters, Journals and Writings of Benjamin Hawkins*, 730.

89. Hawkins to Dallas, Creek Agency, July 8, 1815, in Grant, ed., *Letters, Journals and Writings of Benjamin Hawkins*, 740.

90. *Niles Weekly Register*, June 10, 1815.

91. Contained in Hawkins to Dallas, Fort Hawkins, June 27, 1815, in Grant, ed., *Letters, Journals and Writings of Benjamin Hawkins*, 737.

92. Nicolls to Hawkins, British Post, Apalachicola River, May 12, 1815, NAGB, FO 5/107, 82.

93. Hawkins to Dallas, Fort Hawkins, June 27, 1815, in Grant, ed., *Letters, Journals and Writings of Benjamin Hawkins*, 738.

94. Hawkins to Nicolls, Creek Agency, May 28, 1815, in Grant, ed., *Letter, Journals and Writings of Benjamin Hawkins*, 732–34.

95. Hawkins to Dallas, June 27, 1815, in Grant, ed., *Letters, Journals and Writings of Benjamin Hawkins*, 737.

96. Nicolls to Hawkins, British Post, Apalachicola River, May 12, 1815, NAGB, FO 5/107.

97. Nicolls to Hawkins, Amelia Island, June 12, 1815, Lockey Collection, PKY.

98. Hawkins to Dallas, Fort Hawkins, June 27, 1815, in Grant, ed., *Letters, Journals and Writings of Benjamin Hawkins*, 739.

99. Mitchell to John Whitehead, Milledgeville, Ga., June 1, 1815, "Governor's Letter Books, November 1809–October 1829," reel 1196, GDAH.

100. Nicolls to Hawkins, May 12, 1815, NAGB, FO 5/107, 87.

101. Petition of Cappachimico, McQueen, Emathlela Hadjo, Taitachy, Holochapco, Bowlick, and Micocpah, November 8, 1816, in Arbuthnot to Bagot, Nassau, January 8, 1817, NAGB, CO 23/66, 111.

102. "Substance of Correspondence Relating to Indian Chiefs," Colonial Department, September 25, 1818, NAGB, FO/5/140, 1; Nicolls to Bathurst, Durham Lodge near Eltham, U.K., August 24, 1815, and Nicolls to J. P. Morier, Durham Lodge, September 25, 1815, both in Lockey Collection, PKY.

103. Nicolls to Cochrane, Woolwich, U.K., March 1, 1816, Lockey Collection, PKY.

104. Nicolls to Morier, Durham Lodge near Eltham, U.K., September 25, 1815, Lockey Collection, PKY. This ultimately came to fruition and was seen by white Americans and Creeks as proof of an official British conspiracy to acquire the Floridas or to stir the Indians and blacks of the region to violence against the United States—or perhaps both.

105. Ibid.

106. See Saunt, *A New Order*, chapter 8, for a good discussion of writing and literacy and the southeastern Indians during this period.

107. John Bidwell to William Hamilton, Portsmouth, U.K., September 17, 1818, NAGB, FO 5/140, 2.

108. Foreign Office, September 20, 1815, NAGB, FO 115/24, 83–84.

109. "Substance of Correspondence Relating to Indian Chiefs," Colonial Department, September 25, 1818, NAGB, FO/5/140, 2.

110. Ibid., 3.

111. A. J. Dallas to Gaines, Department of War, June 20, 1815, NARA, Records of the Office of the Secretary of War, Letters Sent, Indian Affairs, vol. C, July 8, 1809–December 31, 1816, reel 3, 228.

112. Ibid.

113. *Niles Weekly Register*, June 10, 1815.

114. Monroe to Anthony St. John Baker, Department of State, July 10, 1815, NARA, Notes from the Department of State to Foreign Ministers and Consuls in the United States, 1793–1824, microfilm 38 (May 5, 1810–June 18, 1821), reel 2, 103.

115. Ibid.

116. Adams to Bathurst, Westminster, November 20, 1815, NAGB, FO 115/24, 97.

117. Nicolls to Cochrane, Woolwich, U.K., March 1, 1816, Lockey Collection, PKY.

Chapter 5. Edward Nicolls and His Black Allies

1. Edward Nicolls's rebuttal point 19, in John Forbes and Co. to Lord Castlereagh, Pensacola, May 20, 1815, enclosed in John Croker to William Hamilton, April 7, 1818, NAGB, FO 72/219.

2. Nicolls to Governor Mateo González Manrique, Pensacola, October 22, 1814, in Forbes-Innerarity Papers, reel 2, PKY.

3. Ibid.

4. British rebuttal point number 10, in Forbes to Castlereagh, Pensacola, May 20, 1815, enclosed in Croker to Hamilton, April 7, 1818, NAGB, FO 72/219.

5. Benjamin Hawkins to Nicolls, Creek Agency, May 24, 1815, in Grant, ed., *Letters, Journals and Writings of Benjamin Hawkins*, 728.

6. Edmund Doyle to unknown recipient, 1817, Greenslade Papers, PKY.

7. George Woodbine to Governor Sebastián Kindelán, St. Augustine, December 30, 1814, in *The Papers of Panton, Leslie and Company*, reel 20.

8. Nicolls to the editor, *Times*, February 16, 1842.

9. Nicolls's rebuttal point number 24, in Forbes to Castlereagh, Pensacola, May 20, 1815, enclosed in Croker to Hamilton, April 7, 1818, NAGB, FO 72/219.

10. Hawkins to Peter Early, District of Fort Hawkins, April 21, 1815, in Grant, ed., *Letters, Journals and Writings of Benjamin Hawkins*, 724; Doyle to unknown recipient, 1817, Greenslade Papers, PKY. Hawkins's intelligence was based on an account of a February visit to Prospect Bluff by the Creek William Hardridge.

11. Doyle to unknown recipient, 1817, Greenslade Papers, PKY.

12. Thompson, *Flight to Freedom*, 91. Many more fugitive slaves from across the Southeast would join the maroon community at Prospect Bluff long after Nicolls had departed. Thus not all members of the community had directly interacted with Nicolls nor directly owed him their freedom.

13. Anderson, "The *Quilombo* of Palmares," 551.

14. Craton, *Testing the Chains*, 70.

15. Fick, *The Making of Haiti*, 105–7.

16. Price, introduction to *Maroon Societies*, 5–10, and Thompson, *Flight to Freedom*, 187–206.

17. Alexander Cochrane to Manrique, *Tonnant* off Pensacola, December 5, 1814, Cochrane Papers, MS 2348, 219, PKY.

18. Cochrane to Nicolls, *Tonnant* off Pensacola, December 5, 1814, Cochrane Papers, MS 2348, 216, PKY.

19. Ibid. It is easy to question the sincerity of Cochrane's anger with Nicolls, given Cochrane's deep personal regard for him and the fact that his actions were militarily successful. Most tellingly, after the war, Cochrane wrote to say he supported Nicolls's petition for a promotion based on his service in North America, assuring him that "[I have done] every thing in my power to induce him [Lord Melville] to take you by the hand and it will give me much pleasure to hear that you have succeeded to your wish." See also Cochrane to Nicolls, Mandesten, June 23, 1816, NAGB, WO 1/144.

20. Robert Spencer to Pultney Malcolm, HM *Carron*, Pensacola Bay, March 12, 1815, Cochrane Papers, MS 2336, 114, PKY.

21. Manrique to Lt. José Urcullo, contained in Manrique to Nicolls, Pensacola, December 17, 1815, Forbes-Innerarity Papers, reel 2, PKY.

22. Robert Henry to Nicolls, Pensacola, September 20, 1814, NAGB, FO 72, 219.

23. Report of Urcullo to Manrique, Pensacola, January 23, 1815, in Forbes-Innerarity Papers, reel 2, PKY.

24. Henry to Manrique, January 12, 1815, Cruzat Papers, PKY.

25. Ibid.

26. Hawkins to Andrew Jackson, Creek Agency, March 24, 1815, in Grant, ed., *Letters, Journals and Writings of Benjamin Hawkins*, 723–24.

27. Henry to Manrique, January 12, 1815, Cruzat Papers, PKY.

28. Report of Urcullo to Manrique, Pensacola, January 23, 1815, Forbes-Innerarity Papers, reel 2, PKY.

29. Nicolls's rebuttal point number 21, in Forbes to Castlereagh, Pensacola, May 20, 1815, enclosed in Croker to Hamilton, April 7, 1818, NAGB, FO 72/219.

30. See Brown and Morgan, ed., *Arming Slaves*, especially Jane Landers, "Transforming Bondsmen into Vassals," 120–45; Hendrik Kraay, "Arming Slaves in Brazil," 146–79; Laurent Dubois, "Citizen Soldiers," 233–55; and Peter Blanchard, "The Slave Soldiers of Spanish South America," 255–73. Also see Buckley, *Slaves in Red Coats*, and Voelz, *Slave and Soldier*, 120–21, 139, 149, 270.

31. Henry to Manrique, January 12, 1815, Cruzat Papers, PKY.

32. Report of Urcullo to Manrique, Pensacola, January 23, 1815, in Forbes-Innerarity Papers, reel 2, PKY.

33. Ibid.

34. Ibid.

35. "Narrative of the Operations of the British in the Floridas," 1815, Cruzat Papers, PKY.

36. Report of Urcullo to Manrique, Pensacola, January 23, 1815, in Forbes-Innerarity Papers, reel 2, PKY. For discussions of female slave resistance, see Elizabeth Fox-Genovese, "Strategies and Forms of Resistance," in Hine, ed., *Black Women in United States History*, 409–432; Hine, *Hine Sight*, 27–36; and White, *Ar'n't I a Woman?*

37. John Innerarity to Forbes, May 22, 1815, in *The Papers of Panton, Leslie and Company*, reel 20.

38. Report of Urcullo to Manrique, Pensacola, January 23, 1815, in Forbes-Innerarity Papers, reel 2, PKY.

39. Doyle to unknown recipient, 1817, Greenslade Papers, PKY.

40. Report of Urcullo to Manrique, Pensacola, January 23, 1815, in Forbes-Innerarity Papers, reel 2, PKY.

41. Manrique to Cochrane, Pensacola, January 25, 1815, Cruzat Papers, PKY.

42. Cochrane to Manrique, *Tonnant* off Mobile, February 10, 1815, Cruzat Papers, PKY.

43. Forbes to Castlereagh, Pensacola, May 20, 1815, enclosed in Croker to Hamilton,

April 7, 1818, NAGB, FO 72/219; John Innerarity to Forbes, Pensacola, May 22, 1815, in *The Papers of Panton, Leslie and Company*, reel 20.

44. Forbes to Castlereagh, Pensacola, May 20, 1815, enclosed in Croker to Hamilton, April 7, 1818, NAGB, FO 72/219; Residents of West Florida to the Governor of West Florida, Pensacola, March 1815, Greenslade Papers, PKY. In the aftermath of New Orleans, Andrew Jackson warned Brigadier General James Winchester that "you cannot be too well prepared or too vigilant—Adml. Cochrane is sore, and Genl Lambert crazy, they may in this situation attempt some act of madness—if their panic does not prevent it." See Andrew Jackson to Winchester, New Orleans, January 30, 1815, in Bassett, ed., *Correspondence of Andrew Jackson*, vol. 2, 154. Britain's defeat at the Battle of New Orleans, the greatest defeat of Cochrane's career to this point, which left him reeling, also meant that Cochrane would have been little concerned with causing a diplomatic rift with the Spanish and that he was paying closer attention to other issues. Nicolls's power of persuasion is the best single explanation for the shift in Cochrane's stance.

45. Edward Codrington's diary, Headquarters near New Orleans, January 13, 1815, Codrington Papers, COD/7/1–6 National Maritime Museum, Greenwich, U.K.

46. Hawkins to Jackson, Creek Agency, March 24, 1815, in Grant, ed., *Letters, Journals and Writings of Benjamin Hawkins*, 723–24.

47. Ibid.

48. Hawkins to Early, District of Fort Hawkins, April 21, 1815, in Grant, ed., *Letters, Journals and Writings of Benjamin Hawkins*, 724.

49. Ibid.

50. Ibid.

51. Vicente Sebastián Pintado to José de Soto, April 29, 1815, Vicente Sebastián Pintado Papers, box 3, folder 1, Library of Congress, microfilm, PKY.

52. John Innerarity to Forbes, Pensacola, May 22, 1815, in *The Papers of Panton, Leslie and Company*, reel 20.

53. Cochrane to Croker, *Tonnant* Havana, February 25, 1815, Cochrane Papers, MS 2347, 151, PKY.

54. Pintado to Soto, April 29, 1815, Vicente Sebastián Pintado Papers, box 3, folder 1, Library of Congress, microfilm, PKY.

55. John Innerarity to Forbes, Pensacola, May 22, 1815, in *The Papers of Panton, Leslie and Company*, reel 20. Sierra was one of Pensacola's most important residents and an employee of the town's hospital, who would later be sent to New Providence to manage the thankless task of filing a lawsuit on behalf of Forbes and Company against Woodbine over lost slaves. During his sojourn at Prospect Bluff, Sierra would stand face to face with a number of his former slaves, who would refuse to return to Pensacola with him. Included among these former slaves was Prince, who would become one of the community's leaders after the departure of the British. Juan Ruiz de Apodaca to West Florida Commander, November 27, 1815, PC, file 158A, reel 356, frame 654, PKY.

56. Pultney Malcolm to Manrique, *Royal Oak* off Mobile Bay, March 15, 1815, Pultney Malcolm Papers, MAL/106, 178, National Maritime Museum, Greenwich, U.K.

57. Pintado to Soto, April 29, 1815, Vicente Sebastián Pintado Papers, box 3, folder 1, Library of Congress, microfilm, PKY.

58. John Innerarity to Forbes, Pensacola, May 22, 1815, in *The Papers of Panton, Leslie and Company*, reel 20.

59. Ibid.

60. Pintado to Soto, April 29, 1815, Vicente Sebastián Pintado Papers, box 3, folder 1, Library of Congress, microfilm, PKY.

61. John Innerarity to Forbes, Pensacola, May 22, 1815, in *The Papers of Panton, Leslie and Company*, reel 20.

62. Pintado to Soto, April 29, 1815, Vicente Sebastián Pintado Papers, box 3, folder 1, Library of Congress, microfilm, PKY.

63. Gaines to Dallas, Acting Secretary of War, Headquarters, Fort Stoddart, Mississippi Territory, May 22, 1815, in *American State Papers*, book 1, *Foreign Relations*, vol. 4 (1815–1822), 552, Library of Congress, American Memory Project, http://memory.loc .gov/ammem/amlaw/lwsp.html.

64. Pintado to Soto, April 29, 1815, Vicente Sebastián Pintado Papers, box 3, folder 1, Library of Congress, microfilm, PKY, and "Memorandum of a gentleman of respectability at Bermuda," St. George, Bermuda, May 22, 1815, in *The Papers of Panton, Leslie and Company*, reel 20.

65. John Innerarity to Forbes, Pensacola, May 22, 1815, in *The Papers of Panton, Leslie and Company*, reel 20.

66. Forbes to Castlereagh, Pensacola, May 20, 1815, enclosed in Croker to Hamilton, April 7, 1818, NAGB, FO 72/219.

67. John Innerarity to Forbes, Pensacola, May 22, 1815, in *The Papers of Panton, Leslie and Company*, reel 20.

68. John Innerarity to Forbes, Mobile, August 12, 1815, Elizabeth Howard West Collection, PKY.

69. "Memorandum of a gentleman of respectability at Bermuda," St. George, Bermuda, May 22, 1815, in *The Papers of Panton, Leslie and Company*, reel 20. Robert Ambrister was one such officer, who had been serving with Nicolls for months with a devotion that would ultimately cost him his life during the First Seminole War. See Robert Ambrister's Commission as auxiliary second lieutenant by Alexander Cochrane, July 25, 1814, in *The Papers of Panton, Leslie and Company*, reel 19; Edmund Doyle to unknown recipient, 1817, Greenslade Papers, PKY.

70. Genovese, *Rebellion*, 53–56, 82–84.

71. Craton, *Testing the Chains*, 164.

72. Ibid., 185.

73. Ibid., 189.

74. Ibid., 213.

75. Ibid.

76. Olwyn Blouet, "Bryan Edwards and the Haitian Revolution," in Geggus, ed., *The Impact of the Haitian Revolution*, 49.

77. Fick, *The Making of Haiti*, 60–64, and Dubois, *Avengers of the New World*, 54–57.

78. David Geggus, "Marronage, Vodou, and the Slave Revolt of 1791," in Geggus, *Haitian Revolutionary Studies*, chapter 5.

79. Fick, *The Making of Haiti*, 49–52, 59–69, 106–7; Dubois, *Avengers of the New World*, 52–56.

80. La Rosa Corzo, *Runaway Slave Settlements in Cuba*, 84–86, 117–19, 220–21.

81. Dubois, *Avengers of the New World*, 54–55.

82. PC, file 147B, reel 483, 960, PKY.

83. Pintado to Soto, April 29, 1815, Vicente Sebastián Pintado Papers, box 3, folder 1, Library of Congress, microfilm, PKY.

84. John Innerarity to Forbes, Pensacola, May 22, 1815, in *The Papers of Panton, Leslie and Company*, reel 20. Not that any of the former slaves would have dared to test this theory, but this was an overstatement designed to make a point about the extent of official freedom promised in the license of decommission.

85. Pintado to Soto, April 29, 1815, Vicente Sebastián Pintado Papers, box 3, folder 1, Library of Congress, microfilm, PKY.

86. Ibid.

87. Cochrane to Malcolm, *Tonnant* off Mobile Bay, February 17, 1815, NAGB, ADM 1/508, 562–65.

88. Malcolm to Spencer, *Royal Oak* off Mobile Bay, March 29, 1815, Pultney Malcolm Papers, MAL/106, 196–97, National Maritime Museum, Greenwich, U.K.

89. Nicolls to Hawkins, British Post, May 12, 1815, Apalachicola River, NAGB, FO 5/107, 83.

90. Forbes to Castlereagh, Pensacola, May 20, 1815, enclosed in Croker to Hamilton, April 7, 1818, NAGB, FO 72/219; Admiral Smith to Croker, Halifax, August 24, 1816, NAGB, ADM 1/510, 24–25.

91. Alexander Kinsman to British Government, Headquarters 3rd Battalion Royal Colonial Marines, Ireland Island, Bermuda, August 18, 1815, NAGB, CO 37/73, 58.

92. Nicolls to Sir John Barrow, Shooter's Hill, London, September 11, 1843, in *Correspondences with Foreign Powers on Slave Trade, 1844*, 13.

93. It was alleged from some quarters that the British were merely feigning loyalty to their black allies and that the former slaves were left at Prospect Bluff for fear that, upon arrival in the Caribbean or Bermuda, it would be exposed that many of them had in fact been stolen from residents of Spanish Florida or from neutral Indians in what would be a political and legal embarrassment. However, considering that hundreds of former slaves at Prospect Bluff had already managed to avoid being returned to their masters and that the British Navy was in the midst of transporting thousands of American slaves to the Caribbean and elsewhere—in a process that was both legally and politically charged and equally public—the British would not have felt compelled to cover up their actions. The Inhabitants of West Florida to the Governor of West Florida, Pensacola, March 1815, Greenslade Papers, PKY.

94. Hawkins to Gaines, Fort Hawkins, June 14, 1815, in Grant, ed., *Letters, Journals and Writings of Benjamin Hawkins*, 735–36.

95. Nicolls to Sir John Barrow, Shooter's Hill, London, September 11, 1843, in *Correspondences with Foreign Powers on Slave Trade, 1844*, 13.

96. James Innerarity to John Innerarity, Mobile, November 25, 1815, Elizabeth Howard West Collection, PKY.

97. Joseph Crawford to the Earl of Aberdeen, Havana, June 12, 1843, in *Correspondences with Foreign Powers on Slave Trade, 1843*, 42–43.

98. Crawford to Aberdeen, Havana, June 12, 1843, in *Correspondences with Foreign Powers on Slave Trade, 1843*, 42–43.

99. Ibid.

100. Ibid.

101. Nicolls to Barrow, Shooter's Hill, London, September 11, 1843, *Correspondences with Foreign Powers on Slave Trade, 1844*, 13.

102. James Carmichael Smith to Bathurst, Government House, Bahamas, August 10, 1831, NAGB, CO 23/78, 58.

103. Petition in Support of Sir James Carmichael Smith, May 7, 1832, NAGB, CO 23/86, 250–53.

104. *Nassau Guardian*, November 23, 1844.

105. Thompson, *Flight to Freedom*, 289–90.

106. Price, introduction to *Maroon Societies*, 4, and Genovese, *Rebellion*, 51.

107. Silvia de Groot, "A Comparison between the History of Maroon Communities in Surinam and Jamaica," in Heuman, ed., *Out of This House of Bondage*, 174–80.

108. Kenneth Bilby, "Swearing by the Past, Swearing to the Future," reprinted in Dubois and Scott, eds., *Origins of the Black Atlantic*, 236–40.

109. Kopytoff, "Colonial Treaty," and Bilby, "Swearing by the Past."

110. Chapters 4–6 of Campbell's *The Maroons of Jamaica* provide an exhaustive overview of the treaties between the Leeward and Windward maroons and the British government.

111. Kopytoff, "Colonial Treaty," 46–47.

112. Wilson, "The Performance of Freedom," 13.

113. De Groot, "A Comparison between the History of Maroon Communities in Surinam and Jamaica" in Heuman, ed., *Out of This House of Bondage*, 180; Brown, "The Performance of Freedom," 26; Kopytoff, "Colonial Treaty," 50.

114. Kopytoff, "Colonial Treaty," 50.

115. Nicolls to Gordon, Durham Lodge near Eltham, U.K., September 24, 1816, Lockey Collection, PKY.

116. Nicolls to Barrow, Shooter's Hill, London, September 11, 1843, in *Correspondences with Foreign Powers on Slave Trade, 1844*, 13.

117. Nicolls to Gordon, Durham Lodge near Eltham, U.K., September 24, 1816, Lockey Collection, PKY.

118. Hawkins to Jackson, Creek Agency, August 4 and 12, 1815, in Grant, ed., *Letters, Journals and Writings of Benjamin Hawkins*, 746–48.

119. At this point Trinidad was the least stable island in the British Caribbean. White

and mixed-race slave owners watched in horror as New Granada burned only a few miles away on the South American mainland in a deeply ideological and racialized revolution that gave "serious grounds to apprehend a permanent organization of freedom and independence among the slaves" of Trinidad. For months, the residents had been watching "our Negroes . . . deserting to any point they can reach without risk or difficulty where they are in a state of freedom and have arms placed in their hands in their arriving at Gueria [Venezuela, creating grave danger for] . . . this colony as well as all the British colonial possessions." It was against this backdrop that the American former-slave soldiers began to arrive in the late summer and fall of 1815.

Upon arrival, the Governor gave them the option of "continuing their former employments of tradesmen and servants," but they "unanimously preferred taking the lands and refused service" with "such a determination [that] manifested their peaceable disposition" while they showed a "strong disposition . . . to keep together or form a separate community." Regardless of their "peaceable disposition," the former slaves were sent to the remote area of Naparine, "so as to meet the wishes of some of the inhabitants who were averse to receiving them in their quarters." Woodford to Bathurst, Trinidad, November 30, 1815, NAGB, CO 295/37, 229; November 10, 1816, NAGB, CO 295/37, 170–71; and August 28, 1816, NAGB, CO 295/40, 109, 125. The residents of Naparine, too, soon became uneasy at the arrival of the former American slaves. An 1816 petition signed by 37 white and 13 "coloured" residents of Naparine explained that they feared the American blacks because of their military experience. Petition on Behalf of the Inhabitants of Naparine, October 7, 1816, NAGB, CO 295/40, 175–81.

The powerfully worded petition, which illustrated a deep fear of slave resistance, was unsuccessful, and the former slaves were allowed to stay in Trinidad. They were organized into villages by their marine companies and placed under the command of their sergeants and corporals. Each family was given sixteen acres of land, to which they received official title in 1847. The refugees' villages thrived and became important parts of Trinidad's broader society. However, the former slaves did not have full legal, political, or social equality with their white neighbors and remained second-class citizens within the British Empire for some time to come. See Titus, *Amelioration and Abolition of Slavery*; John, *Plantation Slaves of Trinidad*; and McNish, *The Merikens*.

The approximately 2,000 former American slaves who were transported to Nova Scotia and New Brunswick between 1813 and 1816 found themselves in a much more difficult and unhappy situation than those in Trinidad. The refugees, who largely arrived in desperate conditions, encountered sustained hostility from the local white population, who aggressively encouraged them to relocate to Africa or the Caribbean or even to return to their masters. The former American slaves' communities remained poor and underdeveloped. When they received farmland it was of poor quality, and both men and women struggled to find employment to supplement their meager agricultural output. Not only did the former slaves fail to achieve anything close to full equality or inclusion within Canadian society, but their distinctly southern Afro-American culture contrasted starkly with the grim Canadian surroundings. Not until the 1830s did the former slaves begin to make their first real social and economic advances, and even these were merely the first small steps for deeply second-class citizens. Whitfield's *Blacks on the Border* is an excellent new study of former American slaves in Canada during this period.

120. Hawkins to John Sevier and William Barnett, August 19, 1815, Fort Hawkins, in Grant, ed., *Letters, Journals and Writings of Benjamin Hawkins*, 748.

121. Nicolls to the editor, *Times*, February 16, 1842.

122. Forbes to Castlereagh, Pensacola, May 20, 1815, enclosed in Croker to Hamilton, April 7, 1818, NAGB, FO 72/219.

Chapter 6. Land, Ecology, and Size

1. Felipe Prieto to Edmund Doyle, September 17, 1815, Cruzat Papers, PKY, qtd. in Saunt, *A New Order*, 284.

2. Saunt, *A New Order*, 284. On two separate occasions it was alleged that the community was either led by Indians or led by a combined group of blacks and Indians. The vast majority of evidence suggests that this was not the case and that the community's leadership was all black.

3. Daniel Patterson to Lieut. Crowley, New Orleans, June 19, 1816, reprinted in *Daily National Intelligencer*, April 23, 1819.

4. Robert Ambrister to Edward Nicolls, Suwannee near Apalachicola, n.d., 1818; *Trials of Arbuthnot and Ambrister*, 70.

5. For more on Gabriel, see Egerton, *Gabriel's Rebellion*, and Sidbury, *Ploughshares into Swords*. For more on Denmark Vesey, see Michael Johnson's "Denmark Vesey and His Co-Conspirators" in *William and Mary Quarterly* 58 and a suite of responses in the following issue (59: 135–202), heatedly debating whether the Denmark Vesey conspiracy ever in fact existed: Gross, "Forum"; Pearson, "Trials and Errors"; Egerton, "Forgetting"; Robertson, "Inconsistent Contextualism"; Morgan, "Conspiracy Scares"; Davis, "Conspiracy"; Jordan, "Charleston Hurricane"; Sidbury, "Plausible Stories"; Paquette, "Jacobins of the Lowcountry"; Johnson, "Reading Evidence." For more on Nat Turner, see Greenberg, ed., *Nat Turner*.

6. The primary sources give no evidence that the community was called a "maroon community" by contemporaries. This fact is unsurprising and therefore should not be used as evidence that the settlement at Prospect Bluff was any less a maroon community because it was not labeled as such. The term would have been less familiar to North Americans and Europeans in the early nineteenth century than it would be later when maroons became common fixtures in pro- and anti-slavery literature and in fiction. What primary sources do make very clear is that contemporaries were describing a community of former slaves living outside the plantation complex, or what is easily identifiable as a maroon community.

7. Joseph Crawford to the Earl of Aberdeen, Havana, June 12, 1843, in *Correspondences with Foreign Powers on Slave Trade, 1843*, 42–43.

8. *Bahama Herald*, December 21, 1853.

9. Lt. Col. Duncan Clinch to Colonel Robert Butler, Camp Crawford, August 2, 1816,

NARA, Joint Military-Navy Engagements, 1759–1898, Office of Naval Records and Library, U.S. Navy, 1775–1910, RG 45, box 181.

10. Daniel Patterson to Secretary of Navy, New Orleans, August 15, 1816, printed in *Daily National Intelligencer*, April 23, 1819.

11. See Howard, *Black Seminoles in the Bahamas*.

12. Edmund Gaines to A. J. Dallas, Acting Secretary of War, Headquarters, Fort Stoddart, Mississippi Territory, May 22, 1815, in *American State Papers*, book 1, *Foreign Relations*, vol. 4 (1815–1822), 552, Library of Congress, American Memory Project, http:// memory.loc.gov/ammem/amlaw/lwsp.html.

13. Petition signed by "Cappahimico, McQueen, Emathlale Hadjo, Holochapco, Bowlegs, and Micocpah," November 8, 1816. Enclosed in Arbuthnot to Bagot, Nassau, June 8, 1817, NAGB, CO 23/66, 112.

14. To the Commander of the U.S. Forces in the Indian Nation from an undetermined sender, April 26, 1816, NARA, Letters Received by the Secretary of War, Registered Series, 1801–1860, microfilm 221 (December 1815–December 1816), reel 69.

15. For example, Mr. L. Sullivan to Viscount Canning, War Office, August 10, 1843, in *Correspondence with Foreign Powers on Slave Trade 1843*, 12. Canning's choice of words is based on his reading of *all* of the official documents in the process of researching a claim by former slaves. Nicolls himself referred to the community as the "post at the Bluff." Colonel Nicolls to Sir John Barrow, Shooter's Hill, London, September 11, 1843, in *Correspondences with Foreign Powers on Slave Trade, 1844*, 13.

16. Nicolls to Barrow, Shooter's Hill, London, September 11, 1843, *Correspondences with Foreign Powers on Slave Trade, 1844*, 13; John Quincy Adams to the American Minister at Madrid, Washington, D.C., November 28, 1818, reprinted in the *Albion, A Journal of News, Politics and Literature*, January 20, 1838.

17. José de Soto to CG Apodaca, November 25, 1815, PC, file 1796, reel 119, 1378, PKY; Mauricio de Zúñiga to Andrew Jackson, Pensacola, May 26, 1816, in Moser et al., eds., *Papers of Andrew Jackson*, 4:42: José de Soto described "Negros profugos y refugados en el Fuerte, que han construido los Yngleses sobre el Rio de Apalachicola" or "black fugitives and refugees who lived in the fort built by the British on the Apalachicola River."

18. Adams to the American Minister at Madrid, Washington, D.C., November 28, 1818, reprinted in the *Albion, A Journal of News, Politics and Literature*, January 20, 1838.

19. *New York Columbian*, November 19, 1819. This periodical is only one among several in which the article was published.

20. For example, Little Prince raged about the "Negro Fort" during the spring of 1816. Clinch to Secretary of War, Fort Gaines, May 9, 1816, NARA, Secretary of War, Letters Received, microfilm 221.

21. For example, "Extract of a letter from a gentleman in New Orleans to a gentleman in this city," reprinted in *Evening Post*, October 28, 1816.

22. Schwartz, *Slaves, Peasants, and Rebels*, 112–18. In Brazil, *mocambo* villages with names such as Ambrosio, Zundu, Gareca, and Calaboca, were common, usually named after prominent individuals. Roger Bastide, "The Other Quilombos," in Price, ed., *Maroon Societies*, 193.

23. Schwartz, *Slaves, Peasants, and Rebels*, 117.

24. Ibid., 125. The name Palmares has received much scholarly attention over the years. *Palmar* (plural *palmares*) is the Portuguese word for "palm grove." The region in which the great *mocambo* was situated did indeed abound with palm trees, and by the 1640s observers were referring to at least two related *mocambos* as Palmares. Within Palmares, the various villages had separate names such as Zambi, Andalaquituche, and Aqualtune, often after their leaders. See Anderson, "The *Quilombo* of Palmares"; Kent, "Palmares," in Price, ed., *Maroon Societies*, 170–90; and Schwartz, *Slaves, Peasants, and Rebels*, 122–28.

25. Schwartz, *Slaves, Peasants, and Rebels*, 127. Many maroon villages in Suriname had names that were African in origin, such as Kosay, Nomerimi, Kromotibo, Buku, Kofihay, and Kwamigron. E. Kofi Agorsah, "Scars of Brutality: Archaeology of the Maroons in the Caribbean," in Ogundiran and Falola, eds., *Archaeology of Atlantic Africa and the African Diaspora*, 338.

26. Schwartz, *Slaves, Peasants, and Rebels*, 125–28.

27. Ibid., 125, and Anderson, "The *Quilombo* of Palmares," 559.

28. Mullin, *Africa in America*, 52–53, provides an important discussion on the use of the word "town" in the naming of Jamaican maroon communities.

29. Interestingly the refugees from Prospect Bluff who relocated to the Bahamas immediately named their settlement Nicholls Town. This decision appears to have shared the same goals as the Jamaican maroons' naming process on two levels: it sought to emphasize permanence, possession, and sovereignty, and it honored their revered founder.

30. Lying on the eastern bank of the Apalachicola River, Prospect Bluff was technically in Spanish East Florida. However, because of its proximity to Pensacola and Fort San Marcos de Apalache, it was generally regarded as falling under the control of the governor of West Florida.

31. Duncan Clinch to Butler, Camp Crawford, August 2, 1816, reprinted in *Army and Navy Chronicle*, February 25, 1836.

32. Gaines to Jackson, Fort Stoddart, Mississippi Territory, May 14, 1816, in Moser et al., eds., *Papers of Andrew Jackson*, 4:31.

33. Duncan Clinch to Robert Butler, Camp Crawford, August 2, 1816, reprinted in *Army and Navy Chronicle*, February 25, 1836.

34. Cypress domes are shallow depressions in the terrain that fill with up to five feet of water and where cypress trees dwell at the center and bushes and smaller plants along the edges.

35. "Gadsden's Sub Report on the Defenses of Florida," in Buell Collection of Historical Documents Relating to the Corps of Engineers, 1801–19, NARA, microfilm 417, reel 3, 808.

36. See Campbell, *The Maroons of Jamaica*; Craton, *Testing the Chains*; and Schafer, "The Maroons of Jamaica: African Slave Rebels in the Caribbean."

37. La Rosa Corzo's *Runaway Slave Settlements in Cuba* is an excellent history of Cuba's eastern *palenques*.

38. La Rosa Corzo, *Runaway Slave Settlements in Cuba*, 74–75.

39. Hoogbergen, *The Boni Maroon Wars in Suriname*, chapter 1.

40. Price's *First-Time* is a fascinating study of Suriname's maroons over the centuries.

41. Hoogbergen, *The Boni Maroon Wars in Suriname*, 7.

42. Mattoso, *To Be a Slave in Brazil*, 139, and Anderson, "The *Quilombo* of Palmares," 551.

43. Schwartz, *Slaves, Peasants, and Rebels*, 122.

44. Mattoso, *To Be a Slave in Brazil*, 140.

45. Woodbine to Pigot, Prospect Bluff, May 25, 1814, Cochrane Papers, MS 2328, PKY. Before construction was complete, there was a foreshadowing of the bizarre and tragic events that would later involve the powder magazine. On a Sunday evening, a bolt of lightning hit a tree next to the magazine, causing a large cask of powder to explode, which severely burnt a soldier.

46. Woodbine to Pigot, Prospect Bluff, May 25, 1814, Cochrane Papers, MS 2328, whole document, PKY. Branch, Old Fort Gadsden Paper; Griffin, Report of Investigations at Old Fort Gadsden; and Poe, "Archaeological Excavations at Fort Gadsden, Florida."

47. Gaines to Jackson, Fort Stoddart, Mississippi Territory, May 14, 1816, in Moser et al., eds., *Papers of Andrew Jackson*, 4:31.

48. Mr. Sullivan to Viscount Canning, War Office, August 10, 1843, in *Correspondence with Foreign Powers on Slave Trade, 1843*, 12.

49. Wilson, *History of the Rise and Fall of the Slave Power in America*, 129, and Saunt, *A New Order*, 283.

50. Covington, "Negro Fort," 79, and Saunt, *A New Order*, 280–81. The new and larger fort replaced Woodbine's earlier establishment. Initially the fort was designed for "the protection of the families of the Indians, while the warriors are in the field." Cochrane to Lambert, *Tonnant* off Mobile Bay, February 17, 1815, NAGB, ADM 1/508, 565.

51. Vicente Sebastián Pintado to José de Soto, April 29, 1815, Vicente Sebastián Pintado Papers, box 3, folder 1, Library of Congress, microfilm, PKY.

52. Ibid.

53. Clinch to Butler, Camp Crawford, August 2, 1816, NARA, List of Vessels of the U.S. Navy, 1797–1816, RG 45, box 181.

54. Gadsden to Jackson, Nashville, August, 1, 1818, NARA, Reports, July 3, 1812–December 4, 1823, RG 77, 338; "Extract of a letter from New Orleans, to the Editor of the *Weekly Register*," printed in *Commercial Advertiser*, September 23, 1816.

55. "Extract of a letter from New Orleans, to the Editor of the *Weekly Register*," printed in *Commercial Advertiser*, September 23, 1816.

56. Mattoso, *To Be a Slave in Brazil*, 139.

57. Schwartz, *Slaves, Peasants, and Rebels*, 124.

58. Anderson, "The *Quilombo* of Palmares," 551.

59. Thompson, *Flight to Freedom*, 187–88.

60. Hoogbergen, *The Boni Maroon Wars in Suriname*, 18–19.

61. Introduction to Price, ed., *Maroon Societies*, 7.

62. See La Rosa Corzo, *Runaway Slave Settlements in Cuba*, and Francisco Pérez de la Riva, "Cuban Palenques," in Price, ed., *Maroon Societies*, 49–59.

63. Thompson, *Flight to Freedom*, 190.

64. Campbell, *The Maroons of Jamaica*, 47.

65. Ibid., 49.

66. Ibid., 47; Craton, *Testing the Chains*, 83; and Thompson, *Flight to Freedom*, 198.

67. Nicolls to Gordon, Kent, September 24, 1816, Lockey Collection, PKY.

68. Nicolls to the editor, *Times*, February 16, 1842.

69. Cochrane to Lambert, *Tonnant* off Mobile Bay, February 17, 1815, NAGB, ADM 1/508, 22. Supporting this estimate is Urcullo's of 500 soldiers, which was presumably an overestimation designed to strengthen his argument that attempting forcefully to remove the former slaves from Pensacola was dangerous.

70. Pintado to Soto, April 29, 1815, Vicente Sebastián Pintado Papers, box 3, folder 1, Library of Congress, microfilm, PKY.

71. Hawkins to Jackson, Creek Agency, March 24, 1815, in Grant, ed., *Letters, Journals and Writings of Benjamin Hawkins*, 723–24.

72. Deposition of Samuel Jervais, Mobile, May 9, 1815, in *The Papers of Panton, Leslie and Company*, reel 20.

73. "Memorandum of a gentleman of respectability at Bermuda," St. George, Bermuda, May 22, 1815, in *The Papers of Panton, Leslie and Company*, reel 20.

74. Gaines to Dallas, Acting Secretary of War, Headquarters, Fort Stoddart, Mississippi Territory, May 22, 1815, in *American State Papers*, book 1, *Foreign Relations*, vol. 4 (1815–1822), 552, Library of Congress, American Memory Project, http://memory.loc.gov/ammem/amlaw/lwsp.html.

75. "Letter from a gentleman on St. Simon's Island, to another in this city [Savannah] dated 18th June, 1815," printed in *Eastern Argus*, July 19, 1815.

76. Hawkins to William Barnett, August 19, 1815, in Grant, ed., *The Letters, Journals and Writings of Benjamin Hawkins*, 748.

77. Hawkins to William Crawford, Creek Agency, February 16, 1816, in Grant, ed., *The Letters, Journals and Writings of Benjamin Hawkins*, 774.

78. "Statement of Ned; a freeman of Colour," in Gaines to Secretary of War, December 1815, NARA, Letters Received, Secretary of War, microfilm 221.

79. Crawford to Jackson, Department of War, March, 15, 1816, in Moser et al., eds., *Papers of Andrew Jackson*, 4:15–16.

80. Gaines to Jackson, Fort Stoddart, Mississippi Territory, May 14, 1816, in Moser et al., eds., *Papers of Andrew Jackson*, 4:31.

81. Clinch to Colonel Butler, Camp Crawford, August 2, 1816, NARA, U.S. Navy, 1775–1910, RG 45, box 181, 5.

82. Commander Zúñiga to C. C. Cienfuegos, Pensacola, August 22, 1816, PC, file 1873, reel 128, PKY.

83. Henry Williams to James Madison, Prospect Bluff, July 28, 1816, James Madison Papers, reel 16, Library of Congress, Washington, D.C., http://lcweb2.loc.gov/ammem/collections/madison_papers/mjmabout2.html; "Extract of a letter from New Orleans, to the Editor of the *Weekly Register*," printed in *Commercial Advertiser*, September 23, 1816. Between 1814 and 1816 the maroon community was Spanish Florida's third largest and best-defended town as well as the largest free black town in North America.

84. Thompson, *Flight to Freedom*, 128. Many slave societies had large overall populations of maroons spread across their territory that often numbered in the many thousands. However, like whites, free blacks, or Indians, these maroons lived in separate communities that had varying relations with each other and the outside world. From this overall perspective, North America had very few maroons. This fact makes the maroon community at Prospect Bluff that much more exceptional. Maroon populations peaked at certain sizes. Communities found it difficult to grow through reproduction or successful flight; and they turned away new members out of respect for treaty stipulations or fear of internal disorder, exhausting limited resources, or attracting attention.

85. Schwartz, *Slaves, Peasants, and Rebels*, 106.

86. Francisco Pérez de la Riva, "Cuban Palenques," in Price, ed., *Maroon Societies*, 54.

87. José France, "Maroons and Slave Rebellions in the Spanish Territories," in Price, ed., *Maroon Societies*, 42.

88. Debbasch, "Le Maniel," in Price, ed., *Maroon Societies*, 144.

89. Thompson, *Flight to Freedom*, 128, and Lokken, "A Maroon Moment," 19.

90. De Groot, "A Comparison between the History of Maroon Communities in Surinam and Jamaica," in Heuman, ed., *Out of This House of Bondage*, 183.

91. Hoogbergen, "The History of the Suriname Maroons," in Brana-Shute, ed., *Resistance and Rebellion in Suriname*, 66.

92. Thompson, *Flight to Freedom*, 128.

93. De Groot, "A Comparison between the History of Maroon Communities in Surinam and Jamaica," in Heuman, ed., *Out of This House of Bondage*, 183; Richard Sheridan, "The Maroons of Jamaica, 1730–1830: Livelihood, Demography and Health," in Heuman, ed., *Out of This House of Bondage*, 158, 161.

Chapter 7. Community and Culture

1. Forbes to Castlereagh, Pensacola, May 20, 1815, enclosed in Croker to Hamilton, April 7, 1818, NAGB, FO 72/219.

2. Edmund Doyle to unknown recipient, 1817, Greenslade Papers, PKY.

3. Governor of East Florida to George Woodbine, St. Augustine, December 31, 1814, EF, reel 84, section 45, PKY.

4. Memorial of John Perpall, New Providence, Bahamas, March 21, 1816, NAGB, CO 23/63, 187.

5. Hawkins to Andrew Jackson, Creek Agency, August 12, 1815, in Grant, ed., *Letters, Journals and Writings of Benjamin Hawkins*, 748.

6. Poitrineau, "Demography and the Political Destiny of Florida," 420–43, and Crider, "The Borderland Floridas," 13–19.

7. Vicente Sebastián Pintado to Jose de Soto, April 29, 1815, Vicente Sebastián Pintado Papers, box 3, folder 1, Library of Congress, microfilm, PKY.

8. Pintado to Soto, May 8, 1815, Pensacola, Vicente Sebastian Pintado Papers, box 3, folder 1, Library of Congress, microfilm, 961, PKY.

9. Pintado to Soto, April 29, 1815, enclosed in Soto to Apodaca, Pensacola, April 29, 1815, PC, file 1796, reel 117, 603, 605, PKY.

10. Ibid., 605.

11. Nicolls's rebuttal point number 19, in Forbes to Castlereagh, Pensacola, May 20, 1815, enclosed in Croker to Hamilton, April 7, 1818, NAGB, FO 72/219.

12. Garçon was described as a "French negro" by Ned. "Statement of Ned; a freeman of Colour," in Gaines to Secretary of War, December 1815, NARA, Letters Received, Secretary of War, microfilm 221.

13. Landers, *Black Society in Spanish Florida*, 178–79. Spain continued officially to import Africans into Florida as late as 1819.

14. Pintado to Soto, April 29, 1815, enclosed in Soto to Apodaca, Pensacola, April 29, 1815, PC, file 1796, reel 117, 602–6, PKY. Cody, "There was no 'Absolom' on the Ball Plantations," and Inscoe, "Carolina Slave Names," both make a persuasive case that African origins could usually be inferred from slave names that were biblical, fantastic, or classical or that included African place names.

15. Woodbine to Cochrane, Prospect Bluff, May 28, 1814, Cochrane Papers, MS 2328, PKY.

16. Gaines to Secretary of War, May 14, 1815, NAGB, FO 5/107.

17. Gaines to A. J. Dallas, Acting Secretary of War, Headquarters, Fort Stoddart, Mississippi Territory, May 22, 1815, in *American State Papers*, book 1, *Foreign Relations*, vol. 4 (1815–1822), 552, Library of Congress, American Memory Project, http://memory.loc .gov/ammem/amlaw/lwsp.html.

18. Ibid.

19. Pintado to Soto, April 29, 1815, Vicente Sebastián Pintado Papers, box 3, folder 1, Library of Congress, microfilm, PKY.

20. "Memorandum of a gentleman of respectability at Bermuda," May 22, 1815, St. George, Bermuda, in *The Papers of Panton, Leslie and Company*, reel 20.

21. *Niles Weekly Register*, September 14, 1816, and Vignoles, *Observations upon the Floridas*, 135.

22. John Innerarity to John Forbes, November 1815, Elizabeth Howard West Papers, PKY.

23. These data appear in the following papers for October and November 1815: *Augusta Chronicle*, *Republican and Savannah Evening Ledger*, *Athens Gazette*, and *Milledgeville Chronicle*. Advertisements for escaped slaves represented a fraction of the actual number of runaways but rather reflected slaves whose owners chose or could afford to advertise, slaves who were not quickly captured, or slaves considered very valuable. Nineteen advertisements in two months were a tremendous number and suggest that something was afoot.

24. Hawkins to William Crawford, Creek Agency, February 16, 1816, in Grant, ed., *Letters, Journals and Writings of Benjamin Hawkins*, 774; *Georgia Journal*, June 26, 1816.

25. "List of Blacks in Confinement at Camp Crawford," August 4, 1816, in James Madison Papers, reel 16, Library of Congress, Washington, D.C.

26. Crawford to Jackson, Department of War, March 15, 1816, NARA, Letters Sent, Secretary of War, microfilm 6, reel 8, 471.

27. Mauricio de Zúñiga to Andrew Jackson, Pensacola, May 26, 1816, in Moser et al., eds., *Papers of Andrew Jackson*, 4:41.

28. Hawkins to Secretary of War, Camp near Chattahoochee, April 2, 1816, NARA, Letters Received, Office of the Secretary of War Relating to Indian Affairs, 1800–1823, microfilm 271, reel 1, 1124.

29. "Return of the Fifth West India Regiment," Fort Augusta, December 1813, NAGB, WO 17/269.

30. Nicolls to Barrow, Shooter's Hill, London, September 11, 1843, in *Correspondences with Foreign Powers on the Slave Trade, 1844*, 13.

31. Pintado to Soto, April 29, 1815, Vicente Sebastián Pintado Papers, box 3, folder 1, Library of Congress, microfilm, PKY.

32. Woodbine to Cochrane, Prospect Bluff, May 25, 1814, Cochrane Papers, MS 2328, PKY.

33. Pintado to Soto, April 29, 1815, Vicente Sebastián Pintado Papers, box 3, folder 1, Library of Congress, microfilm, PKY.

34. Hawkins to Jackson, Creek Agency, August 30, 1814, and Hawkins to the Speakers of the Upper and Lower Creeks, Creek Agency, August 1814, both in Grant, ed., *The Letters, Journals, and Writings of Benjamin Hawkins*, 694; Pintado to Soto, April 29, 1815, Vicente Sebastián Pintado Papers, box 3, folder 1, Library of Congress, microfilm, PKY; Crawford to Jackson, Department of War, March 15, 1816, in Moser et al., eds., *Papers of Andrew Jackson*, 4:16. Crawford was mistaken in his belief that Cherokee slaves were being recruited to join the community at Prospect Bluff.

35. Benjamin Hawkins to Andrew Jackson, Creek Agency, March 24, 1815, in Grant, ed., *The Letters, Journals and Writings of Benjamin Hawkins*, 723–24.

36. Thompson, *Flight to Freedom*, 78–88.

37. Schwartz, *Slaves, Peasants, and Rebels*, 117.

38. Ibid., 125, and Anderson, "The *Quilombo* of Palmares," 119, 545–66. This persistent Angolan dominance and the *quilombo*'s relative homogeneity was captured in its sometimes being called "Little Angola."

39. Anthony McFarlane, "Cimarrones and Palenques: Runaways and Resistance in Colonial Colombia," in Heuman, ed., *Out of This House of Bondage*, 134–35, 148–49.

40. Perez, "The Journey to Freedom."

41. De Groot, "The Maroons of Surinam: Agents of Their Own Emancipation," in Richardson, ed., *Abolition and Its Aftermath*, 71–72.

42. La Rosa Corzo, *Runaway Slave Settlements in Cuba*, 181. Establishing a common language was imperative if a community was to be sustainable, and most communities went to great lengths to make sure this happened as quickly as possible.

43. Debbasch, "Le Maniel," in Price, ed., *Maroon Societies*, 144, and Fick, *The Making of Haiti*, 51.

44. Wilson, "The Performance of Freedom," 55.

45. Kopytoff, "Development of Jamaican Maroon Ethnicity," 38–40.

46. Wilson, "The Performance of Freedom," 55, and Craton, *Testing the Chains*, 77.

These divisions fundamentally shaped the outlook and organization of the two groups, with the Leewards preferring strong and centralized political rule while the Windwards reflected their Indian heritage and were decentralized into confederated villages with much less powerful leaders.

47. Kopytoff, "Development of Jamaican Maroon Ethnicity," 43–44.

48. Campbell, *The Maroons of Jamaica*, 48.

49. Kopytoff, "Development of Jamaican Maroon Ethnicity."

50. Unless otherwise noted, data concerning slaves from Pensacola are listed in Pintado to Soto, April 29, 1815, enclosed in Soto to Apodaca, Pensacola, April 29, 1815, PC, file 1796, reel 117 (whole document, Vicente Sebastián Pintado Papers, box 3, folder 1, Library of Congress, microfilm, PKY); Petition of Slave Owners from Pensacola, May 6, 1815, PC, file 1796, reel 117, 586–624, PKY; "Urcullo's Report," Pensacola, January 23, 1815, Forbes-Innerarity Papers, reel 2, PKY.

51. For example, Tom and his wife Rose; Ben and his wife Mary; Bastaho and his wife Harnetto and their children Ned and Rita; Sally and her children Betty, Adam, and Sally; Elsy and her two children (no names given); and Sally and her children, Carmelete and William, were all members of the community.

52. Hawkins to Jackson, Creek Agency, August 12, 1815, in Grant, ed., *Letters, Journals, and Writings of Benjamin Hawkins*, 748.

53. "File of Witnesses . . . Testimony of Andres Leno," 1815, Cruzat Papers, PKY, and Edmund Doyle to unknown recipient, 1817, Greenslade Papers, PKY.

54. For obvious reasons, former slaves who were stolen by the British or by maroons and/or their Indian allies had the highest probability of having a balanced sex ratio. The evidence makes it clear that when slaves fled to Prospect Bluff under their own power, males heavily predominated. This was a general trend in slave flight, increased by the fact that the British were recruiting slave soldiers in the Southeast.

55. Daniel Patterson to Board of Navy Commissioners, New Orleans, July 6, 1816, NARA, Letters Received, Secretary of the Navy, microfilm 124, reel 76.

56. "List of Blacks in Confinement at Camp Crawford," August 4, 1816, in James Madison Papers, reel 16, Library of Congress, Washington, D.C. Lamb, Elijah, Abraham, and Jo were from Georgia while Butture, Jacob, and William were from Louisiana.

57. Thompson, *Flight to Freedom*, 67–78, and introduction to Price, ed., *Maroon Societies*, 19.

58. Kopytoff, "Development of Jamaican Maroon Ethnicity," 43.

59. Thompson, *Flight to Freedom*, 70, and de Groot, "Maroon Women," 161.

60. R. K. Kent, "Palmares: An African State in Brazil," in Price, ed., *Maroon Societies*, 182.

61. Franklin and Schweninger, *Runaway Slaves*, 63–66.

62. Introduction to Price, ed., *Maroon Societies*, 19–20.

63. Sheridan, "The Maroons of Jamaica, 1730–1830" in Heuman, ed., *Out of This House of Bondage*, 157–58, 163, 168.

64. Kopytoff, "Early Political Development of Jamaican Maroon Societies," 288; Schwartz, *Slaves, Peasants, and Rebels*, 122–28; Hoogbergen, "The History of the Suriname

Maroons," in Sutlive et al., eds., *Resistance and Rebellion in Suriname*, 69; introduction to Price, ed., *Maroon Societies*, 19.

65. Introduction to Price, ed., *Maroon Societies*, 24.

66. Thompson, *Flight to Freedom*, 102–8.

67. Thornton, *Africa and Africans in the Making of the Atlantic World*, 280.

68. Introduction to Price, ed., *Maroon Societies*, 11–12.

69. These were exceptional former slaves whose masters valued them accordingly. The average values for the different sex and age groups were 460 pesos for males between 10 and 20 years of age (this number decreased greatly for a one-armed slave, valued at only 200 pesos); 500 pesos for females between 10 and 20; 605 pesos for males between 20 and 30 years of age and 600 pesos for females of the same age; and 475 pesos for males between the ages of 40 and 50. The most expensive former slave belonged to John Forbes and was valued at the huge sum of 2,000 pesos.

70. Saunt, *A New Order*, 279.

71. Landers, *Black Society*, 162–63.

72. Braund, "The Creek Indians, Blacks, and Slavery," 624.

73. Seminole enslavement of blacks is considered in Wright, *Creeks and Seminoles*, and in Littlefield, *Africans and Seminoles*.

74. Doyle to Forbes, January 14, 1815, MS 2330, Cochrane Papers, 57, PKY.

75. Pintado to Soto, April 29, 1815, Vicente Sebastián Pintado Papers, box 3, folder 1, Library of Congress, microfilm, PKY.

76. Kopytoff, "Development of Jamaican Maroon Ethnicity," 43.

77. De Groot, "Maroon Women," 161.

78. Schwartz, *Slaves, Peasants, and Rebels*, 114, and Mattoso, *To Be a Slave in Brazil*, 141.

79. Introduction to Price, ed., *Maroon Societies*, 19.

80. Ibid.

81. Bilby, "Ethnogenesis in the Guianas and Jamaica: Two Maroon Cases," in Hill, ed., *History, Power, and Identity*, 122.

82. This structure continues today. Hoogbergen, "The History of the Suriname Maroons," in Sutlive et al., eds., *Resistance and Rebellion in Suriname*, 66, and Price, *Saramaka Social Structure*, chapters 4, 7, and 8.

83. Kopytoff, "Early Political Development of Jamaican Maroon Societies," 303–4, and Wilson, "The Performance of Freedom," 10.

84. Kopytoff, "Early Political Development of Jamaican Maroon Societies," 303.

85. Mullin, *Africa in America*, 56–57.

86. Nicolls's rebuttal point number 27, in Forbes to Castlereagh, Pensacola, May 20, 1815, enclosed in John Croker to William Hamilton, April 7, 1818, NAGB, FO 72/219.

87. Joseph Crawford to the Earl of Aberdeen, Havana, June 12, 1843, in *Correspondences with Foreign Powers on the Slave Trade, 1843*, 42–43.

88. Simmons, *Notices of East Florida*, 67.

89. For the much understudied topic of slave masculinity, see Hine and Jenkins, *A Quest for Manhood*, and Wyatt-Brown, "The Mask of Obedience." Happily, slave femininity is the subject of a growing number of studies, including Gaspar and Hine, eds.,

More than Chattel; Morton, ed., *Discovering the Woman in Slavery*; and White, *Ar'n't I a Woman?* On gender across the American population during the Age of Revolution, see Hoffman and Albert, eds., *Women in the Age of the American Revolution*; Kerber, "Beyond Roles, Beyond Spheres"; and Norton, *Founding Mothers and Founding Fathers*.

90. De Groot, "Maroon Women," 162–63.

91. Mullin, *Africa in America*, 53, and Wilson, "The Performance of Freedom," 55.

92. Bastide, "The Other Quilombos," in Price, ed., *Maroon Societies*, 196–97.

93. De Groot, "Maroon Women," 160–73.

94. Wilson, "The Performance of Freedom," 68; Kopytoff, "Early Political Development of Jamaican Maroon Societies," 300; Thompson, *Flight to Freedom*, 76–77; and Campbell, *The Maroons of Jamaica*, 49–53.

95. In *Ar'n't I a Woman*, 142–61, White discusses the assaults on their gender identities that slaves faced.

96. Genovese, *Rebellion*, 53. It is important to note that the vast majority of maroon communities were destroyed or disbanded long before they were able to establish coherent cultural life.

97. Genovese, *Rebellion*, 53

98. Introduction to Price, ed., *Maroon Societies*, 23.

99. Wilson, "The Performance of Freedom," 67.

100. Silvia de Groot, Catherine Christen, and Franklin Knight, "Maroon Communities in the circum-Caribbean," in Knight, ed., *General History of the Caribbean*, vol. 3, 188.

101. Introduction to Price, ed., *Maroon Societies*, 26–30.

102. Hoogbergen, "The History of the Suriname Maroons," in Sutlive et al., eds., *Resistance and Rebellion in Suriname*, 65–68.

103. Schwartz, *Slaves, Peasants, and Rebels*, 123–25, and Anderson, "The *Quilombo* of Palmares," 559. Palmares, even after having become a thoroughly creole community, still loosely modeled itself on the Angolan *ki-lombo*.

104. Schwartz, *Slaves, Peasants, and Rebels*, 124, and Anderson, "The *Quilombo* of Palmares," 556.

105. See Kenneth Bilby, "Maroon Culture as a Distinct Variant of Jamaican Culture," in Agorsah, ed., *Maroon Heritage*, 72–86; Campbell, *The Maroons of Jamaica*; Kopytoff, "Colonial Treaty"; Kopytoff, "Development of Jamaican Maroon Ethnicity"; and Wilson, "The Performance of Freedom."

106. Wilson, "The Performance of Freedom," 68.

107. Ibid.

108. Excellent works on slave religion include Raboteau, *Slave Religion*; Sobel, *Travelin' On*; and Washington, *A Peculiar People*.

109. Simmons, *Notices of East Florida*, 44.

110. J. Carmichael Smyth to Bathurst, Government House, Nassau, August 10, 1831, NAGB, CO 23/78, 58; W. Bethel to Customs Office in London, Customs House, Nassau, August 4, 1831, NAGB, CO 23/78, 58.

111. Baptism Register of Christ Church, 1792–1840, 33–39, Nassau, Bahamas, Bahamas National Archives.

112. Smyth to Bathurst, Government House, Bahamas, February 3, 1832, NAGB, CO 23/78, 58.

113. Hawkins to Crawford, Creek Agency, February 16, 1816, in Grant, ed., *Letters, Journals and Writings of Benjamin Hawkins*, 773; "Abstract of Report of Captain Barnard of the 25th March," contained in Clinch to Secretary of War, Camp Crawford, July 17, 1816, NARA, Letters Received, Secretary of War, microfilm 221, reel 69.

114. Soto to Juan Ruiz de Apodaca, May 13, 1815, PC, file 1796, reel 118, 771, PKY.

115. Smyth to Bathurst, Government House, Bahamas, February 3, 1832, NAGB, CO 23/78, 58.

116. Simmons, *Notices of East Florida*, 76.

Chapter 8. Daily Life

1. Benjamin Hawkins to Peter Early, District of Fort Hawkins, April 21, 1815, in Grant, ed., *Letters, Journals and Writings of Benjamin Hawkins*, 724.

2. Forbes to Castlereagh, Pensacola, May 20, 1815, enclosed in John Croker to William Hamilton, April 7, 1818, NAGB, FO 72/219; James Innerarity to Governor of West Florida, March 1815, Greenslade Papers, PKY.

3. "Extract of a letter from a gentleman in New Orleans to a gentleman in this city," reprinted in *Evening Post*, October 28, 1816.

4. Simmons, *Notices of East Florida*, 45.

5. Edmund Gaines to Secretary of War, Fort Stoddart, May 22, 1815, NAGB, FO 5/107.

6. Pultney Malcolm to Edward Nicolls, *Royal Oak* off Mobile Bay, March 5, 1815, Pultney Malcolm Papers, MAL/106, 169, National Maritime Museum, Greenwich, U.K.

7. Duncan Clinch to Col. Robert Butler, Camp Crawford, August 2, 1816, NARA, List of Vessels of the U.S. Navy, 1797–1816, RG 45, box 181.

8. Henry Williams to James Madison, Prospect Bluff, July 28, 1816, James Madison Papers, reel 16, Library of Congress, Washington, D.C.

9. Poe, "Archaeological Excavations at Fort Gadsden, Florida," 15.

10. Genovese, *Rebellion*, 52–53.

11. Craton, *Testing the Chains*, 64–65.

12. Thompson, *Flight to Freedom*, 257–62. Firearms were highly prized among all groups in colonial societies and people were reluctant to part with them; colonial governments reserved the harshest punishments for those caught trading arms to maroons.

13. Thompson, *Flight to Freedom*, 206.

14. Introduction to Price, ed., *Maroon Societies*, 8.

15. Introduction to Price, ed., *Maroon Societies*, 12. Price describes this dependence as "the Achilles heel of maroon societies throughout the Americas."

16. La Rosa Corzo, *Runaway Slave Settlements in Cuba*, 243–50.

17. Mullin, *Africa in America*, 59.

18. Schwartz, *Slaves, Peasants, and Rebels*, 114.

19. Mattoso, *To Be a Slave in Brazil*, 139.

20. Anderson, "The *Quilombo* of Palmares," 551.

21. Hoogbergen, *The Boni Maroon Wars in Suriname*, 19.

22. Edmund Gaines to Andrew Jackson, Fort Stoddart, Mississippi Territory, May 14, 1816, in Moser et al., eds., *Papers of Andrew Jackson*, 4:31.

23. Pintado to Soto, April 29, 1815, Vicente Sebastián Pintado Papers, box 3, folder 1, Library of Congress, microfilm, PKY.

24. Ibid.

25. Sprague, *The Origins, Progress, and Conclusion of the Florida Wars*, 19.

26. Simmons, *Notices of East Florida*, 44.

27. "A Topographical Memoir of East and West Florida," by H. Young Captain of the Engineers, 1818, NARA, Reports, July 3, 1812–December 4, 1823, RG 45, 320.

28. Wilson, *History of the Rise and Fall of the Slave Power in America*, 129, and Saunt, *A New Order*, 283.

29. Genovese, *Rebellion*, 52, and Introduction to Price, ed., *Maroon Societies*, 10.

30. Thompson, *Flight to Freedom*, 243, and Introduction to Price, ed., *Maroon Societies*, 10–11.

31. Mattoso, *To Be a Slave in Brazil*, 140.

32. Barcia, *Seeds of Insurrection*, 67.

33. Mullin, *Africa in America*, 57.

34. Hoogbergen, *Boni Maroon Wars in Suriname*, 18–19.

35. Report of Captain Amelung to General Jackson, June 4, 1816, New Orleans, *The Papers of Panton, Leslie and Company*, reel 20.

36. Cochrane to Malcolm, February 17, 1815, Mobile Bay, NAGB, ADM 1/508.

37. Vignoles, *Observations upon the Floridas*, 55.

38. Commodore Patterson to Lieut. Crowley, June 19, 1816, New Orleans, reprinted in *Daily National Intelligencer*, April 23, 1819.

39. Campbell, *Historical Sketches of Colonial Florida*, 204. Gaines specifically stated that the fields were devoted to corn.

40. "A Topographical Memoir of East and West Florida," by H. Young Captain of the Engineers, 1818, NARA, Reports, July 3, 1812–December 4, 1823, RG 45, 320. It is not entirely clear whether Young was referring directly to the maroon community at Apalachicola or to a closely related community. However, he provides a careful description of such produce being grown in neatly tended gardens.

41. Marcus Buck to his father, August 4, 1816, Camp Crawford, reprinted in *Army and Navy Chronicle*, February 25, 1836.

42. Giddings, *The Exiles of Florida*, 34.

43. Cochrane to Malcolm, February 24, 1815, Mobile Bay, NAGB, ADM 1/508.

44. George Perryman to Lt. Sands, February 24, 1817, *American State Papers*, book 2, *Indian Affairs*, vol. 2, 155, Library of Congress, American Memory Project, http://memory.loc.gov/ammem/amlaw/lwsp.html.

45. Poe, "Archaeological Excavations," 15.

46. Nicolls to Sir John Barrow, Shooter's Hill, London, September 11, 1843, in *Corre-*

spondences with Foreign Powers on the Slave Trade, 1844, 13; Nicolls's rebuttal point number 26, in Forbes to Castlereagh, Pensacola, May 20, 1815, enclosed in Croker to Hamilton, April 7, 1818, NAGB, FO 72/219.

47. Grant to Bathurst, Nassau, June 30, 1828, NAGB, CO 23/78, 58.

48. Introduction to Price, ed., *Maroon Societies,* 13.

49. "Abstract of Report of Captain Barnard of the 25th March," contained in Clinch to Secretary of War, Camp Crawford, July 17, 1816, NARA, Letters Received, Secretary of War, microfilm 221, reel 69; Caso y Luengo to Soto, September 28, 1815, PC, file 147B, reel 479, PKY; Caso y Luengo to Jose Soto, July 14, 1815, PC, file 1796, reel 118, PKY.

50. See Usner, *Indians, Settlers, and Slaves.* The maroon community's economy did not revolve solely around the exchange of goods. In a sign of its members' economic orientation, many of the community's inhabitants valued hard currency as a payment for service, labor, and goods. Prior to departing, Nicolls faithfully paid his black soldiers in cash for their service. They served for approximately six months, with regular soldiers receiving \$.50 a week and officers, \$4.00 a week, which meant that they received a substantial payment on top of the goods, food, and shelter that the British had given them. It was reported that the survivors at Andros Island "are comfortable in their situation and that many of them have made considerable money." Pintado to Soto, April 29, 1815, Vicente Sebastián Pintado Papers, box 3, folder 1, Library of Congress, microfilm, PKY; Winer Bethel to Customs Office, August 4, 1831, NAGB, CO 23/78, 58.

51. Francisco Caso y Luengo to Don José Mazot, Pensacola, May 14, 1818, reprinted in *National Register, a Weekly Paper,* March 13, 1819.

52. Caso y Luengo to Mazot, Pensacola, May 14, 1818, reprinted in *National Register, a Weekly Paper,* March 13, 1819.

53. James Innerarity to Governor of West Florida, March 1815, Greenslade Papers, PKY.

54. Ferdinand Louis Amelung to Jackson, New Orleans, June 4, 1816, in Moser et al., eds., *Papers of Andrew Jackson,* 4:40.

55. Pintado to Soto, April 29, 1815, Vicente Sebastián Pintado Papers, box 3, folder 1, Library of Congress, microfilm, PKY.

56. Loomis to Benigno Garcia Calderon, Apalachicola Bay, August 5, 1816 reprinted in the *Daily National Intelligencer,* April 23, 1819.

57. James Innerarity to Governor of West Florida, March 1815, Greenslade Papers, PKY.

58. Duncan Clinch to Col. Robert Butler, Camp Crawford, August 2, 1816, NARA, List of Vessels of the U.S. Navy, 1797–1816, RG 45, box 181.

59. Thomas Jesup to Gaines, New Orleans, June 11, 1816, Thomas Sidney Jesup Papers, Special Collections, Duke University.

60. Hawkins to Early, District of Fort Hawkins, April 21, 1815, in Grant, ed., *Letters, Journals and Writings of Benjamin Hawkins,* 724.

61. Deposition of Samuel Jervais, Mobile, May 9, 1815, in *The Papers of Panton, Leslie and Company,* reel 20.

62. Inhabitants of West Florida to the Governor of West Florida, March 1815, Greenslade Papers, PKY.

63. "Memorandum of a gentleman of respectability at Bermuda," St. George, Bermuda, May 22, 1815, in *The Papers of Panton, Leslie and Company*, reel 20.

64. Genovese, *Rebellion*, 53.

65. Introduction to Price, ed., *Maroon Societies*, 13.

66. Schwartz, *Slaves, Peasants, and Rebels*, 112–18.

67. Anderson, "The *Quilombo* of Palmares," 551–52, and Parris, "Alliance and Competition," 193–203.

68. Parris, "Alliance and Competition," 203–10.

69. Thornton, *Africa and Africans*, 291. Over the centuries many maroons from across the hemisphere joined the ranks of pirates.

70. Barcia, *Seeds of Insurrection*, 53–65.

71. Hawkins to John Sevier and William Barnett, Fort Hawkins, August 19, 1815, in Grant, ed., *Letters, Journals, and Writings of Benjamin Hawkins*, 748.

72. *Niles Weekly Register*, September 14, 1816.

73. Prieto to Caso y Luengo, Apalachee, June 17, 1815, Forbes-Innerarity Papers, PKY.

74. John Innerarity to Forbes, Pensacola, May 22, 1815, in *The Papers of Panton, Leslie and Company*, reel 20.

75. Doyle to unknown recipient, 1817, Greenslade Papers, PKY.

76. John Innerarity to Forbes, Pensacola, November 1815, Elizabeth Howard West Collection, PKY.

77. James Innerarity to John Innerarity, Mobile, June 22, 1816, Elizabeth Howard West Collection, PKY.

78. Hambly to John Innerarity, Fort Gaines, May 14, 1816, Elizabeth Howard West Collection, PKY; Hambly to Forbes, Ufalla, May 17, 1816, Elizabeth Howard West Collection, PKY.

79. For example, Hawkins to Speaker of the Lower Creeks, Fort Mitchell, April 30, 1816, NARA, Letters Received, Secretary of War, Registered Series, 1801–1860, microfilm 221, reel 69 (December 1815–December 1816).

80. Thompson, *Flight to Freedom*, 265–72.

81. Genovese, *Rebellion*, 59.

82. Ibid.

83. Ibid., 52.

84. Introduction to Price, ed., *Maroon Societies*, 17.

85. Schwartz, *Slaves, Peasants, and Rebels*, 124, and Wilson, "The Performance of Freedom," 71.

86. De Groot, "A Comparison between the History of Maroon Communities in Surinam and Jamaica," in Heuman, ed., *Out of This House of Bondage*, 178.

87. Campbell, *The Maroons of Jamaica*, 44–52.

88. Wilson, "The Performance of Freedom," 71–72.

89. Ibid., 71.

90. Craton, *Testing the Chains*, 125–39, and Genovese, *Rebellion*, 55.

91. Hoogbergen, "The History of the Suriname Maroons," in Sutlive et al., eds., *Resistance and Rebellion in Suriname*, 84.

92. De Groot, "A Comparison between the History of Maroon Communities in Surinam and Jamaica," in Heuman, ed., *Out of This House of Bondage*, 178.

93. John Innerarity to Forbes, May 22, 1815, in *The Papers of Panton, Leslie and Company*, reel 20.

94. Gaines to Secretary of War, Fort Stoddart, May 22, 1815, U.S. Territorial Papers (Florida), PKY.

95. Vignoles, *Observations upon the Floridas*, 135; Pintado to Soto, April 29, 1815, Vicente Sebastián Pintado Papers, box 3, folder 1, Library of Congress, microfilm, PKY.

96. Amelung to Jackson, New Orleans, June 4, 1816, in Moser et al, eds., *Papers of Andrew Jackson*, 4:40.

97. Thornton, *Africa and Africans*, 282–92.

98. Ibid., 285.

99. Bateman, "African and Indians," and Craton, *Testing the Chains*, 62.

100. Anderson, "The *Quilombo* of Palmares," 559.

101. Thompson, *Flight to Freedom*, 257.

102. Hoogbergen, *The Boni Maroon Wars in Suriname*, 22.

103. Thompson, *Flight to Freedom*, 96–97.

104. Introduction to Price, ed., *Maroon Societies*, 9, and Schwartz, *Slaves, Peasants, and Rebels*, 116, 123.

105. Hawkins to John Sevier and William Blount, Fort Hawkins, August 19, 1815, in Grant, ed., *The Papers, Journals and Writings of Benjamin Hawkins*, 748.

106. Jackson to Mauricio de Zúñiga, Washington, Mississippi Territory, April 23, 1816, in *The Papers of Panton, Leslie, and Company*, reel 20.

107. Duncan Clinch to Gaines, May 1, 1816, in *The Papers of Panton, Leslie and Company*, reel 20.

108. Marcus Buck to His Father, Camp Crawford, August 4, 1816, reprinted in *Army and Navy Chronicle*, February 25, 1836. "Fowl Town" and "Mickasooka" were largely black communities.

109. Clinch to Butler, Camp Crawford, August 2, 1816, reprinted in *Army and Navy Chronicle*, February 25, 1836.

110. "Statement of Ned; a freeman of Colour," in Gaines to Secretary of War, December 1815, NARA, Letters Received, Secretary of War, microfilm 221. A Choctaw chief was described as one of the leaders of the community at the time of its destruction. This overstatement was a reflection of the fact that the renegade Choctaws were the only Native Americans who were at Prospect Bluff when it was destroyed. The community's leaders certainly would have consulted with their Native American allies and residents, but the leadership of the community was entirely black.

111. Covington, "Negro Fort," 82.

112. Hawkins to the Speaker of the Lower Creeks, Fort Mitchell, April 30, 1816, NARA, Letters Received, Secretary of War, Registered Series, 1801–1860, microfilm 221, reel 69 (December 1815–December 1816).

113. Juan José de Estrada to Juin Ruiz de Apodaca, July 10, 1815, EF, reel 13, section 2, PKY.

114. Extract of a Letter from George Perryman to Lt. Sands, February 24, 1817, in *American State Papers:* book 2, *Indian Affairs*, vol. 2, 155, Library of Congress, American Memory Project, http://memory.loc.gov/ammem/amlaw/lwsp.html.

115. Simmons, *Notices of East Florida*, 44.

116. Hambly to John Innerarity, May 14,1816, Fort Gaines, *The Papers of Panton, Leslie and Company*, reel 20.

117. "Extract of a letter from a gentleman in New Orleans to a gentleman in this city," reprinted in *Evening Post*, October 28, 1816.

118. Henry Williams to James Madison, Prospect Bluff, July 28, 1816, James Madison Papers, reel 16, Library of Congress, Washington, D.C.

119. James Innerarity to the Governor of West Florida, March 1815, Greenslade Papers, PKY.

120. Amelung to Jackson, New Orleans, June 4, 1816, in Moser et al., eds., *Papers of Andrew Jackson*, 4:40.

121. Simmons, *Notices of East Florida*, 75, and James Innerarity to John Innerarity, Mandeville, October 4, 1815, Elizabeth Howard West Collection, PKY.

122. Owsley and Smith, *Filibusters*, 107.

Chapter 9. Political and Military Organization

1. "Extract of a letter from a gentleman in New Orleans to a gentleman in this city," reprinted in *Evening Post*, October 28, 1816.

2. Introduction to Price, ed., *Maroon Societies*, 16.

3. Ibid., 18.

4. Thompson, *Flight to Freedom*, 212.

5. Introduction to Price, ed., *Maroon Societies*, 20.

6. Ibid., 22.

7. Thompson, *Flight to Freedom*, 218–23.

8. Barcia, *Seeds of Insurrection*, 65.

9. De La Riva, "Cuban Palenques," in Price, ed., *Maroon Societies*, 51–52.

10. Fick, *The Making of Haiti*, 59–75, and Dubois, *Avengers of the New World*, 51–59.

11. Debbasch, "Le Maniel," in Price, ed., *Maroon Societies*, 142–48.

12. Introduction to Price, ed., *Maroon Societies*, 20.

13. Schwartz, *Slaves, Peasants, and Rebels*, 122–28, and Anderson, "The *Quilombo* of Palmares," 562, 565–66.

14. Thompson, *Flight to Freedom*, 214–16.

15. Introduction to Price, ed., *Maroon Societies*, 21.

16. Hoogbergen, "The History of the Suriname Maroons," in Sutlive et al., eds., *Resistance and Rebellion in Suriname*, 73. These six major tribes continue to exist today.

17. Hoogbergen, "The History of the Suriname Maroons," in Sutlive et al., eds., *Resistance and Rebellion in Suriname*, 66.

18. Kenneth Bilby, "Ethnogenesis in the Guianas and Jamaica," in Hill, ed., *History, Power, and Identity*, 120–23; Craton, *Testing the Chains*, 67–80; and Campbell, *The Maroons of Jamaica*, chapter 2.

19. Wilson, "The Performance of Freedom," 55.

20. Ibid.

21. Craton, *Testing the Chains*, 81.

22. Kopytoff, "Early Political Development of Jamaican Maroon Societies," 296.

23. Ibid., 307.

24. Kopytoff, "Colonial Treaty," 49.

25. Ibid., 49–50.

26. Even in the case of Jamaica, where the Leewards and Windwards rigidly adhered to their treaties, the island's maroons were distinctly second-class subjects who, while enjoying more rights than slaves, were most certainly not full subjects. Furthermore they were disliked by the slave masses and looked down upon by the whites. Perhaps the most interesting similarity between the community at Prospect Bluff and the maroons of Jamaica was each group's fanatical attachment to the deals that they had entered into with the British and the extent to which these deals formed the core of their identity. In Jamaica the communities had been subjugated by these deals, but at Prospect Bluff the former slaves had been empowered by them.

27. Colonel Nicolls to Sir John Barrow, Shooter's Hill, London, September 11, 1843, in *Correspondences with Foreign Powers on the Slave Trade, 1844*, 13. Nicolls stated that Ashley's actions occurred for four days after the fort had exploded, which was impossible. He was clearly mistaken and was referring to four days *during* the American siege.

28. Andrew Jackson to Edmund Gaines, New Orleans, April 8, 1816, in Bassett, ed., in *Correspondence of Andrew Jackson*, vol. 2, 237.

29. Duncan Clinch to Col. Robert Butler, Camp Crawford, August 2, 1816, NARA, List of Vessels of the U.S. Navy, 1797–1816, RG 45, box 181.

30. Bowlegs to Governor of Florida, Suwannee, September 10, 1816, EF, reel 43, section 29, doc. 1816-2, PKY.

31. Daniel Patterson to Lieut. Crowley, June 19, 1816, New Orleans, reprinted in *Daily National Intelligencer*, April 23, 1819.

32. Reprinted in the *New York Columbian*, November 19, 1819.

33. "Extract of a Letter from an Officer Who Was Present at the Destruction of the Negro Fort in East Florida," printed in *Daily National Intelligencer*, September 2, 1816.

34. Mauricio de Zúñiga to Jackson, Pensacola, May 26, 1816, in Moser et al., eds., *Papers of Andrew Jackson*, 4:41.

35. Testimony of D. B. Mitchell, November 17, 1818, *American State Papers*, book 5, *Military Affairs*, vol. 1, 748, Library of Congress, American Memory Project, http://memory.loc.gov/ammem/amlaw/lwsp.html; Overton, *A Vindication of the Measures of the President*, 56; *Georgia Journal* article, reprinted in *City Gazette and Daily Advertiser*, August 23, 1816.

36. Jose de Soto to Juan Ruiz de Apodaca, May 13, 1815, PC, file 1796, reel 118, 771, PKY; "Statement of Ned; a Freeman of Colour," in Gaines to Secretary of War, December 1815,

NARA, Letters Received, Secretary of War, microfilm 221; Prieto to Caso y Luengo, PC, file 1796, reel 118, 964, PKY; Hawkins to Jackson, Creek Agency, August 12, 1815, in Grant, ed., *Letters, Journals, and Writings of Benjamin Hawkins*, 748. In *Historical Sketches of Colonial Florida* (202), Campbell records that a Choctaw had joined the three former slaves as one of the community's leaders by the summer of 1816. While the three men would have consulted with their Indian allies, it seems unlikely that a Choctaw had risen to such a position. Likewise, Garçon at one point told a Spanish official that "an Indian" had assumed command of the fort. This simply was not true, as evidenced by Garçon's role in the defense of the fort in August 1816 (cited in Saunt, *A New Order*, 284). Of the three leaders, Garçon was the only one who led the community all the way until its destruction in July 1816. It appears that the other two leaders had aided in the evacuation of much of the community.

37. William Coker and Susan Parker, "The Second Spanish Period in the Two Floridas," in Gannon, ed., *New History of Florida*, 150–66; Coker and Ingles, *Spanish Censuses of Pensacola*; Jack Holmes, "West Florida, 1779–1821," in George, ed., *Guide to the History of Florida*, 3–76; McAlister, "Pensacola during the Second Spanish Period"; McGovern, ed., *Colonial Pensacola*.

38. Soto to Juan Ruiz de Apodaca, May 13, 1815, PC, file 1796, reel 118, 771, PKY.

39. "Statement of Ned; a Freeman of Colour," in Gaines to Secretary of War, December 1815, NARA, Letters Received, Secretary of War, microfilm 221.

40. Soto to Apodaca, May 13, 1815, PC, file 1796, reel 118, 771, PKY.

41. Ibid.

42. Harry, who was valued at 2,000 pesos, was the most valuable slave in Pensacola and belonged to John Forbes and Company. Soto to Apodaca, May 13, 1815, PC, file 1796, reel 118, 766, PKY.

43. Cody, "There was no 'Absolom' on the Ball Plantations," and Inscoe, "Carolina Slave Names."

44. "Indictment of William Augustus Vesey for Perjury," 1816, Cruzat Papers, PKY.

45. A testament to their leadership abilities came in the career of Abraham, who as a young man spent two years living in the community. Years later Abraham became the most successful black leader in the Second Seminole War. Porter, *The Negro on the Frontier*, 295–338.

46. George Perryman to Lt. Sands, February 24, 1817, *American State Papers*, book 2, *Indian Affairs*, vol. 2, 155, Library of Congress, American Memory Project, http://memory.loc.gov/ammem/amlaw/lwsp.html; "A Topographical Memoir of East and West Florida," by H. Young Captain of the Engineers, 1818, NARA, Reports, July 3, 1812–December 4, 1823, RG 45, 320.

47. Gaines to Jackson, Fort Stoddart, Mississippi Territory, May 14, 1816, in Moser et al., eds., *Papers of Andrew Jackson*, 4:31; Felipe Prieto to Caso y Luengo, Apalachee, June 17, 1815, Forbes-Innerarity Papers, PKY. Interestingly, Hilario was Don José Noriega's only slave, listed as a "well-bred house slave." Nicolls's rebuttal point number 26, Forbes to Castlereagh, Pensacola, May 20, 1815, enclosed in Croker to Hamilton, April 7, 1818, NAGB, FO 72/219.

48. Simmons, *Notices of East Florida*, 67.

49. Pintado to Spencer, March 30, 1815, PC, reel 4, frame 254, PKY.

50. Alexander Arbuthnot to Nicolls, Nassau, August 26, 1817, in *Trial of Arbuthnot and Ambrister*, reprinted in *National Standard*, January 6, 1819.

51. Owsley and Smith, *Filibusters*, 109.

52. Patterson to Secretary of Navy, New Orleans, August 15, 1816, printed in *Daily National Intelligencer*, April 23, 1819; Hawkins to Jackson, Creek Agency, August 12, 1815, in Grant, ed., *Letters, Journals, and Writings of Benjamin Hawkins*, 748.

53. Hawkins to William Crawford, Creek Agency, February 16, 1816, in Grant, ed., *Letters, Journals, and Writings of Benjamin Hawkins*, 773.

54. James Innerarity to Gov. of West Florida, March 1815, Greenslade Papers, PKY.

55. "Statement of Ned; a Freeman of Colour," in Gaines to Secretary of War, December 1815, NARA, Letters Received, Secretary of War, microfilm 221.

56. Mauricio de Zúñiga to Jackson, May 26, 1816, in Moser et al., eds., *Papers of Andrew Jackson*, 4:41.

57. George Perryman to Lt. Sands, February 24, 1817, *American State Papers*, book 2, *Indian Affairs*, vol. 2, 154, Library of Congress, American Memory Project, http://memory.loc.gov/ammem/amlaw/lwsp.html.

58. "Extract of a letter from New Orleans, to the Editor of the *Weekly Register*," printed in *Commercial Advertiser*, September 23, 1816.

Chapter 10. Destruction

1. Andrew Jackson to Mauricio de Zúñiga, Washington, Mississippi Territory, April 23, 1816, in Moser et al., eds., *Papers of Andrew Jackson*, 4:239–40.

2. Jackson to Edmund Gaines, New Orleans, April 8, 1816, in Bassett, ed., *Correspondence of Andrew Jackson*, 237.

3. David Mitchell to Maj. Andrew Maybank, Milledgeville, Ga., May 20, 1816, Governor's Letter Books, November 1809–October 1829," reel 1196, GDAH.

4. "Memorandum of a gentleman of respectability at Bermuda," May 22, 1815, St. George, Bermuda, in *The Papers of Panton, Leslie and Company*, reel 20.

5. "Letter from a gentleman on St. Simon's Island, to another in this city [Savannah] dated 18th June, 1815," printed in *Eastern Argus*, July 19, 1815.

6. *Savannah Journal*, June 26, 1816.

7. *Niles Weekly Register*, September 14, 1816.

8. Notable treatments of the community's destruction include Covington, "Negro Fort," and Frank Owsley and Gene Smith, "A Leftover of War: Negro Fort," in Owsley and Smith, *Filibusters*, 107–17.

9. Owsley and Smith, *Filibusters*, 107.

10. Saunt, *Black, White, and Indian*, chapters 1 and 2.

11. Silver, *Edmund Pendleton Gaines*.

12. Covington, "Negro Fort," 81.

13. Ibid.

14. Ibid.

15. Extract from "The Humble Representation of the Chiefs of the Creek Nation to his Excellency Governor Cameron," 1818, in *Trials of Arbuthnot and Ambrister*, 12

16. Saunt, *A New Order*, 286.

17. Gaines to Jackson, Fort Stoddart, Mississippi Territory, May 14, 1816, in Moser et al., eds., *Papers of Andrew Jackson*, 4:31.

18. Ibid.

19. Saunt, *A New Order*, 287. The agreement to aid in the recovery of the blacks at Prospect Bluff was made in the face of overwhelming Creek force and was probably insincere.

20. Duncan Clinch to Secretary of War, Fort Gaines, May 9, 1816, NARA, Letters Received, Secretary of War, microfilm 221.

21. Gaines to Mitchell, Montgomery, May 24, 1816, NARA, Letters Received, Secretary of War, microfilm 221.

22. Ibid.

23. Owsley and Smith, *Filibusters*, 104.

24. Ibid., 108.

25. Ibid.

26. William Crawford to Jackson, Department of War, March 15, 1816, NARA, Letters Sent, Secretary of War, microfilm 6, reel 8, 471.

27. Jackson to Zúñiga, , Washington, Mississippi Territory, April 23, 1816, in Bassett, ed., *Correspondences of Andrew Jackson*, 239.

28. Mauricio de Zúñiga to Jackson, Pensacola, May 26 1816, in Moser et al., eds., *Papers of Andrew Jackson*, 4:41.

29. Calderon to Zúñiga, Pensacola, August 8, 1816, PC file 1583, reel 15, doc. 265-6, PKY.

30. James Innerarity to John Innerarity, Mobile, June 22, 1816, Elizabeth Howard West Collection, PKY.

31. Gaines to Jackson, Fort Stoddart, Mississippi Territory, May 14, 1816, in Moser et al., eds., *Papers of Andrew Jackson*, 4:31.

32. Ibid.

33. Gaines to Patterson, Fort Montgomery, May 22, 1816, NARA, Miscellaneous Letters Received, Secretary of Navy, 1801–1884, microfilm 124, reel 76 (May 6–September 23, 1816), 21.

34. Patrick, *Aristocrat in Uniform*.

35. William Hambly to John Forbes, Ufella, May 17, 1816, Elizabeth Howard West Collection, PKY.

36. Covington, "Negro Fort," 83.

37. Gaines to Patterson, Fort Montgomery, May 22, 1816, NARA, Miscellaneous Letters Received, Secretary of Navy, 1801–1884, microfilm 124, reel 76 (May 6–September 23, 1816), 21.

38. Hambly to John Innerarity, Fort Gaines, May 14, 1816, Elizabeth Howard West Collection, PKY.

39. Nicolls to Sir John Barrow, Shooter's Hill, London, September 11, 1843, in *Correspondences with Foreign Powers on the Slave Trade, 1844*, 13.

40. Loomis to Patterson, Bay St. Louis, August 15 1816, reprinted in *Daily National Intelligencer*, April 23, 1819.

41. "Extract of a letter from a gentleman in New Orleans to a gentleman in this city," reprinted in *Evening Post*, October 28, 1816.

42. Commodore Patterson to the Secretary of the Navy, New Orleans, August 15, 1816, reprinted in *Daily National Intelligencer*, April 23, 1819.

43. *National Intelligencer*, December 5, 1816, reprinted in the *Times*, December 31, 1816.

44. Saunt, *A New Order*, 287.

45. Clinch to Colonel R. Butler, Camp Crawford, August 2, 1816, NARA, U.S. Navy, 1775–1910, RG 45, box 181, 45.

46. Ibid.

47. Ibid., 3.

48. *Army and Navy Chronicle*, February 25, 1836.

49. Clinch to Butler, Camp Crawford, August 2, 1816, NARA, U.S. Navy, 1775–1910, RG 45, box 181, 3.

50. "Extract of a letter from New Orleans, to the Editor of the *Weekly Register*," printed in *Commercial Advertiser*, September 23, 1816.

51. Marcus Buck to his father, August 4, 1816, Camp Crawford, reprinted in *Army and Navy Chronicle*, February 25, 1836.

52. Clinch to Butler, Camp Crawford, August 2, 1816, NARA, U.S. Navy, 1775–1910, RG 45, box 181, 5. Clinch's sympathy ran only so deep.

53. Marcus Buck to his father, Camp Crawford, August 4, 1816, reprinted in *Army and Navy Chronicle*, February 25, 1836.

54. For example, Covington, "Negro Fort," and Porter, *The Negro on the Frontier*.

55. ACW Hanning to Clinch, Fort Gadsden, June 11, 1819, NARA, Joint Military-Naval Engagements, 1759–1898, Official Naval Records and Library, U.S. Navy, 1775–1910, RG 45, box 181.

56. Clinch to John Calhoun, St. Mary's, October 29, 1819, NARA, Joint Military-Naval Engagements, 1759–1898, Official Naval Records and Library, U.S. Navy, 1775–1910, RG 45, box 181.

57. Owsley and Smith, *Filibusters*, 111.

58. Riordan, "Seminole Genesis."

59. Clinch to Butler, Camp Crawford, August 2, 1816, NARA, U.S. Navy, 1775–1910, RG 45, box 181, 5.

60. Nicolls to Barrow, Shooter's Hill, London, September 11, 1843, in *Correspondences with Foreign Powers on the Slave Trade, 1844*, 13.

61. "Extract of a Letter from an Officer Who Was Present at the Destruction of the Negro Fort in East Florida," *Daily National Intelligencer*, September 2, 1816.

62. Clinch to Butler, Camp Crawford, August 2, 1816, NARA, U.S. Navy, 1775–1910, RG 45, box 181, 5.

63. Nicolls to Barrow, Shooter's Hill, London, September 11, 1843, in *Correspondences with Foreign Powers on the Slave Trade, 1844*, 13.

64. Robert Lyman to Clinch, Nashville Headquarters, Division of the South, May 27, 1819, NARA, Joint Military-Naval Engagements, 1759–1898, Official Naval Records and Library, U.S. Navy, 1775–1910, RG 45, box 181.

65. *Niles Weekly Register*, November 20, 1819.

66. Reprinted in *City Gazetteer and Daily Advertiser*, August 23, 1816.

67. Secretary of War to Jackson, September 27, 1816, NARA, Records of the Office of the Secretary of War, Confidential and Unofficial Letters Sent, microfilm 7, reel 1 (November 26, 1814–August 31, 1835), 86.68. Patterson to Crowley, New Orleans, June 19 1816, reprinted in *Daily National Intelligencer*, April 23, 1819.

69. James Innerarity to Forbes, Mobile, August 5, 1816, Elizabeth Howard West Collection, PKY.

70. Rothman, *Slave Country*, 167–68.

Chapter 11. The Seminole War

1. Committee on Military Affairs to Congress, January 12, 1818, reprinted in the *Niles Weekly Register*, January 16, 1819.

2. Ibid.

3. Edward Nicolls to Sir John Barrow, Shooter's Hill, London, September 11, 1843, in *Correspondences with Foreign Powers on the Slave Trade, 1844*, 13.

4. Petition of Cappachimico, McQueen, Emathlela Hadjo, Taitachy, Holochapco, Bowlick, and Micocpah, November 8, 1816, in Arbuthnot to Bagot, Nassau, January 8, 1817, NAGB, CO 23/66, 111. As late as spring 1821 it was reported that ten Seminoles who "had served with Lt. Nicolls in Florida during the American War" had traveled to the Bahamas to request aid from their British "allies." Grant to Bathurst, Bahamas, April 19, 1821, NAGB, CO 23/70, 5.

5. *Niles Weekly Register*, March 21, 1818.

6. *Army and Navy Chronicle*, February 25, 1836.

7. The conflict is referred to as the Seminole War (rather than First Seminole War) because contemporaries called it this. For discussion of the Seminole War, see Covington, *Seminoles of Florida*; Hiedler and Hiedler, *Old Hickory's War*; Knetsch, *Florida's Seminole Wars*; Missall and Missall, *The Seminole Wars*; Owsley and Smith, *Filibusters*; Remini, *Andrew Jackson and His Indian Wars*; and Wright, *Creeks and Seminoles*.

8. Brown, "Tales of Angola," 7.

9. Ibid. Florida continued to have a high percentage of African slaves because of the persistence of the slave trade. As earlier noted, within this large African population, a sizable number of slaves were Angolan.

10. Ibid., 9.

11. Porter, *Negro on the Frontier*, 221.

12. Francisco Caso y Luengo to Andrew Jackson, Pensacola, May 14, 1818, reprinted in the *National Register*, March 13, 1819.

13. Bowlegs to Governor of Florida, Suwanee, September 10, 1816, EF, reel 43, section 29, PKY.

14. Petition of the Lower Creek Nation to Governor Cameron, 1818, in *Trials of Arbuthnot and Ambrister*, 42.

15. Porter, *Black Seminoles*, 18, and Mulroy, *Freedom on the Border*, 15.

16. Covington, *Seminoles of Florida*, 45.

17. Landers, *Atlantic Creoles in the Age of Revolutions*, 183–85.

18. Testimony of William Hambly, in *Trials of Arbuthnot and Ambrister*, 48.

19. George Perryman to Lt. Sands, February 24, 1817, *American State Papers*, book 2, *Indian Affairs*, vol. 2, 155, Library of Congress, American Memory Project, http://memory.loc.gov/ammem/amlaw/lwsp.html.

20. Committee on Military Affairs to Congress, January 12, 1818, reprinted in the *Niles Weekly Register*, January 16, 1819.

21. "Abstract of Report of Captain Barnard of the 25th March," contained in Clinch to Secretary of War, Camp Crawford, July 17, 1816, NARA, Letters, Secretary of War, microfilm 221, reel 69.

22. Perryman to Sands, February 24, 1817, *American State Papers*, book 2, *Indian Affairs*, vol. 2, 155, Library of Congress, American Memory Project, http://memory.loc.gov/ammem/amlaw/lwsp.html.

23. Testimony of William Hambly, in *Trials of Arbuthnot and Ambrister*, 48.

24. Edmund Doyle to John Innerarity, Prospect Bluff, June 3, 1817, Greenslade Papers, PKY.

25. Cameron to Bathurst, Nassau, November 12, 1817, NAGB, CO 23/65.

26. Doyle to John Innerarity, Prospect Bluff, January 28, 1817, Greenslade Papers, PKY. The Spanish first became aware of Woodbine's return to West Florida in early December 1816. Commander Masot to C. G. Cienfeugos, Pensacola, December, 19, 1816, PC, file 1873, reel 129, 706, PKY.

27. *New York Daily Advertiser*, March 23, 1818.

28. Mitchell to Gaines, Milledgeville, Ga., February 5, 1817, Lockey Collection, PKY.

29. *Niles Weekly Register*, May 10, 1817.

30. William Trimble to Calhoun, New Orleans, February 8, 1818, in Hemphill, ed., *The Papers of John C. Calhoun*, vol. 2, 127.

31. Owsley and Smith, *Filibusters*, 147.

32. Brown, "Tales of Angola," 8.

33. *Niles Weekly Register*, June 6, 1818, and the *Louisiana Gazette* May 12, 1818, reprinted in the *Niles Weekly Register*, June 6, 1818.

34. Testimony of Jacob Harrison, and Testimony of John Lewis Phenix, both in *Trials of Arbuthnot and Ambrister*, 75 and 63 respectively.

35. Robert Ambrister to Edward Nicolls, Suwannee near Apalachicola, 1818, *Trials of Arbuthnot and Ambrister*, 70.

36. Adams to the Minister Plenipotentiary, Washington, D.C., November 28, 1818, reprinted in the *Philadelphia Register and National Recorder*, January 30, 1819.

37. Ibid.

38. Owsley and Smith, *Filibusters*, 145.

39. Bagot to Castlereagh, Washington, D.C., February 5, 1817, NAGB, CO 23/66, 110.

40. Richard Rush to Castlereagh, January 12, 1819, NAGB, FO 5/146.

41. Ibid.

42. Owsley and Smith, *Filibusters*, 149.

43. Covington, *Seminoles of Florida*, 41.

44. Humble Representation of the Chiefs of the Creek Nation to His Excellency Governor Cameron (no date), in *Narrative of a Voyage to the Spanish Main*, 219, cited in Covington, *Seminoles of Florida*, 41.

45. Gaines to David Mitchell, Fort Scott, November 21, 1817, reprinted in the *Times*, January 15, 1818.

46. Ibid.

47. Owsley and Smith, *Filibusters*, 151.

48. April 12 entry, Edward Brett Randolph Diary, SHC, UNC.

49. Porter, *Black Seminoles*, 20.

50. Edward Brett Randolph Diary, SHC, UNC. Though there is no date on the entry, it must be from February 1818.

51. Covington, *Seminoles of Florida*, 43.

52. Owsley and Smith, *Filibusters*, 154.

53. Ibid., 22.

54. Porter, *Black Seminoles*, 21.

55. Testimony of Arbuthnot, in *Trials of Arbuthnot and Ambrister*, 58.

56. Testimony of John Prince, Saint Augustine, January 10, 1828, 27th Congress, 2nd session, Rep. no. 723, May 20, 1842.

57. Gaines to the Seminole Chief, August 1818, in *Narrative of a Voyage to the Spanish Main*, 221–22, quoted in Landers, *Black Society*, 235.

58. John Quincy Adams to the American Minister in Madrid, Washington, D.C., November 28, 1818, reprinted in the *Albion, A Journal of News, Politics and Literature*, January 20, 1838.

59. April 15 entry, Edward Brett Randolph Diary, SHC, UNC.

60. *Niles Weekly Register*, November 15, 1817.

61. Covington, *Seminoles of Florida*, 46.

62. Doyle to John Innerarity, Spanish Bluff, June 17, 1817, Greenslade Papers, PKY.

63. April 18 entry, Edward Brett Randolph Diary, SNC, UNC.

64. See Rosen, "Wartime Prisoners and the Rule of Law."

65. Owsley and Smith, *Filibusters*, 161.

66. Don José Mazot to Jackson, Pensacola, May 23, 1818, reprinted in the *National Register*, March 13, 1819.

67. Jackson to Mazot, Headquarters, Division of the South, May 23, 1818, reprinted in the *National Register*, March 13, 1819.

68. James Monroe to Congress, March 25, 1818, book 1, *Foreign Relations*, vol. 4 (1815–1822), 680–81, Library of Congress, American Memory Project, http://memory.loc.gov/ammem/amlaw/lwsp.html.

69. Brown, "Tales of Angola," 10.

70. Ibid.

71. Doyle to John Innerarity, June 17, 1817, Greenslade Papers, PKY.

72. Brown, "Tales of Angola," 10.

73. Adams to the Minister Plenipotentiary, Washington, D.C., November 28, 1818 reprinted in the *Philadelphia Register and National Recorder*, January 30, 1819.

74. *Niles Weekly Register*, June 6, 1818.

75. Mitchell Testimony, November 17, 1818, *American State Papers*, book 5, *Military Affairs*, vol. 1, 748, Library of Congress, American Memory Project, http://memory.loc.gov/ammem/amlaw/lwsp.html.

76. Overton, *A Vindication of the Measures of the President*, 20.

77. Committee on Military Affairs to Congress, January 12, 1818, reprinted in the *Niles Weekly Register*, January 16, 1819.

78. *Georgia Journal*, 1816.

79. *Daily National Intelligencer*, February 12, 1816.

80. Ibid., November 11, 1817.

81. *Floridian*, May 23, 1823.

82. Ibid., July 19, 1823.

83. Ibid., August 2, 1823.

84. Lewis Edwards to John Calhoun, Charleston, April 3, 1819, in Hemphill, ed., *The Papers of John C. Calhoun*, vol. 4, 8.

85. Jackson to Monroe, The Hermitage, December 7, 1818, in Hemphill, ed., *The Papers of John C. Calhoun*, vol. 3, 360.

86. Calhoun to Jackson, War Department, September 8, 1818, in Hemphill, ed., *The Papers of John C. Calhoun*, vol. 3, 110.

Epilogue

1. Brown, "Tales of Angola," 11.

2. "Advice to the Southern Planters" by "An Eye Witness," *City Gazette and Daily Advertiser*, November 24, 1812.

3. Brown, "Tales of Angola," 12.

4. Will of William Colby, August 31, 1871, Supreme Court of Wills, Nassau, Bahamas, Bahamas National Archives.

5. See Sundiata, *From Slaving to Neoslavery*.

6. "Extract of a Letter from the Agent to Lloyd's at Fernando Po," *Times*, May 2, 1834, 5.

7. See *The Cambridge History of Africa*, chapter 5. Sierra Leone was a rapidly growing colony populated by Caribbean maroons, other refugees from the New World, people intercepted in the slave trade, and indigenous inhabitants.

8. For example in 1830, while appearing before the Parliamentary Select Committee on the state of settlements of Sierra Leone and Fernando Po, Nicolls testified in expert detail—not only about the general state of settlements of freed blacks in Sierra Leone and Fernando Po but also about the climate, disease, environment, soil, suitability of various

crops, future prospects for establishing viable settlements with sustainable economies, differences between local Africans and blacks from the New World, African culture, society, and politics—and he did this by being able to speak "a good deal of that language myself." Edward Nicolls, June 29, 1830, in *Select Committee on State of Settlements of Sierra Leone and Fernando Po*, 44–52.

9. Nicolls, June 29, 1830, in *Select Committee on State of Settlements of Sierra Leone and Fernando Po*, 48.

10. Ibid., 51.

11. *Gentleman's Magazine and Historical Review*, January 1865, 646.

12. *Report of the Committee of the African Civilization Society*, 5.

13. For example, "The Anti-Slavery Society," *Times*, May 14, 1842.

14. "Anti-Slavery, or the World's Convention in London," *Niles's National Register*, August 5, 1843, 363. Other leading anti-slavery proponents with whom Nicolls worked closely included Sir Robert Inglis, Thomas Acland, and MacGregor Laird, who became his son-in-law. *Gentleman's Magazine and Historical Review*, January 1865, 646.

15. A good example appears in the *Times*, February 16, 1842. Interestingly the *African Repository and Colonial Journal* extensively quoted letters between Nicolls and various government officials in its review of Thomas Buxton's *The African Slave Trade and Its Remedy*; see *African Repository and Colonial Journal*, January 1, 1840.

16. *Wesleyan Methodist Magazine* 20, June 1841, 505.

17. *United Service Magazine and Naval and Military Journal*, part 1, 1865, 432.

18. *Gentleman's Magazine and Historical Review*, January 1865, 645.

Bibliography

Abridgment of the Debates of Congress from 1789 to 1856. New York: D. Appleton, 1858.

Adams, Charles Francis, ed. *Memoirs of John Quincy Adams Comprising Portions of His Diary from 1795 to 1848*. Philadelphia: J. B. Lippincot and Company, 1875.

Adelman, Jeremy, and Stephen Aron. "From Borderlands to Borders: Empires, Nation-States, and the Peoples in Between in North American History." *American Historical Review* 104 (June 1999): 814–41.

Agorsah, E. Kofi, ed. *Maroon Heritage: Archaeological, Ethnographic, and Historical Perspectives*. Kingston, Jamaica: Canoe Press, 1994.

Altoff, Gerald. *Amongst My Best Men: African-Americans and the War of 1812*. Put-in-Bay, Ohio: Perry Group, 1996.

Anderson, Robert Nelson. "The *Quilombo* of Palmares: A New Overview of a Maroon State in Seventeenth-Century Brazil." *Journal of Latin American Studies* 28, no. 3 (October 1996): 545–66.

Aptheker, Herbert. "Maroons within the Present Limits of the United States." *Journal of Negro History* 24 (April 1939): 167–84.

Armitage, David, and Michael Braddick, eds. *The British Atlantic World, 1500–1800*. London: Palgrave MacMillan, 2002.

Armitage, David, and Sanjay Subrahmanyam, eds. *The Age of Revolution in Global Context, c. 1760–1840*. Basingstoke, U.K.: Palgrave MacMillan, 2010.

Bailyn, Bernard. *Atlantic History: Concept and Contours*. Cambridge, Mass.: Harvard University Press, 2005.

Barber, John Warner. *Our Whole Country, or, The Past and Present of the United States, Historical and Descriptive*. Vol. 2. Cincinnati: H. Howe, 1861.

Barcia, Manuel. *Seeds of Insurrection: Domination and Resistance on Western Cuban Plantations, 1808–1848*. Baton Rouge: Louisiana State University Press, 2008.

Bardon, Jonathan. *A History of Ulster*. Belfast: Blackstaff Press, 2005.

Bassett, John Spencer, ed. *Correspondences of Andrew Jackson*. Washington, D.C.: Carnegie Institution of Washington, 1927.

———. *Correspondence of Andrew Jackson.* Vol. 2: *May 1, 1814 to December 31, 1819.* Washington, D.C.: Carnegie Institution of Washington, 1926.

Bateman, Rebecca. "African and Indians: A Comparative Study of the Black Carib and Black Seminole." *Ethnohistory* 37 (Winter 1990): 1–24.

Beckles, Hillary. *Black Rebellion in Barbados: The Struggle against Slavery, 1627–1838.* Bridgetown, Barbados: Antilles Publications, 1987.

Berlin, Ira. *Many Thousands Gone: The First Two Centuries of Slavery in North America.* Cambridge, Mass.: Harvard University Press, 1998.

Bilby, Kenneth. *True-Born Maroons.* Gainesville: University Press of Florida, 2005.

Blackburn, Robin. *The Overthrow of Colonial Slavery, 1776–1848.* New York: Verso, 1988.

Blassingame, John, ed. *Slave Testimony: Two Centuries of Letters, Speeches, Interviews, and Autobiographies.* Baton Rouge: Louisiana State University Press, 1977.

Brana-Shute, Gary, ed. *Resistance and Rebellion in Suriname: Old and New.* Williamsburg, Va.: Department of Anthropology, College of William and Mary, 1990.

Branch, Thomas Drew. Old Fort Gadsden. Unpublished paper. Apalachicola National Forest, 1958.

Braund, Kathryn. "The Creek Indians, Blacks, and Slavery." *Journal of Southern History* 57 (November 1991): 601–36.

———. *Deerskins and Duffels: The Creek Indian Trade with Anglo America, 1685–1815.* Lincoln: University of Nebraska Press, 1993.

Brenton, Edward. *The Naval History of Great Britain: From the Year 1783–1822.* Vol. 5. London: C. Rice, 1825.

Brooks, Richard. *The Royal Marines: A History.* Annapolis, Md.: U.S. Naval Institute Press, 2002.

Brown, Canter. *Florida's Peace River Frontier.* Gainesville: University Presses of Florida, 1991.

———. "The 'Sarrazota, or Runaway Negro Plantations': Tampa Bay's First Black Community, 1812–1821." *Tampa Bay History* 12 (1990): 5–19.

Brown, Canter, and David Jackson, eds. *Go Sound the Trumpet: Selections of Florida's African American History.* Tampa: University of Tampa Press, 2005.

———. "Tales of Angola: Free Blacks, Red Stick Creeks, and International Intrigue in Spanish Southwest Florida, 1812–1821." In *Go Sound the Trumpet,* ed. Canter Brown and David Jackson, 1–20. Tampa: University of Tampa Press, 2005.

Brown, Christopher Leslie. *Moral Capital: Foundations of British Abolitionism.* Chapel Hill: University of North Carolina Press for the Omohundro Institute of Early American History and Culture, Williamsburg, Va., 2006.

Brown, Christopher Leslie, and Philip Morgan, eds. *Arming Slaves: From Classical Times to the Modern Age.* New Haven, Conn.: Yale University Press, 2006.

Brown, Matthew. *Adventuring through Spanish Colonies: Simón Bolívar, Foreign Mercenaries, and the Birth of New Nations.* Liverpool, U.K.: Liverpool University Press, 2007.

Buckley, Roger. *The British Army in the West Indies: Society and the Military in the Age of Revolution.* Gainesville: University Press of Florida, 1998.

―――. *Slaves in Red Coats: The British West India Regiments, 1795–1815*. New Haven, Conn.: Yale University Press, 1979.

Bullard, Mary. *Black Emancipation at Cumberland Island in 1815*. Delean Springs, Fla.: Mary Bullard, 1983.

Buxton, Thomas. *The African Slave Trade and Its Remedy*. London: Murray, 1840.

The Cambridge History of Africa. Vol. 5: *C. 1790–c. 1870*. Cambridge: Cambridge University Press, 2001.

Campbell, James. *Historical Sketches of Colonial Florida*. Cleveland: Williams Publishing Company, 1892.

Campbell, Mavis. *The Maroons of Jamaica, 1655–1796: A History of Resistance, Collaboration, and Betrayal*. Granby, Mass.: Bergin and Garvey Publishers, 1988.

Canny, Nicolas, ed. *The Oxford History of the British Empire: The Origins of Empire*. Oxford, U.K.: Oxford University Press, 1998.

Cassell, Frank. "Slaves in the Chesapeake Bay Area and the War of 1812." *Journal of Negro History* 57 (1972): 144–55.

Chaplin, Joyce. "Creating a Cotton South." *Journal of Southern History* 57 (May 1991): 171–200.

Childs, Matt. *The 1812 Aponte Rebellion in Cuba and the Struggle against Atlantic Slavery*. Chapel Hill: University of North Carolina Press, 2006.

Cody, Cheryll Ann. "There was no 'Absolom' on the Ball Plantations: Slave-Naming Practices in the South Carolina Low Country, 1720–1865." *American Historical Review* 92 (June 1987): 563–96.

Coe, Charles. *Red Patriots: The Story of the Seminoles*. Cincinnati: Editor Publishing Company, 1898.

Coker, William. "The Last Battle of the War of 1812: New Orleans? No, Fort Bowyer!" *Alabama Historical Quarterly*, no. 1 (1981): 43–63.

Coker, William, and Douglas Ingles. *The Spanish Censuses of Pensacola, 1784–1820: A Genealogical Guide to Spanish Pensacola*. Pensacola: Perdido Bay Press, 1980.

Coker, William, and Thomas Watson. *Indian Traders of the Southeastern Spanish Borderlands: Panton, Leslie and Company and John Forbes and Company, 1783–1847*. Pensacola: University of West Florida Press, 1986.

Coles, Harry. *The War of 1812*. Chicago: University of Chicago Press, 1965.

A Concise Narrative of the Seminole Campaign by an officer attached to the Expedition. Nashville: McLean and Tunshell, 1819.

Constructing Race. Thematic issue of *William and Mary Quarterly*, 3rd Series, vol. 44, no. 1 (January 1997).

Correspondences with Foreign Powers on the Slave Trade, 1843, (Class B) Presented to Parliament. London: William Clowes and Sons, 1843.

Correspondences with Foreign Powers on the Slave Trade, 1844, (Class B) Presented to Parliament. London: William Clowes and Sons, 1844.

Correspondence to and from George Chalmers Colonial Agent for the Bahamas, 1792–1825. Nassau, New Providence: Bahamas National Archives, n.d.

Covington, James. "The Negro Fort." *Gulf Coast Historical Review* 5 (1990): 78–91.

————. *The Seminoles of Florida*. Gainesville: University Press of Florida, 1993.

Craton, Michael. *Testing the Chains: Resistance to Slavery in the British West Indies*. Ithaca, N.Y.: Cornell University Press, 1982.

Craton, Michael, and Gail Saunders. *Islanders in the Stream: A History of the Bahamian People*. Vol. 1: *From Aboriginal Times to the End of Slavery*. Athens: University of Georgia Press, 1999.

Crider, Robert. "The Borderland Floridas, 1815–1821: Spanish Sovereignty under Siege." PhD diss., Florida State University, 1979.

Cronon, William. "Revisiting the Vanishing Frontier: The Legacy of Frederick Jackson Turner." *Western Historical Quarterly* 18 (April 1987): 157–76.

Cronon, William, George Miles, and Jay Gitlin, eds. *Under an Open Sky: Rethinking America's Western Past*. New York: W. W. Norton, 1992.

Cusick, James. *The Other War of 1812: The Patriot War and the American Invasion of Spanish Florida*. Gainesville: University Press of Florida, 2003.

Daniels, Christine, and Michael Kennedy, eds. *Negotiated Empires: Centers and Peripheries in the New World, 1500–1820*. New York: Routledge, 2002.

Davis, David Brion. *The Problem of Slavery in the Age of Revolution, 1770–1832*. Ithaca, N.Y.: Cornell University Press, 1975.

————. *The Problem of Slavery in Western Culture*. Ithaca, N.Y.: Cornell University Press, 1967.

Davis, Rachel. *The Black Experience in Natchez, 1720–1880*. Natchez, Miss.: Eastern National, 1999.

Davis, Thomas J. "Conspiracy and Credibility: Look Who's Talking, about What—Law Talk and Loose Talk." *William and Mary Quarterly* 59 (January 2002): 167–74.

————. *A Rumor of Revolt: The "Great Negro Plot" in Colonial New York*. New York: Free Press, 1985.

Degler, Carl. *Neither Black nor White: Slavery and Race Relations in Brazil and the United States*. Madison: University of Wisconsin Press, 1971.

De Groot, Silvia. "Maroon Women as Ancestors, Priests and Mediums in Surinam." *Slavery and Abolition* 7, no. 2 (September 1986): 160–74.

De la Teja, Jesus, and Ross Frank, eds. *Choice, Persuasion, and Coercion: Social Control on Spain's North American Frontiers*. Albuquerque: University of New Mexico Press, 2005.

Dessens, Nathalie. *From Saint Domingue to New Orleans: Migration and Influences*. Gainesville: University Press of Florida, 2007.

Dowd, Gregory. "The Panic of 1751: The Significance of Rumors on the South Carolina–Cherokee Frontier." *William and Mary Quarterly* (July 1996): 527–60.

————. *A Spirited Resistance: The North American Indian Struggle for Unity, 1745–1815*. Baltimore: Johns Hopkins University Press, 1992.

Drescher, Seymour. *Capitalism and Anti-Slavery: British Mobilization in Comparative Perspective*. London: Macmillan, 1987.

————. *Econocide: British Slavery in the Era of Abolition*. Pittsburgh: University of Pittsburgh Press, 1977.

The Dublin Almanac and General Register of Ireland for the Year 1838: To Which Are Added Lists of Both Houses of Parliament. Dublin: Pettigrew and Oulton, 1838.

Dubois, Laurent. *Avengers of the New World: The Story of the Haitian Revolution*. Cambridge, Mass.: Belknap Press of Harvard University Press, 2004.

———. "Citizen Soldiers: Emancipation and Military Service in the Revolutionary French Caribbean." In *Arming Slaves*, ed. Christopher Leslie Brown and Philip Morgan, 233–54. New Haven, Conn.: Yale University Press, 2006.

———. *A Colony of Citizens: Revolution and Slave Emancipation in the French Caribbean, 1787–1804*. Chapel Hill: University of North Carolina Press, 2004.

Dubois, Laurent, and Julius Scott, eds. *Origins of the Black Atlantic*. New York: Routledge, 2010.

Duffy, Michael. *Soldiers, Sugar, and Seapower: The British Expeditions to the West Indies and the War against Revolutionary France*. Oxford, U.K.: Clarendon Press, 1987.

Dyer, Oliver. *General Andrew Jackson: Hero of New Orleans and Seventh President of the United States*. New York: Robert Banner's Sons, 1891.

Egerton, Douglas. *Death or Liberty: African Americans and Revolutionary America*. New York: Oxford University Press, 2009.

———. "Forgetting Denmark Vesey; or, Oliver Stone Meets Richard Wade." *William and Mary Quarterly* 59 (January 2002): 143–52.

———. *Gabriel's Rebellion: The Virginia Slave Conspiracies of 1800 and 1802*. Chapel Hill: University of North Carolina Press, 1993.

Elliott, J. H. *Empires of the Atlantic World: Britain and Spain in America*. New Haven, Conn.: Yale University Press, 2006.

Ellsworth, Lucius, ed. *The Americanization of the Gulf Coast, 1803–1850*. Pensacola: University Press of Florida, 1972.

Eltis, David. *Economic Growth and the Ending of the Transatlantic Slave Trade*. Oxford, U.K.: Oxford University Press, 1987.

Emerson, Edwin. *A History of the Nineteenth Century by Year*. Vol. 2. New York: P. F. Collier and Son, 1902.

Engerman, Stanley, and Robert Paquette, eds. *The Lesser Antilles in the Age of European Empires*. Gainesville: University Press of Florida, 1996.

Ethridge, Robbie. *Creek Country: The Creek Indians and Their World*. Chapel Hill: University of North Carolina Press, 2003.

Evans, Clement Anselm. *Confederate Military History*. Atlanta, Ga.: Confederate Publishing Company, 1898.

Fairbanks, George. *History of Florida: From Its Discovery by Ponce de Leon in 1512, to the Close of the Florida War, in 1842*. Philadelphia: J. B. Lippincott and Company, 1871.

Faragher, John Mack. "The Frontier Trail: Rethinking Turner and Reimagining the American West." *American Historical Review* 98, no. 1 (February 1993): 106–17.

Fehrenbacher, Paul. *The Slaveholding Republic: An Account of the United States Government's Relations to Slavery*. Oxford, U.K.: Oxford University Press, 2001.

Fick, Carolyn. *The Making of Haiti: The Saint Domingue Revolution from Below*. Knoxville: University of Tennessee Press, 1990.

Finkleman, Paul. *Slavery and the Founders: Race and Liberty in the Age of Jefferson*. Armonk: M. E. Sharpe, 1996.

Follett, Richard. *The Sugar Masters: Planters and Slaves in Louisiana's Cane World, 1820–1860*. Baton Rouge: Louisiana State University Press, 2005.

Forbes, James Grant. *Sketches, Historical and Topographical of the Floridas; More Particularly of East Florida*. New York: C. S. Van Winkle, 1821.

Ford, Worthington Chauncey, ed. *Writings of John Quincy Adams*. Vol. 5: *1814–1816*. New York: MacMillan, 1915.

Franklin, John Hope, and Loren Schweninger. *Runaway Slaves: Rebels on the Plantation*. New York: Oxford University Press, 1999.

Fredrickson, George. *The Black Image in the White Mind: The Debate on Afro-American Character and Destiny*. Middletown, Conn.: Wesleyan University Press, 1987.

Frehling, William. *The Reintegration of American History: Slavery and the Civil War*. New York: Oxford University Press, 1994.

Frey, Silvia. *Water from the Rock: Black Resistance in a Revolutionary Age*. Princeton, N.J.: Princeton University Press, 1993.

Frost, John. *Indian Battles, Captivities, and Adventures: From the Earliest Period to the Present Time*. New York: Derby and Jackson, 1858.

Fuller, Herbert. *The Purchase of Florida: Its History and Diplomacy*. Cleveland: Burrows Brothers Company, 1906.

Furstenberg, François. "Beyond Freedom and Slavery: Autonomy, Virtue, and Resistance in Early American Political Discourse." *Journal of American History* 89 (March 2003): 1295–330.

Games, Alison. "Atlantic History: Definitions, Challenges, and Opportunities." *American Historical Review* 111, no. 3 (June 2006): 741–57.

———. *The Web of Empire: English Cosmopolitans in an Age of Expansion, 1560–1660*. New York: Oxford University Press, 2008.

Gannon, Michael, ed. *The New History of Florida*. Gainesville: University Press of Florida, 1996.

Gaspar, David, and David Geggus, eds. *A Turbulent Time: The French Revolution and the Greater Caribbean*. Bloomington: University of Indiana Press, 1997.

Gaspar, David, and Darlene Hine, eds. *More than Chattel: Black Women and Slavery in the Americas*. Bloomington: University of Indiana Press, 1996.

Geggus, David. *Haitian Revolutionary Studies*. Bloomington: University of Indiana Press, 2002.

———. *Slavery, War, and Revolution: The British Occupation of Saint Domingue, 1793–1798*. Oxford, U.K.: Oxford University Press, 1983.

Geggus, David, ed. *The Impact of the Haitian Revolution in the Atlantic World*. Columbia: University of South Carolina Press, 2001.

Genovese, Eugene. *From Rebellion to Revolution: Afro-American Slave Revolts in the Making of the Modern World*. Baton Rouge: Louisiana State University Press, 1979.

———. *Roll, Jordan, Roll: The World the Slaves Made*. New York: Vintage, 1974.

George, Christopher. "The Mirage of Freedom: African Americans in the War of 1812." *Maryland Historical Quarterly* 91 (Winter 1996): 427–50.

George, Paul, ed. *A Guide to the History of Florida*. New York: Greenwood Press, 1989.

Giddings, Joshua. *The Exiles of Florida: or, The Crimes Committed by Our Government against the Maroons Who Fled from South Carolina and Other Slave States, Seeking Protection under Spanish Laws*. Columbus, Ohio: Follett, Foster, and Company, 1858.

Goodwin, Philo. *Biography of Andrew Jackson: President of the United States, Formerly Major General in the Army of the United States*. New York: R. Hart Townes, 1837.

Grant, C. L., ed. *Letters, Journals and Writings of Benjamin Hawkins*. Vol. 2: *1802–1816*. Savannah: Beehive Press, 1980.

Greenberg, Kenneth, ed. *Nat Turner: A Slave Rebellion in History and Memory*. New York: Oxford University Press, 2004.

Greene, Jack. *All Men Are Created Equal: Some Reflections on the Character of the American Revolution—An Inaugural Address*. Oxford, U.K.: Oxford University Press, 1976.

———. *Peripheries and Center: Constitutional Development in the Extended Polities of the British Empire and the United States, 1607–1788*. Athens: University of Georgia Press, 1986.

Greene, Jack, and Philip Morgan, eds. *Atlantic History: A Critical Appraisal*. Oxford, U.K.: Oxford University Press, 2009.

Green Fields: Two Hundred Years of Louisiana Sugar. Lafayette: Center for Louisiana Studies, 1980.

Griffin, John. Report of Investigations at Old Fort Gadsden, Apalachicola National Forest, Florida, in January, 1950. Unpublished report. Florida Parks Service, 1950.

Gross, Robert A. "Forum: The Making of a Slave Conspiracy, part 2." *William and Mary Quarterly* 59 (January 2002): 135–36.

Grossman, James, ed. *The Frontier in American Culture*. Berkeley: University of California Press, 1994.

Gutiérrez, Ramón A., and Elliott Young. "Transnationalizing Borderlands History." *Western Historical Quarterly* 41 (Spring 2010): 27–53.

Hall, Gwendolyn Midlo. *Africans in Colonial Louisiana: The Development of Afro-Creole Culture in the Eighteenth Century*. Baton Rouge: Louisiana State University Press, 1992.

Hämäläinen, Pekka, and Samuel Truett. "On Borderlands." *Journal of American History* 98 (September 2011): 338–61.

Hayes, J. E., ed. *Creek Indian Letters, Talks, and Treaties, 1705–1839*. Part 3: *1813–1829*. Atlanta: Georgia Department of Archives and History, 1939.

———. *East and West Florida and Yazoo Land Sales 1764–1850*. Atlanta: Georgia Department of Archives and History, 1941.

Hechter, Michael. *Internal Colonialism: The Celtic Fringe in British National Development, 1536–1966*. London: Kegan Paul International, 1975.

Hemphill, W. Edwin, ed. *The Papers of John C. Calhoun*. Vol. 2: *1817–1818*. Columbia: University of South Carolina Press, 1963.

———. *The Papers of John C. Calhoun*. Vol. 3: *1818–1819*. Columbia: University of South Carolina Press, 1967.

———. *The Papers of John C. Calhoun*. Vol. 4: *1819–1920*. Columbia: University of South Carolina Press, 1969.

Hendrick, George, and Willine Hendrick. *The Creole Mutiny: A Tale of Revolt aboard a Slave Ship*. Chicago: Ivan R. Dee, 2003.

Henri, Florette. *The Southern Indians and Benjamin Hawkins, 1796–1816*. Norman: University of Oklahoma Press, 1986.

Heuman, Gad, ed. *Out of This House of Bondage: Runaways, Resistance and Marronage in Africa and the New World*. London: International Specialized Book Services, 1982.

Hickey, Donald. *The War of 1812*. Champaign: University of Illinois Press, 1989.

Hiedler, David, and Jeanne Hiedler. *Old Hickory's War: Andrew Jackson and the Quest for Empire*. Mechanicsburg, Pa.: Stackpole Books, 1996.

Higginson, Thomas Wentworth. *Memoir of Thomas Wentworth Higginson*, in *Army Life in a Black Regiment*. Boston: Osgood and Company, 1870.

Hildreth, Richard. *The History of the United States*. Vol. 6. New York: Harper and Brothers, 1880.

Hill, Jonathan, ed. *History, Power, and Identity: Ethnogenesis in the Americas, 1492–1992*. Iowa City: University of Iowa Press, 1996.

Hill, Myrtle. *Evangelical Protestantism in Ulster Society, 1740–1890*. London: Taylor and Francis, 1992.

Hine, Darlene Clark. *Hine Sight: Black Women and the Re-Construction of American History*. Brooklyn: Carlson Publishing, 1994.

Hine, Darlene Clark, and Earnestine Jenkins. *A Quest for Manhood: A Reader in United States Black Men's History and Masculinity*. Bloomington: Indiana University Press, 1999.

Hine, Darlene Clark, ed. *Black Women in United States History*. Brooklyn: Carlson Publishing, 1990.

Hobsbawm, E. J. *The Age of Revolution, 1789–1848*. Cleveland: World, 1962.

Hoffman, Paul. *Florida's Frontiers*. Bloomington: Indiana University Press, 2002.

Hoffman, Ronald, and Peter Albert, eds. *Women in the Age of the American Revolution*. Charlottesville: University of Virginia Press, 1983.

Holmes, Andrew. *The Shaping of Ulster Presbyterian Belief and Practice, 1770–1840*. Oxford, U.K.: Oxford University Press, 2006.

Hoogbergen, Wim. *The Boni Maroon Wars in Suriname*. New York: E. J. Brill, 1990.

Horsman, Reginald. *The War of 1812*. New York: Random House, 1969.

Howard, Rosalyn. *Black Seminoles in the Bahamas*. Gainesville: University Press of Florida, 2002.

Hunt, Alfred. *Haiti's Influence on Antebellum America: Slumbering Volcano in the Caribbean*. Baton Rouge: Louisiana State University Press, 1988.

Hurtado, Albert. "Parkmanizing the Spanish Borderlands: Bolton, Turner, and the Historians' World." *Western Historical Quarterly* 26 (Summer 1995): 149–67.

Ingersoll, Thomas. *Mammon and Manon in Early New Orleans: The First Slave Society in the Deep South, 1718–1819*. Knoxville: University of Tennessee Press, 1999.

Inscoe, John. "Carolina Slave Names: An Index to Acculturation." *Journal of Southern History* 49 (November 1983): 527–54.

Jackson, Robert, ed. *New Views of Borderlands History.* Albuquerque: University of New Mexico Press, 1998.

James, C. L. R. *The Black Jacobins: Toussaint L'Ouverture and the San Domingo Revolution.* New York: Vintage: 1963.

Jay, William. *A View of the Action of the Federal Government on Behalf of Slavery.* New York: American Anti-Slavery Society, 1839.

Jennings, Francis. *The Invasion of America: Indians, Colonialism, and the Cant of Conquest.* Chapel Hill: University of North Carolina Press, 1975.

John, A. Meredith. *The Plantation Slaves of Trinidad, 1783–1816: A Mathematical and Demographic Enquiry.* Cambridge, U.K.: Cambridge University Press, 2004.

Johnson, Benjamin. "Problems and Prospects in North American Borderlands History." *History Compass* 4 (January 2006): 1–7.

Johnson, Benjamin H., and Andrew R. Graybill, eds. *Bridging National Borders in North America: Transnational and Comparative Histories.* Durham, N.C.: Duke University Press, 2010.

Johnson, Michael. "Denmark Vesey and His Co-Conspirators." *William and Mary Quarterly* 58 (October 2001): 915–76.

———. "Reading Evidence." *William and Mary Quarterly* 59 (January 2002): 193–202.

Johnson, Walter, ed. *The Chattel Principle: Internal Slave Trades in the Americas* New Haven, Conn.: Yale University Press, 2005.

———. *Soul by Soul: Life inside the Antebellum Slave Market.* Cambridge, Mass.: Harvard University Press, 1999.

———. "White Lies: Human Property and Domestic Slavery aboard the Slave Ship *Creole*." *Atlantic Studies* (August 2008): 237–63.

Johnston, Alexander. *American Political History, 1763–1876*, vol. 2: *The Slavery Controversy, Civil War and Reconstruction, 1820–1876.* New York: Knickerbocker Press, 1905.

Jordan, Winthrop D. "The Charleston Hurricane of 1822; Or, the Law's Rampage." *William and Mary Quarterly* 59 (January 2002): 175–78.

———. *White over Black: American Attitudes Toward the Negro, 1550–1812.* Chapel Hill: University of North Carolina Press, 1995.

Kastor, Peter. *The Nation's Crucible: The Louisiana Purchase and the Creation of America.* New Haven, Conn.: Yale University Press, 2004.

Kenny, Kevin, ed. *Ireland and the British Empire.* Oxford, U.K.: Oxford University Press, 2004.

Kerber, Linda. "Beyond Roles, Beyond Spheres: Thinking about Gender in the Early Republic." *William and Mary Quarterly* 46 (July 1989): 565–85.

Klein, Herbert. *Slavery in the Americas: A Comparative Study of Virginia and Cuba.* Chicago: University of Chicago Press, 1967.

Klein, Rachel. *The Unification of a Slave State: The Rise of the Planter Class in the South Carolina Backcountry, 1760–1808.* Chapel Hill: University of North Carolina Press, 1990.

Klooster, Wim. *Revolutions in the Atlantic* World. New York: New York University Press, 2009.

Knetsch, Joe. *Florida's Seminole Wars: 1817–1858*. Charleston: Arcadia Publishing, 2003.

Knight, Franklin, ed. *General History of the Caribbean*. Vol. 3: *The Slave Societies of the Caribbean*. London: UNESCO Publishing, 1997.

Knight, Lucian. *A Standard History of Georgia and Georgians*. Chicago: Lewis Publishing Company, 1917.

Kopytoff, Barbara. "Colonial Treaty as Sacred Charter of the Jamaican Maroons." *Ethnohistory* 26 (Winter 1979): 45–64.

———. "The Development of Jamaican Maroon Ethnicity." *Caribbean Quarterly* 22 (1976): 33–55.

———. "The Early Political Development of Jamaican Maroon Societies." *William and Mary Quarterly* 35 (1978): 287–307.

Lalor, John, ed. *Cyclopedia of Political Science, Political Economy, and the Political History of the United States*. New York: Charles E. Merrill and Company, 1890.

Lambert, David. "Producing/Contesting Whiteness: Rebellion, Anti-Slavery and Enslavement in Barbados, 1816." *Geoforum* (January 2005): 29–43.

Lambert, David, and Alan Lester, eds. *Colonial Lives across the British Empire: Imperial Careering in the Long Nineteenth Century*. Cambridge, U.K.: Cambridge University Press, 2006.

Landers, Jane. *Atlantic Creoles in the Age of* Revolutions. Cambridge, Mass.: Harvard University Press, 2010.

———. "Black Community and Culture in the Southeastern Borderlands." *Journal of the Early American Republic* 18 (Spring 1998): 117–34.

———. "Black-Indian Interactions in Spanish Florida." *Colonial Latin America Historical Review* 3 (1993): 141–62.

———. *Black Society in Spanish Florida*. Urbana: University of Illinois Press, 1999.

———. "Gracia Real de Santa Teresa de Mose: A Free Black Town in Spanish Florida." *American Historical Review* 95 (February 1990): 9–30.

———. "Slave Resistance on the Southern Frontier: Fugitives, Maroons, and Banditti in the Age of Revolution." *El Escribano* (1995): 12–24.

Langley, Lester. *The Americas in the Age of Revolution, 1750–1850*. New Haven, Conn.: Yale University Press, 1996.

La Rosa Corzo, Gabino. *Runaway Slave Settlements in Cuba: Resistance and Repression*. Trans. Mary Todd. Chapel Hill: University of North Carolina Press, 2003.

Leaming, Hugo. *Hidden Americans: Maroons of Virginia and Carolina*. New York: Garland, 1995.

Letters and Writings of James Madison. Vol. 3: *1816–1828*. Philadelphia: J. B. Lippincott and Company, 1865.

Lewis, Alfred. *When Men Grew Tall or the Story of Andrew Jackson*. New York: D. Appleton, 1907.

Limerick, Patricia Nelson, Clyde Milner II, and Charles Rankin, eds. *Trails towards a New Western History*. Lawrence: University Press of Kansas, 1991.

Littlefield, Daniel. *Africans and Seminoles: From Removal to Emancipation.* Westport, Conn.: Greenwood Press, 1977.

Lockhart, James, and Stuart Schwartz. *Early Latin America: A History of Colonial Spanish America and Brazil.* Cambridge, U.K.: Cambridge University Press, 1983.

Lockley, Timothy James, ed. *Maroon Communities in South Carolina: A Documentary Record.* Columbia: University of South Carolina Press, 2009.

Lokken, Paul. "A Maroon Moment: Rebel Slaves in Early Seventeenth-Century Guatemala." *Slavery and Abolition* 25 (December 2004): 44–58.

Lynch, James. *The Bench and Bar of Mississippi.* New York: E. J. Hale and Son, 1881.

Mahon, John. *The War of 1812.* Cambridge, Mass.: Da Capo Press, 1991.

Malone, Michael. "Beyond the Last Frontier: Toward a New Approach to Western History." *Western Historical Quarterly* 20 (November 1989): 409–27.

Mancke, Elizabeth, and Carole Shammas, eds. *The Creation of the British Atlantic World.* Baltimore: Johns Hopkins University Press, 2005.

Martin, Joel. *Sacred Revolt: The Muskogee's Struggle for a New World.* Boston: Beacon, 1991.

Mason, Matthew. "The Battle of the Slaveholding Liberators: Great Britain, the United States, and Slavery in the Early Nineteenth Century." *William and Mary Quarterly* 59 (July 2002): 665–96.

———. *Slavery and Politics in the Early American* Republic. Chapel Hill: University of North Carolina Press, 2006.

Mattoso, Katia De Queiros. *To Be a Slave in Brazil, 1550–1888.* Trans. Arthur Goldhammer. New Brunswick, N.J.: Rutgers University Press, 1986.

McAlister, L. N. "Pensacola during the Second Spanish Period." *Florida Historical Quarterly* 37 (January–April 1959): 281–327.

McGovern, James, ed. *Colonial Pensacola.* Pensacola: Pensacola News Journal, 1974.

Memoir of General David Blackshear, Including Letters from Governors Irwin, Jackson, Mitchell, Early, and Rabun, and from Major-General McIntosh, Brigadier-General Floyd, and Other Affairs of the Army in the War of 1813–1814 on the Frontier and Sea Coast of Georgia; and Also Members of Congress. Philadelphia: J. B. Lippincott and Company, 1858.

Memoirs of General Andrew Jackson, Together with the Letter of Mr. Secretary Adams, in Vindication of the Execution of Arbuthnot and Ambrister and the Other Public Acts of Gen. Jackson, in Florida. Bridgeton, N.J.: Simeon Siegfried, 1824.

Meriwether, Robert, ed. *The Papers of John C. Calhoun.* Vol. 1: *1801–1817.* Columbia: University of South Carolina Press, 1959.

Merrell, James. "The Racial Education of the Catawba Indians." *Journal of Southern History,* no. 3 (August 1984): 363–84.

Merton, Dillon. *Slavery Attacked: Southern Slaves and Their Allies, 1619–1865.* Baton Rouge: Louisiana State University Press, 1990.

Miers, Suzanne. *Britain and the Ending of the Slave Trade.* New York: Africana Publishing Company, 1975.

Milligan, John. "Slave Rebelliousness and the Florida Maroons." *Prologue* 6 (Spring 1974): 1–18.

Missall, John, and Mary Lou Missall. *The Seminole Wars: America's Longest Indian Conflict*. Gainesville: University Press of Florida, 2004.

Monette, John. *History of the Discovery and Settlement of the Valley of the Mississippi*. New York: Harper and Brothers, 1846.

Montgomery, David. *The Student's American History*. Boston: Ginn and Company, 1897.

Moore, John. *The Emergence of the Cotton Kingdom in the Old Southwest*. Baton Rouge: Louisiana State University Press, 1988.

Morgan, Edmund. *American Slavery, American Freedom*. New York: W. W. Norton, 2003.

Morgan, Philip. "Conspiracy Scares." *William and Mary Quarterly* 59 (January 2002): 159–66.

———. *Slave Counterpoint: Black Culture in the Eighteenth Century Chesapeake and Lowcountry*. Chapel Hill: University of North Carolina Press for the Omohundro Institute of Early American History and Culture, Williamsburg, Va., 1998.

Morgan, Philip, and Andrew O'Shaughnessy. "Arming Slaves in the American Revolution." In *Arming Slaves*, ed. Christopher Leslie Brown and Philip Morgan, 180–208. New Haven, Conn.: Yale University Press, 2006.

Morton, Patricia, ed. *Discovering the Woman in Slavery: Emancipating Perspectives in the African American Past*. Athens: University of Georgia Press, 1996.

Moser, Harold, David Hoth, Sharon MacPherson, and John Reinhold, eds. *The Papers of Andrew Jackson*. Vol. 3: *1814–1815*. Knoxville: University of Tennessee Press, 1992.

Moser, Harold, David Hoth, and George H. Hoemann, eds., *The Papers of Andrew Jackson*. Vol. 4: *1816–1820*. Knoxville: University of Tennessee Press, 1994.

Mullin, Gerald. *Flight and Rebellion: Slave Resistance in Eighteenth Century Virginia*. New York: Oxford University Press, 1974.

Mullin, Michael. *Africa in America: Slave Acculturation and Resistance in the American South and Caribbean, 1763–1831*. Urbana: University of Illinois Press, 1992.

Mulroy, Kevin. *Freedom on the Border: The Seminole Maroons in Florida, the Indian Territory, Coahuila, and Texas*. Lubbock: Texas Tech University Press, 1993.

Narrative of a Voyage to the Spanish Main on the Ship "Two Friends." London: John Miller, 1819.

Nash, Gary. *The Forgotten Fifth: African Americans in the Age of Revolution*. Cambridge, Mass.: Harvard University Press, 2006.

Norton, Mary Beth. *Founding Mothers and Founding Fathers: Gendered Power and the Forming of American Society*. New York: W. W. Norton, 1996.

Ogundiran, Akinwumi, and Toyin Falola, eds. *Archaeology of Atlantic Africa and the African Diaspora*. Bloomington: Indiana University Press, 2007.

O'Reilly, William. "Genealogies of Atlantic History." *Atlantic Studies* 1, no. 1 (2004): 66–84.

Overton, John. *A Vindication of the Measures of the President and His Commanding Generals, in the Commencement and Termination of the Seminole War*. Washington, D.C.: Gales and Seaton, 1819.

Owsley, Frank. "British and Indian Activities in Spanish West Florida during the War of 1812." *Florida Historical Quarterly* 46 (October 1967): 111–23.

———. *Struggle for the Gulf Borderland: The Creek War and the Battle of New Orleans.* Gainesville: University Presses of Florida, 1981.

Owsley, Frank, and Gene Smith. *Filibusters and Expansionists: Jeffersonian Manifest Destiny, 1800–1821.* Tuscaloosa: University of Alabama Press, 1997.

Palfrey, John. *Papers on the Slave Power: First Published in the "Boston Whig."* Boston: Merrill and Cobb, 1846.

Palmer, R. R. *The Age of Democratic Revolution.* 2 vols. Princeton, N.J.: Princeton University Press, 1959, 1964.

Paquette, Robert. "'A Horde of Brigands?': The Great Louisiana Slave Revolt of 1811 Reconsidered." *Historical Reflections* 35 (Spring 2009): 72–96.

———. "Jacobins of the Lowcountry: The Vesey Plot on Trial." *William and Mary Quarterly* 59 (January 2002): 185–92.

———. "Social History Update: Slave Resistance and Social History." *Journal of Social History* 24 (1991): 681–84.

Parris, Scott. "Alliance and Competition: Four Case Studies of Maroon-European Relations." *Nieuwe West-Indische Gid* 55 (1981): 193–203.

Parton, James. *Life of Andrew Jackson.* Vol. 2. New York: Mason Brothers, 1861.

Patrick, Rembert. *Aristocrat in Uniform, General Duncan L. Clinch.* Gainesville: University of Florida Press, 1963.

———. *Florida Fiasco: Rampant Rebels.* Athens: University of Georgia Press, 1954.

Pearson, Edward. "Trials and Errors: Denmark Vesey and His Historians." *William and Mary Quarterly* 59 (January 2002): 137–42.

Perdue, Theda. "Race and Culture: Writing the Ethnohistory of the Early South." *Ethnohistory* 51 (Fall 2004): 701–23.

Perez, Berta. "The Journey to Freedom: Maroon Forebears in Southern Venezuela." *Ethnohistory* 47 (Summer 2000): 611–34.

Perkins, Samuel. *General Jackson's Conduct in the Seminole War, Delineated in a History of That Period: Affording Conclusive Reasons Why He Should Not Be the Next President.* Brooklyn, Conn.: Advertiser Press, 1828.

———. *Historical Sketches of the United States, from the Peace of 1815 to 1830.* New York: S. Converse, 1830.

Pickett, Albert James. *History of Alabama, and Incidentally of Georgia and Mississippi, from the Earliest Period.* Charleston: Walker and James, 1851.

Poe, Stephen. "Archaeological Excavations at Fort Gadsden, Florida." *Notes in Anthropology* 8 (1963): 1–35.

Poitrineau, Abel. "Demography and the Political Destiny of Florida during the Second Spanish Period." *Florida Historical Quarterly* 56 (April 1988): 420–43.

Porter, Kenneth Wiggins. *The Black Seminoles: A History of a Freedom-Seeking People.* Gainesville: University Press of Florida, 1996.

———. *The Negro on the Frontier.* London: Ayer Company Publishing, 1971.

Price, Richard. *First-Time: The Historical Vision of an Afro-American People.* Baltimore: Johns Hopkins University Press, 1983.

———. *Saramaka Social Structure: Analysis of a Maroon Society in Surinam*. Río Piedras, Puerto Rico: Institute of Caribbean Studies, 1975.

Price, Richard, ed. *Maroon Societies: Rebel Slave Communities in the Americas*. 2nd ed. Baltimore: Johns Hopkins University Press, 1979.

Quarles, Benjamin. *The Negro in the American Revolution*. Chapel Hill: University of North Carolina Press, 1961.

Raboteau, Albert. *Slave Religion: The "Invisible Institution" in the Antebellum South*. New York: Oxford University Press, 1978.

Reilly, Robin. *The British at the Gates: The New Orleans Campaign in the War of 1812*. New York: Putnam's, 1974.

Remini, Robert. *Andrew Jackson*. Vol. 1: *The Course of American Empire, 1767–1821*. Baltimore: Johns Hopkins University Press, 1998.

———. *Andrew Jackson and His Indian Wars*. New York: Penguin, 2002.

———. *The Battle of New Orleans: Andrew Jackson and America's First Military*. New York: Penguin, 2001.

———. *The Legacy of Andrew Jackson: Essays on Democracy, Indian Removal, and Slavery*. Baton Rouge: Louisiana State University Press, 1990.

Report of the Committee of the African Civilization Society to the Public Meeting of the Society, Held at Exeter Hall . . . the 21st of June, 1842. London: John Murray, 1842.

Restall, Matthew, ed. *Black and Red: African-Native Relations in Colonial Latin America*. Albuquerque: University of New Mexico Press, 2005.

Richardson, David, ed. *Abolition and Its Aftermath: The Historical Context, 1790–1916*. London: Frank Cass, 1985.

Riley, Glenda. "The Specter of a Savage: Rumors and Alarmism on the Overland Trail." *Western Historical Quarterly* 15 (October 1984): 427–44.

Riordan, Patrick. "Finding Freedom in Florida: Native Peoples, Africans and Colonists, 1670–1816." *Florida Historical Quarterly* 75 (Summer 1996): 24–43.

———. "Seminole Genesis, Native Americans, African Americans and Colonists on the Southern Frontier from Prehistory through the Colonial Era." Ph.D. diss., Florida State University, 1996.

Robertson, David. "Inconsistent Contextualism: The Hermeneutics of Michael Johnson." *William and Mary Quarterly* 59 (January 2002): 153–58.

Rodriguez, Junius. "Ripe for Revolt: Louisiana and the Tradition of Slave Insurrection, 1803–1865." Ph.D. diss., Auburn University, 1992.

Rosen, Deborah. "Wartime Prisoners and the Rule of Law: Andrew Jackson's Military Tribunals during the First Seminole War." *Journal of the Early Republic* (Winter 2008): 559–95.

Rothman, Adam. *Slave Country: American Expansion and the Origins of the Deep South*. Cambridge, Mass.: Harvard University Press, 2005.

Royer, John. *The Monument to Patriotism: Being a Collection of Biographical Sketches*. Pottstown, N.Y.: J. Royer, 1825.

Sale, Maggie. *The Slumbering Volcano: American Slave Ship Revolts and the Production of Rebellious Masculinity*. Durham, N.C.: Duke University Press, 1997.

Saunt, Claudio. *Black, White, and Indian: Race and the Unmaking of an American Family.* New York: Oxford University Press, 2005.

——. *A New Order of Things: Property, Power, and the Transformation of the Creek Indians, 1733–1816.* Cambridge, U.K.: Cambridge University Press, 1999.

Saunt, Claudio, Barbara Krauthamer, Tiya Miles, Celia Naylor, and Circe Sturm. "Rethinking Race and Culture in the Early South." *Ethnohistory* 53 (Spring 2006): 399–405.

Schafer, Daniel. "The Maroons of Jamaica: African Slave Rebels in the Caribbean." Ph.D. diss., University of Minnesota, 1973.

Schama, Simon. *Citizens: A Chronicle of the French Revolution.* New York: Alfred A. Knopf, 1989.

Schmidt-Nowara, Christopher, and John M. Nieto-Phillips, eds. *Interpreting Spanish Colonialism: Empires, Nations, and Legends.* Albuquerque: University of New Mexico Press, 2005.

Schwartz, Stuart. *Slaves, Peasants, and Rebels: Reconsidering Brazilian Slavery.* Urbana: University of Illinois Press, 1992.

Schweninger, Loren, ed. *Race and Free Blacks: Petitions to Southern Legislators, 1777–1867.* Bethesda, Md.: University Publications of America, 1998.

Scott, Julius. "The Common Wind: Currents of Afro-American Communication in the Era of the Haitian Revolution." Ph.D. diss., Duke University, 1986.

Select Committee on State of Settlements of Sierra Leone and Fernando Po, Minutes of Evidence before Select Committee: Houses of Parliament. London, 1831.

Shoemaker, Nancy. "How Indians Got to Be Red." *American Historical Review* 102 (June 1997): 624–44.

Sidbury, James. "Plausible Stories and Varnished Truths." *William and Mary Quarterly* 59 (January 2002): 179–84.

——. *Ploughshares into Swords: Race, Rebellion, and Identity in Gabriel's Virginia, 1730–1810.* Cambridge, U.K.: Cambridge University Press, 1997.

Silver, James. *Edmund Pendleton Gaines, Frontier General.* Baton Rouge: Louisiana State University Press, 1949.

Simmons, William Haynes. *Notices of East Florida.* 1822; Gainesville: University of Florida Press, 1973.

Sinclair, David. *The Land That Never Was: Sir Gregor MacGregor and the Most Audacious Fraud in History.* Cambridge, Mass.: Da Capo Press, 2003.

Snyder, Christina. *Slavery in Indian Country: The Changing Face of Captivity in Early America.* Cambridge, Mass.: Harvard University Press, 2010.

Sobel, Mechal. *Travelin' On: The Slave Journey to an Afro-Baptist Faith.* Princeton, N.J.: Princeton University Press, 1988.

Sprague, John. *The Origins, Progress, and Conclusion of the Florida Wars.* New York: D. Appleton, 1848.

Stagg, J. C. A. *Borderlines in Borderlands: James Madison and the Spanish-American Frontier, 1776–1821.* New Haven, Conn.: Yale University Press, 2009.

———. *Mr. Madison's War: Politics, Diplomacy and Warfare in the Early American Republic, 1783–1830*. Princeton, N.J.: Princeton University Press, 1983.

Stagg, J. C. A., ed. *The Papers of James Madison*. Vol. 5: *July 10, 1812–February 17, 1813*. Charlottesville: University of Virginia Press, 2004.

Starkey, Armstrong. *European and Native American Warfare, 1675–1815*. Norman: University of Oklahoma Press, 1998.

Sugden, John. "The Southern Indians in the War of 1812: The Closing Phase." *Florida Historical Quarterly* (January 1982): 275–312.

Sundiata, Ibrahim. *From Slaving to Neoslavery: The Bight of Biafra and Fernando Po in the Era of Abolition, 1827–1930*. Madison: University of Wisconsin Press, 1996.

Sutlive, Vinson H., Mario D. Zamora, Virginia Kerns, and Tomoko Hamada, eds. *Resistance and Rebellion in Suriname: Old and New*. Williamsburg, Va.: Department of Anthropology, College of William and Mary, 1990.

Tadman, Michael. *Speculators and Slaves: Masters, Traders, and Slaves in the Old South*. Madison: University of Wisconsin Press, 1989.

Tannenbaum, Frank. *Slave and Citizen: The Negro in the Americas*. New York: Alfred Knopf, 1947.

The Papers of Panton, Leslie and Company (microfilm collection). Woodbridge, Conn.: Research Publications, 1986.

Thompson, Alvin. *Flight to Freedom: African Runaways and Maroons in the Americas*. Kingston, Jamaica: University of the West Indies Press, 2006.

Thornton, John. *Africa and Africans in the Making of the Atlantic World, 1400–1800*. 2nd ed. Cambridge, U.K.: Cambridge University Press, 1992.

Tise, Larry. *Proslavery: History of the Defense of Slavery in America, 1701–1840*. Athens: University of Georgia Press, 1987.

Titus, Noel. *The Amelioration and Abolition of Slavery in Trinidad, 1812–1834: Experiments and Protests in a New Slave Colony*. Bloomington, Ind.: AuthorHouse, 2009.

Trials of Arbuthnot and Ambrister, Charged with Exciting the Seminole Indians to War with the United States. London: James Ridgway, 1819.

Truett, Samuel, and Elliott Young, eds. *Continental Crossroads: Remapping U.S.–Mexico Borderlands History*. Durham, N.C.: Duke University Press, 2004.

Usner, Daniel. *Indians, Settlers, and Slaves in a Frontier Exchange Economy: The Lower Mississippi Valley before 1783*. Chapel Hill: University of North Carolina Press for the Omohundro Institute of Early American History and Culture, Williamsburg, Va., 1992.

Vignoles, Charles. *Observations upon the Floridas*. New York: E. Bliss and E. White, 1823.

Voelz, Peter. *Slave and Soldier: The Military Impact of Blacks in the Colonial Americas*. New York: Garland, 1993.

Wallerstein, Immanuel. *The Modern World-System III: The Second Era of Great Expansion of the Capitalist World-Economy, 1730–1840*. New York: Academic Press, 1989.

Waselkov, Gregory. *A Conquering Spirit: Fort Mims and the Red Stick War of 1813–1814*. Tuscaloosa: University of Alabama Press, 2006.

Washington, Margaret Creel. *A Peculiar People: Slave Religion and Community Culture among the Gullahs*. New York: New York University Press, 1988.

Watson, William. *The Civil War and Reconstruction in Florida*. New York: Longmans, Green and Company, 1913.

Weber, David. *Myth and the History of the Hispanic Southwest*. Albuquerque: University of New Mexico Press, 1988.

——. *The Spanish Frontier in North America*. New Haven, Conn.: Yale University Press, 1992.

——. "Turner, the Boltonians, and the Borderlands." *American Historical Review* 91 (February 1986): 66–81.

Weiss, John McNish. *The Merikens: Free Black American Settlers in Trinidad 1815–1816*. London: McNish and Weiss, 2002.

White, Ashli. *Encountering Revolution: Haiti and the Making of the Early Republic*. Baltimore: Johns Hopkins University Press, 2010.

White, Deborah Grey. *Ar'n't I a Woman? Female Slaves in the Plantation South*. Rev. ed. New York: W. W. Norton, 1999.

Whitfield, Harvey Amani. *Blacks on the Border: The Black Refugees in British North America, 1815–1860*. Burlington: University of Vermont Press, 2006.

Wilentz, Sean. *Andrew Jackson*. New York: Times Books, 2005.

Williams, John Lee. *A View of West Florida*. 1823; Gainesville: University Presses of Florida, 1976.

Wilson, Henry. *History of the Rise and Fall of the Slave Power in America*. Vol. 1. Boston: James Osgood and Company, 1878.

Wilson, Kathleen. "The Performance of Freedom: Maroons and the Colonial Order in Eighteenth Century Jamaica and the Atlantic Sound." *William and Mary Quarterly* 66 (January 2009): 46–86.

Wright, J. Leitch. *Creeks and Seminoles: The Destruction and Regeneration of the Musogulge People*. Lincoln: University of Nebraska Press, 1986.

Wyatt-Brown, Bertram. "The Mask of Obedience: Male Slave Psychology in the Old South." *American Historical Review* 93 (December 1988): 1228–252.

Index

Dunmore, Lord, 17–18
Durant, Alexander, 39
Dutch, 100, 120–21, 137, 184

Early, Governor Peter (Georgia), 19, 67–68, 86, 93, 183, 217, 220
East Florida: American fears about conditions in, 143; American military and, 89; free blacks in, 60; Native Americans in, 86; Patriot Invasion of, 35–37; population of, 76, 85; slaves from, 45, 77, 116, 143, 148, 155, 234
Education, 20, 169–70, 211, 252
Escambia River, 218, 239
Estrada, Governor Juan José de (East Florida), 220
Expansion: American, 2, 5, 233, 235, 259; of slavery, 4–5, 14, 33, 67, 159, 216, 243
Explosion, of Fort at Prospect Bluff, 227–28, 231, 248

Farms: in maroon communities across hemisphere, 136, 140–41, 158, 164; at Prospect Bluff, 125, 134, 172, 177–78, 181
Fathers, 161, 163
Fedon's Rebellion, 112
Fernandina Island, 35, 60
Fernando Po, 22, 24–25, 252–53
Fifth West India Regiment, 28, 87, 104, 116, 143, 151, 155, 211
First Battalion Royal Colonial Marines, 51–53, 115
Flint River, 133, 192, 240
Florida. See East Florida; West Florida
Forbes and Company. See House of Forbes and Company
Former slave soldiers, 14, 26, 64, 101, 104, 107, 117, 161
Fort at Prospect Bluff: as base of activity, 75, 77, 181, 192, 195, 203; as "British-built," 9, 146, 150, 160, 176, 210; construction of, 138–39; destruction of, 7, 163, 173, 178–79, 189, 193, 201, 203, 207, 209–10, 218–19, 221–33, 239–41, 248–49; naming of, 129–32; population of, 143–44; refugees from, 235, 237–38; turned over to blacks and Indians, 89, 94, 96–97, 101, 110, 127–28, 161, 183, 215
Fort Barrancas, 51, 72–73, 106, 228
Fort Gadsden, 242, 251
Fort Jackson, 69

Fort Mims, 38, 43
Fort Mose, 5, 11
Fort San Marcos, 186
Fort San Miguel, 48, 60
Fort Scott, 239–41
Fowltown, 80, 179, 240
France, 20, 102, 112–13, 208
"Free papers," 118, 120, 124, 126–27, 161, 163, 195, 201
Free people of color, 7, 61, 77, 142–43, 148, 200, 204, 206
French Revolution, 14, 22, 208
Frontier: "Indian," 86; slave, 13, 64, 83, 98, 126, 134, 216, 230, 242, 259; southeastern, 66, 68, 71, 93, 220, 229, 243; southern, 3, 39, 68, 74, 81, 83, 87, 92, 151, 192, 217, 235, 239, 244–45, 247, 249; as theoretical concept, 34; western, 12

Gabriel's Rebellion, 13, 33, 127, 255
Gadsden, James, 135, 245
Gaines, Edmund: background, 217; and destruction of fort at Prospect Bluff, 134, 218–20, 222–24, 229; involvement in Seminole War, 239, 240, 243; observations on Prospect Bluff maroons, 91, 95, 143–44
Ganga Zumba, 166, 197–98
Garçon, 129, 149, 196, 201, 205–7, 210, 225–26, 228, 234
Gender, 8, 147, 155, 160–61, 163, 165–67, 170, 179
Gentry, 110, 182, 208, 211
Georgia: British plans against, 74, 86–87; fear of racial disorder within, 36–37, 79–80, 86, 183, 215, 217; militia, 44, 68, 86; Native Americans in, 90; residents of, 35, 38, 81, 92; runaway slaves from, 2, 78, 150–52, 235–36; and Seminole War, 243; slavery in, 13, 33, 43; theft of livestock from, 179
Georgia Journal, 68, 230, 248
German Coast uprising, 13
Giddings, Joshua, 4
Goulburn, Henry, 18
Grand marronage, 6, 100, 132, 212, 214
Great Dismal Swamp, 6
Grenada, 15, 112–13
Gulf Coast, 13, 26, 31, 39–40, 43, 49, 66–67, 74, 180
Gulf of Mexico, 1, 133–35, 222
Gunboat 149, 223
Gunboat 154, 223, 227
Guthrie, Captain John, 121–22

Hadjo, Hillis (Josiah Francis), 42, 48, 94, 242
Haitian Revolution, 13, 20, 113–14, 154, 189
Hambly, William, 125, 127, 185–87, 193, 208–9, 218, 228–29, 240–41
Hardridge, William, 78, 107–8
Havana, 46, 65, 73, 108, 184, 237
Hawkins, Benjamin, 37, 69, 79, 81–82, 92–93, 99, 117, 125, 143–44, 151–52, 185, 187, 192–93, 209–10, 216, 218–19
Henry, Robert, 84, 103–5, 107–8
Higginson, Thomas Wentworth, 1
Hilario, 149, 207
House of Forbes and Company, 50–51, 77, 79, 105, 125, 127, 134, 148, 150, 161, 180–81, 185–87, 210, 230, 238, 241, 246
Humanity, 8, 22, 52–53, 55–56, 61, 73, 83, 110, 120, 123, 165, 253, 258, 260
Hunting: of maroons, 136, 140–41, 158, 177–78, 232; of Prospect Bluff maroons, 159–60, 179, 224–25, 228
Husbands, 118, 161, 163, 188

Indian Territory, 75, 99, 168
Innerarity, James, 50, 60, 186–87, 193
Innerarity, John, 56, 59, 77–78, 99, 148, 150, 186–87
Ireland, 19, 20, 51, 66

Jackson, Andrew: biographies of, 3; and Creek War, 48, 90–91, 219; defense of Mobile, 65–66; and destruction of fort at Prospect Bluff, 214, 217–18, 221–23, 230; fears of racial disorder, 39, 57, 67, 69–71, 80, 192; invasion of Pensacola, 71, 73, 74, 76; observation on the government at Prospect Bluff, 201–3; Proclamation to People of Louisiana, 70; and Seminole War, 240–49; as Territorial Governor of Florida, 250
Jamaica: as British colony, 28, 151; maroon agriculture, 177; maroon culture, 166–67, 169; maroon demographics, 156–57; maroon dwellings, 141, 176; maroon economy, 181; maroon families, 161–62, 164; maroon gender, 161, 164; maroon government, 199; maroon knowledge of anti-slavery thought, 111, 116; maroon military organization, 141–42, 211; maroon names, 132; maroon origins, 100, 153–54, 158; maroon relations with outsiders, 184, 190; maroon sizes, 145; physical environment of, 136–38; treaties between maroons and the British government, 120–24, 185, 200

Jervais, Samuel, 143, 150, 183
Jesup, Thomas, 182

Kinache, 192, 219, 239–40, 242
Kindelán, Governor Sebastián, 75–77, 85, 220
King of England, 54, 56, 84, 122–23

Lachua, 75–76, 148, 159, 233
Lake Miccosukee Village, 242–43
Latin America, 15, 31, 33, 204, 208
Law: as ingredient in British rights, 128, 211; at Prospect Bluff, 204, 208–10, 258
Leeward maroons, 121–22, 132, 136, 141, 153–54, 162, 164, 166, 188–89, 199–200
Le Maniel, 145, 153, 184, 197
Liberalism, 8, 22, 24
Liberty: British, 22, 54; as political concept, 7, 53, 55, 110, 208; and Prospect Bluff maroons, 118–19, 122, 125, 128; for slaves, 84, 106, 113; in United States, 25, 29
License of decommission, 115
Literacy, 94, 169–70, 206
Little Prince, 81, 218, 219
Liverpool, Lord, 90
Loomis, Sailing Master Jarius, 223–24, 227
Louisiana, 6, 13, 32, 43–44, 70, 77, 135, 149–50, 159, 205, 229, 236
Louisiana Purchase, 13
Lowcountry, 13, 19, 31, 45, 159
Luffborough, Midshipman, 224–25

MacGregor, Gregor, 28, 41, 236
Mad Bear, 79
Madison, James, 12, 18, 221
Makandal, 113, 197
Manrique, Governor Mateo González (West Florida), 46, 48, 51, 64, 71, 77, 99, 102, 106–7
Marriage, 160, 162–63, 165, 167
Matthews, George, 35
McIntosh, John Houston, 35–36
McIntosh, William, 80, 193, 216, 224, 242
McPherson, William, 105, 108, 110
McQueen, Peter, 38, 42, 48, 84, 192, 219
Methodism, 20
Micco, Hopoy, 91
Micco, Hepoeth, 91
Minatti, 251
Mississippi Territory, 13, 43, 150, 217
Mitchell, David, 37, 93, 215, 237, 247
Mobile, 38, 48–51, 65–66, 68, 71, 74, 77, 88, 106, 129, 189

Proclamation by Alexander Cochrane to American slaves, 17–19, 26, 28–29, 43–44, 54, 72, 75, 117, 161, 181, 236

Proclamation by Edward Nicolls to the First Battalion of Royal Colonial Marines, 51–58, 69, 72, 84, 106, 161, 181, 237

Pro-slavery, 41, 55–56, 112, 114, 124

Quilombo, 100, 131, 138, 152, 156, 176–77, 184, 191, 198

Randolph, John, 14

Rawlins, Captain, 143, 150

Red Sticks: agency of, 9; and American attack on Prospect Bluff, 217–20; Angola, 232; and Article 9, Treaty of Ghent, 88; as British allies, 40, 42, 45, 48, 75, 77, 81, 88–89, 215–16, 236, 238–39, 249; Creek War, 38, 219; Dance, 169, 235; flight to Florida, 39, 48, 67; generational rift, 82; and Prospect Bluff maroons, 127, 129–30, 180, 191–92, 194, 214; relations with blacks, 44, 60, 63–64, 83–85, 103, 152, 160, 168, 251; Seminole War, 231, 233, 239–40, 242–43, 245, 247–48, 259; treaty with Nicolls, 89–97

Religion, 14, 22, 161, 163, 166, 168–69, 211

Republicanism, 7, 33

Restorationist, 111, 167, 212, 257

Royalist, 122–23

Royal Marines, 12, 20, 29, 40, 48–49, 56, 64–65, 101, 116–17, 210, 225, 237, 253

Royal Navy, 16, 20, 31, 41, 90, 108, 117, 143, 252

Rumors, 8, 43–45, 68, 71, 87, 112–14, 187, 248

Saint Domingue, 15, 36, 100, 112–13, 153–54, 184, 189, 197

Santo Domingo, 22, 120

Second Maroon War (Jamaica), 15, 113

Second West India Regiment, 27–29, 236

Seminoles: as allies of British, 2, 39–42, 45, 48, 64, 75, 77–78, 88, 90, 92, 97, 103, 236, 238, 249; Angola, 232; destruction of fort at Prospect Bluff, 223, 225, 228; generational rift, 82–83; interactions with blacks, 44, 47, 60, 63, 76, 81–85, 151–52, 160; Nero, 234; Patriot War, 36; refugees from Prospect Bluff among, 210, 232–33, 235, 251, 259; relations with Prospect Bluff maroons, 127, 129–30, 168, 180, 187, 191–94, 214, 218–19; rivalry with Creeks, 80; Seminole War, 231–32,

239–41, 243–45, 247–48; treaty with Nicolls, 91, 93, 96; violence against United States, 68, 71, 215, 217

Seminole War: and acquisition of Florida, 248–49, 259; American explanation of, 130, 245–47; American war aims, 193; black-Indian alliance in, 192; connection to Prospect Bluff maroons, 5; military conflict, 240, 244; Nicolls's contact with allies during, 96; Nicolls's role in, 232; nineteenth-century accounts of, 2–3; observation by American veteran of, 39; refugees from, 119

1739 Treaties (between Jamaican maroons and British government), 121, 123, 145, 154, 156, 189, 199–200

Sex ratio, 156–57, 162, 182

Sierra, Dr. Don Eugenio, 60, 206

Sierra Leone, 253

Simmons, William Haynes, 170, 173, 176, 193

Size of population at Prospect Bluff, 142–45

Slave rebels, 7, 10, 15, 98, 100, 128, 173, 194, 205, 255–57

Slave resistance: during Age of Revolution, 7, 40; American fear of, 14, 131, 230, 243; British understanding of, 16; Creek fear of, 80–81, 108; Prospect Bluff maroon community as example of, 10, 126, 128, 213–14, 243

Society for the Extinction of the Slave Trade and for the Civilization of Africa, 253

Soto, José de, 57–58, 130

South, 2–3, 13–14, 18, 32, 36–37, 40, 55, 66–67, 69–70, 87, 201, 236

South Carolina, 6, 13, 74, 87

Southeast: Age of Revolution in, 133, 135, 139; American forces in, 65, 73, 87, 242; Atlantic borderland status of, 34, 35; black–Native American relations in, 45–47, 231, 245, 251; British mission to, 40–41, 236; environment, 177; fear of racial disorder in, 67–68, 96, 146, 222; history of, 4–5, 255–56; impact of Prospect Bluff maroon community on, 175, 214–15, 217; Native Americans in, 63, 78–79, 88, 154, 216, 218; Nicolls in, 9, 51–52, 56, 05, 125; prior to 1814, 32–33, 37–39; Seminole War in, 241; slaves from, 75, 77, 127, 167, 169, 190; societies of, 205–6; stability of, 92–93, 237; War of 1812 in, 8, 12, 19, 26–27

Sovereignty, 7, 73, 122, 129, 132, 203–4, 208–9, 221, 226

Spencer, Robert, 90, 102, 108

Nathaniel Millett is associate professor of history at Saint Louis University. His research interests include the Atlantic World and borderlands of colonial and Revolutionary North America and the Caribbean as well as African American and Native American history. He lives in St. Louis with his wife and daughter.

CONTESTED BOUNDARIES
Edited by Gene Allen Smith, Texas Christian University

Contested Boundaries focuses on conflicts—political, social, cultural, and economic—along the ever-changing territorial boundaries of the American empire to explore the fluidity that characterized these borderlands as they transformed into modern nation states.

CPSIA information can be obtained
at www.ICGtesting.com
Printed in the USA
LVHW091931101218
599930LV00007B/1149/P

9 780813 060866